T0207451

Lecture Notes in Computer Science 13795

More information about this series at https://link.springer.com/bookseries/558

Qiaohong Zu · Yong Tang ·
Vladimir Mladenovic · Aisha Naseer ·
Jizheng Wan (Eds.)

Human Centered Computing

7th International Conference, HCC 2021
Virtual Event, December 9–11, 2021
Revised Selected Papers

 Springer

Editors
Qiaohong Zu
Wuhan University of Technology
Wuhan, China

Vladimir Mladenovic
University of Kragujevac
Kragujevac, Serbia

Jizheng Wan
University of Birmingham
Birmingham, UK

Yong Tang
South China Normal University
Guangzhou, China

Aisha Naseer
Huawei Technologies Co., Ltd.
Oak Way, UK

ISSN 0302-9743   ISSN 1611-3349 (electronic)
Lecture Notes in Computer Science
ISBN 978-3-031-23740-9   ISBN 978-3-031-23741-6 (eBook)
https://doi.org/10.1007/978-3-031-23741-6

This Springer imprint is published by the registered company Springer Nature Switzerland AG
The registered company address is: Gewerbestrasse 11, 6330 Cham, Switzerland

Preface

This volume presents the proceedings of the 7th International Conference on Human Centered Computing (HCC 2021) conference, which was held virtually during December 9–10, 2021. For many of us and for the HCC community, 2021 was yet another extraordinary year: we started to see some semblance of normality in everyday research and study while a tremendous effort was still required before we could proudly announce that 'the dark days are behind us'. Even though research and collaboration were not any easier in 2021, we still tried to collaborate and communicate with each other, albeit virtually. HCC2021 was trying to offer such a platform within and beyond the HCC family.

In 2021, we continued adapting to and thriving in the 'new normal': we focused on 'big' data processing and communication networks, investigating how technologies can be of assistance when we can no longer take face-to-face communication for granted; we advocated for smart society themes in a world which is facing unprecedented environmental and logistical challenges; and we continuously promoted studies on socio-technological issues that hopefully can help us in learning from the past and moving forward with the essential knowledge.

HCC 2021 brought together a wide range of state-of-the-art research from different disciplines. We received a total of 86 full paper submissions. All submissions went through a rigorous three-phase reviewing process: each paper went through a quick plagiarism check; this was followed by two peer reviews based on a paper's technical strength, significance of the study, completeness, and overall presentation. Finally, for selected papers, one meta-review was completed by a senior Program Committee member.

In the end, the Program Committee accepted 17 regular papers and 10 short papers to be included in the HCC 2021 conference proceedings. Big data and machine learning was inevitably still the "hottest" topic, contributing 13 papers with a good balance between theory and optimization. Clearly, innovative applications of established methodologies is still an area experiencing rapid growth. For communication and mobile networks, which attracted eight papers, we witnessed a growing interest in "unconventional" device-to-device communication (e.g., UAV networks)—we expect interest in similar topics to grow in the forthcoming events. On the other hand, the boundary between smart systems and big data has become less distinct as edge devices have started to harvest more data than the amount that can be processed locally, calling for better engineering approaches to communication networks and big data processing. We also selected one paper trying to give a 'green' touch to the heavily polluted transportation industries. The quality of the HCC 2021 proceedings was ensured by the arduous efforts of the Program Committee members and invited reviewers, to whom we owe our deepest gratitude and appreciation.

Similar to the wider research community, the HCC conference series went through a challenging year in 2021. Looking back from 2022, we are sincerely grateful to the authors and organizers for their contributions and persistence, without which we would not have enjoyed another year of fruitful discussion. We are also grateful to Springer's editorial staff for their hard work in publishing these post-conference proceedings in the LNCS series.

December 2021

Qiaohong Zu
Yong Tang
Vladimir Mladenovic
Aisha Naseer
Jizheng Wan

Organization

Conference Co-chairs

Yong Tang   South China Normal University, China
Qiaohong Zu   Wuhan University of Technology, China
Vladimir Mladenovic   University of Kragujevac, Serbia

Program Committee Co-chairs

Aisha Naseer   Huawei Technologies, UK
Srinandan Dasmahapatra   University of Southampton, UK

Program Committee

Fatima Ayoub   Maynooth University, Ireland
Innes Arana   Robert Gordon University, UK
Herbert Daly   University of Wolverhampton, UK
Matjaz Debevc   Maribor University, Slovenia
Tillal Eldabi   University of Surrey, UK
Liping Gao   University of Shanghai for Science and
                                Technology, China
Jing He   IBM, UK
Zhifa He   Wuhan University, China
Andreas Holzinger   Medical University of Graz, Austria
Cunping Hou   Tianjin University, China
Bin Hu   Beijing Institute of Technology, China
Mona Jaber   Queen Mary University of London, UK
Bin Jia   IBM, UK
Hiromichi Kobashi   Fujitsu, Japan
Teerath Kumar   Dublin City University, Ireland
Dun Lu   Fudan University, China
Vladimir Mladenovic   University of Kragujevac, Serbia
Cathy Mulligan   Instituto Superior Técnico, Portugal
Nhamoinesu Mtetwa   Glasgow University, UK
Michael Ng   University of Southampton, UK
Ayyaz Qureshi   Glasgow Caledonian University, UK
Hamza Raiz   Dublin City University, Ireland
Uwe Riss   SAP Research, Germany

Debjani Roy	BT, UK
Meina Song	Beijing University of Posts and Telecommunications, China
Lampros Stergiolas	The Hague University of Applied Sciences, Netherlands
Yong Tang	South China Normal University, China
Feng Tao	University of Southampton, UK
Maria Vargas-Vera	Adolfo Ibanez University, Chile
Hans Friedrich Witschel	FHNW, Switzerland
Linda Yang	University of Portsmouth, UK
Chen Yu	Huazhong University of Science and Technology, China
Changyou Zhang	Institute of Software, Chinese Academy of Sciences, China
Yan Zhang	Glasgow Caledonian University, UK
Yu Zhang	Wuhan University of Technology, China
Shikun Zhou	University of Portsmouth, UK
Gang Zou	Ericsson, Sweden

Publication Chairs

Jizheng Wan	Birmingham University, UK
Bo Hu	Fujitsu Research, UK

Organization Committee

Vladimir Mladenovic	University of Kragujevac, Serbia
Jingwen Yan	Wuhan University of Technology, China
Yong Zhang	Beijing University of Posts and Telecommunications, China

Partners

University of Kragujevac, Serbia
South China Normal University, China
Wuhan University of Technology, China

Contents

Communication

Smart City

Algorithms

A Fast Shortest Path Searching Method Based on A* and Simulated Annealing

Qiang Cui[1] and Sihua Gao[2(✉)]

[1] Systems Engineering Research Institute, Beijing, China
[2] School of Computer Science and Technology, Civil Aviation University of China, Tianjin, China
shgao@cauc.edu.cn

Abstract. Finding the shortest path in a transportation network is an important and common problem in practice. A* is usually recognized as an efficient approach to the shortest path problem. However, the time and space requirements make A* hard efficiently find the shortest path in a massive and complicated transportation network. Reducing useless nodes generated is an efficient way to improve A*. In view of spatial distribution characters of transportation networks, this paper presents a fast shortest path searching method named A*_SA. The main idea of A*_SA is that when expanding node n, only those children whose h-cost is equal to or smaller than h(n) + C are generated and stored. Motivated by simulated annealing, in order to avoid getting stuck in local optima, the children with larger h-cost are also be stored with a certain probability. Experimental results prove the efficiency of A*_SA.

Keywords: The shortest path · A* · Simulated annealing

1 Introduction

Due to the continuous development of modern science and technology, transportation networks are becoming ever more massive and complicated, that brings more choices for passengers. Moreover, people usually want to find out the best way from one place to another. That is the shortest path problem. There are many approaches to solve the shortest path problem, including blind search algorithms [2] (such as Dijkstras algorithm, depth-first search, breadth-first search, and so on) and heuristic search algorithms.

Blind search works with no domain knowledge and sequentially expands nodes according to a predefined order. Blind search usually generates many useless nodes and the search efficiency is poor. Guided by domain knowledge, heuristic search can dynamically adjust the search direction to get the target node as soon as possible. Heuristic search is generally considered to be more efficient than blind search. However, heuristic search algorithms cannot guarantee the optimal solution in applications. For large scale networks like transportation networks, time or memory constraints rule out the possibility of finding an optimal solution and suboptimal solutions are almost always acceptable.

Q. Zu et al. (Eds.): HCC 2021, LNCS 13795, pp. 3–14, 2022.
https://doi.org/10.1007/978-3-031-23741-6_1

Especially, with the advent of big data, speed becomes more and more important. Therefore, heuristic search has got significant attention recently. As pointed in [9], heuristic search is coming of age.

A majority of work in heuristic search is focused on A* [3], a popular heuristic search algorithm. Like other heuristic search algorithms, A* is guided by the cost function $f(n) = g(n) + h(n)$, where $g(n)$ is the cost of the path from the origin node to node n and $h(n)$ is a heuristic function estimating the cost from n to the destination node. A* is often recognized as an efficient approach to the shortest path problem. However, the time and space requirements make A* hard efficiently find the shortest path in a large scale network. These algorithms can be divided into two categories:

(1) The first kind belongs to parallel algorithms. With the exponential growth of computing power, along with the ubiquitous availability of different hardware platforms - such as multi-processor and multi-core computers, computer clusters, and graphics processing units (GPUs), many parallel algorithms have been proposed to improve A*.

(2) The second kind is focused on the improvement of search strategy. Although each expanded node is currently the most promising node based on domain knowledge, A* still always generates many useless nodes. This is mainly due to that when expanding node n, all child nodes including good ones or poor ones are stored in *OPEN* (a data structure used to store nodes to expand). Those poor children gradually become useless nodes in next iterations, and the number of useless nodes grows rapidly with search progress. Useless nodes not only occupy a lot of memory, but also incur high time overhead. One hand, when selecting a node to expand, A* must scan all nodes in *OPEN* to find the node with minimum f-cost. Useless nodes will cause A* to spend more time to find the node with minimum f-cost. On the other hand, to generate all child nodes and compute their f-costs is also time-consuming. If these useless nodes can be avoided, A* can be improved in terms of run-time and space consumption. So, a popular method to improve A* is to reduce the number of useless nodes. For example, Yoshizumi et al. [10] introduced a variant of A* called Partial Expansion A*(PEA*). PEA* generates all children nodes but does not store all of them in OPEN when expanding node n. It only selects promising children to store, which reduces the length of *OPEN*.

(3) Ariel Felner et al. [7] improved PEA* and presented a method called Enhanced Partial Expansion A* (EPEA*). By using the Operator Selection Function (OSF), EPEA* can find those promising nodes ahead and only generated those promising nodes, avoiding generating unpromising nodes as in PEA*.

Motivated by EPEA*, this paper presents a fast shortest path searching method named A*_SA. In application, the efficiency of A* depends to a large extent on the use of domain knowledge. Research [6] shows that given two nodes in a transportation network, the shortest route between them must be in a narrow area centered on a straight line connecting the two nodes. Then, $h(n_c)$ is equal to or smaller than $h(n)^2 + Cost(n, n_c)^2$. In view of that $h(n)$ is only an assess of the real distance between n to the target node and there is usually difference between $h(n)$ and the real distance, only those children whose h-cost is equal to or smaller than $h(n) + C$ are regarded as promising nodes for simplicity. So, the main idea of A*_SA is that when expanding node n, only those children whose h-cost is equal to or smaller than $h(n) + C$ are generated and stored. Moreover, in order to avoid getting stuck in local optima, the children with larger h-cost are also generated and stored with a certain probability as in simulated annealing.

The paper is organized as follows. The shortest path finding algorithm based on A* and the simulated annealing algorithm are described in Sect. 2. Section 3 presents A*_SA in detail and analyzes the time and space complexity of it in theory. Sections 4 tests A*_SA through experiments. Section 5 concludes the paper.

2   A* and Simulated Annealing

2.1   A*

Starts from the origin node, the shortest path finding algorithm based on A* alternately selects the node n with minimum f-cost from *OPEN* and expands n until the destination node is obtained. The pseudo code of it is shown in Algorithm 1.

Suppose b is the maximum branching factor of the search tree and d is the depth of the least-cost solution, the space complexity of A* is $O(b^d)$. As shown in Algorithm 1, the most time-consuming part of A* is from Line 6 to Line 32, where generates and stores every child node n_c of node n. In the *ith* expansion, there are $ib - i + 1$ nodes in *OPEN* and i nodes in *CLOSE*, the time used to find the node n with the lowest $f(n)$ from *OPEN* is $ib - i + 1$ (Line 9). In order to avoid duplication, before generating a child node n_c, A* first makes sure that it has not been generated by other nodes (from Line 10 to Line 31). In the *ith* expansion, the time used to test duplication is $O(ib^2)$, then the time consumption in the *ith* expansion is $O(ib^2)$. The time complexity of the whole A* is $O((db)^2)$.

2.2   Simulated Annealing

Simulated annealing is often used as a global optimization algorithm and was first successfully introduced to the field of combination optimization in 1983 [5].

Algorithm 1 A*

Require: graph G, the origin node s, the destination node t
Ensure: the shortest paths P between s and t in G
 1:   $g(s) - 0$;
 2:   Compute $h(s)$;
 3:   $f(s) - g(s) + h(s)$;
 4:   $OPEN - \{s\}$;
 5:   $CLOSE - \{\}$;
 6:   **while** $OPEN = \Phi$ **do**
 7:        Get n with lowest $f(n)$ from $OPEN$;
 8:        $OPEN - OPEN - \{n\}$;
 9:        N—the set of all the child nodes of n;
10:       **for all** n_c $e\ N$ **do**
11:            **if** $n_c = t$ **then**
12:                GOTO Line 33;
13:            **else**
14:                $g\_t - g(n) + cost(n, n_c)$;
15:                $h\_t - h(n_c)$;
16:                **if** $n_c\ eOPEN$ **then**
17:                    **if** $(g\_t + h\_t < f(n_c))$ **then**
18:                        $g(n_c)\quad - g\_t;\ h(n_c)\quad -h\_t;\ f(n_c) - g\_t + h\_t$;
19:                    **end if**
20:                **else** $\{ n_c\quad eCLOSE \}$
21:                    **if** $(g\_t + h\_t < f(n_c))$ **then**
22:                        $g(n_c)\quad - g\_t;\ h(n_c)\quad -h\_t;\ f(n_c) - g\_t + h\_t$;
23:                        $OPEN - OPEN + \{ n_c \}$;
24:                        $CLOSE - CLOSE + \{ n_c \}$;
25:                    **end if**
26:                **else** $(n_c / eCLOSE) \text{AND} (n_c / eOPEN)$
27:                    $g(n_c)\quad - g\_t;\ h(n_c)\quad -h\_t;\ f(n_c) - g\_t + h\_t$;
28:                    $OPEN - OPEN + \{ n_c \}$;
29:                **end if**
30:            **end if**
31:       **end for**
32:   **end while**
33:   get P according to $CLOSE$;
34:   **return** P .

The main idea of simulated annealing is that when searching in a solution space, not only good solutions can be accepted, but also poor solutions can be accepted with a certain probability that makes it avoid local optimum to a certain extent. In view of its simplicity and effectiveness, simulated annealing has been successfully applied to many fields, such as rout planning [4], distributed generation deployment [8] and other fields. The pseudo code of simulated annealing is shown in Algorithm 2, where suppose a maximization problem is solved by Simulated Annealing.

Algorithm 2 Simulated Annealing
1: initialize T and ε;
2: $s - su$;
3: **while** termination conditions are not met **do**
4:      generate a neighbor s_{new} of s;
5:      $dE - f(snew) - f(s)$
6:      **if** $dE > 0$ **then**
7:          $s - snew$;
8:      **else** {$exp(dE/T) > random(0, 1)$}
9:          $s - snew$;
10:    **end if**
11:    $T - T * \varepsilon$;
12: **end while**

3   A* SA

The overall structure of A* SA is same with that of A*, that is, alternately selects and expands the node n with minimum f-cost from *OPEN* until the target node is obtained. The main difference between A*_SA and A* is that when expanding node n, only those children whose h-cost is equal to or smaller than $h(n) + C$ are generated and stored in *OPEN*. Moreover, motivated by simulated annealing, in order to avoid the local optimal solution, the children with larger h-cost can be generated and stored in *OPEN* with a certain probability.

C is a key parameter in A*_SA. If the C is too large, a lot of useless nodes would be generated. If the C is too small, some useful nodes may be discarded and no solution can be found. However, there is no theoretical guidance on how to set up C. In order to avoid no solution, A* SA adopts a kind of cycle mechanism. That is, initially, C is set as 0. If no solution is found after running A* SA with the current C, then C is increased by α in next iteration until a solution is found.

The pseudo code of A*_SA is shown in Algorithm 3. In the worst case, all the nodes have been generated as in A*, so the space complexity of A* is $O(b^d)$.

Suppose xb children nodes are regarded as promising nodes in every expansion, where $0 < x < \leftarrow 1$. Suppose b is the maximum branching factor of the search tree and d is the depth of the least-cost solution, the space complexity of A*_SA is same to that of A*, that is, $O(b^d)$.

In the *ith* expansion, there are $ixb - i + 1$ nodes in OPEN and i nodes in *CLOSE*, the time used to find the node n with the lowest $f(n)$ from *OPEN* is $ixb - i + 1$ (Line 11). The time used to test duplication (from Line 14 to Line 46) is $O(ixb^2)$, then the time consumption in the ith expansion is $O(ixb^2)$. The time used to executing A*_SA for one time is $O((dxb)^2)$. In sometimes, A*_SA needs to be executed several times. And in every run, x is increased gradually. Therefore, in the worst case, the time complexity of the whole A*_SA is $O((db)^2)$, same with that of A*.

For the transportation networks, the *h*-cost function is defined as the spherical distance between node n and the target node. It is worth pointing out that A*_SA can be applied to other fields by designing appropriate *h*-cost functions.

4 Experiments

In order to evaluate the efficiency of A*_SA, this section tests it through experiments. The experiments include two parts. The first part tests the influence of C on A*_SA. In the second part, A*_SA is compared with A* and EPEA*. In order to make it more comparable, A*_SA, A* and EPEA* were all coded in C and experiments were all carried out on a personal IBM PC with 2.0-GHZ CPU and 1-GB RAM running over Windows 7. In A*_SA, T is set as 100, ε is set as 0.95. It is worth pointing out that A*_SA has some randomicity and the run-time or the number of nodes stored may be different for every run. So the following results of A*_SA is the average of 100 runs.

4.1 The Influence of C on A* SA

In order to test the influence of C, A*_SA is tested on a global airline network. The global airline network includes 3818 nodes and 64387 links, where each node represents an airport, each link is a regular flight between two airports and the length of every link is defined as the spherical distance between the two airports corresponded by two nodes. In experiments, 100 origin-destination pairs of nodes were randomly selected and tested. For the limited space, only the results of 5 pairs are listed in Fig. 1 and Fig. 2.

Algorithm 3 A*_SA

Require: graph G, the origin node s, the destination node t
Ensure: the shortest paths P between s and t in G

1:   $C-0$;
2:   initialize α;
3:   $g(s)-0$;
4:   Compute $h(s)$;
5:   $f(s)-g(s)+h(s)$;
6:   $OPEN-\{s\}$;
7:   $CLOSE-\{\}$;
8:   Initialize T as a very big number;
9:   Initialize ε as a decimal number between 0 and 1;
10: **while** $OPEN$ is not empty **do**
11:     Get n with lowest $f(n)$ from $OPEN$;
12:     $OPEN-OPEN-\{n\}$;
13:     N—the set of all the child nodes of n;
14:     **for all** n_c $\in N$ **do**
15:       **if** $n_c = t$ **then**
16:         GOTO Line 48;
17:       **else**
18:         $flag-0$;
19:         $h\_t-h(n_c)$;
20:         $E-h(n)+C-h\_t$
21:         **if** $(h\_t < h(n)+C)$ **then**
22:           $flag-1$;
23:         **end if**
24:         **if** $((h\_t > h(n)+C))\text{AND}(e^{E/T}-random(0,1)>0)$ **then**
25:           $flag-1$;
26:         **end if**
27:         **if** $flag == 1$ **then**
28:           $g\_t-g(n)+cost(n,n_c)$;
29:           **if** $n_c \in OPEN$ **then**
30:             **if** $(g\_t+h\_t < f(n_c))$ **then**
31:               $g(n_c)$ $-g\_t$; $h(n_c)$ $-h\_t$; $f(n_c)-g\_t+h\_t$;
32:             **end if**
33:           **else** $\{n_c \in CLOSE\}$
34:             **if** $(g\_t+h\_t < f(n_c))$ **then**
35:               $g(n_c)$ $-g\_t$; $h(n_c)$ $-h\_t$; $f(n_c)-g\_t+h\_t$;
36:               $OPEN-OPEN+\{n_c\}$;
37:               $CLOSE-CLOSE+\{n_c\}$;
38:             **end if**
39:           **else** $\{(n_c \notin CLOSE)\text{AND}(n_c \notin OPEN)\}$
40:             $g(n_c)$ $-g\_t$; $h(n_c)$ $-h\_t$; $f(n_c)-g\_t+h\_t$;
41:             $OPEN-OPEN+\{n_c\}$;
42:            **end if**
43:         **end if**
44:         $T-T*\varepsilon$;
45:       **end if**
46:     **end for**
47: **end while**
48: get P according to $CLOSE$;
49: **if** P is empty **then**
50:     $C-C+\alpha$;
51:     GOTO Line 3;
52: **end if**
53: **return** P.

Figure 1 and Fig. 2 respectively show the run-time and the number of nodes generated by A*_SA with different C on 5 pairs of nodes. OD1, OD2, OD3, OD4 and OD5 represent 5 origin-destination pairs of nodes tested. The vertical axis in Fig. 1 is the run time in milliseconds and that in Fig. 2 shows the number of nodes generated. The horizontal axis in Fig. 1 and Fig. 2 are both the value of α (C is initialized as 0 and is increase by α in every iteration as shown in Algorithm 3).

From Fig. 1 and 2, the following points can be obtained:

(1) For different pairs of nodes, the influence of C is different. For example, with the increasing of C, the run-time for OD5 remains unchanged; however, the run-time for other 4 pairs has been changed obviously. This is due to that for OD5, when $C = 0$, a solution is found and the algorithm stops. So the run-time is not affected by C. For other 4 pairs, when $C = 0$, no solution can be found, then A*_SA must be run several times. Then, the value of C can affect their running time.

(2) With the increasing of C, for OD1, OD2, OD3 and OD4, the run-time has similar change trend. That is, with the creasing of C, the run-time decreases; when C reaches a certain value, the run-time gradually increases. The value of C determines the range of nodes to expand. When C is small, increasing C means that more nodes can be expand and some better nodes may be expanded as early as possible. So, run-time can be shut down. However, when C is enough large, increasing C may lead to many more useless nodes to expand. Thus, to generate and store those nodes can only extend the run-time. For nodes generated, there are similar results.

(3) For the same test data, the change of run-time with the increase of C is similar with that of nodes generated.

(4) For different test data, the best set of C with that A*_SA has the minimum run-time or nodes generated is different. For example, for OD3, the best set of C is 3000; for OD4, the best set of C is 5000. Therefore, the best set of C depends on the test data.

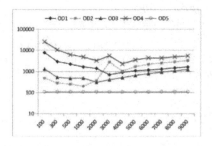

Fig. 1. Run-time (ms) of A* SA with different C on 5 pairs of nodes

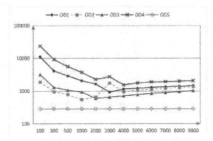

Fig. 2. Nodes generated by A* SA with different C on 5 pairs of nodes

4.2 Comparison of A* SA with A* and EPEA*

In order to be compared with A* and EPEA*, A* SA is tested on both the real global airline network introduced in 4.1 and simulated data. In experiments, the α in A* SA is set as 1000.

Test on the Real Global Airline Network

In experiments, 40 origin-destination pairs of nodes were randomly selected. The test results are shown in Fig. 3 and Fig. 4.

In Fig. 3, the vertical axis is the run time in milliseconds and the horizontal axis represents 40 test data. In Fig. 4, the vertical axis is the number of nodes generated, the horizontal axis is same with that in Fig. 3. From Fig. 3 and 4, the following points can be got:

(1) For different test data, the performance of A*_SA, A* and EPEA* are different. In terms of running time, for the 40 test data, A*_SA is faster than the other two algorithms on the 36 data sets; on the 2 test data, EPEA* is the fastest; on another 2 test data, A* is the fastest. For the number of nodes generated, A*_SA is better (the number of nodes generated represents the space overhead. The smaller the number of nodes generated, the better) than A* and EPEA* on 24 test data; EPEA* is best on 12 test data and on other 4 test data, the number of nodes generated by A*_SA is same with that by EPEA* and is smaller than that by A*.
(2) For 40 test data, the average run-time of A*, EPEA* and A*_SA is respectively 821 ms, 1617 ms and 66 ms; the average run-time of A*_SA and EPEA* is respectively 8% and 196% of that A*. The average number of nodes generated by A*, EPEA* and A*_SA is respectively 594, 219 and 165. The average number of nodes generated by A*_SA and EPEA* is respectively 37% and 27% of that by A*.

From above, in general, for both time and space requirements, A* SA is better than A*. Compared with A*, EPEA* saves space but at expense of running time. Compared with EPEA*, the running time of A*_SA is greatly reduced, but the space overhead is increased slightly.

Test on Simulated Data

In order to test the performance of A*_SA with the scale of graphs, four simulated

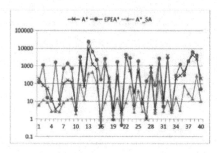

Fig. 3. The run-time (ms) of A* SA, A* and EPEA* on different test data

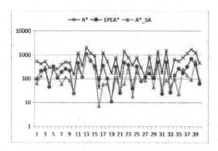

Fig. 4. The nodes generated by A* SA, A* and EPEA* on different test data

graphs with different average branching factors are generated. The number of nodes, the number of links and the average branching factor of every simulated graph is shown in Table 1. As shown in Table 1, the number of nodes in four simulated graphs are all the same, but the average branching factors are gradually increasing.

Table 1. Four simulated graphs

	Graph1	Graph2	Graph3	Graph4
Number of Nodes	4000	4000	4000	4000
Number of links	668569	3342850	4800000	6685700
Average branching factor	167	835	1200	1670

100 pairs of nodes are randomly selected from every simulated graphs. The average run-time and the average number of nodes generated by A*, EPEA* and A*_SA on the 100 test data are listed in Table 2 and Table 3 respectively. In Table 2, the ratio columns indicate the ratio of the run-time of EPEA* or A*_SA to that of A*. In Table 3, the ratio columns indicate the ratio of number of nodes generated by EPEA* or A*_SA to that by A*.

Table 2. The average run-time of A*, EPEA* and A* SA on simulated data

Data	A*	EPEA*	Ratio	A* SA	Ratio
Graph1	759	4893	6.44	37	0.048
Graph2	1150	33170	28.84	53	0.046
Graph3	1305	63587	48.72	43	0.033
Graph4	1612	150694	93.48	50	0.031

Table 3. The number of nodes generated by A*, EPEA* and A* SA on simulated data

Data	A*	EPEA*	Ratio	A* SA	Ratio
Graph1	1602	313	0.195	250	0.156
Graph2	2134	388	0.182	528	0.247
Graph3	2292	409	0.178	649	0.283
Graph4	2766	431	0.156	942	0.341

From Table 1, Table 2 and Table 3, the following several points can be got:

(1) With the increasing of average branching factor, the average run-time and the average number of nodes generated by A*, EPEA* and A*_SA increases.
(2) In terms of run-time, on four simulated networks, A*_SA is much faster than A* and EPEA*. Moreover, with the increasing average branching factor, compared with A*, EPEA* becomes worse and the speed advantage of A* SA is more and more obvious.
(3) In terms of the number of nodes generated, A* is the most space consuming. With the increasing average branching factor, the ratio of the number of nodes generated by A*_SA to that by A* gradually increases and the ratio of EPEA* to A* is decreased continuously.

In conclusion, the experimental results on simulated data are consistent with those on the global airline network, that is, A*_SA outforms A* in terms of running time and space overhead; EPEA* improve A* in terms of space overhead but at the expense of running time; Compared with EPEA*, the running time of A*_SA is greatly reduced, but the space overhead is increased slightly. Moreover, with the increasing average branching factor, the speed advantage of A*_SA and space advantage of EPEA* become more and more obvious, but respectively at the expense of space overhead and running time.

5   Conclusion

Motivated by EPEA* and the spatial distribution of transportation networks, a shortest path searching method named A*_SA based on A* and simulated annealing is proposed in this paper. The main idea of A*_SA is that when expanding node n, only those children whose h-cost is equal to or smaller than $h(n) + C$ are generated and stored. Moreover, in order to avoid getting stuck in local optima, the children with larger h-cost than n are also be stored with a certain probability as in simulated annealing. In theory, in the worst case, A*_SA has the same time and space complexity with A*. In order to test the efficiency of A* SA in application, A*_SA is compared with A* and EPEA* through experiments on the global airline network and simulated networks. Experimental results show that A*_SA outforms A* in terms of running time and space overhead; EPEA* improve A* in terms of space overhead but at the expense of running time. Compared with EPEA*, the running time of A*_SA is greatly reduced, but the space overhead is increased slightly. Moreover, with the increasing average branching factor, the speed advantage of A*_SA and space advantage of EPEA* become more and more obvious, but respectively at the expense of space overhead and running time. These results prove the efficiency of A*.

Acknowledgments. This work was supported by grants from the Major Program of Tianjin Basic Application and Cutting-edge Technology Research Plan (14JCZDJC32500).

References

1. Burns, E., Lemons, S., Ruml, W., Zhou, R.: Best-first heuristic search for multi-core machines. In: International Joint Conference on Artificial Intelligence (IJCAI) (2009)
2. Delling, D., Sanders, P., Schultes, D., Wagner, D.: Engineering route planning algorithms. Lect. Notes Comput. Sci. **5515**, 117–139 (2009)
3. Hart, P.E., Nilsson, N.J., Raphael, B.: A formal basis for the heuristic determination of minimum cost paths. IEEE Trans. Syst. Sci. Cybern. **4**(2), 100–107 (1968)
4. Li, J., Zhou, M., Sun, Q., Dai, X., Yu, X.: Colored traveling salesman problem. IEEE Trans. Cybern. **45**(11), 2390–2401 (2015)
5. Kirkpatrick, S., Gelatt, C.D., Jr., Vecchi, M.P.: Optimization by simulated annealing. Science **220**(4598), 671–680 (1983)
6. Lu, F., Lu, D., Cui, W.: Time shortest path algorithm for restricted searching area in transportation networks. J. Image Graph. **4**(10), 849–953 (1999). (in Chinese)
7. Meir, G., et al.: Enhanced partial expansion A*. J. Artif. Intell. Res. **50**, 141–187 (2014)
8. Mitra, J., Vallem, M.R., Singh, C.: Optimal deployment of distributed generation using a reliability criterion. IEEE Trans. Ind. Appl. **52**, 1989–1997 (2016)
9. Roni, S., Lelis, L.H.S.: What's hot in heuristic search. In: Proceedings of the Thirty AAAI Conference on Artificial Intelligence (2016)
10. Toshiya, H., Anton, K., Carsten, D.: Multiplexed metropolis light transport. ACM Trans. Graph. **33**(4), 1–10 (2014)

A Combining Forecasting Method Based on Seasonal Unit Root Test and Support Vector Regression

Songyuan Gu[1], Yuanyuan Qin[2], and Anwen Lu[3]([⊠])

[1] China Electronics Technology Group Corporation, Beijing, China
[2] China Academy of Electronics and Information Technology, Beijing, China
qinyuanyuan@cetc.com.cn
[3] North China Electric Power University, Baoding, China
1092879984@qq.com

Abstract. For catching and processing seasonality in seasonal time series, a combining forecasting method based on seasonal unit root test, i.e., the Dickey-Hasza-Fuller (DHF) test and support vector regression (SVR) is proposed, which is denoted as DHF-SVR method. The DHF-SVR method employs DHF test to identify seasonality in series and utilizes seasonal differencing operator to process the seasonal time series; for solving the difficulty of adaptive selection of maximum lag order, a SVR hyper-parameters tuning method based on a genetic algorithm (GA) with real-integer hybrid encoding is proposed. The experimental comparison demonstrates that the proposed DHF-SVR method could improve the forecasting performance in comparison with the comparative methods.

Keywords: Time series forecasting · Seasonal unit root test · Support vector regression · Hyper-parameters optimization

1 Introduction

Some dynamic systems, especially some monthly and quarterly data in economic and commerce fields, often show certain repetitive and periodic characteristics in each cycle due to the influence of seasonal effects. For the sake of improving our forecasting performance when facing such data in reality, the study in this paper is conducted. In the time series forecasting research of machine learning, Ref. [1] found empirically that neural networks could not capture seasonality and trend variations of original series without pre-processing, while de-seasonality operator and detrending operator could significantly reduce the forecasting error, in particular, seasonal adjustment was adopted to remove seasonality and trends in the series in this literature. Combining models based on SARIMA and SVR were adopted in Ref. [2, 3] to solve seasonal time series forecasting problems by modeling the nonlinear residuals of SARIMAs utilizing SVR. In this paper, DHF test and seasonal differencing operator are used as the pre-processing methods of seasonal time series and combined with SVR to forecast seasonal time series, and a genetic algorithm (GA) with real-integer hybrid encoding is utilized to deal with the synchronization optimization of SVR maximum lag order and hyper-parameters.

© The Author(s), under exclusive license to Springer Nature Switzerland AG 2022
Q. Zu et al. (Eds.): HCC 2021, LNCS 13795, pp. 15–24, 2022.
https://doi.org/10.1007/978-3-031-23741-6_2

2 Seasonal Time Series Forecasting Method

The DHF-SVR method employs DHF test to identify seasonality in series and utilizes seasonal differencing operator to process it; for solving the difficulty of the adaptive selection of the maximum lag order, a SVR parameters tuning method based on GA with real-integer hybrid encoding is proposed. The specific framework of the proposed method is shown in Fig. 1.

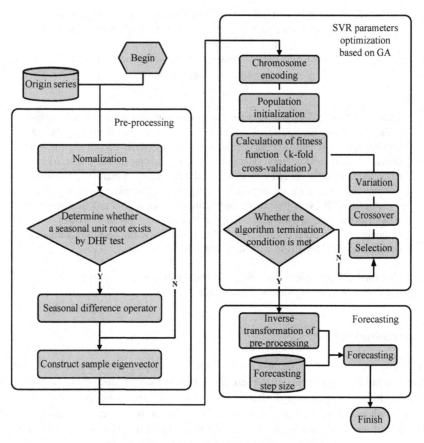

Fig. 1. Framework of the DHF-SVR method

2.1 Data Pre-processing

It is of great importance to take data pre-processing for raw data to improve forecasting performance. The data pre-processing of the DHF-SVR method includes data normalization, seasonal unit root test and processing, which could benefit forecasting results by avoiding numerical problems caused by dimension inconsistency of data and catching and eliminating the influence of seasonality.

2.1.1 Data Normalization

In order to avoid numerical problems caused by dimension inconsistency in training process, it is also necessary to apply normalization to pre-process continuous time series data. Data normalization could map data to same order of magnitude, eliminate impact of dimensions, enhance comparability between data, and reduce computational complexity. The min-max normalization formula is as follows

$$x_t' = \frac{x_t - x_{\min}}{x_{\max} - x_{\min}}$$

2.1.2 Dickey-Hasza-Fuller Test and Seasonal Differencing

Dickey, Hasza, and Fuller extended the Dicky-Fuller test to time series with seasonal unit roots, and proposed DHF test [4, 5] to verify existence of seasonal unit roots. When there are seasonal unit roots in the series, seasonal differencing operators would be used to remove the seasonal unit roots. The DHF test is based on the following regression model

$$y_t = \alpha y_{t-s} + \sum_{j=1}^{l} \Delta_s y_{t-j} + [\text{set of fixed regressors}] + \varepsilon_t$$

where s represents the length of the seasonal period and Δ_s represents the seasonal differencing operator. The fixed regression term could contain seasonal dummy variables, a linear trend and a constant. Empirical experience shows that the absence of these fixations may cause scale distortion. Therefore, it is a safe strategy to add these fixed terms into the model [5].

2.2 SVR Parameters Optimization Based on GA with Real-Integer Hybrid Encoding

In the DHF-SVR method, in order to find the optimal maximum lag order of the model while optimizing SVR hyper-parameters, a GA with real-integer hybrid encoding is used to encode and optimize the SVR maximum lag order and SVR hyper-parameters synchronously. The optimization process of GA with real-integer hybrid encoding is as follows.

2.2.1 Hybrid Encoding of SVR Hyper-parameters and Maximum Lag Order

Through the analysis of the influence of SVR parameters selection on SVR performance, the following 4 parameters for GA optimization are finally determined: penalty coefficient C, insensitive loss coefficient ε, Gaussian RBF kernel function bandwidth σ and maximum lag order l, namely the number of input features. Since the SVR hyper-parameters C, ε, σ are optimized in real number space, and the maximum lag order l is a positive integer, the real integer hybrid encoding of GA chromosome is performed on these 4 parameters. The specific encoding structure of a chromosome is shown as Fig. 2.

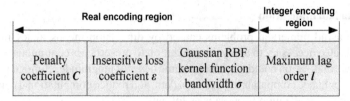

Fig. 2. Encoding structure of a chromosome

2.2.2   Fitness Function Selection and Population Initialization

MSE with 5-fold cross-validation of training set is utilized as the fitness function of GA in optimization. After chromosome encoding, the population is initialized by random generation.

2.2.3   Selection

Among selection operators, the standard 'roulette' selection algorithm is most commonly used, which calculates the probability of an individual to be selected in proportion to the individual fitness value. In order to avoid the 'precocious' problem of the 'roulette' selection algorithm in the early stage of the optimization process and the difficulty in selecting the superior individual children in the later stage, Goldberg's [6] adaptive scaling method is used in the optimization of SVR parameters of GA with real-integer hybrid encoding: scale the fitness value of the individual appropriately and then calculate its probability to be selected. The specific method of fitness scaling is to linearize the fitness value through three parameters a, b and c

$$\text{Fit}'(x) = a * \text{Fit}(x) + b$$

where

$$a = \frac{(c-1) * \text{Fit}_{\text{mean}}}{\text{Fit}_{\text{max}} - \text{Fit}_{\text{min}}}$$

$$b = \frac{\text{Fit}_{\text{mean}} * (\text{Fit}_{\text{max}} - c * \text{Fit}_{\text{mean}})}{\text{Fit}_{\text{max}} - \text{Fit}_{\text{mean}}}$$

and c is a parameter to be determined. The smaller the value of c, the greater the scaling effect, and generally c takes 1.5.

2.2.4   Crossover

GA with real-integer hybrid encoding uses arithmetic intersection to generate new individuals. Meanwhile, since there are integral genes in the chromosomes, it's necessary to process them separately after crossover to ensure the correctness of gene expression. The specific crossover form is described below. Let the two chromosomes selected for crossover be

$$c_1 = (x_1^1, x_1^2, \cdots, x_1^n)$$
$$c_2 = (x_2^1, x_2^2, \cdots, x_2^n)$$

After arithmetic crossover, the two chromosomes become

$$\hat{c}_1 = (\hat{x}_1^1, \hat{x}_1^2, \cdots, \hat{x}_1^n)$$
$$\hat{c}_2 = (\hat{x}_2^1, \hat{x}_2^2, \cdots, \hat{x}_2^n)$$

where

$$\hat{x}_1^i = \begin{cases} r * x_1^i + (1-r) * x_2^i & \text{if } x_1^i \text{ is real type} \\ \text{round}(r * x_1^i + (1-r) * x_2^i) & \text{if } x_1^i \text{ is integer} \end{cases}$$

$$\hat{x}_2^i = \begin{cases} r * x_2^i + (1-r) * x_1^i & \text{if } x_1^i \text{ is real type} \\ \text{round}(r * x_2^i + (1-r) * x_1^i) & \text{if } x_1^i \text{ is integer} \end{cases}$$

2.2.5 Mutation

The uniform mutation method is utilized in the SVR parameters optimization of GA with real-integer hybrid encoding, which selects a gene in a chromosome with a certain probability and then mutates it with random mutation within its value range. The specific mutation form of GA considering real-integer gene hybrid encoding is as follows

$$\hat{x}_i = \begin{cases} LB_i + r * (UB_i - LB_i) & \text{if } x_i \text{ is real type} \\ \text{round}(LB_i + r * (UB_i - LB_i)) & \text{if } x_i \text{ is integer} \end{cases}$$

where UB_i, LB_i are the upper and lower bounds of the value range of gene x_i.

2.3 DHF-SVR Forecasting Model

After the synchronous optimization for SVR hyper-parameters and maximum lag order by the GA with real-integer hybrid encoding proposed in the previous section, an optimal SVR model is obtained, and the inverse transformation of the previous pre-processing is still needed for this SVR model to establish the final nonlinear time series forecasting model based on SVR. The final nonlinear time series forecasting model can be formally described as

$$f(t) = \text{mapminmax}^{-1}(\Delta_s^{-m}(\sum_{i=1}^{n} (\alpha_i - \alpha_i^*)K(\mathbf{x}_i, \mathbf{x}) + b^*))$$

where Δ_s^{-m} is the m-order seasonal differencing restoring operator; mapminmax^{-1} is the inverse transformation of the min-max normalization.

3 Experimental Validation and Forecasting Performance Evaluation

In this section, for evaluating the performance of the DHF-SVR method proposed in this paper, 108 data elements, the dataset of monthly industry sales for printing and writing paper, were taken as the forecasting performance evaluation data, and for the reason that we focus on the forecasting performance improvement based on SVR, the forecasting results were compared in forecasting performance with SSVR, a forecasting method combining seasonal adjustment and SVR proposed in Ref. [7]. The original series sample is shown as Fig. 3. For convenience of comparison with the SSVR method, the last 12 data elements of the dataset were divided into test set, which is the same as in Ref. [7], to test the extrapolation forecasting performance of the proposed method. The specific partition of the dataset is shown in Table 1..

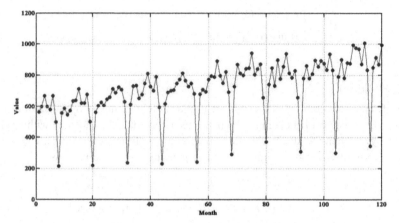

Fig. 3. Original series curve

Table 1. Experimental dataset partition

Dataset	Data range	Sample size
Training set	Jan. 1963–Dec. 1971	108
Test set	Jan. 1972–Dec. 1972	12

LibSVM [8–10] was utilized as the SVR development library. The value range of each parameter in the SVR hyper-parameters optimization and the GA parameters are shown in Table 2..

After pre-processing and testing for seasonal unit root, the SVR hyper-parameters optimization began. The GA evolution process and the optimized parameter values are shown in Fig. 4, which depicts the evolution of global optimum fitness and average fitness.

Using the optimized SVR hyper-parameters and maximum lag order, the SVR model was established. The processed series curve and the fitting situation of the training set are shown in Fig. 5.

After pre-processing and the SVR hyper-parameters optimization, the optimal DHF-SVR time series forecasting model was established and employed to make one step

Table 2. Parameter configurations of SVR and GA

Type	Parameter	Value range
DHF test	Significance level	0.05
SVR	C	0.1–1000
	ε	0.0001–0.06
	σ	0.01–100
	l	1–8
GA	Population size	20
	Generation	100
	Crossover probability	0.6
	Mutation probability	0.2
	Fitness function	MSE with 5-fold cross-validation

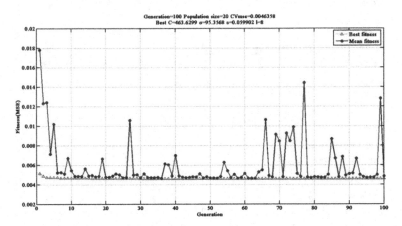

Fig. 4. Evolution process of GA

forward forecasting for the 12 samples in the test set. In addition to the comparison with the SSVR, the proposed method was also compared with the method denoting as SVR-GA$_{RIHE}$ method which is optimized by GA with real-integer hybrid encoding but is processed without DHF test and seasonal differencing. Since the forecasting data of each sample in the test set was not disclosed in Ref. [7], only the absolute errors was compared with the SVR-GA$_{RIHE}$ method. The comparison curves with the SVR-GA$_{RIHE}$ method is shown in Fig. 6, and the comparison curves of absolute error (AE) is shown in Fig. 7. It is shown in these figures that the forecasting performance and the stability of the DHF-SVR method are significantly better than that of the SVR-GA$_{RIHE}$ method.

The comparison data of the forecasting results between the DHF-SVR method, the SSVR method and the SVR-GA$_{RIHE}$ method are shown in Table 3., which manifest that the forecasting performance of the DHF-SVR method is significantly better than the

22   S. Gu et al.

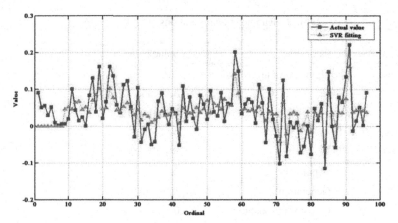

Fig. 5. SVR fitting of training set after pre-processing

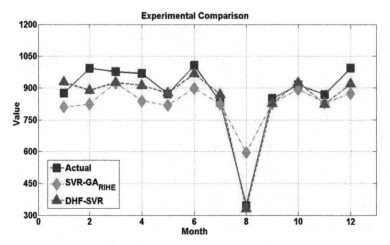

Fig. 6. Forecasting results comparison

SVR-GA$_{RIHE}$ method without DHF test and seasonal differencing operator processing, even so, the SVR-GA$_{RIHE}$ method performing synchronous optimization of maximum lag order is still superior to the SVR without seasonal adjustment in Ref. [7] in all statistics. This highlights the significance of the synchronous optimization of the maximum lag order. Compared with the SSVR method, the MAPE of the DHF-SVR method improves by (5.47–4.80)/5.47 = 12.2% and the RMSE is also superior to the SSVR method.

Table 3. Forecasting performance comparison

Comparative statistics	DHF-SVR	SSVR	SVR-GA$_{RIHE}$
MAE	42.98	–	86.63
MAPE	4.80%	5.47%	12.92%
RMSE	50.904	50.96	110.58

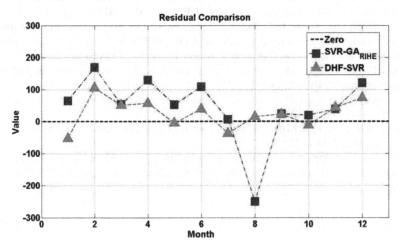

Fig. 7. Forecasting AE comparison

4   Conclusion

For solving the problem of forecasting performance improvement for time series with seasonality, a seasonal time series combining forecasting method (DHF-SVR method) based on DHF test and SVR was proposed in intelligent forecasting of univariate non-linear time series based on machine learning in this paper. Influence of seasonality could be eliminated and forecasting performance could be further improved by the proposed DHF-SVR method due to the employment of the DHF test and the SVR parameters optimization based on GA with real-integer hybrid encoding, which was verified by the experimental comparisons between the DHF-SVR, the SSVR and the SVR-GA$_{RIHE}$ methods. Though our work shows certain improvement in seasonal time series forecasting, future work would be conducted in novel approaches such as deep learning or prophet methods.

References

1. Zhang, G.P., Qi, M.: Neural network forecasting for seasonal and trend time series. Eur. J. Oper. Res. **160**(2), 501–514 (2005)

2. Chen, K.Y., Wang, C.H.: A hybrid SARIMA and support vector machines in forecasting the production values of the machinery industry in Taiwan. Expert Syst. Appl. **32**(1), 254–264 (2007)
3. Cheng, H.B., Jiang, D.L.: Hybrid models of SARIMA and support vector machine to forecast the requirement of military supplies in wartime. Mil. Oper. Res. Syst. Eng. **30**(2), 45–49 (2016)
4. Du, Y.H., Wang, R.F.: An overview of seasonal time series theory. J. Tech. Econ. Manag. **18**(5), 67–84 (2009)
5. Ghysels, E., Lee, H.S., Noh, J.: Testing for unit roots in seasonal time series: some theoretical extensions and a Monte Carlo investigation. J. Econom. **62**(2), 415–442 (1994)
6. Pasamontes, L.B., Torres, F.G., Zwick, D., et al.: Support structure optimization for offshore wind turbines with a genetic algorithm. In: ASME 2014 33rd International Conference on Ocean, Offshore and Arctic Engineering. American Society of Mechanical Engineers (2014)
7. Pai, P.F., Lin, K.P., Lin, C.S., et al.: Time series forecasting by a seasonal support vector regression model. Expert Syst. Appl. **37**(6), 4261–4265 (2010)
8. Bergmeir, C., Benítez, J.M.: On the use of cross-validation for time series predictor evaluation. Inf. Sci. **191**, 192–213 (2012)
9. Chang, C.C., Lin, C.J.: LIBSVM: a library for support vector machines. ACM Trans. Intell. Syst. Technol. **2**(3), 1–27 (2011)
10. Zaidi, S.: Novel application of support vector machines to model the two phase boiling heat transfer coefficient in a vertical tube thermosiphon reboiler. Chem. Eng. Res. Des. **98**, 44–58 (2015)

Adaptive ICP Registration Algorithm Based on the Neighborhood of SIFT Feature Points

Yawei Hong, Wentao Li, and Yongfu Chen[✉]

School of Mechanical Science and Engineering,
Huazhong University of Science and Technology, Wuhan, China
Chenyf@hust.edu.cn

Abstract. The ICP algorithm has been widely used for point cloud registration, but it has low computational efficiency under large-scale point cloud data. Moreover, it only uses the structural information of point cloud in the solving process.

Its accuracy and efficiency will be greatly affected in scenes lacking of obvious structural features and scenes with low overlap. In this paper, we propose a semidense ICP algorithm based on the neighborhood of SIFT feature points. Instead of the whole points or the sparse SIFT feature points, it selects the neighborhood of SIFT feature points as the matching range of the nearest matched point pair. We also introduce a new objective function with adaptive weights for the ICP algorithm, which balances the importance of the structural features and image features by dynamically adjusting the weights, and ensures that the ICP iteration can converge correctly. Experimental results show that the proposed method achieves higher accuracy and efficiency than several related methods. Especially, its effectiveness is also verified in scenes without obvious structural features or texture features and scenes with low overlap rate of two frame point clouds.

Keywords: RGB-D · Point cloud registration · SIFT · ICP · Adaptive weight

1 Introduction

Point cloud registration is a fundamental task for many 3D computer vision applications, such as 3D reconstruction, 3D recognition, and SLAM [1]. The purpose of registration is to transform a set of point clouds in various views into the same coordinate system, which is optimal for model recovery or pose estimation. Besl et al. proposed the ICP algorithm [2], which provides a reliable tool for point cloud registration. The ICP algorithm can get much fast speed for registration. It does not need to extract the features of the point sets or preprocess the point set. In recent years, research on ICP algorithm has focused on speed and robustness and many variant algorithms are proposed.

After the initial alignment, the traditional ICP algorithm performs fine registration of the target point sets P and source point sets Q by iteratively associating points through a nearest-neighbor search and estimating the rigid transformation T by calculating the mean square error of the objective function (1). By iterating through the above process

Q. Zu et al. (Eds.): HCC 2021, LNCS 13795, pp. 25–37, 2022.
https://doi.org/10.1007/978-3-031-23741-6_3

until the error is negligible or the maximum number of iterations is reached, the best transformation matrix T can be obtained.

$$f_{(k)} = \arg\min_{p_i \in P, q_i \in Q} \sum_{i=1}^{N_x} \|p_i \cdot T - q_i\|^2 \tag{1}$$

Theoretically, only the points of the overlapping part can get real matched point pairs. However, the ICP performs the nearest neighbor matching for the global search of all points, which has high time complexity. On the other hand, the mismatched point pairs may make the ICP converge to the wrong direction. When the overlap region of two point sets is small, the robustness is very poor. The traditional ICP is easily failed when the point sets lack obvious structural features. In this case, the correct correspondences based on the MSE between point clouds are difficult to establish. How to improve the registration accuracy, efficiency and the robustness of ICP has become a hotspot for many scholars. The contribution of this paper can be summarized as follows:

- This paper proposes a semi-dense ICP algorithm based on the neighborhood of SIFT feature points. Based on the SIFT feature points, the algorithm selects its neighborhood as the matching range.
- A new objective function with adaptive weights for the ICP algorithm is proposed. The distance of SIFT feature points which represents texture features is added to the objective function, and the weights of each item can be adjusted dynamically.
- Our algorithm also includes an outlier rejection method. We set a dynamic threshold at each iteration, and the threshold depends on both the distance of nearest matched point pair and the spatial distance of the SIFT feature pairs.

The remainder of this paper is organized as follows. Section 2 reviews the related work. Section 3 demonstrates the details of our proposed method. Section 4 provides the experiment results and analyses. Section 5 is the summary and outlook.

2   Related Work

Although ICP is simple and easy to converge, it is limited by the initial position of the point cloud and the convergence is sensitive to outliers and noises. Many points on the source point sets do not have ideal correspondences on the target points sets. To improve the performance of ICP, many variants of ICP have been proposed.

Dense point cloud matching can retain the complete information of the point cloud, but the amount of calculation is large. There are some methods to speed up the ICP. The $k - d$ tree is typically used to replace the linear scan for the closest point search. Nchter proposed an improved method called cached $k - d$ tree, which is 50% faster than traditional $k - d$ tree. Kim et al. [3] proposed a coarse-to-fine registration method, which combined the HMPS with the LDPS method to speed up the registration. Griffiths proposed the ICL/ICT, which triangulates the points of two concentrated points, and completes the match by finding the corresponding triangle area. Chen et al. proposed to use the point-to-surface distance in the objective function when finding the correspondence. It reduces the amount of calculation, but the robustness is not good.

Bae et al. [4] used curvature and normal vector to strengthen the matching relationship. It improved the accuracy to a certain extent. Du et al. [5] used the characteristics of the corners in the image to get robust results. Chetverikov et al. proposed the TrICP algorithm. In each iteration, only the $n\%$ matched point pairs with the smallest distance are reserved to calculate the transformation, which can effectively eliminate mismatches in non-overlapping regions. Ridene et al. [6] proposed a robust ICP algorithm with RANSAC and adaptive threshold to reduce the outliers. To overcome the problem of partially overlapping between two frames, Du proposed a clipping-based ICP algorithm which is independent on parameters. In addition, non-ICP algorithm have been proposed. For example, the NDT algorithm based on the probability density model uses the D-dimensional Gaussian function as the registration model. Myronenko [7] presented a probabilistic method with GMM centroids registration, and used maximum likelihood estimation to solve the probability density estimation problem.

Although the above methods can improve the accuracy and speed to a certain extent, these methods only focus on the structural information. When the point set lacks obvious structural features, it is difficult to work. With the advent of RGB-D cameras, color images and depth images can be obtained at the same time when collecting target objects. Therefore, many scholars and researchers integrate RGB image information into the ICP registration algorithm, and propose several based on the color ICP algorithm [8, 9], the results show that when the scene lacks obvious structural features, adding color information can significantly reduce the registration error.

Hao et al. proposed the 4D ICP, which introduced coordinate and hue information to establish correct correspondences. However, all points participate in the registration, it is not robust enough to noise and outliers, and its complexity is also high. Korn et al. [10] proposed a plane-to-plane ICP with lab color space and use $k - d$ tree to speed up calculation, but this algorithm is susceptible to light. Liang et al. proposed to use the HSV information filter to unify the luminosity features such as brightness and saturation of the light source, and add it to the ICP registration algorithm. The results show that better results can be obtained even in the absence of obvious structural features.

Zheng et al. [11] used the scale-invariant feature transformation of images to reduce the error of the process in generating corresponding relationship in registration. In [12], the SIFT descriptor is introduced in the ICP iteration process to improve the registration when the point cloud lacks structural features. In the algorithm [9], the matching range is limited to the sparse SIFT feature point set. The sparse method can reduce a large amount of data that needs to be calculated and greatly improve the calculation speed. However, it will have problems if the scene lacks obvious texture features.

In most ICP, a fixed coefficient is used to weight the contribution of matched point pairs to the objective function, which may not provide the best performance. In the Z-SIFT algorithm [13], the coefficient corresponding to the SIFT feature pairs is set to 2, and the weights of other point pairs are still set to 1. The corresponding SIFT feature point pair is more likely to be correspondence. The matching point pair obtained by finding the closest point is more likely to be correspondence. This algorithm can improve the accuracy and speed of registration to a certain extent, but the residual weight of the corresponding point pair is still fixed. Sometimes, the improvement effect is not obvious.

In the method of Jana et al. [14], the weight of each pair is allocated according to the angle between the normal vectors of the matching point pair.

3 Proposed Method

The input is RGB-D data, including rgb and depth images. We use SIFT features extracted from the rgb images to perform RANSAC for the initial registration. Then, we perform our ICP for the fine registration to obtain the final transform. In the iteration, we consider both structural features and the spatial distances of the SIFT feature pairs. Considering that different matched pairs in the objective function have different probabilities of being actual matched pairs, the matched pairs may have different effects on the objective function. Also, the new objective function can adjust the weight adaptively. The proposed method selects the neighborhood of SIFT feature points as the matching range of the ICP algorithm. It not only reduces the amount of calculation, but also reduces the probability of mismatching. The proposed algorithm flow is shown in Fig. 1, the following sections describe each step of the proposed algorithm.

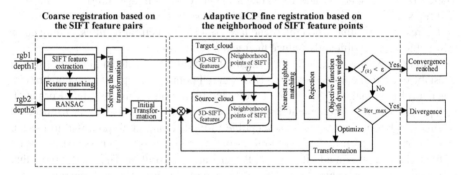

Fig. 1. Flowchart of the proposed registration algorithm for RGB-D data.

3.1 Coarse Registration Based on SIFT Feature Points

Before executing ICP, the point cloud should be coarsely registered to get a better initial pose, otherwise the iteration will be difficult to converge or fall into a local optimum. Firstly, we extract the SIFT feature points from the rgb images and get the SIFT feature point pairs by matching. There are still some mismatching in the previous results, especially in the case of small overlap area between images, so we use the RANSAC to eliminate the mismatched point pairs. We get the corresponding SIFT feature point set defined as $S = \{(m_1, n_1), ..., (m_k, n_k)\}$.

Based on the corresponding SIFT feature pairs, the transformation matrix can be solved by using unit quaternion method. The obtained initial transformation can be used as the initial pose of ICP registration algorithm.

3.2 Matching Strategy Based on the Neighborhood of SIFT Feature Points

As mentioned in the previous chapter, the matching range of the ICP is the entire point cloud. The time complexity of matching is $O(MN)$. If all points are involved in matching, it takes a long time. The points in the non-overlapping region actually have no correspondence. If these points are also involved in the matching stage, it is possible to generate mismatched point pairs, which are likely to cause errors in the calculation results and increase unnecessary calculations. With the decrease of point cloud overlap rate, the registration performance of the ICP algorithm will decrease greatly.

Based on the SIFT feature points, this paper uses its implicit index relationship to limit the matching range to the neighborhood of SIFT feature points. The schematic diagram of this method is shown in Fig. 2. Given the target point sets $P = \{p_i | i = 1, 2, 3, \ldots, N_x\}$ and source point sets $Q = \{q_i | i = 1, 2, 3, \ldots, N_x\}$.

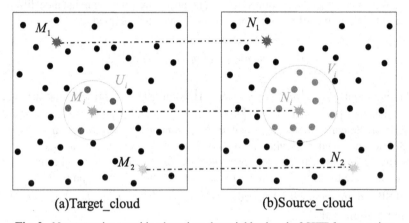

(a)Target_cloud   (b)Source_cloud

Fig. 2. Nearest point matching based on the neighborhood of SIFT feature points

$M = \{m_i | i = 1, 2, 3, \ldots, K\}$ and $N = \{n_i | i = 1, 2, 3, \ldots, K\}$ represent SIFT point sets obtained from P and Q. (m_i, n_i) stands for the corresponding SIFT feature pair which contains an implicit correspondence between P and Q. For each point m_i in M, we get the nearest x neighboring points in P, denoted as $U_i = \{U_{ij} | j = 1, 2, 3, \ldots, x\}$. Similarly, for each point n_i, we get the nearest $2x$ neighboring points in Q, denoted as $V_i = \{V_{ij} | j = 1, 2, 3, \ldots, 2x\}$. Only the points in the set $U = \{U_i | i = 1, 2, 3, \ldots, K\}$ can participate in the iterative search for the nearest point. When each point in U_i searches for the nearest corresponding point, the matching range is set V_i.

The SIFT feature pairs belong to the overlapping part of the two point sets under different viewing angles. Therefore, it can be considered that the nearest x points in the neighborhood of SIFT feature points also belong to the overlapping part of point cloud. We set the number of V_i as $2x$, so that each point in U_i can find the corresponding point. This further reduces the amount of calculation and the number of iterations, improves the computational efficiency, and makes the algorithm not easy to get localized.

3.3 Dynamically Eliminate Mismatched Point Pairs

As the iteration goes on, the outliers should be removed in each iteration. Otherwise, they will affect the accuracy of the result, and lead to difficult or wrong convergence. The proposed algorithm proposes an outlier rejection method. We set a dynamic threshold in each iteration. At the kth iteration, the corresponding point pair with the Euclidean distance greater than the threshold t^k is considered to be a mismatched point pair, and it does not participate in the calculation of the transformation matrix T^k.

The threshold depends on both the distance of nearest matched point pair and the spatial distances of the SIFT feature pairs. The dynamic threshold for the outlier rejection is defined as follow:

$$t^k = c \cdot \sqrt{er^k \cdot df^k} \tag{2}$$

where c is a constant, and er^k counts the root mean square Euclidean distance difference of all point pairs in the effective point pair set s^k, which is defined as:

$$er^k = \sqrt{mean_{p_i \in s^k}\left(\left\|p_i \cdot T^{k-1} - q_i^k\right\|^2\right)} \tag{3}$$

Among them, $s^k = \{p_i | d_i^k < 3 \cdot std(d^k)\}$ point set, d_i^k represents the distance of nearest matched point pair, $d_i^k = \left\|p_i \cdot T^{k-1} - q_i^k\right\|$, $std(d^k)$ represents the standard deviation of all nearest matched point pair. All point pairs with a Euclidean distance less than 3 times the standard deviation are added to the effective point pair set s^k, and the remaining point pairs can be considered to be wrong result with a higher probability. Finally, calculate the er^k of all the point pairs in the effective point pair set s^k.

All SIFT point pairs with distance $d_i > mean_{p_i \in s^k}\left(\left\|p_i \cdot T^0 - q_i\right\|^2\right) + 2std(d)$ also need to be eliminated.

It is generally believed that the smaller the distance of the SIFT feature pair, the higher the reliability of the feature point pair can be matched correctly. Firstly, the distances of all SIFT feature pairs are calculated, we place the first $m\%$ pair of SIFT feature point pairs with smaller distance into set S^m, and calculate the average Euclidean distance df^k by Eq. (4).

$$df^k = mean_{m_i \in s^m}\left(\left\|m_i \cdot T^0 - n_i\right\|^2\right) \tag{4}$$

3.4 Design of Objective Function with Adaptive Weights

In the proposed algorithm, the distance of SIFT feature pair and the distance of nearest matched point pair should be considered at the same time. It is obvious that SIFT feature points have a greater probability of becoming a real matched point pair.

The new objective function to be minimized in the kth iteration to find T^k is denoted as follow:

$$f_{(k)} = \sum_{p_i \in U} \alpha_i \left\|p_i \cdot T^k - q_i^k\right\|^2 + \sum_{(m_i, n_i) \in S} \beta_i \left\|m_i \cdot T^k - n_i\right\|^2 \tag{5}$$

where q_i^k is the corresponding point in the point cloud V with the closest distance to each point p_i in the point cloud U:

$$q_i^k = \underset{q_i \in V}{argmin}\left(\left\| p_i \cdot T^{k-1} - q_i \right\|^2 \right) \tag{6}$$

This method minimizes the spatial distance of points with structural features and the spatial distance of SIFT feature point pairs representing image texture features. By classifying the two kinds of matched point pairs and giving different weight parameters, the iteration can be effectively constrained to the correct convergence direction, and the robustness and correctness of registration can be improved.

Among the point pairs obtained by the nearest neighbor matching, the degree of influence on the results is different in the solution. The more similar the matched point pair is, the more likely it is to be the correct matched point pair. And, it should be given a higher weight. Curvature information of point cloud can well represent local features of point cloud. We propose the following weight calculation formula:

$$\alpha_i = \sqrt{\frac{0.01}{|\sigma(p_i) - \sigma(q_i^k)|}} \tag{7}$$

where $\sigma(p_i)$ 和$\sigma(q_i^k)$ represent the curvature information of a pair of matched points. A common method to calculate the curvature is to fit a local surface and then calculate the curvature at the point. However, this method is time-consuming. We usually approximate the surface curvature by calculating the eigenvalues of the covariance matrix of the local region. And the calculation process is as follows. For each point p_i, the point covariance matrix of the neighborhood point set centered on it is calculated:

$$\Sigma_i^s = \frac{1}{|V_i|} \sum_{p_i \in V_i} (p_i - \mu_i)^T (p_i - \mu_i) \tag{8}$$

where μ_i is the average value of the neighborhood point set. Due to the symmetry of the covariance matrix, SVD decomposition is performed to obtain:

$$\Sigma_i^s = R \begin{pmatrix} \lambda_1 & 0 & 0 \\ 0 & \lambda_2 & 0 \\ 0 & 0 & \lambda_3 \end{pmatrix} R^T \tag{9}$$

Assume that $\lambda_1 < \lambda_2 < \lambda_3$, the corresponding feature vector of the smallest feature root λ_1 is the normal vector $\vec{v}_1$ of the tangent plane at the point set V_i, and the curvature of p_i can be approximated as:

$$\sigma_i = \frac{\lambda_1}{\lambda_1 + \lambda_2 + \lambda_3} \tag{10}$$

The value of β_i is also very important. If the weight is too large, the result mainly relies on a relatively small number of SIFT feature points, which may degenerate into sparse ICP registration. On the contrary, the regular terms based on RGB image texture features become less important, so a reasonable balance of weight is needed. Based on the above argument, β_i is set as:

$$\beta_i = c' \cdot \frac{1}{dist(m_i, n_i)} \cdot \frac{er^k}{es^k} \tag{11}$$

where, er^k represents the RMS of Euclidean distance of matched point pairs, and es^k represents the RMS of Euclidean distance of all SIFT feature pairs. The calculation of er^k is shown in Eq. (3). es^k is defined as:

$$es^k = \sqrt{mean_{(m_i, n_i) \in S} \left(\left\| m_i \cdot T^{k-1} - n_i \right\|^2 \right)} \tag{12}$$

In Eq. (11), c' is a constant, $dist(m_i, n_i)$ represents the spatial distance of SIFT point pair (m_i, n_i). The smaller $dist(m_i, n_i)$ is, the more similar the SIFT feature pairs is and the more likely it is to be matched correctly. The larger er^k is, the smaller es^k is, the higher the matching accuracy is compared with other matched point pairs.

4   Experimental Results and Analysis

In this section, we will conduct experimental verification, especially its effectiveness in scenes lacking of obvious structural features and scenes with low overlap. It is compared with FPFH + ICP algorithm based on structure, sparse ICP based on SIFT and dense ICP based on SIFT. The experiments are performed on the fr1_xyz dataset in TUM. According to the real trajectory of the camera, the real relative pose transformation between any two frames of images can be obtained. By comparing with the pose transformation calculated by the registration algorithm, the relative pose error (RPE) can be obtained to measure the accuracy of the registration algorithm. In the experiment, we take 101 frames from the dataset at an equal time interval. We register each pair of adjacent data. The experimental results were evaluated with the automatic evaluation tool provided by TUM website, and the evaluation results are shown in Table 1.

Table 1. Experimental results of several algorithms on TUM dataset

Evaluation	FPFH + ICP	Sparse ICP based on SIFT	SIFT + ICP	Our method
$Rmse(RPE_{trans})$	0.021 m	0.0187 m	0.016 m	0.0124 m
$Mean(RPE_{trans})$	0.016 m	0.012 m	0.0117 m	0.0105 m
$Median(RPE_{trans})$	0.011 m	0.0099 m	0.0092 m	0.00837 m
$std(RPE_{trans})$	0.009 m	0.0097 m	0.011 m	0.00731 m
$Min(RPE_{trans})$	0.00053 m	0.00051 m	0.00047 m	0.000415 m
$Rmse(RPE_{rot})$	0.92°	0.83°	0.867°	0.71°
$Mean(RPE_{rot})$	0.632°	0.572°	0.618°	0.549°
$Median(RPE_{rot})$	0.00954°	0.00838°	0.00899°	0.00759°
$std(RPE_{rot})$	0.51°	0.437°	0.597°	0.412°
$Min(RPE_{rot})$	0.042°	0.047°	0.0389°	0.036°

The proposed algorithm is superior to the other algorithms in all indicators. It has higher accuracy and smaller registration error. Compared with the previous algorithms, the RMSE of translation errors are reduced by 40.9%, 38.5% and 22.5% respectively. Also, the RMSE of rotation errors are reduced by 22.8%, 23.4%, 18% respectively.

In order to compare the running speed of several algorithms, we count the average running time of single registration in several groups of experiments, and the experimental results are shown in Fig. 3. The results show that the average time consumption of the proposed algorithm is much lower than that of SIFT + ICP and FPFH + ICP, and the average time is basically the same as that of the sparse ICP based on SIFT. From the overall results, the time consumption of the proposed algorithm is reduced by 76.3% and 80.4% compared with the other two algorithms respectively.

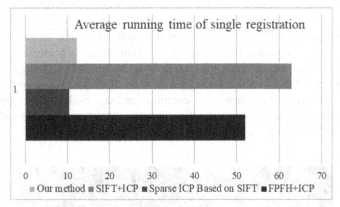

Fig. 3. The average time consumption of the four algorithms in the TUM dataset

The points participating in matching and the matching range are limited to the overlapping region of two frames. It can ensure that the points participating in the matching are valid. Based on the implicit correspondence provided by SIFT point pair, the searching range of nearest neighbor points can be greatly reduced. Also, the design of dynamic weight and the removal of mismatched point pairs during each iteration can accelerate the convergence of the algorithm and improve the registration speed.

The above experiments show that the accuracy based on structural and texture features is better than that based only on structural information (FPFH + ICP). In order to verify the effectiveness in scenes lacking obvious structure, we select three groups of data without obvious structural features in the RGB-D Object Dataset for experiments.

The results in Table 2 show that the proposed method can still converge when scenarios lack structural features, and the accuracy is higher than the other algorithms. The results based on the FPFH + ICP are very poor, because the algorithm does not add the texture information, but only the structure information based on point cloud. In this case, it is usually unable to extract significant points or find matched point pairs, and it is easy to converge to the wrong direction.

Table 2. RMSE of the distance between matched point pairs after registration (mm)

Algorithm	Test1	Test2	Test3
SIFT + ICP	7.438	6.115	6.233
FPFH + ICP	12.990	10.853	8.135
SIFT + ICP	3.102	4.325	2.983
Our method	2.843	5.578	3.103

In order to verify the registration effect of our algorithm in different overlap rates, especially in scenes with low overlap. We extract 4 frames of data at intervals on the TUM, and register the 2nd, 3rd and 4th frame with the 1st frame respectively. In the three groups of experiments, the overlap rate of point clouds is gradually smaller, and in the last group of experiments, the overlap rate is only 40%. Through simulation experiments, the RMS of point cloud spacing in the three groups of experiments was obtained as a function of the number of iterations, and the results were compared with other algorithms. Figure 4 shows the registration effect of the proposed algorithm in low overlap scene. The Iterative effect is shown in Fig. 5, 6 and 7.

Fig. 4. The registration result of the proposed algorithm in low overlap scene

The proposed method performs better than the other two algorithms. With the decrease of the overlap rate, the accuracy of the results obtained by our method decreases slightly, but it can still converge. However, the accuracy of other algorithms deteriorates significantly with the decrease of overlap rate. In the last two sets of experiments, they can not converge. In classic ICP, it is prone to get wrong correspondence. This may lead to incorrect convergence direction or slow down the convergence speed. In the proposed method, the searching scope of participating points and corresponding points can be limited to the overlap region of the two frames. There is no mismatching and the iterative process can be pointed in the right direction.

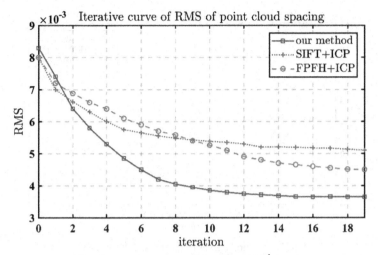

Fig. 5. Iteration curves of the 1st and 2nd frames

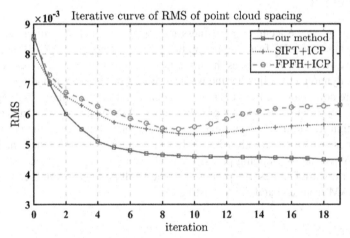

Fig. 6. Iteration curves of the 1st and 3rd frames

It can be seen from the results that our method is generally superior to the compared algorithms. Moreover, it still has good registration accuracy and efficiency in scenes without significant structural features and scenes with low overlap degree.

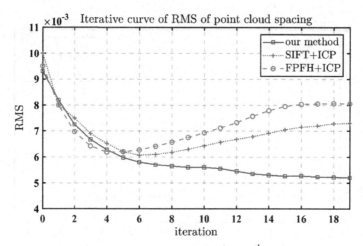

Fig. 7. Iteration curves of the 1st and 4th frames

5 Conclusion

In order to improve the accuracy, robustness and speed of the ICP algorithm, we consider both the distance of SIFT feature pair and the distance of nearest matched point pair in the objective function. It balances the importance of the structural features and image features by dynamically adjusting the weights. Based on the corresponding relation of SIFT feature point pair, we limit the matching data points and the matching range of the points. This semi-dense method can greatly improve the registration speed and make our ICP algorithm iterate in the right direction. Simulation results verify the effectiveness of the proposed method, which achieves higher accuracy and efficiency than several methods. When the overlapping part is relatively small or the point sets lack obvious structural or texture features, the proposed method still performs well. It can be widely used in SLAM front-end and 3D reconstruction.

References

1. Wolff, K., Kim, C., Zimmer, H., et al.: Point cloud noise and outlier removal for image-based 3D reconstruction. In: International Conference on 3D Vision, pp. 118–127 (2016)
2. Besl, P., Mckay, N.: A method for registration of 3-D shapes. IEEE Trans. Pattern Anal. Mach. Intell. **14**, 239–256 (1992)
3. Kim, D., et al.: A fast ICP algorithm for 3-D human body motion tracking. IEEE Signal Process. Lett. **17**(4), 402–405 (2010)
4. Bae, K., Lichti, D.: A method for automated registration of unorganized point clouds. LSPRS J. Photogramm. Remote Sens. **63**(1), 36–54 (2008)
5. Du, S., et al.: Precise iterative closest point algorithm with corner point constraint for isotropic scaling registration. Multimedia Syst. **25**(2), 119–126 (2017). https://doi.org/10.1007/s00530-017-0573-6
6. Ridene, T., Goulette, F.: Registration of fixed-and-mobile - based terrestrial laser data sets with DSM. In: IEEE International Symposium on Computational Intelligence in Robotics and Automation, pp. 375–380 (2010)

7. Myronenko, A., Song, X.: Point set registration: coherent point drift. IEEE Trans. Pattern Anal. Mach. Intell. **32**(12), 2262–2275 (2010)
8. Pandey, G., McBride, J., et al.: Visually bootstrapped generalized ICP. In: IEEE International Conference on Robotics and Automation, pp. 2660–2667 (2011)
9. Lexian, L.: Precise iterative closest point algorithm for RGB-D data registration with noise and outliers. Neurocomputing **399**, 361–368 (2020)
10. Korn, M., Holzkothen, M., Pauli, J.: Color supported generalized-ICP. In: International Conference on Computer Vision Theory and Applications, pp. 592–599 (2015)
11. Zhongyang, Z., Yan, L.: LiDAR point cloud registration based on improved ICP method and SIFT feature. In: IEEE PIC, pp. 588–592 (2015)
12. Lemuz, R., Arias, M.: Iterative closest SIFT formulation for robust feature matching. In: Advances in Visual Computing, pp. 502–513 (2006)
13. Lulu, H., Sen, W., Pappas, T.: 3D surface registration using Z-SIFT. In: IEEE International Conference on Image Processing, pp. 1985–1988 (2011)
14. Procházková, J., Martišek, D.: Notes on iterative closest point algorithm. In: 17th Conference on Applied Mathematics APLIMAT, pp. 876–884 (2018)

A PSO Based Multi-view Hierarchical Clustering Method

Zhongyu Zhou[1] and Jianfu Li[2(✉)]

[1] Research and Development Center, TravelSky Technology Limited, Beijing, China
[2] School of Computer Science and Technology, Civil Aviation University of China, Tianjin, China
jianfu_lili@163.com

Abstract. In the era of big data, multi-view data becomes more and more common. Many clustering algorithms have been developed into multi-view clustering to process multi-view data, except for hierarchical clustering. Although it has advantages over other clustering algorithms, hierarchical clustering lags behind due to the lack of a well-defined objective function. In the past five years, many people have devoted themselves to the study of the objective function for hierarchical clustering, and have proposed some objective functions. Inspired by the existing multi-view clustering algorithms and the emerging objective functions for hierarchical clustering, this paper proposes a multi-view hierarchical clustering method called MVHCPSO. The main idea of MVHCPSO is to use the particle swarm optimization algorithm and tree rearrangement operations to fuse multi-view data. The test results on simulated datasets and real datasets show that MVHCPSO is effective.

Keywords: Multi-view clustering · Hierarchical clustering · Particle swarm optimization · Tree rearrangement

1 Introduction

In the era of big data, multi-view data becomes more and more common and multi-view clustering has attracted more and more attentions. In the recent two decades, multi-view clustering has been developed rapidly and many multi-view clustering algorithms have been presented. The multi-view clustering algorithms are developed on the basis of existing single-view clustering algorithms. The basic idea of multi-view clustering is to improve the accuracy of single-view clustering by using the consistency and complementarity between multi views data. Many single-view clustering algorithms [1] have been developed into multi-view clustering to process multi-view data, such as multi-view spectral clustering, multi-view subspace clustering, multi-view k-means, and so on. However, none of hierarchical clustering algorithms have been developed to multi-view clustering.

A hierarchical clustering is a recursive partitioning of a dataset into successively smaller clusters. Due to that it does not require any parameters and provides richer

Q. Zu et al. (Eds.): HCC 2021, LNCS 13795, pp. 38–49, 2022.
https://doi.org/10.1007/978-3-031-23741-6_4

information at all levels of granularity simultaneously displayed in an intuitive form, hierarchical clustering has more advantages. However, compared with other clustering algorithms, the development of hierarchical clustering is much slower. As pointed out by Dasgupta [2] in 2016, the main reason why hierarchical clustering has lagged behind is the lack of a well-defined objective function. Although there are two popular objective functions for hierarchical clustering in phylogenetics [3]: maximum likelihood function and maximum parsimony function, these two objective functions are very complex, often implicitly embody constraints, and not suitable for general data in data mining [2]. Since Dasgupta [2] firstly proposed an objective function for hierarchical clustering with general pairwise similarities between points in 2016, many people have devoted themselves to the study of the objective function for hierarchical clustering, and have proposed some objective functions [4].

Inspired by existing multi-view clustering algorithms and the emerging objective functions for hierarchical clustering, this paper proposes a multi-view hierarchical clustering method. In implementation, the existing multi-view clustering algorithm usually establishes a clustering error function to reflect the clustering error of each view, and then continuously adjusts the clustering results to reduce the clustering error in the way of gradient descent until the desired result is obtained or the termination condition is reached. However, we cannot apply directly the implementation of existing multi-view clustering algorithms to multi-view hierarchical clustering due to the following two reasons.

(1) Existing multi-view clustering represents each single-view clustering by a cluster assignment matrix or a vector with fixed size. The simple and consistent representation facilitates the fusion of multiple clustering results. On the contrary, a hierarchical clustering is represented by a tree, which is much more complicated than a matrix or a vector. This brings difficulties to the sharing and integration between various views.

(2) Although there are currently some objective functions for hierarchical clustering, their discreteness inherently restricts them from adjusting the clustering results dynamically according to the clustering error function like exiting multi view clustering algorithms.

In view of the above two reasons, this paper uses the particle swarm optimization (PSO) and tree rearrangement operations widely used in phylogenetic to fuse multi views data. For convenience, the new method is called MVHCPSO(**m**ulti-**v**iew **h**ierarchical **c**lustering based on **PSO**).

The remainder of this paper is organized as follows. Section 2 briefly introduces PSO and tree rearrangements. In Sect. 3, MVHCPSO is proposed and detailed. Section 4 conducts comparative experiments. Finally, Sect. 5 concludes the paper.

2 PSO and Tree Rearrangements

2.1 PSO

PSO [5] is a population based random search algorithm and proposed in 1995. The core idea of PSO is to find the optimal solution through cooperation and information sharing among particles in the swarm.

PSO firstly initializes the swarm as a group of random particles. Each particle represents a possible solution to the optimization problem and has two properties, state and velocity. PSO iteratively adjusts particles' state and velocity until the termination condition is reached.

In the $(k + 1)$th iteration, particle i is updated according to the following formulas (1) and (2)

$$v_i^{k+1} = w \times v_i^k + c_1 \times r_1 \times \left(p_i - x_i^k\right) + c_2 \times r_2 \times \left(p_g - x_i^k\right) \tag{1}$$

$$x_i^{k+1} = x_i^k + v_i^{k+1} \tag{2}$$

where v_i^{k+1} (v_i^k) is the velocity of particle i in the $(k + 1)$th (kth) iteration and x_i^{k+1} (x_i^k) is the state of particle i in the $(k + 1)$th (kth) iteration; p_i is the state of the local optimal solution found by the particle i, p_g is the state of the global optimal solution found by the entire particle swarm so far. A solution is evaluated by a fitness function f, which is defined according to the specific optimization problem. The parameters, c_1 and c_2 are two positive constant named as learning factors, usually set as $c_1 = c_2 = 2$; r_1 and r_2 are random variables in $[0, 1]$; w is a weight factor and usually positive.

The condition to stop the above iterations is generally to reach the predetermined number of iterations or the particle swarm is no longer been updated in predetermined multiple iterations.

The pseudocode of PSO is shown in Fig. 1.

2.2 Tree Rearrangements

A hierarchical clustering result is usually an unrooted binary tree where each leaf represents a data point and each internal node represents a cluster containing its descendant leaves. The tree arrangements [6] are a serial of operations to change the topology structure of a tree. Common tree arrangements include NNI (Nearest Neighbor Interchange), SPR (Subtree Prune and Regraft), TBR (Tree Bisection and Reconnection) and p-ECR (p-Edge Contraction and Refinement).

NNI is to exchange the four subtrees connected by an internal branch, SPR is to select and reinsert a subtree into elsewhere in the tree. In TBR, to randomly select and delete branch from a tree, so that the current tree is divided into two sub-trees, and then connect the two sub-trees by connecting any two edges from the two sub-trees respectively, resulting in different trees. The amount of change of the new tree obtained by the above three rearrangements relative to the original tree is fixed and can not be adjusted according to actual needs. On the contrary, p-ECR means to contract p edges all at once, creating unresolved nodes in the process, then to refine these unresolved nodes to give back a binary tree. Thus, p-ECR can use the parameter p to just the degree of change. Moreover, in our previous work [7], we gave an effective implementation p-ECRNJ for p-ECR. In this paper, we use p-ECRNJ to update the state of a particle. p-ECRNJ mainly includes the following two steps.

(1) To randomly select p branches to contract all at once;
(2) To refine unresolved nodes to give back a binary tree by Neighbor Joining (NJ) [8], a popular single-view hierarchical clustering.

For detailed information of p-ECRNJ, please refer to the reference [7].

Input: c_1, c_2, w
Output: Optimal solution
1. $k \leftarrow 0$;
2. for each particle i do
3.   initialize v_i^k and x_i^k;
4. $p_i \leftarrow x_i^k$;
5. $p_g \leftarrow$ the best one of $p_i\{i=1,2,...m\}$, where m is total number of particles;
6. while the termination condition is not reached do
7.   for each particle i do
8. $r_1 \leftarrow$ rand(0,1), $r_2 \leftarrow$ rand(0,1);// a random real number between 0 and 1
9.   update v_i^{k+1} by formula (1);
10.   update x_i^{k+1} by formula (2);
11.   if ($f(x_i^{k+1})$ is better than $f(x_i^k)$)
12. $p_i \leftarrow x_i^k$;
13.   if $f(p_i)$ is better than $f(p_g)$
14. $p_g \leftarrow p_i$;
15. Return p_g.

Fig. 1. The pseudocode of PSO

3 The MVHCPSO Method

Let $D_1,..., D_i, ..., D_V$ denote the multi-view data, where $D_i \in R^{n \times n}$ is a distance matrix between data points, V and n are respectively the number of views and data points in each view. MVHCPSO mainly includes the following three steps:

(1) Cluster each view data D_i separately by a hierarchical clustering algorithm to obtain a clustering tree T_i. It should be noted that the hierarchical clustering algorithm for clustering each view of data can be the same or different. In the experiments of this paper, NJ is used in this step to cluster each view of data;
(2) Use the set of $T_i \{i = 1, 2, ..., V\}$ as the initial particle swarm, and then continuously update each particle according to the PSO algorithm;
(3) Output the best solution as the final clustering result.

In above three steps, the second step is the core of MVHCPSO, that is, PSO based information integration. This part adopts the basic framework of PSO, that is, each particle continuously updates its velocity and state according to formulas (1) and (2). However, in the context of hierarchical clustering, the mathematical operations in the formulas have been given new definitions as follows.

3.1 Fitness Function

The fitness function to evaluate a hierarchical clustering tree T_i in MVHCPSO is the objective function proposed by reference [4] as shown in formula (3), where $D_i(x, y)$ denotes distances between two leaf nodes x and y in D_i, $T_i(x, y)$ is the subtree rooted at the lowest common ancestor of x and y in T_i and $|T_i(x, y)|$ is the number of leaves $T_i(x, y)$ contains:

$$f(T_i) = \sum_{(x,y)\in T_i} D_i(x, y) \times |T_i(x, y)| \tag{3}$$

The tree T_i with higher $f(T_i)$ is better.

The pseudocode to compute $f(T_i)$ is shown in Fig. 2. The most time consuming part is *Step* 3.1.5, which is to calculate the minimum common subtree between any two leaf nodes x and y. Its time complexity is $O(n)$, so time complexity of *Step* 3 and the total time complexity to compute $f(T_i)$ is $O(n^3)$.

Input: T_i, D_i
Output: $f(T_i)$
1. *sum*←0;
2.*Leas*←all leaf nodes of T_i;
3.for(x=0;x< *Leas.size*()-1;x++)
4.   for(y=x+1; y< *Leas.size*(); y++)
5.   *nodex*←*Leas*[*x*];
6.   *nodey*←*Leas*[*y*];
7.   *a*←D_i [*nodex.id*][*nodey.id*];
8.   *node*←*nodex*;
9.   *while*(1) //*O(n)*
10   *if*(*node*==*T.root* || *nodey*∈ **node. leaves**)   *break*;
11.   *node*←*node.father*
12.   *b*←|*node.leaves*|;
13.   *sum*+=*a*b*;
14. return *sum*.

Fig. 2. The pseudocode to compute $f(T_i)$

3.2 Velocity Update

The velocity of every particle i in the $(k+1)$th iteration is updated according to formula (1). However, in the context of hierarchical clustering, x_i^{k+1} (x_i^k) is the hierarchical clustering tree T_i in the $k+1$th (kth) iteration, p_i denotes the best clustering tree which has ever passed by the particle i till now, p_g denotes the best clustering tree which has ever passed by the whole swarm. Since p_i, p_g and x_i^k are trees and can not be subtracted mathematically, we use the topological distance between trees to represent the difference between trees, that is, $p_i - x_i^k$ and $p_g - x_i^k$ denote the topology distance between p_i and x_i^k and that between p_g and x_i^k respectively. In the experiments in this paper, the topological distance between the two trees T_i and T_j on the same set of data points is defined as the number of different internal branches contained by the two trees. Deleting an internal branch e from tree T will divide T into two separate subtrees TS_1 and TS_2, and divide the original data point set S into two sets S_1 and S_2, where S_1 is the leaf node of the subtree TS_1 and S_2 is the leaf node set of TS_2. If the data points set division derived from the two branches from the tree T_i and T_j are the same, the two branches are the same. Since there are $n - 3$ internal branches for an unrooted binary tree including n data points, the topological distance between the two trees is an integer with a maximum of $n - 3$ and a minimum of 0. The pseudocode to compute the topological distance $Dis(T_1, T_2)$ between two trees T_1 and T_2 shown in Fig. 3. The first and second steps are to get the internal nodes of the two trees with $O(n)$ time complexity. The third step is to calculate the sets of leaf nodes in the subtree rooted at each internal node in T_1, which corresponds to the data points set division generated by an internal branch. Step 4 is to calculate the sets of leaf nodes in the subtree rooted at each internal node in T_2. The time complexity of Step 3 and Step 4 are both $O(n^2)$. Step 6 is to calculate the number of the same internal branches between two trees by judging whether the leaf sets corresponding to the two internal nodes are equal. The time cost of judging whether two sets are equal is $O(n^2)$ (Step 6.1.1), so the time complexity of step 6 is $O(n^4)$. Thus, the time complexity to compute $Dis(T_1, T_2)$ is $O(n^4)$.

From the above definition, we can see that $p_i - x_i^k$ and $p_g - x_i^k$ are always greater than or equal to 0, which is different from that in the basic PSO. In the basic PSO, $p_i - x_i^k$ and $p_g - x_i^k$ can be positive or negative. In this way, the search direction of particles can be adjusted by $p_i - x_i^k$ and $p_g - x_i^k$, , so that other parameters (c_1, r_1, c_2 and r_2) are always positive. In MVHCPSO, if the parameters are also set as positive as in the basic PSO algorithm, the particles will fly in a certain direction at an increasing velocity as the iteration progresses, that is not in line with the nature of the PSO algorithm. In order solve the problem, r_1 and r_2 are allowed to be positive or negative in MVHCPSO.

Input: T_1, T_2
Output: $Dis(T_1, T_2)$
1.$nodes1$← internal node of T_1//$O(n)$
2.$nodes2$← internal node of T_2//$O(n)$
3.for($i=0;i<nodes1.size();i++$)//$O(n^2)$
4    $Leaves1[i]$ ←the leaf nodes of the subtree rooted at $nodes1[i]$ in T_1;
5.for($i=0;i<nodes2.size();i++$)//$O(n^2)$
6. $Leaves2[i]$ ←the leaf nodes of the sub rooted at nodes2[i] in T_2;
7. num←0;
8. for($i=0;i<nodes1.size();i++$)////$O(n^4)$
9.   for($j=0;j<nodes2.size();j++$)
10.   if($Leaves1[i]$== $Leaves2[j]$)// $O(n^2)$
11. $break$;
12.   if(j== $nodes2.size()$)
13. num++;
14. return $nodes1.size()$-num.

Fig. 3. The pseudocode to compute $Dis(T_1, T_2)$

3.3   State Update

The state of every particle i in the $(k + 1)$th iteration is updated according to formula (2). Since x_i^k denotes the topology of particle i in the k-iteration and v_i^{k+1} is a real number representing the velocity, there is no way to mathematically sum them. In this paper, every x_i^{k+1} is obtained through operating the p-ECRNJ as mentioned in Sect. 2.2 on x_i^k, and p is defined as $\left\lceil \left| v_i^{k+1} \right| \right\rceil$, where $\lceil x \rceil$ is the minimum integer that greater than x.

As shown in reference [7], the time complexity of p-ECRNJ is $O(p^4)$.

3.4   Termination Conditions

The termination condition in MVHCPSO is that the maximum times k_{max} of iterations is reached.

3.5   The Pseudocode and Time Complexity of MVHCPSO

The pseudocode of MVHCPSO is shown in Fig. 4. The first step is to cluster D_i to get hierarchical clustering tree T_i. The time cost of this step depends on the clustering algorithm. The time complexity of NJ used in experiments is $O(n^3)$, where n is the number of data points in D_i. Then, the time complexity of $Step$ 1 is $O(Vn^3)$. $Step$ 3 is to initialize the swarm and compute $f(T_i)$ for very T_i. As shown in Sect. 3.1 that the total time complexity to compute $f(T_i)$ is $O(n^3)$, the time complexity of $Step$ 3 is $O(Vn^3)$.

Step 4 is to select the p_i with best $f(p_i)$ as p_g, and the time complexity is $O(V)$. In Step 5, the particles are iteratively updated. The most time-consuming part is Step 5.1. The time complexity to compute p_i $(p_g) - x_i^k$ (Step 5.1.1 and Step 5.1.2) is $O(n^4)$ and the time complexity to update v_i^{k+1} using (1) (Step 5.1.4) and calculate p according to v_i^{k+1} (Step 5.1.5) is $O(1)$. And the time used to apply p-ECRNJ to x_i^k to get x_i^{k+1} (Step 5.1.6) is $O(p^4)$. In general, p is much less than n. So, the time complexity of Step 5.1 is $O(Vn^4)$, and that of Step 5 is $O(k_{max}Vn^4)$. The time complexity of MVHCPSO is $O(k_{max}Vn^4)$.

From above analysis, we can see that the time complexity of MVHCPSO is $O(k_{max}Vn^4)$, and the time complexity of NJ is only $O(n^3)$. Therefore, considering multiple views of data brings additional time overhead to MVHCPSO, that is consistent with the nature of multi-view clustering. However, if the clustering results of MVHCPSO is better than those of NJ, then this extra time overhead is considered worthwhile.

Input: $D_1,\ldots, D_i, \ldots, D_V$, a, b, k_{max}, w, c_1, c_2
Output: hierarchical clustering T
1. for each D_i do
2.   cluster D_i to get hierarchical clustering tree T_i;
3. $k \leftarrow 0$;
4. for each particle i do//$O(Vn^3)$
5. $x_i^k \leftarrow T_i$;
6.   initialize v_i^k as a random real number between $[-a, a]$;
7. $p_i \leftarrow x_i^k$;
8.   compute $f(x_i^k)$;
9. $p_g \leftarrow \{p_i | \max\limits_{i=1:2\ldots v} f(p_i)\}$;
10. while ($k<k_{max}$) do//$O(Vn^4)$
11.   for each particle i do
12.   calculate p_i-x_i^k;// $O(n^4)$
13.   calculate p_g-x_i^k; // $O(n^4)$
14. $r_1 \leftarrow$ rand(-b,b), $r_2 \leftarrow$ rand(-b,b);// a random real number between -1 and 1
15.   update v_i^{k+1} by formula (1);//$O(1)$
16. $p \leftarrow \lceil \|v_i^{k+1}\| \rceil$;//$O(1)$
17.   apply p-ECRNJ on x_i^k to get x_i^{k+1};// $O(p^4)$
18.   if $(f(x_i^{k+1}) > f(x_i^k))$
19. $p_i \leftarrow x_i^k$;
20.   if $(f(p_i) > f(p_g))$
21. $p_g \leftarrow p_i$;
22. $k \leftarrow k+1$;
23. output p_g.

Fig. 4. The pseudocode of MVHCPSO

4 Experiments

In order to verify the effectiveness of MVHCPSO, this section compared MVHCPSO with NJ through experiments. In MVHCPSO, parameter are set as follows: a is set as 10, b is set as 1, k_{max} is set as 50, c_1 and c_2 are set as 2, w is set as 0.1. Experiments include two parts: test on simulated data sets and that on real data sets.

4.1 Test on Simulated Data Sets

This part tests MVHCPSO on two simulated data sets from the reference [9]. Both datasets consist of 2,000 model trees, each corresponding to three sequence sets generated by the model tree under different evolutionary conditions. In the first dataset, the model trees include 24 leaves; in the second datasets, the model trees include 96 leaves. We randomly selected 100 model trees with 24 taxa and 100 ones with 96 taxa and three sequence sets corresponded by very model tree are seen as a 3-view data set. Then, we get 200 data sets, each of which has three views, 24 or 96 data points. Experiment results on the two simulated data sets are listed in Table 1 and Table 2.

Table 1. Test results on the simulated data sets with 24 taxa

	V1_24	V2_24	V3_24	MVHCPSO	Ratio1	Ratio2	Ratio3
1	3080	2920	2920	3128	1.56%	7.12%	7.12%
2	3164	3205	3210	3648	15.30%	13.82%	13.64%
3	2930	2930	2887	3423	16.83%	16.83%	18.57%
4	2334	2347	2369	2723	16.67%	16.02%	14.94%
5	2905	2783	3114	3311	13.98%	18.97%	6.33%
6	3296	3308	3214	3942	19.60%	19.17%	22.65%
7	2666	2749	2666	3134	17.55%	14.01%	17.55%
8	2562	2900	2719	2919	13.93%	0.66%	7.36%
9	2985	2699	2679	3102	3.92%	14.93%	15.79%
10	3234	3242	3247	3950	22.14%	21.84%	21.65%
11	3287	3399	3312	3920	19.26%	15.33%	18.36%
12	2706	2641	2372	2721	0.55%	3.03%	14.71%
13	2265	2262	2395	2929	29.32%	29.49%	22.30%
14	2602	2704	2549	3106	19.37%	14.87%	21.85%
15	2663	2888	1850	3146	18.14%	8.93%	70.05%
16	4085	3760	3903	4399	7.69%	16.99%	12.71%
Average	2923	2921	2838	3344	14.74%	14.50%	19.10%

Table 2. Test results on the simulation data sets with 96 taxa

	V1_96	V2_96	V3_96	MVHCPSO	Ratio1	Ratio2	Ratio3
1	200978	202466	203794	237790	18.32%	17.45%	16.68%
2	150733	151383	151892	174268	15.61%	15.12%	14.73%
3	153618	151123	158171	177935	15.83%	17.74%	12.50%
4	160897	181272	175785	183165	13.84%	1.04%	4.20%
5	194967	193961	192639	227600	16.74%	17.34%	18.15%
6	166381	171578	170890	198128	19.08%	15.47%	15.94%
7	156136	158411	153002	176521	13.06%	11.43%	15.37%
8	178873	193954	188558	209053	16.87%	7.78%	10.87%
9	171808	169610	170537	190621	10.95%	12.39%	11.78%
10	152286	150738	151257	167064	9.70%	10.83%	10.45%
11	173104	161335	172816	179513	3.70%	11.27%	3.88%
12	138233	138052	137563	164811	19.23%	19.38%	19.81%
13	191509	191158	186874	220432	15.10%	15.31%	17.96%
14	187557	191841	185854	216217	15.28%	12.71%	16.34%
15	168023	170118	165560	192894	14.80%	13.39%	10.65%
16	205169	204786	202954	234483	14.29%	14.50%	15.54%
Average	171892	173862	163696	196906	14.53%	13.32%	13.79%

Due to space limitations, Table 1 only shows the test results on 16 multi-view data sets with 24 taxa. In Table 1, the first column is the number of the test data set; columns 2 through 4 from the left are the objective function values of the trees obtained by NJ on each view data; and the fifth column lists the objective function values of the trees returned by MVHCPSO on multi view data. It is worth noting that, because of the randomness of PSO, the values in column 5 are the average of 20 runs. Right three columns compared the clustering results of MVHCPSO and the clustering results of NJ on each single view data and each item is calculated by $(f(T_{MVHCPSO}) - f(T_{NJ}))/f(T_{NJ}) * 100\%$, where $f(T_{MVHCPSO})$ is the objective function value of the tree obtained by MVHCPSO on multi-view data, $f(T_{NJ})$ is the objective function value of the tree obtained by NJ on a single view data. The last row in Table 1 is the average of all the data in the column.

Similar to Table 1, Table 2 shows the results on the second simulated dataset.

From Table 1 and Table 2, we can see that:

(1) The values in the right three columns in Table 1 and Table 2 are all positive, which mean that MVHCPSO on multi-view data is better than NJ on every three single views data.

(2) For different test data, MVHCPSO has different advantages over NJ. For example, for the first test data in Table 1, the improvement percentage of MVHCPSO compared with NJ with the first single view data is 1.56%; for the 10th test set, the

improvement percentage of MVHCPSO compared with NJ on the first single view is 22.14%.

(3) Compared with different views, MVHCPSO has different advantages. For example, the improvement percentage of MVHCPSO compared with NJ on three single view data in Table 1 is 14.74%, 14.50% and 19.10% in average; those in Table 2 are 14.53%, 13.32% and 13.79%.

4.2 Test on Real Data Sets

This part tests MVHCPSO on two real data sets SensIT Vehicle data and Handwritten numerals from the reference [10].

For SensIT Vehicle data, we randomly sample 50 data for each class and see the signals by acoustic and seismic sensor as different views. So, we have a data set with 100 data, with two views. In handwritten numerals, digits are classified into 10 classes from 0 to 9 and digits are represented in terms of the six feature sets: fou, fac, kar, pix, zer and mor. We randomly select 10 pattern for each class and see very feature set as a view. Then, we get a multi view data with 6 views and 100 data points in each view. The test results on the two real data sets are listed in Table 3, where the "V_i" (i = 1, 2,..., 6) column is the objective function values of the trees returned by NJ on that view data, the "MVHCPSO" column is the objective function values of the trees returned by MVHCPSO on multi view data. Similar to Table 1 and Table 2, the values in the "MVHCPSO" column are the average of the results of 20 runs.

From Table 3, we can see that the objective function values of MVHCPSO are all bigger than that of NJ on single view data on the two real datasets. On SensIT Vehicle, the improvement percentage of MVHCPSO compared with NJ on two single view data is (1969422 − 1929746)/1929746 * 100% and (1969422 − 1789615)/1789615 * 100% respectively, that is, 2.06% and 10.04%. On Handwritten numbers, the improvement percentage of MVHCPSO compared with NJ on six single view data is (1004319 − 962244)/962244 * 100%, (1004319 − 900017)/900017 * 100%, (1004319 − 950938)/950938 * 100%, (1004319 − 983094)/983094 * 100%, (1004319 − 909421)/909421 * 100%, (1004319 − 922172)/922172 * 100% respectively, that is, 4.37%, 11.59%, 5.61%, 2.16%, 10.44% and 8.91%.

Table 3. Test results on the two real data sets

	V1	V2	V3	V4	V5	V6	MVHCPSO
SensIT Vehicle	1929746	1789615					1969422
Handwritten numbers	962244	900017	950938	983094	909421	922172	1004319

From the above test results on simulated data sets and real data sets, we can see that the results of MVHCPSO on multi view data are better than that of NJ based on single view data with different improvement percentages, which proves that MVHCPSO can effectively fuse the information in various views.

5 Conclusion

Based on PSO, this paper proposes a new multi-view hierarchical clustering called MVHCPSO and describes it in detail. In theory, the time complexity of MVHCPSO is $O(k_{max}Vn^4)$, which is higher than its single-view clustering algorithm NJ. However, the experimental results on simulated data sets and real data sets show that the clustering results obtained by the MVHCPSO are all better than those by NJ.

Since the new algorithm MVHCPSO is based on the traditional hierarchical clustering algorithms, it has all the disadvantages of the traditional hierarchical clustering algorithm, such as high complexity and the clustering results are not high enough. With the rapid development of deep learning technologies in the last decade, many clustering and multi-view clustering algorithms have been greatly improved. So far, some researches have begun to use neural network or reinforcement learning to improve the hierarchical clustering. In the future, we will consider using neural network or deep learning technology to improve multi view hierarchical clustering.

References

An Overview of Recent Multi-View Clustering

1. Fu, L., Lin, P., Vasilakos, A.V., Wang, S.: An overview of recent multi-view clustering. Neurocomputing **402**, 148–161 (2020)
2. Sanjoy, D.: A cost function for similarity-based hierarchical clustering. In: Proceedings of the Forty-Eighth Annual ACM Symposium on Theory of Computing, pp. 118–127. Association for Computing Machinery, New York (2016)
3. Yang, Z.: Computational Molecular Evolution. Oxford University Press, Oxford (2006)
4. Cohen-Addad, V., Kanade, V., Mallmann Trenn, F., Mathieu, C.: Hierarchical clustering: objective functions and algorithms. In: Proceedings of the Twenty-Ninth Annual ACM-SIAM Symposium on Discrete Algorithms, pp. 378–397. Society for Industrial and Applied Mathematics, 3600 University City Science Center Philadelphia, PA (2018)
5. Kennedy, J., Eberhart, R.: Particle swarm optimization. In: Proceedings of IEEE International Conference on Neural Networks, vol. 4, pp. 1942–1948 (1995)
6. Caceres, A.J.J., Castillo, J., Lee, J., John, K.S.: Walks on SPR neighborhoods. IEEE/ACM Trans. Comput. Biol. Bioinf. **1**, 236–239 (2013)
7. Li, J.-F., Guo, M.-Z.: Improving the efficiency of p-ECR moves in evolutionary tree search methods based on maximum likelihood by neighbor joining. In: The Symposium of Computations in Bioinformatics and Bioscience, pp. 60–67 (2007)
8. Saitou, N., Nei, M.: The neighbor-joining method: a new method for reconstructing phylogenetic trees. Mol. Biol. Evol. **4**, 406–425 (1987)
9. Desper, R., Gascuel, O.: Fast and accurate phylogeny reconstruction algorithms based on the minimum-evolution principle. J. Comput. Biol. **5**, 687–705 (2002)
10. Cai, X., Nie, F., Huang, H.: Multi-view k-means clustering on big data. In: Proceedings of the Twenty-Third International Joint Conference on Artificial Intelligence, pp. 2598–2604 (2013)

GCN-ARIMA Based Sales Demand Prediction

Boquan Gao and Jingjing Cao[✉]

School of Transportation and Logistics Engineering, Wuhan University of Technology, No. 1178 Heping Road, Wuhan 430063, People's Republic of China
bettycao@whut.edu.cn

Abstract. Since its appearance, neural network and time series related works had been tremendously developed. The GNN, CNN based Graph Convolutional Network was proposed recently, and made obvious contribution in solving link prediction and vector classification problems. With the development of chain operation, more and more data analysis institutions had started to provide network based sales and inventory level prediction service. This paper dedicated to propose a new prediction mean by joint employing the network analysis mean and single vector time series prediction mean to achieve a significantly more accurate prediction result. Employing GCN as the network analysis part and the ARIMA model as single vector time series prediction part. The GCN model is especially suitable for analyzing embedding information on non-Euclidean graph while the ARIMA model is able to utilize rather small amount of data to achieve an accurate prediction result, by combining these two models, this paper have achieved a better prediction result on non-Euclidean graph. And a supply chain related dataset was used to certify the efficiency of GCN-ARIMA model.

Keywords: GCN · ARIMA · Prediction · Sales-network

1 Introduction

With the development of logistics industry in our country, related commercial entities are no longer satisfied with traditional rough and qualitative sales prediction measures. The classical prediction method like: exponential smoothing method, regression analysis method, moving average method and soon had made great contribution in the business world. But holding a more accurate prediction method can surely help a corporation greatly decrease the chance of handling a lack of stock situation while effectively lower the level of unnecessary stock. These can significantly lower the cost of logistic company. Therefore, related quantitative prediction measures are proposed to solve these problems. Recent years, with the development of artificial intelligence, humankind now have a much more powerful tool ever before. Measures such like: Long Short-Term Memory (LSTM), Graph Convolutional Network (GCN), Autogressive Intergrated Moving Average Model (ARIMA) are raised to solve this kind of problem.

All these measures had proved their effectiveness in multiple occasions, however, there still are issues ought to settle. In the past research, in a sales network, simply dealing with the history information of a single vector may can not get a satisfying

Q. Zu et al. (Eds.): HCC 2021, LNCS 13795, pp. 50–60, 2022.
https://doi.org/10.1007/978-3-031-23741-6_5

result of prediction. Because each part of the network are intimately connected. A time-series based method can extract the tendency and time influence of the data easily. However, there still has many stochastic influences in the real business world. And in some occasions, these might be the key to solve the problem.

Simply using method like ARIMA, LSTM [1] or SVM [2] will be likely to neglect some "hidden" information, while tools like GCN and other graph based measures can only learn these part information of the entirety and lose sight on the specific individual data. These features had made the using of these model will be likely to cause some distortion of prediction result, which shall lead to huge commercial loss.

In consideration of above problems, Yanguo Huang had came up with a GCN-LSTM based measure [3]. By combining these two models, this new method should has the capability to dig information globally. However, Huang's work mainly focus on short term traffic flow forecast, the LSTM model might be suitable for that situation, but not appropriate for the sales prediction in logistics industry. So this paper will mainly focus on rather longer term prediction.

This paper uses a dataset of sales quantity in 6 different chain shops as the input of our model, in order to verify the efficiency of this new method.

2 GCN-ARIMA Model Description

The supply network is a non-euclidean net, which means many traditional methods like CNN [4] or GNN [5] can not be used to solve this issue. These traditional methods were only designed for computing information on Euclidean Graph, they can not deal with irregular target. Hence we choose to use the GCN model to learn the embedding infor-mation of the whole network, which was originally designed to analyze the connection between vectors of a graph. Unlike other methods, the GCN model focus on the target connection of neighbor vectors rather than the fixed eight neighbor vectors of our target, this feature allows the GCN model to extract information even on non-Euclidean graph. After the process of GCN step, a ARIMA method can be used to learn the periodical change of each supply center.

2.1 Graph Convolutional Network

The concept of Graph Convolutional Network was first put forward by Joan Bruna from New York University in 2013. It is a model developed from GNN and CNN model, but as this paper had mentioned before, these method are only suitable for Euclidean graph, which means all vector on the map has to be evenly spread, the distances between each vector are the same. This feature made these models can only be used in matrix computing or something alike, in a word, they have a strict limitation. While GCN model was designed to extract information from non-euclidean graph. The core idea of GCN [6] is to do discrete convolution operation to each part of the graph, by that way, the model can still fuse the value of the vector itself and its neighbor's together while do not have to be limited by the shape of the graph. Therefore, the GCN can easily dig out some hidden connection in the graph that might be easily neglected by other models. This feature is kind of like the Grey forecasting model. Many information not that easy to be described individually yet expressed by a "polymeride", are usually called embedding. With this feature, many complex predictions in the real world can be done easily, like social network analysis, traffic flow prediction, and of course sales prediction.

This feature made the GCN model especially good at handling classification and prediction problem. It even can be used in text classification [7], semantic recognition and other linguistics problem solving.

In a graph G = (V, E), with a input of X. A single layer of GCN operation can be described below:

$$H^{l+1} = \sigma\left(LH^lW^l\right)$$

this equation can most concisely describe the core idea of GCN model, the L here represents the Laplacian operator [8], which represents the convolution operation of the model, the Laplacian operator in this occasion can be unfolded into this equation:

$$L = \tilde{D}^{-\frac{1}{2}}\tilde{A}\tilde{D}^{-\frac{1}{2}}$$

with these two equations, we can give out a specific formula for the GCN model:

$$H^{l+1} = \sigma\left(\tilde{D}^{-\frac{1}{2}}\tilde{A}\tilde{D}^{-\frac{1}{2}}H^lW^l\right)$$

the H^l represents the *lth* layer of the GCN operation, for the first layer of the model, the $H^1 = X$. The $\tilde{D}$ represents the diagonal matrix of current matrix, the specific computing method shall be introduced later in this paragraph. While the A as the adjacency matrix expresses the relation between each vector of the graph. $\tilde{A} = A + I$, the I in this formula means a $N*N$ unit matrix. The reason we add a I matrix is to make express that each vector is also connected to itself, this feature will be needed in later computing. To be specific, if there is an edge between vector i and j, then $a_{ij} = 1$, otherwise $a_{ij} = 0$. And the $\tilde{D}_i = \Sigma_j\widetilde{A_{ij}}$. The W^l represents the *lth* weight matrix that the model needs to learn. Beware the w matrix here is not a global matrix, instead it should be calculate separately in each layer. Finally, the $\sigma(\ldots)$ represents the activation function. In this paper, we choose to use the *RELU* function as the activation function, the formula of *RELU* is shown below:

$$f(x) = \begin{cases} x, & x > 0 \\ 0, & x \leq 0 \end{cases}$$

2.2 Autoregressive Integrated Moving Average

The Autoregressive integrated moving average (ARIMA) is proposed to solve time series prediction puzzles. It is a model that developed from the Autoregressive integrated moving average (ARMA) model, the ARIMA model mainly consists three parts. The Autoregressive operation (AR) [9], the integrate operation (I), and then Moving average operation (MA) [10].

The ARIMA model is a time-series data based prediction model, which means the training of this model mainly relies on the past data. For most traditional time-series data based prediction model. A larger amount of bygone can obtain a better prediction result, so does the ARIMA model. However, a great advantage of the ARIMA model is that it does not have to utilize a large amount of known data to make a rather precise result. And it can handle the volatility even better than traditional prediction model, such as: exponential smoothing method, regression analysis method and moving average method.

This model has three parameters, p represents the lag of the data itself, called the AR parameter; d represents the number of difference operation we need to do in order to get a stable time series data, it is called Integrated parameter; q represents the lag of deviation during our calculation, usually use MA parameter to describe it. With these back knowledge, the formula of the ARIMA operation can be described below:

$$\widehat{y_t} = \mu + \theta_1 * y_{t-1} + \cdots \theta_p * y_{t-p} + \epsilon_1 * e_{t-1} + \cdots \epsilon_q * e_{t-q}$$

in this formula, the μ is the constant term; the θ_p represents AR operation parameter, a slop coefficient; the d decides the form of y_t, for the case d $= 1$, $\widehat{y_t} = \widehat{Y_t} - Y_{t-1}$; and the e_{t-q} represents the error value of the prediction model, for the case q $= 1$, $e_{t-1} = Y_{t-1} - \widehat{Y_{t-1}}$.

The reason we need to do difference operation to the original data is that the ARIMA model requires the Input data has to be stable, which can be reflected in the value of p and q. Overlarge value of p and q can cause the time complexity of this algorithm rises Exponentially. While the value of d also can not goes too high. Normally the value of d should be no more than 3. Otherwise the time complexity will also rises greatly, meanwhile a time-series data that holds that much severe volatility may not suitable to be predicted by this model. Other more suitable models should be considered in that occasion.

2.3 GCN-ARIMA Model

The GCN-ARIMA sales prediction model can be described as: joint using the embedding E that learned through the GCN model and a time series data $X_{t-s}, X_{t-s+1}, \ldots X_{t-1}$ that collected from each vector in the network, to predict the sales of moment t. The formula can be states as below:

$$X_t = F\left(E, \left[X_{t-s}, X_{t-s+1}, \ldots X_{t-1}\right]\right)$$

the X_t here represents the output matrix of the model. The $F()$ function here represents the GCN-ARIMA model.

The GCN-ARIMA model consists two parts, the Graph Convolutional Network model and the Autoregressive integrated moving average model. As it shown in Fig. 1, this model uses a time series data which has a length of s as the input data, process the data with 3 GCN layer to extract the spatial feature of the non-euclidean graph then record the data of this step as part of the input for ARIMA model. After processing the data of X_{t-1}, the ARIMA model shall calculate the finally forecast sales value.

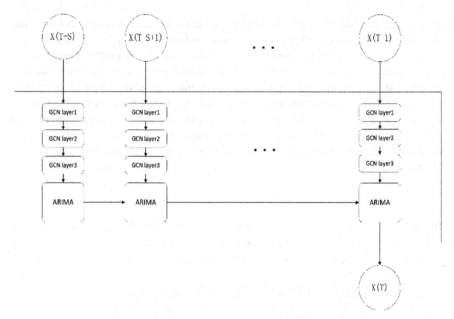

Fig. 1. The schematic diagram of GCN-ARIMA model

The original dataset had been divided into training set and testset. Where as the data concludes many clearly unreasonable unit, therefore a data preprocessing step is necessary. After this step, the processed data can be transmitted to the model, then use the test set to verify the model. Repeating this step until get a satisfying result. The whole progress is shown as Fig. 2.

3 Data and Result Analysis

3.1 Original Dataset

The original dataset comes from a 6 shop concluded chain sales network, this paper collected 5 different brands of cola sales data cross 72 days, correct to day. Therefore, there are 2160 individual data in our dataset.

The graph here for logistical industry is a isomorphic graph. In a logistic graph, each node represents a distribution outlet or a warehouse in the real world. In this particular paper, the nodes stand for retail shops, while the edges that connect the shops means shops that being connected have influence to each other, reflected by their sales performance. In this paper, restricted by the size of experiment data, a fully connected homogeneous graph with six nodes and fifteen edges is used to do the computation. The information in each node only contains one meaning, that is the sales performance at a particular point-in-time. The input data shall be a series of graphs shaped like this logistic graph.

The reason this paper picked GCN instead of other models is that the input dataset is a rather small one, the cost of computation for changing map isn't unacceptable. Past researches had proved that GCN method can usually extract embedding from a graph more accurately than traditional models like GraphSage or Random Walk model. These models especially models like GraphSage that does not works base on inductive learning, might have a better result in handling large scale of (10000 nodes or even more) graph based data. Based on these two reasons, a GCN model was selected to extract embedding information from the logistic graph.

Part of the raw data are shown below in Fig. 3, it should be noted that this dataset concludes many distortion and missing with a huge fluctuation range. Therefore adequate pre-processing measures are taken to get a clean and appropriate input dataset, to fill the missing part and normalize the raw data.

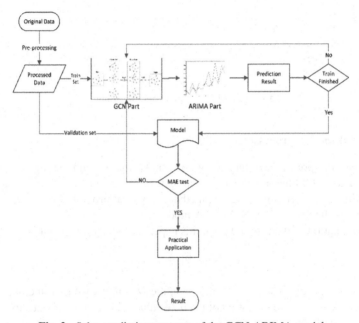

Fig. 2. Sales prediction progress of the GCN-ARIMA model

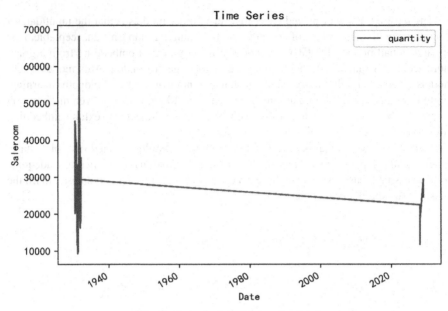

Fig. 3. Part of original cola sales data

3.2   Input Data Pre-processing

In this paper, the pre-processing mainly consists two parts, eliminating the evidently distortion data and fill the blank that caused by these distorted data. Then normalize all the data with zero-mean normalization method. Data that processed by these two steps can be used as the input of GCN-ARIMA model.

The elimination of distortion data in this paper shall obey this formula:

$$\left| D_i - \overline{D} \right| > 3\sigma_D$$

the D_i here represents each date of sales data, the $\overline{D}$ is mean value of the date and the σ_D represents the standard deviation of the date value. This formula means to eliminate all data that clearly has a wrong date.

The missing data supplement operation in this paper shall obey this formula:

$$\widehat{x_{i+n}} = \frac{x_{i+n+1} - x_i}{n}$$

the x_{i+n} represents the n missing data between x_i and x_{i+n+1}. The i here has a range of $[1, \infty], i \in Z$.

The normalize operation in this paper shall obey the zero-mean normalization:

$$y_i = \frac{x_i - \bar{x}}{\sigma}$$

the y_i represents the normalized data, the $\bar{x}$ is the mean value of original sales data, the σ means the standard deviation of the sales data.

The hardware environment is Intel(R) Core(TM)i7-8750H CPU@2.20 GHz, Nvidia Geforce GTX 1050Ti 4 GB, 24 GB RAM; the software environment is Windows 10 operating System, Python 3.8, Pytorch 1.7.1.

3.3 Evaluation of the Result

The aim of the GCN-ARIMA model is to predict sales value more accurately than traditional methods, therefore this paper uses MAE (Mean Absolute Error) for evaluation. The formula of MAE and is shown below.

$$MAE = \frac{1}{n} \sum_{i=1}^{n} \left| \widehat{Y}_i - Y_i \right|$$

the $\widehat{Y}_i$ represents the prediction value of the GCN-ARIMA model, the Y_i represents the true value of the sales data.

The experiment uses ARIMA model, GCN-ARIMA model and traditional Moving Average model to predict the sales value of a same chain-shop network. By randomly using 30 days of the past selling data as the input of the model, the experiment predicted the incoming 7 days sales value as the output of the model. Part of the experiment result are shown below.

Table 1. Experiment result of prediction for different model

Shop	MAE		
	Moving average	ARIMA	GCN-ARIMA
Athens-1	3672.44	2857.62	2952.27
Irakleion	4112.64	3259.71	3004.12
Patra	7012.85	5672.99	5211.34
Thessaloniki	3871.26	2296.71	1984.70
Athens-2	1992.45	1301.53	1029.86
Larisa	6091.38	3825.89	3776.91

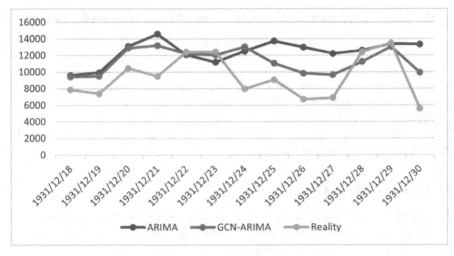

Fig. 4. Part of prediction result at vector Athens-2

Conclude from Table 1, it should be noted that in most cases, the MAE value of the GCN-ARIMA model is much smaller than ARIMA model, which means the GCN-ARIMA model can predict the sales value more accurately than the traditional ARIMA model. However there still has some exception, for example when it comes to the prediction of shop Athens-1. It seems that the GCN-ARIMA model had failed. So an analyzation for the experiment data is needed.

Figures 5 and 6 show the original sales data of shop Athens-1 and shop Athens-2, which separately represents the worst and best prediction of GCN-ARIMA model. It is clear that sales data from Athens-1 shop has much more fluctuant than it in Athens-2, while data from other shops are more likely to Athens-2's. They are more periodic and stable than Athens-1's data, rarely has much fluctuation. This might be caused by the feature of ARIMA model. The ARIMA model focus on recent data much more than remote data, while models like LSTM are likely to use the data from remote and recent more evenly. It can be concluded that the GCN-ARIMA model can handle periodic data better than ARIMA model, but it still needs some improvement in handling fluctuant data (Fig. 4).

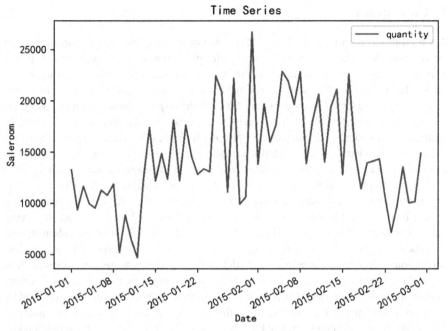

Fig. 5. Original data from shop Athens-1

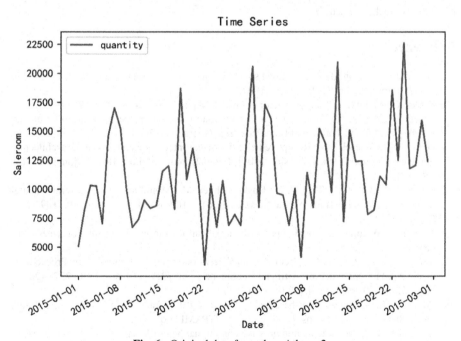

Fig. 6. Original data from shop Athens-2

4 Conclusion

Research about chain-shop network sales prediction had become a hot research direction recent years. Abundant graph based time-series prediction methods had been proposed to provide a more proper solution to this sort of puzzle. This paper proposed a new GCN-ARIMA method that joint collecting both spatial and horary information of a sales network. By using the GCN model to dig out the hidden spatial information and using the ARIMA model to calculate the time series changing of the data, this model can globally settle complex issues in the real world. Especially for issues that the restriction conditions and environment variables could hardly be described with specific mathematical formula, vast majority of real-life matters posses above features. Besides, this model can dissolve small-scale graph based problem better than many traditional methods. Therefore, this new method can be estimate as a practical serviceable solution, and had proved it is more effective than traditional ARIMA model and Moving Average model in solving sales value prediction problem. This model still holds some unsolved problem in data pre-processing phase. Under certain circumstance that original dataset holds a large data fluctuation, this model may not perform that well, this issues needs further research to settle. At the mean time, other substitutable methods might be used to replace current models. The ARIMA model that is used to extract time-series data might be replaced by some up to date model like prophet algorithm or holt-winters time-series data analysis model. While the GCN part that used to extract spatial information might be replaced by other methods like GAT(Graph Attention Network) or DeepGCNs models. These might be done by further research.

References

1. Hochreiter, S., Schmidhuber, J.: Long short-term memory. Neural Comput. **9**(8), 1735–1780 (1997). https://doi.org/10.1162/neco.1997.9.8.1735
2. Cortes, C., Vapnik, V.: Support-vector networks. Mach. Learn. **20**(3), 273–297 (1995)
3. Huang, Y., Zhang, S., Wen, J., Chen, X.: International Conference on Transportation and Development 2020: Traffic and Bike/Pedestrian Operations (2020)
4. Hubel, D.H., Wiesel, T.N.: Receptive fields, binocular interaction and functional architecture in the cat's visual cortex. J. Physiol. **160**, 106 (1962). https://doi.org/10.1113/jphysiol.1962.sp006837
5. Scarselli, F., Gori, M., Tsoi, A.C., Hagenbuchner, M., Monfardini, G.: The graph neural network model. IEEE Trans. Neural Netw. **20**(1), 61–80 (2009). https://doi.org/10.1109/TNN.2008.2005605
6. Kipf, T.N., Welling, M.: Semi-supervised classification with graph convolutional networks (2017)
7. Yao, L., Mao, C., Luo, Y.: Graph convolutional networks for text classification. In: Proceedings of the AAAI Conference on Artificial Intelligence, vol. 33, no. 01, pp. 7370–7377 (2019). https://doi.org/10.1609/aaai.v33i01.33017370
8. Wang, X.: Laplacian operator-based edge detectors. IEEE Trans. Pattern Anal. Mach. Intell. **29**(5), 886–890 (2007). https://doi.org/10.1109/TPAMI.2007.1027
9. Bollerslev, T.: Generalized autoregressive conditional heteroskedasticity. J. Econom. **31**(3), 307–327 (1986). https://doi.org/10.1016/0304-4076(86)90063-1
10. Stuart Hunter, J.: The exponentially weighted moving average. J. Qual. Technol. **18**(4), 203–210 (1986). https://doi.org/10.1080/00224065.1986.11979014

Dynamic Adjustment of the Learning Rate Using Gradient

Shuai You[1], Wanyi Gao[2,3(✉)], Ziyang Li[4], Qifen Yang[1], Meng Tian[5], and Shuhua Zhu[6]

[1] College of Information Science and Technology, Jinan University, Guangzhou, China
shuai2@stu2019.jnu.edu.cn, Qifeny@stu2020.jnu.edu.cn
[2] School of Economics, Jinan University, Guangzhou, China
[3] College of Business and Economics, The Australian National University, Canberra, Australia
gaowy@jnu.edu.cn
[4] College of Art, Northeast Agricultural University, Harbin, China
[5] School of Information and Communication Engineering, Jingzhou Institute of Technology,
Jingzhou, China
[6] Network and Educational Technology Center, Jinan University, Guangzhou, China
zsh@jnu.edu.cn

Abstract. Gradient descent method is the preferred method to optimize neural networks and many other machine learning algorithms. Especially with the wide use of deep learning in recent years, gradient descent algorithm has become more and more important. In gradient descent algorithm, learning rate is a very important parameter. The setting of learning rate directly affects the performance of the final model. The existing learning rate optimization algorithms adjusts learning rate based on the idea of step-by-step reduction. Different from this idea, this paper based on human walking law proposes a new optimization algorithm, the consolidate step-by-step algorithm (CSBS), which determines the learning rate according to the gradient of each iteration. In this paper, MNIST data set is used to verify the performance of the algorithm. The experimental results show that the CSBS algorithm accelerates the convergence speed of the model and reduces the sensitivity to the initial parameters.

Keywords: Gradient descent · Learning rate · Deep learning · Convergence rate

1 Introduction

Because deep learning has strong learning ability, it is widely used in various fields. Such as recommendation system [9], natural language processing [10], image recognition [11], etc. An important factor to promote the development of deep learning is the application of gradient descent algorithm in back propagation. The gradient descent algorithm indicates that the parameters are updated along the gradient direction. As another parameter, learning rate determines the moving distance of parameter update [8]. Only when the direction and learning rate work at the same time, the algorithm can obtain better performance [7]. Otherwise, unreasonable learning rate setting will lead to some problems: too small learning rate will lead to slow convergence, too large learning rate will hinder convergence, and cause the loss function to fluctuate or even diverge near the minimum value [1].

© The Author(s), under exclusive license to Springer Nature Switzerland AG 2022
Q. Zu et al. (Eds.): HCC 2021, LNCS 13795, pp. 61–69, 2022.
https://doi.org/10.1007/978-3-031-23741-6_6

In order to optimize the gradient descent algorithm, many learning rate optimization algorithms have appeared. Polyak [2] introduces momentum into SGD to speed up the training speed of the model. The algorithm accumulates the moving average of the previous gradient exponential decay. Inspired by Nesterov accelerated gradient algorithm [3], Sutskever [4] introduced Nesterov into the gradient descent algorithm. Although these algorithms have achieved good experimental results, they introduce another parameter. Based on the historical information of the gradient, some new adaptive learning algorithms have appeared, including AdaGrad [5], RMSProp, Adam [6], etc. AdaGrad dynamically adjusts the learning rate through the cumulative sum of squares of the gradient. The gradient sum of squares is modified to an exponential moving average in RMSProp algorithm to obtain better performance in a non-convex environment. Adam introduces the offset correction and the first-order and second-order moments into the model to update the learning rate.

From a new point of view, this paper proposes a new dynamic learning rate optimization algorithm — Consolidate Step by Step (CSBS), which can dynamically adjusts the learning rate in the gradient descent process, so that the model can finally achieve a better performance.

2   Gradient Methods in Deep Learning

With the development of science and technology, many optimization algorithms have been born in the field of gradient descent. The optimization algorithms is divided into two categories: One is the momentum introduced to speed up the training speed of the model, and the other is the adaptive dynamic adjustment of the learning rate. Among them, the first category of optimization algorithms is represented by Momentum and Nesterov; The second category is represented by AdaGrad, RMSProp, Adam, etc. Later, the combination of two category of optimization algorithms was born, and the famous Nadam is one of them. In Fig. 1, we show the development process of these optimization algorithms.

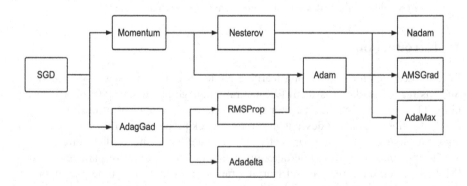

Fig. 1. Development of gradient optimization algorithm

This random gradient can be written in the following form:

$$w_{k+1} = w_k - \alpha_k \tilde{\nabla} f(w_{k+1}) \tag{1}$$

where $\tilde{\nabla} f(w_k)$ is the gradient of some loss function computed on a batch of data x_{i_k} and α_k is the learning rate.

In order to promote the training of the model, the concept of momentum is introduced and a random momentum method is formed. These methods can generally be written as:

$$w_{k+1} = w_k - \alpha_k \tilde{\nabla} f(w_k - \gamma_k(w_k - w_{k-1})) + \beta_k(w_k - w_{k-1}) \tag{2}$$

The core of the another adaptive gradient algorithms is to use the historical information in the gradient descent process to affect the current gradient. These method can generally be written as:

$$w_{k+1} = w_k + \alpha_k H_k^{-1} \tilde{\nabla} f(w_k + \gamma_k(w_k - w_{k+1})) + \beta_k H_k^{-1} H_{k-1}(w_k - w_{k-1}) \tag{3}$$

where $H_k := H(w_1, w_2, ..., w_k)$ is a positive definite matrix. Though not necessary, the matrix H_k is usually defined as:

$$H_k = diag(\{\sum_{i=1}^{k} \eta_i g_i \circ g_i\}^{\frac{1}{2}}) \tag{4}$$

where "$\circ$" denotes the entry-wise or Hadamard product, $g_k = \tilde{\nabla} f(w_k + \gamma_k(w_k - w_{k-1}))$ and η_k is some of coefficients specified for each algorithm. That is a diagonal matrix whose entries are that square roots of a linear combination of square of past gradient components.

Finally, we summarize the setting of the learning rate of common optimization algorithms in deep learning and form Table 1.

Table 1. Parameter settings of algorithm in deep learning.

	SGD	AdaGrad	RMSProp	Adam
G_k	/	$G_{k-1} + D_k$	$\beta_2 G_{k-1} + (1 - \beta_2)D_k$	$\frac{\beta_2}{1-\beta_2^k}G_{k-1} + \frac{1-\beta_2}{1-\beta_2^k}D_k$
α_k	α	/	α	$\alpha\frac{1-\beta_1}{1-\beta_1^k}$
β_k	/	/	/	$\frac{\beta_1(1-\beta_1^{k-1})}{1-\beta_1^k}$

In Table 1, $D_k = diag(g_k \circ g_k)$ and $G_k := H_k \circ H_K$. We omit the additional added to the adaptive methods, which is only needed to ensure non-singularity of the matrices H_k.

3 CSBS Algorithm

In the second section, we introduce some gradient methods of deep learning. From these algorithms, we know that setting a large learning rate at the beginning can make the experimental results converge quickly. With the continuous convergence of the model, if the learning rate remains large, the loss function will fluctuate near the minimum value. In order to solve this problem, the existing optimization algorithms adopt the method of gradually reducing the learning rate, so that the model can continuously reduce the learning rate in the process of continuous training, and then obtain better experimental performance [12]. The reason for this phenomenon may be that the initial point is far from the optimal solution, so a large learning rate can make the model converge faster. However, with the training of the model, the closer it is to the optimal solution, so it needs to adjust the parameters carefully. In this case, a small learning rate is more suitable than a large learning rate.

In this paper, we dynamically adjust the learning rate according to the gradient. We note that the gradient is a vector formed by combining the partial derivatives of each variable in the function. Vectors contain not only length, but also direction. Therefore, if the vector is directly used in the gradient descent algorithm, there will be a scenario with the same direction but different moving distance. The existing gradient descent algorithms ignore the length of the gradient and use the learning rate to determine the moving distance.

For the convenience of later explanation, we define a new distance formula (Eq. 5) to represent the change of parameter search space and a new function (Eq. 6) to represent the change of gradient.

$$Distance = (x_n - x_o)^2 + (y_n - y_o)^2 + (z_n - z_o)^2 \tag{5}$$

$$Change = \alpha \tilde{\nabla} f(w) \tag{6}$$

In Eq. 5, (x_n, y_n, z_n) represents the position of the parameters after gradient change, and (x_o, y_o, z_o) indicates the position of the parameters before gradient change. So Eq. 5 represents the moving distance of the parameters. And in Eq. 6, we use the gradient change part $\alpha \tilde{\nabla} f(w)$ to express the degree of parameter change.

In fact, the distance in Eq. 5 can be regarded as the search space for parameter change. The greater the value, the greater the distance the search changes. But, according to our experience, things with similar characteristics will show similar or even the same performance. According to this idea, $g_1 = (1, 2, 3)$ and $g_2 = (2, 4, 6)$ have the same direction, but their corresponding $Distance_1 = 15$ and $Distance_2 = 56$ are very different. This is unreasonable. Equation 6 represents the change of gradient. If a gradient changes greatly, the degree of the gradient change will be very drastic. When the gradient is large, if we still maintain a large learning rate, it will lead to significant changes in parameters and miss the optimal solution, which may be a reason for the small setting of fixed learning rate in SGD. Setting a small learning rate can solve this problem, but when the gradient is very small, its descent speed is slow. At this time, coupled with a small learning rate, it will lead to a smaller moving distance. Therefore, no suitable learning rate can solve these two problems at the same time.

In order to solve this problem in gradient descent method, a new learning rate optimization algorithm is proposed based on human walking law. We observed that everyone's stride size was fixed. However, in different cases, it will change its stride size to achieve the best walking speed. When the road is flat, people move a fixed stride size. When a slope occurs, the stride size decreases accordingly. Aiming at this phenomenon in life, this paper proposes a consolidate step-by-step algorithm. The core idea of CSBS is to fix a moving distance r in the process of gradient descent, and then adjust the moving distance according to the gradient. The larger the slope, the faster the moving distance will decrease, which makes the model more stable during training. We define the following formula to measure the slope:

$$|group_i| = \frac{g^i_{max} - g^i_{min}}{g^i_{max} + 0.0001} \tag{7}$$

Here, we regard a group of partial derivatives g^i starting from the same node as group $group_i$, and then dynamically adjust the initial moving distance using the gradient of $group_i$. At the same time, in order to prevent the denominator from being zero, 0.0001 is added. When the directional derivatives of a group of variables have little difference, it indicates that the slope is gentle, and the slope changes with the maximum and minimum of the directional derivatives. The specific steps of the algorithm are shown in Table 2.

Table 2. CSBS algorithm flowchart

CSBS Algorithm:
1: Initialization:fiexd moving distance r
2: while stop condition not met do:
3:      A small batch of m samples $\{x_1, x_2, ..., x_m\}$ is collected from the training set,
4:      where x_i corresponds to y_i
5:      Calculate gradient value:$g = \frac{1}{m}\nabla_\theta \sum_i L(f(x^i; \theta), y^i)$
6:      for i in g.column.length:
7:           Calculate slope:$group_i = \frac{g^i_{max} - g^i_{min}}{0.0001 + g^i_{max}}$
8:      constructed the slope vector of matrix $group$
9:      Update learning rate:$a = \frac{r}{1 + |group|}$
10:     Apply updates:$\theta = \theta - ag$
11: end while

4 Experience and Result Analysis

4.1 Experimental Setup

We build a neural network on MNIST data set to verify the performance of the algorithm, its network structure is shown in Fig. 2. Here, in order to clearly display the

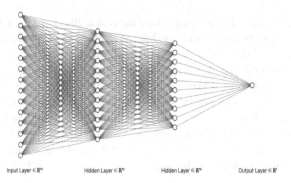

Fig. 2. Neural network structure

neural structure, the number of nodes in the network does not use real data. It will be described in detail later.

In Fig. 2, we firstly use a flat layer to input all pixels in the image into the neural network. The number of nodes in the input layer is 785. Two hidden layers are then used to process the data. The first hidden layer uses 50 nodes and the second hidden layer uses 10 nodes, corresponding to 10 tags in the MNIST dataset. Each sample has a corresponding probability value corresponding to the corresponding label. Finally, the softmax function is used to predict the corresponding tag from the corresponding probability value. The activation function we use in the hidden layer is the sigmoid function. Since MNIST is a multi-classification problem, the loss function is a cross entropy loss function.

4.2 Compare with Other Algorithm

In order to verify the difference between CSBS algorithm and other classical algorithm, this paper adopts the comparative experiment. The CSBS model is compared with SGD, AdaGrad, RMSProp, and Adam. Some hyper-parameters in RMSProp and Adam are set as default values, $\rho = 0.9$ in RMSProp, $\rho_1 = 0.9$ and $\rho_2 = 0.999$ in Adam. The epoch of the experiment is set to 100 and mini-batch = 50.

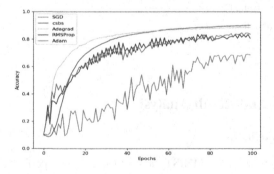

Fig. 3. Comparison of algorithm in deep learning

Table 3. Train accuracy and test accuracy of algorithm in deep learning

	SGD	AdaGrad	RMSProp	Adam	CSBS
Trian Acc	63.75%	**88.84%**	81.37%	83.60%	**90.23%**
Test Acc	64.69%	**88.70%**	81.46%	85.07%	**90.03%**

Figure 3 shows the changes in the accuracy of different gradient descent algorithms during training. Table 3 shows the final performance of different gradient descent algorithms on the training set and test set after 100 epochs. From Fig. 3 and Table 3, we can draw the following conclusions:

- The performance of the adaptive gradient descent algorithm is better than that of the fixed learning rate gradient descent algorithm. This shows that adjusting the learning rate according to the actual situation is conducive to the training of the algorithm.

- The performance of the CSBS model is better than other models. In Table 3, we can observe that after 100 epochs, the accuracy of CSBS model on the training set is 1.39% higher than Adagrad, which is the best reference model, and the accuracy on the test set is 1.33% higher than Adagrad. This proves the effectiveness of our proposed algorithm. The reason for this result is that the adaptive gradient descent model will accumulate the previous gradient sum to adjust the learning rate. Excessive gradient accumulation will make the learning rate tend to zero and end in advance. CSBS model does not accumulate the previous gradient, but adjusts the learning according to the gradient of each iteration, so there is no case of ending the training in advance.

- Compared with other model training curves, the training curves of CSBS algorithm and AdaGrad algorithm are smoother, indicating that there is no excessive model oscillation in the training process. The main reason for this phenomenon is that if the learning rate is fixed, when the gradient is large, the model will move a large distance along the gradient direction, resulting in missing the optimal solution. However, the CSBS model will adjust the learning rate of the model according to the gradient. When the gradient is large, this will reduce the learning rate; The smaller the gradient, the greater the learning rate. A balance is maintained between the learning rate and the gradient size so that there is no large oscillation in each iteration.

4.3   Different Learning Rate Experiment

In order to observe the effect of different initial learning rate on the experimental results, we did a comparative experiment. Set the training epoch of the model to 100 and the learning rate to different values such as [0.01,0.1,0.2,0.3,0.4,0.5,0.6,0.8,1.0], and observe the performance of the model.

In Fig. 4(a), we can find that different initial learning rates have an impact on the accuracy of the experimental results. When the initial learning rate is too small, our experimental results will converge too slowly. However, it can be observed from Fig. 4(b) that with the increase of epoch we train, the model may also reach the corresponding accuracy. If the initial learning rate is too large, the model will fluctuate

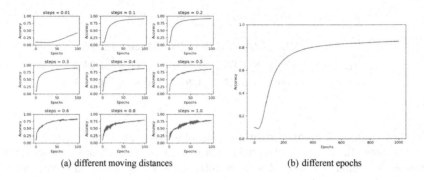

(a) different moving distances   (b) different epochs

Fig. 4. Different learning rate experiment

and the accuracy will decrease. This is because the learning rate is too large, the worse the regularization effect of the gradient, just like the fixed learning rate in SGD is too large. At the same time, it can be seen that the fluctuation of accuracy caused by the initial learning rate is relatively small, indicating that CSBS has low sensitivity to the initial learning rate of the model, which is conducive to researchers' setting of hyperparameter.

5   Conclusion

In this paper, according to the human walking law, the learning rate is dynamically adjusted by using the gradient. When the gradient is small, the moving distance increases accordingly; When the gradient is large, the moving distance decreases accordingly. So as to control the optimization process of the model.

Experiments show that the CSBS algorithm proposed has better performance than other optimization algorithms in training data set and test data set, and the fitting curve of the algorithm is more smooth. Through different initialization comparison problems, we also find that the CSBS algorithm is less sensitive to the initial moving distance. This will help us to adjust the model parameters during model training.

In future work, we will try to complement the disadvantages of the CSBS algorithm with other optimization algorithms, so that CSBS can converge faster and achieve the accuracy of the model even if it has a large learning rate.

Acknowledgments. This work was partially supported by National Natural Science Foundation of China (Grant No. 61972179), Guangdong Basic and Applied Basic Research Foundation (Grant No. 2020A1515011476).

References

1. Ruder, S.: An overview of gradient descent optimization algorithms. arXiv preprint arXiv:1609.04747 (2016)
2. Polyak, B.T.: Some methods of speeding up the convergence of iteration methods. USSR Comput. Math. Math. Phys. **4**(5), 1–17 (1964)

3. Nesterov, Y.: A method of solving a convex programming problem with convergence rate $O(1/k^2)$[C]. In: Soviet Mathematics Doklady (1983)
4. Sutskever, I., Martens, J., Dahl, G., et al.: On the importance of initialization and momentum in deep learning. In: International Conference on Machine Learning, pp. 1139–1147. PMLR (2013)
5. Duchi, J., Hazan, E., Singer, Y.: Adaptive subgradient methods for online learning and stochastic optimization. J. Mach. Learn. Res. **12**(7), 2121–2159 (2011)
6. Kingma, D., Ba, J.: Adam: a method for stochastic optimization. Comput. Sci. (2014)
7. Smith, L.N.: Cyclical learning rates for training neural networks. In: 2017 IEEE Winter Conference on Applications of Computer Vision (WACV), pp. 464–472. IEEE (2017)
8. Babichev, D., Bach, F.: Constant step size stochastic gradient descent for probabilistic modeling. arXiv preprint arXiv:1804.05567 (2018)
9. Kiran, R., Kumar, P., Bhasker, B.: DNNRec: a novel deep learning based hybrid recommender system. Expert Syst. Appl. **144**, 113054 (2020)
10. Otter, D.W., Medina, J.R., Kalita, J.K.: A survey of the usages of deep learning for natural language processing. IEEE Trans. Neural Netw. Learn. Syst. **32**(2), 604–624 (2020)
11. Özyurt, F.: Efficient deep feature selection for remote sensing image recognition with fused deep learning architectures. J. Supercomput. **76**(11), 8413–8431 (2019). https://doi.org/10.1007/s11227-019-03106-y
12. Konar, J., Khandelwal, P., Tripathi, R.: Comparison of various learning rate scheduling techniques on convolutional neural network. In: 2020 IEEE International Students' Conference on Electrical, Electronics and Computer Science (SCEECS), pp. 1–5. IEEE (2020)

Data and Analytics

Predicting Personalities of Ancient Chinese Emperors Based on Relational Knowledge Transfer Model

Huanyi Xiao[1,2], Fugui Xing[1,2], Miaorong Fan[1,2], Hua Li[3], and Tingshao Zhu[1,2(✉)]

[1] Institute of Psychology, Chinese Academy of Sciences, Beijing, China
tszhu@psych.ac.cn
[2] Department of Psychology, University of Chinese Academy of Sciences, Beijing, China
[3] Institute of Qilu-Cultural Studies, Shandong Normal University, Jinan, China

Abstract. In this paper, we propose a Relational Knowledge Transfer (RKT) model to predict Chinese ancient emperors' personalities. It make good use of relational history semantic knowledge including Chinese emperors' self-claimed character "朕", statistics knowledge about correlation coefficient, and psychological knowledge including personality scores having normal distribution, to produce the virtual training datasets. With the Domain-Adversarial Training of Neural Network's learning ability, we transferred human knowledge to the machine well with little manual data annotation effort. Compared with original version of PAP-TL tool, latest version of RKT model achieved the state of art in terms of the prediction accuracy of the Big Five personality scores of ancient Chinese emperors, with RMSE on average decreased from 9.16 to 5.40 (by 41%). This RKT model can be further applied to predict the personalities of Chinese of a specific group or period in the more than 2000 years ancient history.

Keywords: Transfer learning · CC-LIWC · Big Five personality · Zero-shot learning · DANN · Normal distribution

1 Introduction

It is of considerable significance to analyze the ancients' personality traits for us to learn from history, especially from the celebrities. During the two thousand years of monarchy history in ancient China, as the supreme rulers, emperors played important roles in history. Personality is a psychological construct aimed at explaining the wide variety of human behavior, thought and interpersonal communication. And interestingly, it is across culture [1]. For ancient emperors' personalities, the contemporary traditional method, self-report, is impossible to be conducted on historical individuals. Prior studies mostly are based on qualitative analysis, and only focused on one individual emperor [2, 3].

With the development of artificial intelligence, Transfer Learning provides a new way to identify the personality of ancient people [4]. However, it requires a great amount of manual data annotation. In order to alleviate the burden of machine learning, Palatucci

Q. Zu et al. (Eds.): HCC 2021, LNCS 13795, pp. 73–81, 2022.
https://doi.org/10.1007/978-3-031-23741-6_7

proposed Zero-Shot Learning (ZSL) [5]. Zero-shot learning is a special scenario of transfer learning [6]. In the zero-shot learning, people hope that zero sample learning can be realized through some methods. Bernardino proposed Embarrassingly Simple ZSL, which combines a linear model together with a principled choice of regularizers that allow for a simple and efficient implementation [7]. Feature transformation-based models aim to learn a transformation or projection of the data with some distribution matching metrics between source and target domains [8]. Due to the unavailability of target labels, in conditional alignment based deep network adaptation models, clustering labels or progressively updated target pseudo-labels (label refinement) are generally exploited [8]. Relational Knowledge Transfer (RKT) extracts the relational knowledge in semantic knowledge space [6].

In this paper, we propose a novel RKT model for ZSL to predict Chinese ancient emperors' personalities, which is simple and effective. It make good use of relational knowledge to produce two kinds of virtual training datasets to transform human knowledge from knowledge space to label space directly. With Domain-Adversarial Training of Neural Network (DANN)'s learning ability [9], the accuracy of predicting personality of ancient emperors increased a lot.

The rest of the paper is organized as follows. Related work is discussed in Sect. 2. In Sect. 3, we describe the proposed methodology of personality recognition in details, including description of the data set, feature extraction process and the process of generating virtual training dataset algorithms to automatically recognize ancient Chinese emperors' Big Five personality traits. Experimental evaluation results are presented in Sect. 4, followed by the conclusion and future work in Sect. 5.

2   Related Work

The RKT method we proposed applied the Classical Chinese Linguistic Inquiry and Word Count (CC-LIWC) tool proposed by Fan [10], and Personality of Ancient People based on Transfer Learning (PAP-TL) tool proposed by Xing [4].

Because the language ancient Chinese used is classical Chinese, we used the software CC-LIWC for our analyses. It is currently the only one LIWC version which can analyze classical Chinese texts. It defined 80 different linguistic categories, such as "adverb", "negate", "family". It can calculate the percentage of usage of each of these categories of a text file.

As per Pennebaker, linguistic style is an independent and meaningful way of exploring personality [11]. Big Five personality model is an prevalent paradigm in personality psychology as well as the widely accepted approach in computing oriented personality research. The Big Five personality traits include 5 dimensions as openness, conscientiousness, extroversion, agreeableness, neuroticism [12]. Mairesse proposed to use linguistic cues for the automatic recognition of personality in conversation and text [13].

The Personality of Ancient People based on Transfer Learning (PAP-TL) tool [4] uses machine learning method to transfer the knowledge from source domain to target domain. It can be used to predict ancient Chinese's personality traits and obtain their personality scores as labels. Its source domain data is the text data of microblog users, including the SCLIWC [14] word frequency characteristics and big five personality score tags of 1706 active microblog users. It measure the personality score by The Big Five personality scale BFI-44, and the word frequency is calculated by the "Wenxin" system [14]. Based on the same word categories of the SCLIWC and CC-LIWC, finally, the shape of the feature space in our source domain is 1706 × 64.

Based on the original PAP-TL tool [4], we tried to enhance it with the RKT model, which is composed of virtual training instances and Domain-Adversarial Training of Neural Network (DANN) (Fig. 1).

3   The Relational Knowledge Transfer Model (RKT)

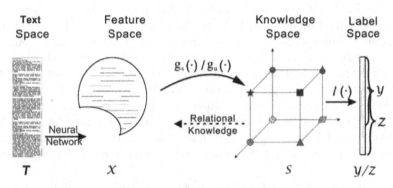

Fig. 1. The Relational Knowledge Transfer (RKT) framework.

In our RKT framework, X denotes the feature space, that is, the word frequencies of linguistic categories. $Y = \{y_1,..., y_p\}$ denotes a set of p seen contemporary Sina Weibo Users' personality scores and $Z = \{z_1,..., z_q\}$ a set of q unseen ancient emperors' personality scores. The RKT firstly transfers the correlation from knowledge space S to feature space X; then it uses this correlation to restore the manifold structure of unknown values by producing virtual labelled data; finally, it learns mapping g(x) from the linear feature space X into the semantic knowledge space S.

Since Chinese first emperor QinShihuang unified China in 221 B.C., Chinese emperors called themselves "朕" (Chinese character, Zhen), which means I/me. The official history books (Twenty-Six History) recorded many emperors spoken utterances and imperial edict records. We collected all the sentences with the emperors self-claimed Chinese Character "朕" in the Twenty-Six History books, and denoted this text as T.

As per Rothmann, there is an indication that the personality scores are relatively normally distributed [15]. As per Xue, the personality scores of Sina Weibo users conform to normal distribution [16]. And according to the central limit theorem (CLT), that the distribution of a sample variable approximates a normal distribution (i.e., a "bell curve") as the sample size becomes larger, assuming that all samples are identical in size, and regardless of the population's actual distribution shape [17], we can assume that the personality scores of ancient figures (approximately) are normally distributed too.

Psychologists estimate a person's personality by asking him to fill in a psychological inventory [18]. However, for history figures, they can't fill in such inventories. We will need to extract related knowledge to fill the unseen labels in the target domain, which is ancient emperors' personality scores in this case. Inspired by the stratified sampling idea, we chose some very different emperors as samples. We tried to collect as many modern Chinese books as possible from online/physical book stores and libraries, finally, we got 42 books whose authors had explicit evaluations about some ancient Chinese emperors. We counted the books, ranked the emperors and got "the top 10 enlightened emperors list" and "the top 10 fatuous emperors list". From the top10 lists, we randomly chose two enlightened emperors, two fatuous emperors and two emperors out of the list. We collected the spoken utterances and imperial edict records of these 6 emperors in official history books (Twenty-Six History).

We chose 4 post-graduates who have fundamental knowledge of emperors to participate in the experiment. They studied the 6 emperors' parts in the official history books and filled in the Big Five Inventory BFI-44 (others-rating version) [19]. So we obtained the 6 emperors' 5 dimensions personality scores tested by Big Five Inventory. And then we calculated the mean value of the scores, regarded them as the 6×5 observed score labels, which are also regarded as the Big Five personality mean value of ancient Chinese emperors and the mean μ of the normal distributions of the emperors' personality scores. We assume that the standard deviations of the personality scores of emperors are same as those of Chinese Weibo users, which were obtained from Xing's study [4]. With the mean μ and standard deviation σ, we can generate some batches of random numbers which conform to normal distribution [20], and used them as the virtual personality scores.

For unseen class prediction, Donghui proposed to learn semantic mapping $g_u(x)$ directly, and the semantic mapping function for unseen categories can be learned directly from only generated data X_{aug} and semantic knowledge Φ_{aug} [6]. In our case, some LIWC word categories have correlation with Big Five scores [11]. Let x_i denotes the word frequency of such word category, and c_i denotes the correlation coefficient. We define below empirical hypothesis function to generate some virtual Big Five personality score labels, and ensure them to fit in the score scale presented in Xue's study [16] by linear mapping based on psychological knowledge.

$$y_i = \sum_{i-1}^{n} x_i * c_i \tag{1}$$

We used below two algorithms to generate virtual training datasets for the neural network to transfer the human relational knowledge to machine.

In Algorithm 1, by slicing all the emperors' utterances texts T randomly, we can extract some features. We combine the features – the word frequencies of the linguistic word categories denoted as x_i, and the labels – the personality scores y_{ti} calculated by empirical Eq. 1 together to constitute the training datasets D_{aug1}.

Algorithm 1: Generate Augmented Training Datasets Based on Hypothesis Function

---

Data: text of T

Result: the augmented training datasets D_{aug1}

1 **for** $i = 1, 2, ..., N$ **do**

2 $\quad$ Slice T into mini-batches with stochastic size as t_i.

3 $\quad$ Apply CC-LIWC tool on t_i, and get word frequencies of linguistic categories as x_i.

4 $\quad$ Apply $Eq(1)$ on x_i to get virtual personality scores y_{ti}, and constitute the augmented training datasets D_{aug1}.

5 **end**

6 Return D_{aug1}.

In Algorithm 2, with the mean μ and standard deviation σ mentioned above, we can generate random numbers which conform to normal distribution. Similar to Algorithm 1, by slicing all the emperors' utterances texts T randomly, we get the features x_i. And then we match the labels and the random numbers which are regarded as virtual personality score labels to constitute the augmented training datasets D_{aug2}.

Algorithm 2: Generate Augmented Training Datasets Based on Normal Distribution

---

Data: text of T

Result: the augmented training datasets D_{aug2}

1 **for** $i = 1, 2, ..., N$ **do**

2 $\quad$ Generate random number based on normal distribution as y_{ti2}.

3 **end**

4 **for** $i = 1, 2, ..., N$ **do**

5 $\quad$ Slice T into mini-batches with stochastic size, which is denoted as t_i.

6 $\quad$ Apply CC-LIWC tool on t_i, and get word frequencies of linguistic categories x_i.

7 $\quad$ Randomly match x_i and y_{ti2} to constitute the augmented training datasets D_{aug2}.

8 **end**

9 Return D_{aug2}.

Running Algorithm 2, we got the virtual Big Five personality scores, which constitute normal distributions. As is shown in Fig. 2.

Follow the approach in [21], in our RKT model version 3, the training datasets are finally built by randomly picking samples from two datasets D_{aug1} and D_{aug2}, which is denoted as m for every mini-batches. As is shown in Fig. 3.

We enhanced the original PAP-TL tool with Domain-Adversarial Training of Neural Network (DANN) [9]. The DANN model contains three parts: (a) a feature extractor, (b) a Big-five personality regressor, (c) a domain classifier. The feature extractor non-linearly transforms input datasets to features. The regressor takes the features as its input, does a linear transform, and estimate the big-five personality scores. The domain classifier also

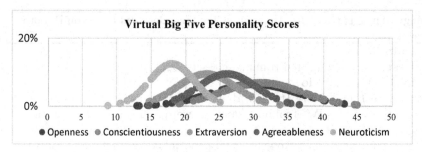

Fig. 2. Virtual big five personality scores

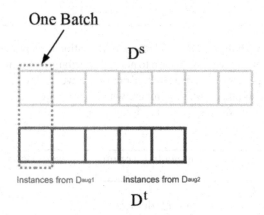

Fig. 3. Method of building the batches of training datasets

takes the features as input, and classify whether the input is from the source domain or the target domain. The loss of this model contains two parts, one is from the regression task, the other is from the classification task. To prevent gradient explosion and improve the robustness of training, we choose SmoothL1Loss (2) as the loss of the regression task. And for the classification task, we use negative binary cross entropy (3) as the loss.

To transfer knowledge from source domain to target domain, the feature extractor is trained to 'fool' the classifier. To realize the adversarial training, we insert a gradient reverse layer between the feature extractor and the domain classifier in the back propagation phase during training, and use the negative gradient to update the parameters of the feature extractor.

$$L_{reg}(y, \hat{y}) = \begin{cases} 0.5\|y - \hat{y}\|_2^2 & \|y - \hat{y}\| < 1 \\ \|y - \hat{y}\|_1 - 0.5 & \|y - \hat{y}\| \geq 1 \end{cases} \tag{2}$$

$$L_d(y, \hat{y}) = -y \log(\hat{y}) - (1 - y) \log(1 - \hat{y}) \tag{3}$$

$$L = L_{reg} + \lambda L_d \tag{4}$$

$$\lambda = \frac{2}{1 + \exp(-10p)} - 1 \tag{5}$$

To balance personality regression and domain classification, we use a hyperparameter λ to control the importance of domain classification, so the total loss is a linear combination of two losses above (4). And this hyperparameter is increasing in the training process (5). In Eq. (5), p denotes the progress of training.

Algorithm 3 : DANN for transfer learning

Data: samples from the source domain $S = \{(x_i, y_i)_{i=1}^n\}$, samples from the target domain $T = \{x_i\}_{i=1}^n$, number of iterations N, initialized neural network parameters θ

Result: network parameters θ after training

1 **for** $i = 1, 2, ..., N$ **do**

2 $\quad$ Sample minibatch of m_1 examples
$\quad$ $\{(x_s^{(1)}, y_s^{(1)}), (x_s^{(2)}, y_s^{(2)}), ..., (x_s^{(m_1)}, y_s^{(m_1)})\}$ from S

3 $\quad$ Sample minibatch of m_2 examples $\{(x_t^{(1)}, x_t^{(2)}, ..., x_t^{(m_2)}\}$ from T

4 $\quad$ Update hyperparameter λ use (4)

5 $\quad$ $\hat{y}_s = G_{\hat{y}}(G_f(x_s))$

6 $\quad$ $p_s = G_p(G_f(x_s))$

7 $\quad$ $p_t = G_p(G_f(x_t))$

8 $\quad$ Update θ by descending its stochastic gradient:

9 $\quad$ $\nabla_\theta[\frac{1}{m_1}\sum_{i=1}^{m_1} L_{reg}(y_i, \hat{y}_s^{(i)}) + \lambda(\frac{1}{m_1}\sum_{i=1}^{m_1} L_d(p_s, 0) +$
$\quad$ $\frac{1}{m_2}\sum_{i=1}^{m_2} L_d(p_s, 1))]$

10 **end**

---

4 Results

In our experiments, the predictive ability of the personality recognition approaches was evaluated by Root Mean Square Error (RMSE), a frequently used measure of differences between the predicted score and the observed score tested by Big Five Inventory in personality recognition research. It can be calculated using Eq. (6), where n denotes the number of unseen instances, $(s_{x_i}^{y_j})^*$ the predicted value for personality trait y_j, and $(s_{x_i}^{y_j})$, the observed one. Since RMSE is a measure of error, thus, the lower, the better. We carried out the model training and testing experiments and calculated the average RMSE after applying each enhancement approaches. We used the original PAP-TL as the baseline algorithm.

$$RMSE = \sqrt{\frac{1}{n}\sum_{i=1}^{n}[(s_{x_i}^{y_j})^* - s_{x_i}^{y_j}]^2} \qquad (6)$$

We used the above mentioned 6 emperors data as test set, in which the features are the word frequencies of linguistic word categories of the 6 emperors, with shape of 6 × 64. The human average observed values for the 5-dimension scores are the labels, with label shape of 6 × 5. Compared with original version of PAP-TL tool, latest version of RKT which enhanced with DANN and two virtual training datasets (D_{aug1} and D_{aug2}), achieved best performance in terms of the prediction accuracy of the Big Five personality scores of ancient emperors, with the RMSE on average decreased from 9.16 to 5.40 (by 41%). The results achieved are presented in Fig. 4.

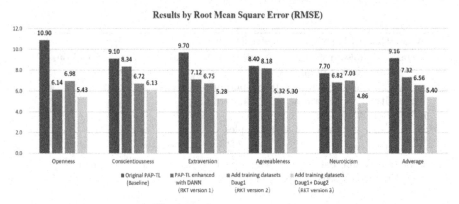

Fig. 4. Performance comparison

5 Conclusion

The RKT model trained by augmented virtual instances can predict Chinese ancient emperors' personalities in a more simple and accurate way compared with the original PAP-TL tool, and achieve the state of art in terms of predicting the Big Five personality scores of ancient Chinese emperors. It make good use of relational knowledge including Chinese emperors' self-claimed character "朕", statistics knowledge about correlation coefficient, and psychological knowledge including personality scores having normal distribution, to produce the virtual training datasets. With DANN's learning ability, the RMSE on average have decreased by 41%.

At present, only all the sentences in official history books (Twenty-Six History) containing "朕" of the emperors are collected. In the future, the model can be further applied to predict the personalities of Chinese officers and concubines of emperors whose self-claimed are Chinese characters "臣" and "妾", and the Chinese of a specific group or period in the more than 2000 years ancient history. Theoretically, given enough various ancient figures' utterance texts, it is possible to construct the personality predicting model of general population of the ancient Chinese with few human observed labels. And exploring optimal feature space, especially the feature distribution is also in our plan.

References

1. Mccrae, R.R., Jüri Allik, E.: The five factor model of personality accross cultures. In: Marsella, A.J. (ed.) International and Cultural Psychology Series, p. 336. Kluwer Academic/Plenum Publishers, New York (2002)

2. Heidi, S.: Wu Zetian's personality and important interpersonal relationships. Wuhan University (2014)

3. Xianjiao, C.: The Personality of Ming Shenzong. Hunan Normal University (2013)

4. Xing, F., et al.: Predicting Personality of Ancient People based on Transfer Learning. IFAC PapersOnLine **53**(5), 470–475 (2020)

5. Palatucci, M.P.D., Hinton, G., Mitchell, T.M.: Zeroshot learning with semantic output codes. In: Proceedings of the 22nd International Conference on Neural Information Processing Systems, pp. 1410−1418 (2009)

6. Wang, D., et al.: Relational knowledge transfer for zero-shot learning. In: Thirtieth AAAI Conference on Artificial Intelligence (2016)

7. Romera-Paredes, B., Ox, E., Torr, P.H.: An embarrassingly simple approach to zero-shot learning. ICML, pp. 2152–2161 (2015)

8. Zhang, L., Gao, X.: Transfer adaptation learning: A decade survey. arXiv preprint arXiv: 1903.04687 (2019)

9. Ganin, Y., et al.: Domain-adversarial training of neural networks. J. Mach. Learn. Res. **17**(17), 1–35 (2016)

10. Miaorong, F., et al.: Classical Chinese LIWC: A Brief Introduction and Pilot Analysis (2019)

11. Pennebaker, J.W.: Linguistic styles: language use as an individual difference. J. Pers. Soc. Psychol. **77**(6), 1296–1312 (1999)

12. Tausczik, Y.R., Pennebaker, J.W.: The psychological meaning of words: LIWC and computerized text analysis methods. J. Lang. Soc. Psychol. **29**(1), 24–54 (2010)

13. Mairesse, F.M.A.W., Mehl, M.R., Moore, R.K.: Using linguistic cues for the automatic recognition of personality in conversation and text. Artif. Intell. Res. 30, 457–500 (2010)

14. Gao, R., et al.: Developing Simplified Chinese Psychological Linguistic Analysis Dictionary for Microblog. Springer International Publishing, Cham (2013)

15. Rothmann, S., Coetzer, E.P.: The big five personality dimensions and job performance. SA J. Ind. Psychol. **29**(1), 68–74 (2003)

16. Xue, D., et al.: Personality recognition on social media with label distribution learning. IEEE Access **5**, 13478–13488 (2017)

17. Rosenblatt, M.: A central limit theorem and a strong mixing condition. Proc. Natl. Acad. Sci. U.S.A. **42**(1), 43 (1956)

18. Hendriks, A.A.J., Hofstee, W.K.B., Raad, B.D.: The Five-Factor Personality Inventory (FFPI). Personality and Individual Differences 27(2), 307–325 (1999)

19. Carciofo, R., et al.: Psychometric evaluation of chinese-language 44-Item and 10-Item big five personality inventories, including correlations with chronotype, mindfulness and mind wandering. PLoS ONE **11**(2), e0149963 (2016)

20. Roy, R.: Comparison of different techniques to generate Normal random variables. Journal of East Central Europe **545**, 5–6 (2002)

21. Zhang, X., et al.: Deep Transfer Network: Unsupervised Domain Adaptation. arXiv preprint arXiv:1503.00591 (2015)

Visualization of Convolutional Neural Networks with Attention Mechanism

Meng Yuan[1], Bao Tie[1(✉)], and Dawei Lin[2]

[1] Jilin University, Changchun 130012, China
yuanmeng_1996@126.com, baotie@jlu.edu.cn
[2] Northeast Electric Power University, Jilin 132012, China

Abstract. With the continuous development of deep learning, convolutional neural networks are gradually playing an increasingly important role in classification models. Adding attention mechanisms based on convolutional neural networks to improve the classification effect of the model has been proven a lot. However, only theoretically understanding how attention mechanisms enhance the model's performance is a lack of intuition. Therefore, to explore the role of the attention mechanism in the model, this article will start from visualization and analyze how the attention mechanism improves the model's performance in combination with theory. The method makes attention more intuitive and more accessible for non-professionals to understand the working principle of attention mechanism, facilitating the promotion of attention mechanism and convolutional neural networks.

Keywords: Convolutional neural network · Visualization · Attention · Interpretability analysis

1 Introduction

With the deepening of deep learning research, convolutional neural networks have proved to be a useful model for tackling a wide range of visual tasks [8–10, 12] At each convolutional layer in the network, a collection of filters expresses neighbor-hood spatial connectivity patterns along input channels-fusing spatial and channel-wise information together within local receptive fields. By interleaving a series of convolutional layers with nonlinear activation functions and downsampling operators, CNNs can produce image representations that capture hierarchical patterns and attain a global theoretical receptive field [1]. The central task of computer vision is to capture the most significant attributes in the target image that are most conducive to completing the target task. Many attention mechanisms proposed at present have been proven to help better convolutional networks to complete this task, thereby improving performance [1, 4, 13, 15, 16].

However, these methods often explain in theory how to improve the performance of the model, which not only requires a large amount of theoretical knowledge as a basis but is also unintuitive. This article will study why the convolutional neural network is added to the attention mechanism to improve the model's performance through visualization

Q. Zu et al. (Eds.): HCC 2021, LNCS 13795, pp. 82–93, 2022.
https://doi.org/10.1007/978-3-031-23741-6_8

and theoretical analysis. This article uses a widely used attention mechanism (Efficient Channel Attention) and a visualization method (visualize the intermediate output) to conduct experiments on three datasets (MNIST, Fashion-MNIST, and CIFAR-10) and combine the visualization results to analyze different experimental results.

The other parts of this article are arranged as follows. Section 2 introduces the working principles of the attention mechanism and visualization method that we added to the benchmark convolutional neural network. Section 3 presents the three datasets we used and the preprocessing techniques for the data. Section 4 conducts three visualization experiments and analyzes why the attention mechanism affects the model's performance. Section 5 summarizes the research content and deficiencies in this article and prospects for future work.

2 Background

2.1 Efficient Channel Attention for Deep Convolutional Neural Networks

Since Squeeze-and-Excitation Networks (SE) [1] was proposed, many approaches have focused on opening up more complex attention modules for higher performance, which will undoubtedly increase the complexity of the model. The Effective Channel Attention (ECA) module described below overcomes the contradiction between performance and complexity by focusing on a few parameters but delivering significant performance gains.

ECA is an improvement of the SE method. It generates channel attention through fast one-dimensional convolution, whose kernel size is determined by the nonlinear mapping adaptation of channel bits. ECA avoids dimensional degradation and effectively captures cross-channel interactions. As illustrated in Fig. 1, after channel-wise global average pooling (GAP) without dimensionality reduction, ECA captures local cross-channel interaction by considering every channel and k neighbors. Why choose a GAP without a drop dimension here? The experiment of changing the calculation of attention in three basic SE methods demonstrates that avoiding dimensionality reduction is helpful to learn adequate channel attention [3]. Therefore, ECA modules are designed without channel dimensionality reduction.

With the global average pooling of non-fall dimensions, we will get the aggregated feature y $\in \mathbb{R}^c$. Let all channels share the same learning parameters, i.e.,

$$\omega_i = \sigma \left(\sum_{j=1}^{k} \omega^j y_i^j \right), \gamma_i^j \in \Omega_i^k \tag{1}$$

This method allows for a fast one-dimensional convolution with a kernel size of k, i.e.

$$\omega = \sigma \mathrm{C1D_k}(y) \tag{2}$$

where C1D indicates 1D convolution. Here, the method in q (2) is called by efficient channel attention (ECA) module, which only involves k parameters. ECA module guarantees both efficiency and effectiveness by appropriately capturing local cross-channel

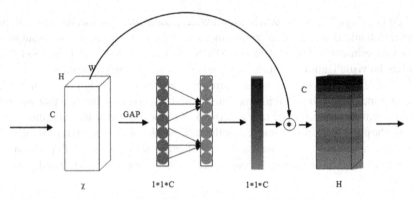

Fig. 1. The schematic diagram ECA. Global average pooling (GAP) obtains aggregated features, and convolution generates channel weights.

interaction [3]. The following is to determine the exchange coverage (i.e., the core size 1d convolution) to capture the local cross-channel interaction adequately.

Sharing a similar philosophy as [11, 14, 17], it is reasonable that the coverage of interaction (i.e., kernel size k of 1D convolution) is proportional to channel dimension C. It is well known that channel number C is usually a power of 2, and there is a non-linear mapping relationship between channel number C and kernel size k. Therefore, a possible mapping relationship between channel number C and kernel size is used here.

$$C = \phi(k) = 2^{(\gamma * k - b)} \tag{3}$$

Then, given channel dimension C, kernel size k can be adaptively determined by

$$k = \psi(C) = \left| \frac{log_2(C)}{\gamma} + \frac{b}{\gamma} \right|_{odd} \tag{4}$$

where |t| odd indicates the nearest odd number of t, set γ and b to 2 and 1 in [3]. Through the mapping ψ, high-dimensional channels have more extended range interaction while low-dimensional ones undergo shorter range interaction using a non-linear mapping.

As in Fig. 1, one-dimensional convolution is performed using the identified kernel size k, and the Sigmoid function is used to learn channel attention. Finally, the same operation is performed using the formula (5):

$$\widetilde{\chi}_c = F_{scale}(u_c, s_c) \tag{5}$$

where $\tilde{\chi} = [\widetilde{\chi_1}, \widetilde{\chi_2}, \ldots \widetilde{\chi_c}]$ and $F_{scale}(u_c, s_c)$ refers to channel-wise multiplication between the scalar s_c and the feature map $u_c \in \mathbb{R}^{H \times W}$ [1]. The shape of the model output $\tilde{\chi}$ is restored to H × W × C.

2.2 Visualization Method

It is often said that deep learning models are "black boxes", meaning that what models learn means that it is difficult to extract and present in a way that humans can understand.

But for convolutional neural networks, it is not entirely correct. Convolutional neural networks learn that representations are well suited for visualization, mainly because they represent solving concepts. Since 2013, a variety of techniques have been developed to visualize and interpret these representations. In this paper, we used the method of visualizing the intermediate output (intermediate activation) of the convolutional neural network to study how the attention mechanism affects the model's performance.

Our approach is helpful to understand how the continuous layer of the convolutional neural network transforms inputs and beneficial to understand the meaning of each filter of the convolutional neural network. Visual intermediate activation allows you to present a feature map of the outputs of each convolution and pooled layer under a given input. Visualization allows us to see how the information is broken down into different filters learned by the network. Each channel corresponds to relatively independent features, so in this article, we draw the contents of each channel into a two-dimensional image, as shown in Fig. 4, Fig. 5, Fig. 6.

3 Datasets

3.1 Three Public Datasets

In this article, three exposed datasets, MNIST, Fashion-MNIST, and CIFAR-10 are used. The distribution of data across three datasets is described in Table 1.

Table 1. The distribution of the three datasets.

Datasets	Size of train set	Size of test set	Category	data format
MNIST	60000	10000	10	28*28
Fashion-MNIST	60000	10000	10	28*28
CIFAR-10	60000	10000	10	32*32

The MNIST handwritten character dataset consists of a set of 28 × 28 pixel grayscale images with a training set of 60,000 and a test set of 10,000, including handwritten characters 0 through 9, for a total of 10 digital tags. The Fashion-MNIST fashion item dataset has the same size and specifications as the MNIST dataset.

The CIFAR-10 dataset consists of 60000 32 × 32 RGB color images in 10 classes, with 6000 images per class. There are 50000 training images and 10000 test images. The dataset is divided into five training batches and one test batch, each with 10000 images. The test batch contains exactly 1000 randomly-selected images from each class. The training batches contain the remaining images in random order, but some training batches may contain more images from one class than another. Between them, the training batches contain exactly 5000 images from each class. The classes are completely mutually exclusive. There is no overlap between automobiles and trucks. Here are the classes in the dataset as Fig. 2. These classes are mutually exclusive and do not overlap.

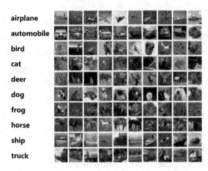

Fig. 2. The classes in the CIFAR-10 dataset. The categories in the figure are indexed from top to bottom as 0–9

3.2 Data Preprocessing

We need to preprocess the data before we start training, and the images are normalized. Before this, the training picture and the test picture are saved in an array of uint8 type, the range of values is [0,255], we need to transform it into a variety of float32, the value range is 0 to 1.

Then, turning the data into the shape of the network requirements. Therefore, we need to adjust the data shape. MNIST and Fashion-MNIST are set to 1, CIFAR-10 dataset is set to 3, as the images are grayscale and colorful. At the same time, the picture size of MNIST and Fashion-MNIST datasets is adjusted to 28, the picture size of the CIFAR-10 dataset is adjusted to 32. We used one-hot encoding for the labeling of the data. The preprocessing of the data is complete.

4 Experiment

We implemented our model on Keras, which is a deep learning framework. All the models were trained and tested on a machine with Intel(R) Core (TM) i7-10700f CPU with 32 GB memory and an NVIDIA GeForce RTX 2070 SUPER GPU with 8 GB memory. We accomplished the training stage with a batch size of 64 for all the experiments in this paper. The Adam optimizer is used to train our model with an initial learning rate which equals 0.001. In the MNIST and Fashion-MNIST datasets, we introduced 10 epochs and 30 epochs in CIFAR-10.

4.1 CNN Classification Model

In this paper, one CNN model was selected as baselines. We named CNN for this image classification CNN-Base. As Table 2 shows, the CNN-Base model went through three convolutions and two pooling layers, followed by two full-connected layers after expanding into a line structure.

Table 2. CNN-base model for grayscale image and color image.

Layer	Grayscale		Color	
	Output shape	Param #	Output shape	Param #
Conv2d	(None,26,26,32)	320	(None,30,30,32)	896
Max-pooling2d_1	(None,13,13,32)	0	(None,15,15,32)	0
Conv2d_2	(None,11,11,64)	18496	(None,13,13,64)	18496
Max-pooling2d_2	(None,5,5,64)	0	(None,6,6,64)	0
Conv2d_3	(None,3,3,64)	36928	(None,4,4,64)	36928
Flatten_1	(None,576)	0	(None,1024)	0
Dense_1	(None,64)	36928	(None,64)	65600
Dense_2	(None,10)	650	(None,10)	650

4.2 CNN and ECA Classification Model

Previous experiments have proved that the ECA method is a very effective channel attention mechanism. Here we use CNN with the ECA module as a comparison, visualize the classification results, and discuss the reasons for the effect of attention mechanisms in the classification.

According to previous experiments, adding the SE method in different locations will affect [2]. Due to the ECA method being an improvement of the SE method, we add ECA to different positions of the convolutional neural network to find the location, which helps us observe the visualization results.

Three datasets are used here to add the ECA method after each convolution and pooling layer of the CNN-Base model to find the most suitable location for the ECA method to add. Table 3, Table 4, and Table 5 illustrate the results of adding ECA modules to different layers. The bold and underlined values represent the best and worse values after adding ECA, respectively. And () are the accuracy and loss values without ECA.

Table 3. ECA method after each convolution and pooling layer of CNN-Base model on MNIST. Bold values represent the best results in the comparison methods. The underlined value is the worst result (0.9892/0.0367).

Layer	Acc	Loss
Cov2d_1(Conv2D)	0.9893(+)	0.0391
Max_pooling2d_1	0.9897(+)	0.0334
Cov2d_2(Conv2D)	**0.9906(+)**	**0.0334**
Max_pooling2d_2	0.9899(+)	0.0366
Cov2d_3(Conv2D)	<u>0.9883(-)</u>	0.0386

Table 4. ECA method after each convolution and pooling layer of CNN-Base model on Fashion-MNIST. Bold values represent the best results in the comparison methods. The underlined value is the worst result (0.9063/0.2636)

Layer	Acc	Loss
Cov2d_1(Conv2D)	**0.9094(+)**	**0.2608**
Max_pooling2d_1	0.9011(−)	0.2702
Cov2d_2(Conv2D)	0.9042(−)	0.2733
Max_pooling2d_2	0.8976(−)	0.2881
Cov2d_3(Conv2D)	0.9086(+)	0.2630

Table 5. ECA method after each convolution and pooling layer of CNN-Base model on CIFAR-10. Bold values represent the best results in the comparison methods. The underlined value is the worst result (0.8632/0.6844)

Layer	Acc	Loss
Cov2d_1(Conv2D)	0.8392(−)	0.6560
Max_pooling2d_1	0.8335(−)	**0.6496**
Cov2d_2(Conv2D)	**0.8656(+)**	0.6854
Max_pooling2d_2	0.8622(−)	0.6888
Cov2d_3(Conv2D)	0.7961(−)	0.7241

Table 6. Explore the impact of the ECA module on the data used for visualization. () indicates the data number of the original data.

Layer	Positive influence				Negative influence			
	MNIST (3)		Fashion-MNIST (1)		Fashion-MNIST (4)		CIFAR-10 (5)	
	ACC	Loss	ACC	Loss	ACC	Loss	ACC	Loss
CNN-Base	0.9892	0.0367	0.9063	0.2636	0.9063	0.2636	0.8632	0.6844
CNN-Base + ECA	0.9906	0.0334	0.9094	0.2608	0.8976	0.2881	0.7961	0.7241

Tables 3, 4 and 5 show that adding the ECA method to different positions will bring other effects. In addition, the impact of the ECA module on different datasets is also different. We can find that the model with the ECA module performs well on MNIST. Four of the five different positions have improved accuracy after the addition. However, the model with the ECA module does not perform well on the other two datasets. Two locations on Fashion-MNIST have improved performance after adding ECA, while only one spot on CIFAR-10 has improved model performance.

To make the visual effect of the influence of the ECA module on the model performance more apparent, we selected the third result on MNIST, the first and fourth results on Fashion-MNIST, and the fifth result on CIFAR-10. Among them, the third result of MNIST and the first result of Fashion-MNIST are used to explore the positive influence of the ECA module, and the other two experiments are used to analyze the negative impact of the ECA module. The specific data selected are shown in Table 6.

As shown in Table 6, in the several sets of data we selected, after adding ECA, the accuracy increased by 0.0014 and 0.0031 on MNIST and Fashion-MNIST, respectively. On the other two sets of data, there was a decrease of 0.0087 and 0.0671, respectively. In the next section, we will visualize the positive and negative effects of ECA, respectively.

4.3 Visual Instance

As shown in Fig. 3, we will select the 36th (index 35) in the MNIST and Fashion-MNIST datasets and the 6666th (index 6665) in the CIFAR-10 dataset. We are interpreting the classification results from a visual perspective. Visually illustrate the positive influence of ECA in section *The Positive influence of ECA*. Visually represent the negative influence of ECA in *The Negative influence of ECA*.

Fig. 3. Three selected examples of data. It corresponds to MNIST, Fashion-MNIST, and CIFAR-10 from left to right.

The Positive Influence of ECA

Figure 4 is the experimental result on MNIST. The left side is the visualization image without the ECA module, and the right side is the visualization image with the ECA method added. The three convolutional layers and two top pooling layers of the model are represented from top to bottom.

According to Table 6, the CNN-Base model has reached an accuracy rate of 0.9892 on MNIST, but the accuracy rate is still slightly improved after adding the ECA method on MNIST. On the one hand, the result can illustrate that CNN-Base has extracted the features fully of images in MNIST and performed effective classification. On the one hand, the result can demonstrate that CNN-Base has fully extracted the characteristics of images in MNIST and performs effective classification. On the other hand, the result can show that on the basis that the model can extract features well, the addition of the ECA module can help the model assign more weight to the part that is conducive to image classification, that is, to retain information that is conducive to category and filter out irrelevant information.

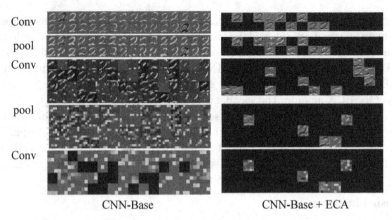

Fig. 4. Visualization of the intermediate filter on the MNIST dataset.

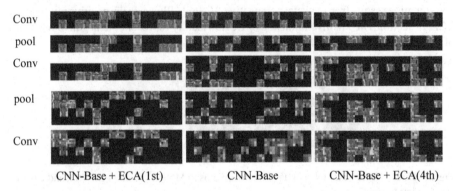

Fig. 5. Visualization of the intermediate filter on the Fashion-MNIST dataset. CNN-Base + ECA (1st) means adding the ECA module after the first layer of CNN-Base. CNN-Base + ECA (4th) means adding the ECA module after the fourth layer of CNN-Base.

Figure 4 may verify our idea. According to prior knowledge, each filter has a different sensitivity to graphics when extracting features. Each filter will remove the elements in the image as comprehensively as possible according to its preferences. As shown in the left image of Fig. 4, each filter extracts a large number of features. However, since the content removed by each filter has the same impact on the final classification, some irrelevant information or even noise information may affect the final classification result. The role of the ECA module here is to help the model assign more weights to the parts that are conducive to the final classification, filter out irrelevant information so that the model can get better results. This result is also shown in the right image of Fig. 4. Only part of the filter extracts the information in the picture, and this information is the part that has a positive impact on the final classification. Other useless data has been filtered out. We conducted a similar experiment on Fashion-MNIST, and the experimental results are shown in Fig. 5.

The most intuitive observation from Fig. 5 is that the left image is less than the middle image than the right image. The left image in Fig. 5 shows the positive effect after ECA is added to the first convolution. The medium image is the CNN-Base model we chose. The picture on the right is a visual view of adding the ECA method after the fourth layer (the second pooling layer) and getting the adverse effect. In this section, we will discuss the positive impact of ECA on model performance.

According to previous research on convolutional neural networks, shallow networks are more used to extract image features than deep networks for image classification. From the visualization image of CNN-Base in Fig. 5, the result shows that the effect of CNN-Base in extracting features on Fashion-MNIST is not very satisfactory. The addition of ECA in the shallow layer has the same impact on MNIST and helps extract features, improving the model's performance.

As a consequence, the ECA module has a positive impact on CNN-Base in two main aspects. 1, In the shallow layer, help the model extract features more effectively, assign a high weight to helpful information and filter useless information. 2, on the premise that the model itself can extract features well, assign higher weights to the parts conducive to the final classification results to help the model filter out useless information.

The Negative Influence of ECA

In this section, we compare the two sets of data selected above to study the reasons for the negative impact of the ECA module on the model performance. The visualization results are shown in the middle and right images in Fig. 5 and Fig. 6.

According to Fig. 5 and Table 6, under the premise that CNN-Base does not extract features well, adding the ECA module in the deep layer does not improve the model's performance but reduces the model's performance. The reason may be that some helpful information was missed when the originally extracted features were not complete. On this basis, the deep ECA method pays more attention to the classification of the existing extracted features, so weighted categories on limited features will not achieve good results.

In Fig. 6, we used RGB color images for comparison to verify the reasons for the negative effects mentioned above. An intuitive feeling is that the number of filters in the last convolutional layer in the right image in Fig. 6 is significantly more than the number in the CNN-Base in the left image. At the same time, we can see that although image features have been extracted as much as possible in CNN-Base, the classification effect is not very ideal. The reason may be that too few convolutional layers cannot wholly extract adequate information in the RGB color image, thereby omitting the helpful information in the original image. Under this premise, the reasons for the harmful effects of ECA are the same as those in Fig. 6.

Therefore, we believe there are two main reasons for the negative effects after adding the ECA method. 1. The baseline model cannot extract image features well, resulting in the lack of useful information. 2. The added position of the ECA module is later, which makes ECA pay more attention to the classification in the absence of information rather than the feature extraction of the original image.

Conv

pool

Conv

pool

Conv

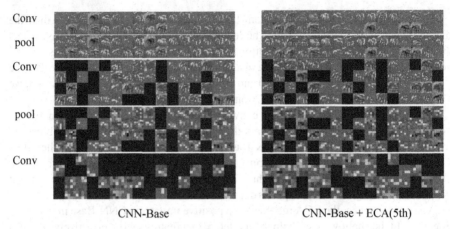

CNN-Base   CNN-Base + ECA(5th)

Fig. 6. Visualization of the intermediate filer on the CIFAR-10 dataset. CNN-Base + ECA (5th) means adding the ECA module after the fifth layer of CNN-Base.

5   Conclusion

In this paper, we use the method of visualizing the intermediate filter of the convolutional neural network to study why the attention mechanism (ECA module is used in this article) affects the model's performance. Experiments were conducted on three datasets (MNIST, Fashion-MNIST, and CIFAR-10) from two aspects (positive and negative). Experimental results illustrate that different addition positions of ECA on other datasets will cause different effects for the same baseline model.

The different effects can be attributed to two aspects: 1, The location of ECA addition. ECA always assigns more weight to helpful information. The convolutional neural network performs feature extraction in the shallow layer and classification in the deep layer. Therefore, adding ECA in appropriate locations will improve the network performance. 2, The choice of the baseline model. The baseline model is not sufficient for feature extraction. Adding ECA can only assign weights to limited feature information and not help the model extract new feature information. It may miss useful information and cause performance degradation. Therefore, we should not use the attention mechanism blindly, and the improvement of model performance is not entirely dependent on the addition of attention mechanisms. We suggest that when using the attention mechanism, you should first pay attention to the choice of the baseline model, and secondly, pay attention to where the attention mechanism is added.

Some of the problems in this article also cannot be ignored, such as simple dataset, insufficient baseline model layers, single attention mechanism method used, and so on. In the future, we hope to use more complex datasets, baseline models, and other excellent attention mechanisms (for example, Squeeze-and-excitation networks (SE), Convolutional Block Attention Module (CBAM) [4], Criss-Cross Attention (CCNet) [5], GPU Effificient Networks (Genet) [6], Pyramid Split Attention (PSA)) [7] for visual analysis.

References

1. Jie, H., et al.: Squeeze-and-excitation networks. In: IEEE Transactions on Pattern Analysis and Machine Intelligence, p. 99 (2017)
2. Nair, V., Hinton, G. E.: Rectified linear units improve restricted boltzmann machines. In: International Conference on Machine Learning (2010)
3. Wang, Q., et al.: ECA-Net: Efficient channel attention for deep convolutional neural networks. In: 2020 IEEE/CVF Conference on Computer Vision and Pattern Recognition (CVPR). IEEE (2020)
4. Woo, S., Park, J., Lee, J.Y., Kweon, I.S.: CBAM: Convolutional Block Attention Module. In: Ferrari, V., Hebert, M., Sminchisescu, C., Weiss, Y. (eds.) ECCV 2018. LNCS, vol. 11211, pp. 3–19. Springer, Cham (2018). https://doi.org/10.1007/978-3-030-01234-2_1
5. Huang, Z., et al.: CCNet: Criss-cross attention for semantic segmentation. IEEE Trans. Pattern Anal. Mach. Intell. https://doi.org/10.1109/TPAMI.2020.3007032
6. Lin, M., et al.: Neural architecture design for GPU-efficient networks (2020)
7. Zhang, H., et al.: EPSANet: an efficient pyramid split attention block on convolutional neural network. ArXiv abs/2105.14447 (2021)
8. Krizhevsky, A., et al.: ImageNet classification with deep convolutional neural networks. In: Proceedings Conference on Neural Information Processing Systems, pp. 84–90 (2012)
9. Toshev, A., Szegedy, C.: DeepPose: human pose estimation via deep neural networks. In: Proceedings of the IEEE Conference on Computer Vision and Pattern Recognition, pp. 1653–1660 (2014)
10. Long, J., Shelhamer, E., Darrell, T.: Fully convolutional networks for semantic segmentation. IEEE Trans. Pattern Anal. Mach. Intell. **39**(4), 640–651 (2015)
11. Zhang, T., et al.: Interleaved group convolutions. In: 2017 IEEE International Conference on Computer Vision (ICCV). IEEE (2017)
12. Ren, S., He, K., Girshick, R., Sun, J.: Faster R-CNN: towards realtime object detection with region proposal networks. In: Proceedings of the 28th International Conference on Neural Information Processing Systems. vol. 1, pp. 91–99 (2015)
13. Hu, J., Shen, L., Albanie, S., Sun, G., Vedaldi, A.: Gather-excite: exploiting feature context in convolutional neural networks. In: NeurIPS (2018)
14. Xie, S., Girshick, R., Dollár, P., Tu, Z., He, K.: Aggregated residual transformations for deep neural networks. In: 2017 IEEE Conference on Computer Vision and Pattern Recognition (CVPR), pp. 5987–5995 (2017). https://doi.org/10.1109/CVPR.2017.634
15. Yunpeng, C., et al.: A2-Nets: double attention networks. In: Neural Information Processing Systems (2018)
16. Huayu, L.: Channel locality block: a variant of squeeze-and-excitation. arXiv:1901.01493 (2019)
17. Ioannou, Y., et al.: Deep roots: improving CNN efficiency with hierarchical filter groups. In: IEEE Conference on Computer Vision and Pattern Recognition (CVPR). IEEE (2017)

Course Recommendation System Based on SSM Framework

Qingyu Liang[1], Zhengyang Wu[1,2(✉)], Ronghua Lin[1], and Li Huang[1]

[1] School of Computer Science, South China Normal University, Guangzhou, China
wuzhengyang@m.scnu.edu.cn
[2] Guangzhou Key Laboratory of Big Data and Intelligent Education, Guangzhou, China

Abstract. With the continuous increase of online courses and the rapid growth of network data, how to improve the recommendation accuracy and real-time performance of personalized recommendation system is a key issue. In order to improve the recommendation quality and real-time performance of the recommendation system, this paper uses SSM (Spring, Spring MVC, Mybatis) Framework, the most popular and latest framework of the enterprise, as the framework of the recommendation system, and uses the hybrid recommendation algorithm (Socialized Recommendation algorithm) that integrates Collaborative Filtering recommendation algorithm and social relationship to make course recommendation. In this paper, the course and relational data of scholar.com are used as data sets for research, so as to provide richer social relationships and more references for experiments.

Keywords: Recommendation system · SSM · Collaborative filtering · Socialized recommendation

1 Introduction

The continuous development of network technology and the popularity of intelligent mobile terminals make online learning more and more popular. With the continuous expansion of online learning courses and the rapid growth of the number and types of courses, the problem of "information overload" [1] becomes more and more serious. Students need to spend a lot of time looking for courses suitable for them, which seriously affects the speed of students' search for personalized information. In order to solve this problem, personalized course recommendation system came into being. Due to the huge amount of data, the recommendation accuracy and real-time performance of the recommendation system are always contradictory [2]. This paper studies the course recommendation system based on SSM framework, hoping to further improve the quality and real-time performance of the recommendation system.

In order to improve the real-time performance and robustness of the recommender system, SSM (Spring, Spring MVC, Mybatis) framework is used as the framework of the recommender system. SSM framework is one of the most popular and novel frameworks used by enterprises. It has the characteristics of lightweight, fast and high efficiency.

Q. Zu et al. (Eds.): HCC 2021, LNCS 13795, pp. 94–106, 2022.
https://doi.org/10.1007/978-3-031-23741-6_9

SSM framework consists of Spring, Spring MVC and Mybatis. Through the IOC/DI feature of Spring [9], the dependency relationship between objects is controlled by Spring. Eliminates the need to use complex EJBs (Enterprise Java Beans) [7], facilitating decoupling and simplifying development. Through the AOP (Aspect Oriented Programming) feature of Spring [9], we only need to focus on the coding of core issues, and Spring is responsible for the non-core code. Spring provides integration support for other excellent open source frameworks [8].

Spring MVC is a lightweight Web framework that uses MVC design ideas to decouple the Web layer, making development clearer and easier. Spring MVC separates the roles of controller, model object, dispenser, and handler object, and this separation makes them easier to customize [12] for extensibility and flexibility.

Mybatis is a set of Object Relation Mapping (ORM) framework, which can simplify the persistence layer, provide mapping labels, and support custom SQL, data storage process and advanced Mapper mapping [5]. Compared with Hibernate, MyBatis is simple and easy to use, which can carry out more detailed SQL optimization and reduce query fields, while Hibernate is more difficult to build complex SQL statements [10]. The execution of one-to-many association may lead to the execution of unexpected SQL statements, execution of too many SQL statements or loading too many objects into memory [11].

At present, traditional and mainstream recommendation algorithms in the recommendation field are mainly divided into three categories: Content-based recommendation algorithm, Collaborative Filtering recommendation algorithm and hybrid recommendation algorithm [13, 15]. Collaborative filtering recommendation algorithm is the most popular and widely used algorithm in the current recommendation algorithm [2]. In real scenarios of Internet applications, the number of users is far greater than the number of items, the historical behavior data of users is very sparse, and the maintenance of the user similarity Matrix is very difficult, compared with the User-based Collaborative Filtering algorithm, the Item-based Collaborative Filtering algorithm has better performance, and produces high-quality recommendations in real time [26], so the Item-based collaborative filtering algorithm is better.

Hybrid recommendation algorithm is the fusion of many kinds of recommendation technologies, which integrates the advantages of other recommendation algorithms [3]. Moreover, when the user access density is too small, the user behavior data used to calculate user similarity is too sparse, making the calculation result inaccurate. Traditional recommendation systems have inherent limitations [14], such as data sparsity and cold start, because they do not take into account the clear social relationship between users [15]. Social networks provide additional user association information, which can help build model analysis between users and items and improve the quality of personalized recommendations. Recommendation algorithm combined with social information is one of the effective means to solve the problem of data sparsity [16].

In order to improve the quality of the recommendation system, this paper uses the hybrid recommendation algorithm for recommendation, which not only uses the Item-based Collaborative Filtering recommendation algorithm, but also considers the relationship between users and integrates the recommendation of users' social relationship, so as to improve the accuracy of Collaborative Filtering recommendation.

2   Related Work and Techniques

2.1   SSM Framework

SSM framework is the integration of Spring, Spring MVC and Mybatis framework. It is the most popular framework in enterprises and can create high-performance, easily tested and reusable code [8]. The flow chart of SSM framework is shown in Fig. 1:

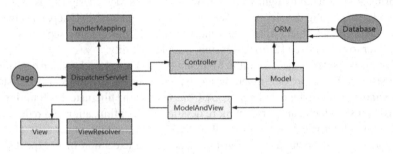

Fig. 1. The flow chart of the SSM framework.

When the page sends an HTTP request, the Spring MVC DispatcherServlet invokes the appropriate Controller (or Handler) according to HandlerMapping. The controller receives the request and invokes the appropriate service method based on the GET or POST methods used. The service method sets up the data of the Model according to the defined business logic (the Model interacts with the database according to the ORM of Mybatis) and returns the ModelAndView to the front-end controller. The scheduling service will get help from the ViewResolver and return the defined View for the requester [9]. SSM framework is described in detail below:

Mybatis is a set of object relational Mapping framework established on the basis of iBatis, which can simplify the persistence layer, provide mapping labels, and support custom SQL, stored procedures and advanced mapping [4]. SQL statements are written in XML files for unified management and optimization, decoupling between SQL and program code, and using simple XML or annotations for configuration and original mapping [12], some major codes can be quickly generated. Mybatis mapper is responsible for recording mapping rules, configuring cache, saving SQL related information, dynamic SQL and session transaction control [10].

Spring is a lightweight inversion of control/Dependency Injection (IoC/DI) and AOP oriented container framework that fits seamlessly into the Web environment [7]. Through Spring's IoC/DI feature, Java reflection mechanism is used to realize the interdependence of object creation and coordination [6]. The dependency between objects is controlled by Spring, and the SqlSessionFactoryBean is used to create objects. Injection when needed for easy decoupling. Spring's AOP feature requires only code writting to focus on the core issues, and non-core code is handled by Spring.

Spring MVC, a successor to the Spring Framework, provides a model-View-controller architecture and off-the-shelf components for developing flexible and loosely coupled Web applications [9]. Spring MVC separates data Model, View and Controller from each other, which makes the data Model generated after back-end processing highly separated from the front-end View display, so that a data Model can be presented in many different ways.

2.2 Collaborative Filtering Recommendation

Collaborative Filtering is the first proposed and most widely used method in recommendation system, which has been widely concerned and studied by industry and academia. Collaborative Filtering recommendation algorithm includes User-based Collaborative Filtering recommendation algorithm and Item-based Collaborative Filtering recommendation algorithm. In the real scenario of Internet application, it is better to adopt Item-based collaborative filtering recommendation algorithm. There are many ways to improve the collaborative filtering recommendation algorithm, which can be divided into three directions. The first improvement direction is to add the algorithm of matrix decomposition, which uses the user's rating information matrix for matrix decomposition to mine the low-dimensional hidden feature space, and represents the user and the item in this low-dimensional space, thus improving the ability to process sparse matrix. For example, Hafed Zarzour et al.[17] proposed a collaborative filtering recommendation algorithm based on reduction and clustering technology, using K-means algorithm and singular value decomposition (SVD) to cluster similar users and reduce the dimension respectively. Weimin Li et al. [18] proposed a matrix decomposition algorithm based on user features to find the global optimal solution while maintaining user preference features. The second direction of improvement is to add more features and use automatic feature crossing to add composite features. For example, Yuchin Juan proposed the fieldaware factorization machine(FFM) algorithm for recommendation, introduced the information of the feature domain, and made the multi-domain implicit vector carry out feature crossover [19]. The third improvement direction is to add users' social relations to provide more social information for reference. For example, in order to solve the problem of sparsity, Hao Ma et al. [20] used a generalized matrix decomposition to make recommendations in combination with the explicit social relationships of latent factor analysis.

2.3 Social Relationship Recommendation

The huge complexity of social networks and the heterogeneity of shared elements provide rich reference information for recommendation systems[21]. People with social relations tend to influence each other. With similar characteristics, social network data can fully reveal the similarity of users' preferences. The measurement of preference similarity between users and friends (also known as trust) is an important factor affecting social recommendation algorithm. Trust can be measured in terms of ratings or trust data. Many scholars have explored the recommendation of social relationships. Hao Ma et al. [20] adopted the method of probability matrix decomposition to model social information, used score similarity function to calculate the trust intensity between users, and took social network as a regular constraint item to learn user preferences. Meiling Wang et al. [22] proposed the user's ability measure function and trustworthiness measure function, and obtained the estimated user preferences by combining them with the score similarity function in the way of adaptive weighting. Mohsen Jamali et al. [23] proposed a random walk algorithm in scoring networks and social networks to spread trust by restricting the similarity of average preferences between users and their friends. In general, the most commonly used method to construct social recommendation model is the social recommendation model based on matrix decomposition. In recent years, many scholars have used community discovery algorithm to obtain indirect social relations between users to construct social recommendation model.

3 Introduction of the System

3.1 System Framework

The course recommendation system in this paper adopts a hierarchical development structure, which is divided into Entity layer, Operation layer (Dao layer or Mapper layer), Business layer, Control layer and View layer. The system structure diagram is shown in Fig. 2:

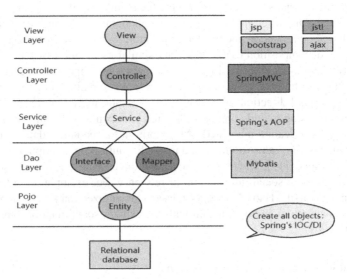

Fig. 2. System structure.

(1) Configuration: The core of using SSM framework is to configure Mybatis, Spring, Spring MVC configuration file and web.xml. You need to configure which packages to scan, which objects Spring uses to create with beans, configure annotations, configure transaction enhancements and pointcuts for transaction management, configure view parsers, release static resources, and so on.
(2) Relational database: Build up database, database table, and then insert data.
(3) Entity Layer: Establish entity class, one database table corresponds to one class, and the data members of the class correspond to the attributes of the database table one by one.

(4) Dao Layer: Mainly does the work of data persistence layer and encapsulates some tasks of database mapping. Dao Layer uses Mybatis to realize one-to-one mapping of entity classes and fields in database tables by defining interfaces and mapper mapping files. First, define an interface. Then create a mapping file Mapper with the same name as the interface, and implement SQL operations of the database in Mapper. Other parts of the application program will interact with the database through the interface with the same name. If the class field name is different from the database field name, you also need to define a ResultMap result set mapping.

(5) Service Layer: Mainly responsible for the logic design of the business module, and invokes the operation layer DAO for business operation. The AOP of Spring is configured in the configuration file to enhance the transaction processing of the business logic layer.

(6) Controller layer: Controller is responsible for controlling specific business modules, using Spring MVC to interact with the data of the front and back ends, and calling the service of the business logic layer to realize corresponding functions.

(7) View Layer: Front-end page using JSP, JSTL tag library, Bootstarp [24] front-end framework, Ajax asynchronous request, HTML, CSS3, Jquary, to achieve page display and interaction.

3.2 Hybrid Recommendation Algorithm

Considering that only using the Collaborative Filtering recommendation algorithm will have the problem of data sparsity, leading to the inaccurate recommendation results, this paper uses the hybrid recommendation algorithm and adds the recommendations of users' social relationships to improve the accuracy of the Collaborative Filtering recommendation algorithm. Collaborative Filtering algorithms combined with social relationships are also called Social Recommendation algorithms [16]. The algorithm used in this paper are as follows:

First, the user-item scoring matrix is constructed based on the user-item scoring data.

Then, calculate the similarity between the items. There are many methods to calculate similarity, such as cosine similarity, Pearson similarity, Euclidean distance, Jaccard similarity and so on. Cosine similarity is measured by the cosine Angle between vectors. In order to correct the deviation of different users with different scoring scales, the modified cosine similarity method improves this shortcoming by subtracting the average score of users for all items. The modified cosine similarity is used to calculate the similarity.

Calculate the modified cosine similarity between items:

$$\mathrm{Sim}(I_x, I_y) = \frac{\sum\limits_{k=1}^{t} (R_{k,x} - \overline{R}_x) \times (R_{k,y} - \overline{R}_y)}{\sqrt{\sum\limits_{k=1}^{t} (R_{k,x} - \overline{R}_x)^2} \times \sqrt{\sum\limits_{k=1}^{t} (R_{k,y} - \overline{R}_y)^2}} \tag{1}$$

where, $R_{k,x}$ represent the score of user U_k on item I_x, $R_{k,y}$ represent the score of user U_k on item I_y, and $\overline{R}_y$ is the average score of item I_x, where is the average score of item I_y. The larger $\mathrm{Sim}(I_x, I_y)$ is, the greater the similarity between item I_x and item I_y is.

Then, calculate the Item-based Collaborative Filtering prediction score. In order to correct the deviation of different users with different scoring scales, the mean value of item scoring is often used for correction.

After the calculation of item similarity, the candidate item set of target user i can be obtained, and then the score can be predicted. User i's prediction score $R_{i,x}$ for item x is:

$$R_{i,x} = \overline{R}_x + \frac{\sum\limits_{y=1}^{t} Sim(I_x, I_y) \times (R_{i,y} - \overline{R}_y)}{\sum\limits_{y=1}^{t} |Sim(I_x, I_y)|} \tag{2}$$

where, $R_{i,y}$ represent the score of user U_i on item I_y, $\overline{R}_x$ is the average score of item I_x, and $\overline{R}_y$ is the average score of item I_y.

In this way, the Item-based Collaborative Filtering recommendation algorithm is used to obtain the score prediction of designated user i for each item, denoted as P(i). Then you calculate the recommendations that fit into the design relationship. The next step is to calculate recommendations that fit into social relationships.

Firstly, user relationship matrix is constructed based on user social relationship data. To prevent some users from having too few neighbors, for a user with less than 10 neighbors, iterate over the next neighbor of his neighbor and then update as his neighbor to the user relationship matrix. According to the user relationship matrix, the Top-N policy is adopted to select the nearest neighbor of user i, denoted as $K(U_i)$.

Then calculate the user similarity between user i's nearest neighbors:

$$Sim'(U_i, U_j) = \frac{\sum\limits_{k=1}^{t} (R_{i,k} - \overline{R}_i) \times (R_{j,k} - \overline{R}_j)}{\sqrt{\sum\limits_{k=1}^{t} (R_{i,k} - \overline{R}_i)^2} \times \sqrt{\sum\limits_{k=1}^{t} (R_{j,k} - \overline{R}_j)^2}} \tag{3}$$

where, $R_{i,k}$ stand for user U_i's score on item I_k, $R_{j,k}$ stand for user U_j's score on item I_k, $\overline{R}_i$ is the average value of user U_i's score, and $\overline{R}_j$ is the average value of user U_j's score. The larger $Sim'(U_i, U_j)$ is, the more similar U_i and U_j is.

Then, calculate user i's score on each item x to predict $R_{i,x}$:

$$R_{i,x} = \overline{R}_i + \frac{\sum\limits_{U_j \in K(U_i)} Sim'(U_i, U_j) \times (R_{j,x} - \overline{R}_j)}{\sum\limits_{U_j \in K(U_i)} |Sim'(U_i, U_j)|} \tag{4}$$

where, $R_{j,x}$ represent U_j's score on item I_x, $\overline{R}_i$ is the average value of U_i score, and $\overline{R}_j$ is the average value of U_j score.

In this way, the social relationship between users is integrated to obtain the score prediction of designated user i for each item, denoted as P'(i).

Then, the score prediction $\Phi(i) = \lambda P(i) + (1-\lambda)P'(i)$, $\lambda \in (0,1)$ of user i for each item is synthetically calculated, the initial value is 0.5, and the subsequent experiment is optimized.

Finally, user i makes a ranking of $\Phi(i)$ for each item score and recommends the TopN items with the highest score.

In summary, the steps of the hybrid recommendation algorithm are as follows:

Input: User history behavior information records, user social relationship data.
Output: List of items recommendations.
Step 1: Construct user-item scoring matrix based on user history behavior information.
Step 2: Calculate the similarity between items according to Formula (1).
Step 3: Calculate the score prediction of designated user i for each item according to Formula (2), denoted as P(i).
Step 4: Construct the user relationship matrix based on the user's social relationship data. If the number of neighbors of the user is small, continue to update the user relationship matrix.
Step 5: Select user i's nearest neighbor using the Top-N policy based on the user relationship matrix.
Step 6: Calculate the user similarity between the nearest neighbors of user i according to Formula (3).
Step 7: Calculate the score prediction of user i for each item according to Formula (4), denoted as P'(i).
Step 8: Combine P(i) and P'(i) to calculate user i's score prediction of each item $\Phi(i) = \lambda P(i) + (1-\lambda)P'(i)$.
Step 9: Sort with $\Phi(i)$ of item score prediction, and recommend TopN items with the highest score.

4   System Implementation

The course recommendation system has the following functions: User Information Maintenance, Course Information Maintenance, User Relationship Visualization, Course Statistics Visualization, Personalized Recommendation, and the most core function is Personalized Recommendation. Personalized Recommendation function will use hybrid recommendation algorithm – the improved algorithm of Collaborative Filtering recommendation algorithm to recommend. The course, user and user relationship data and user-course access data in the database of this system come from scholar.com [25]. New users can also be registered and new courses can be added. The recommendation algorithm will use these data to make recommendations.

The homepage of the system is shown in Fig. 3:

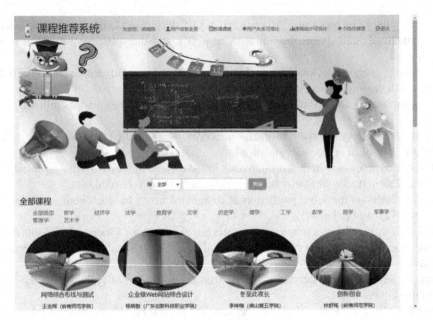

Fig. 3. The homepage of the system.

5   Experiment and Result Analysis

5.1   Data Set

The experiment used data sets from academic social network scholar.com's course visit information and real social network information. The data set of scholar.com not only has a large amount of data, but also can provide the reference of the relationship between users for recommendation, thus improving the accuracy of recommendation. By the end of June 2021, there are 3168 courses, 150,563 users, 52,166 connections, and 1237,485 courses visited data in half a year. Users' access information to courses is a kind of historical behavior information of users. Users' predicted scores for items can also be calculated by using the user scoring formula to make recommendations. In the experiment, the data set was randomly divided into 5 equal parts, 4 of which were used as the training set and the remaining one as the test set.

5.2   Evaluation Indicators

MAE is the most commonly used method to evaluate the recommendation quality of recommendation algorithms. MAE measures the accuracy of the prediction by calculating the deviation between the predicted user ratings and the actual user ratings. The smaller the value of MAE, the higher the recommendation quality. Let the set of predicted user ratings be represented as$\{p_1, p_2,..., p_n\}$, the corresponding actual user score set is $\{r_1,$

$r_2,\ldots, r_n\}$, then the calculation formula of average absolute deviation MAE is:

$$\text{MAE} = \frac{\sum_{i=1}^{n} |p_i - r_i|}{n}$$

5.3 Experimental Results and Analysis

The principle is the same for calculating the deviation between the predicted user access data and the actual user access data using MAE. The experiment is mainly to compare the MAE of the top-N nearest neighbor number change and the MAE of the weight λ value change of the prediction score.

1. Comparison of Top-N nearest neighbors of user relationships
   This experiment calculates the influence of the number of Top-N nearest neighbors on the accuracy of recommendation. The unit length is 5, and the initial value of the weight of the predicted score λ is 0.5. The experiment results are shown in Fig. 4:

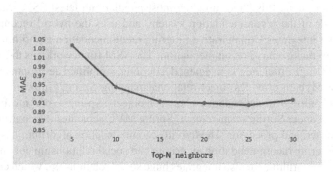

Fig. 4. MAE values of different top-N neighbor numbers.

According to the experimental results, when the number of Top-N neighbors is 15, THE MAE value is close to the lowest, and the subsequent increase of the number of neighbors has little influence on MAE. In order to improve the running speed of the algorithm, update the user relationship matrix as little as possible, and the best value of top-n neighbor number is 15. At this point the algorithm has the best recommendation effect.

2. Comparison of the weight λ value of the prediction score
   This experiment calculates the influence of different weight λ value on the recommended accuracy. The unit length is 0.1, and the initial nearest neighbor number of Top-N is 15. The experiment result is shown in Fig. 5:

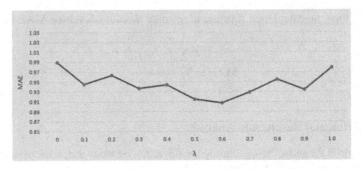

Fig. 5. MAE values of λ values with different weights.

According to the experimental results, when MAE is the lowest and the value of the weight λ is 0.6, the algorithm has the best recommendation effect.

6   Conclusions

In order to improve the recommendation quality and real-time performance of the recommendation system, this paper uses the most popular and latest SSM framework as the framework of the recommendation system, and uses the hybrid recommendation algorithm that integrates Collaborative Filtering recommendation algorithm and social relationship to make course recommendation. The SSM framework has the advantages of lightweight, high efficiency, convenient decoupling, simplified development, and easy maintenance. Mybatis provides object-relational mapping. Spring's injection mechanism gives Spring control over dependencies between objects. Spring's AOP mechanism puts non-core code under Spring management. Spring MVC separates the controller, model object, dispenser, and processor. The hybrid recommendation algorithm based on Collaborative Filtering recommendation algorithm and social relationship not only uses the most classical algorithm, but also integrates huge social relationship, which can improve the accuracy of recommendation. In this paper, the measurement of social relations is rough and there are still many shortcomings. The future research direction is to integrate users' multi-dimensional information, measure users' social relations more fully, and mine users' potential needs to provide more and more accurate resources.

References

1. Isinkaye, F.O., Folajimi, Y.O., Ojokoh, B.A.: Recommendation systems: principles, methods and evaluation. Egypt. Inform. J. **16**(3), 261–273 (2015)
2. Jiemin, C., Yong, T., Jianguo, L., Yibin, C.: Research on personalized recommendation algorithm. J. South China Normal Univ. **46**(5), 1–8 (2014)
3. He, C., et al.: Scientific paper recommendation method based on academic community. J. South China Normal Univ. **44**(3), 1–4 (2012)
4. Guo, Y., Chen, M., Wei, K.: Research of recycling resource website based on spring and MyBatis framework. In: 2015 International Conference on Information Technology and Intelligent Transportation Systems (ITITS), pp. 307–314 (2015)

5. Li, Q., Qing, A.: Design and implementation of student life service platform based on SSM framework. Comput. Knowl. Technol. **17**(13), 80–82 (2021)
6. Yongchang, R., Deyi, J., Tao, X., Ping, Z.: Research on software development platform based on SSH framework structure. Procedia Eng. **15**, 3078–3082 (2011)
7. Arthur, J., Azadegan, S.: Spring framework for rapid open source J2EE Web application development: a case study. In: Sixth International Conference on Software Engineering, Artificial Intelligence, Networking and Parallel/Distributed Computing and First ACIS International Workshop on Self-Assembling Wireless Network, pp. 90–95 (2005)
8. Mane, D., Chitnis, K., Ojha, N.: The spring framework: an open source java platform for developing robust Java applications. Int. J. Innovative Technol. Explor. Eng. **3**, 137–143 (2013)
9. http://www.tutorialspoint.com/spring/index.htm
10. Shiyong, X., Tianxiang, D., Rongzheng, Z., Rongsen, W.: Research on Mybatis mapper model based on SQL template. In: 2020 International Conference on Computer Engineering and Application (ICCEA), pp. 502–505 (2020)
11. Węgrzynowicz, P.: Performance antipatterns of one to many association in hibernate. In: 2013 Federated Conference on Computer Science and Information Systems, pp. 1475-1481 (2013)
12. Hou, Y.: Design and implementation of the framework for Spring+SpringMVC+MyBatis in the development of web application. In: 2017 International Conference on Computer Technology, Electronics and Communication (ICCTEC), pp. 368–371 (2017)
13. Li, M., Zhao, X., Yu, Y., et al.: Research progress of recommendation algorithm. Small Microcomput. Syst. **43**(03), 544–554 (2022)
14. Chen, S., Owusu, S., Zhou, L.: Social network based recommendation systems: a short survey. In: 2013 International Conference on Social Computing, pp. 882–885 (2013)
15. Suhaim, A.B., Berri, J.: Context-aware recommender systems for social networks: review, challenges and opportunities. IEEE Access **9**, 57440–57463 (2021)
16. Yiteng, P., Fazhi, H., Haiping, Y.: A social recommendation algorithm based on implicit similarity of trust relationship. Chin. J. Comput. **41**(1), 65–81 (2018)
17. Zarzour, H., Al-Sharif, Z., Al-Ayyoub, M., Jararweh, Y.: A new collaborative filtering recommendation algorithm based on dimensionality reduction and clustering techniques. In: 2018 9th International Conference on Information and Communication Systems (ICICS), pp. 102–106 (2018)
18. Li, W., et al.: Personalization recommendation algorithm based on trust correlation degree and matrix factorization. IEEE Access **7**, 45451–45459 (2019)
19. Juan, Y., Zhuang, Y., Chin, W.-S., Lin, C.-J.: Field-aware factorization machines for CTR prediction. In: Proceedings of the 10th ACM Conference on Recommender Systems (RecSys'16), pp. 43–50. Association for Computing Machinery, New York, NY, USA (2016)
20. Ma, H., Yang, H., Lyu, M.R., King, I.: SoRec: social recommendation using probabilistic matrix factorization. In: Proceedings of the 17th ACM conference on Information and knowledge management (CIKM'08). Association for Computing Machinery, New York, NY, USA, pp. 931–940 (2008)
21. Gasparetti, F., Sansonetti, G., Micarelli, A.: Community detection in social recommender systems: a survey. Appl. Intell. **51**(6), 3975–3995 (2020). https://doi.org/10.1007/s10489-020-01962-3
22. Wang, M., Ma, J.: A novel recommendation approach based on users' weighted trust relations and the rating similarities. Soft. Comput. **20**(10), 3981–3990 (2015). https://doi.org/10.1007/s00500-015-1734-1
23. Jamali, M., Ester, M.: TrustWalker: a random walk model for combining trust-based and item-based recommendation. In: Proceedings of the 15th ACM SIGKDD International Conference on Knowledge Discovery and Data mining (KDD'09), pp. 397–406. Association for Computing Machinery, New York, NY, USA (2009)

24. https://www.bootcss.com/
25. https://www.scholat.com/
26. Linden, G., Smith, B., York, J.: Amazon.com recommendations: item-to-item collaborative filtering. IEEE Internet Comput. 7(1), 76–80 (2003)

Using Entropy for Trust Measure in Collaborative Filtering

Xiaojuan Cai[1], Wenan Tan[1,2(✉)], Xiao Zhang[1], and Xin Zhou[1]

[1] Nanjing University of Aeronautics and Astronautics, Nanjing 211106, China
wtan@foxmail.com
[2] Shanghai Polytechnic University, Shanghai 201209, China

Abstract. The recommendation system achieves user preferences by analyzing users' historical behaviors, find user groups similar to target users, predict target users' ratings of items of interest and make recommendations. Therefore, various techniques have been proposed to develop similarity measures. Research on recommendation algorithms that integrate user trust information has made considerable progress. However, only the definition of trust relationship based on the degree of social relationship can't truly reflect the trust relationship between users. Focusing on the shortcomings of current trust algorithms, this paper proposes an implicit trust calculation method that integrates user entropy. By using the information entropy of user ratings to improve the previous similarity measurement, the user's trust degree is integrated to make more accurate selection of neighborhoods, and the situation of high trust and low interest similarity is reduced. The effectiveness of the algorithm is verified through experiments, it is proved that it is superior to the previous similarity measure, and compared with the traditional recommendation algorithm, the prediction accuracy has been improved.

Keywords: Recommendation system · User trust · User entropy · Collaborative filtering

1 Introduction

In many commercial systems, users tend to search for products based on the ratings of other users. This recommendation system has been implemented in many fields, such as books, music, movies, and online learning. Collaborative filtering (CF) is a common and efficient technology used in recommendation systems [1]. Many commercial systems, such as Amazon and eBay, have successfully implemented collaborative filtering recommendations. The basic idea of collaborative filtering is to find people who share the same interests with current users, and recommend items they might like to target users based on the rating behavior of these users. This method is based on the user's collaborative filtering algorithm. From a project perspective, project-based collaborative filtering is to recommend similar projects to target users that are similar to their favorite projects. These two collaborative filtering algorithms constitute a memory-based collaborative filtering algorithm. They are named this way because they store all user ratings in memory.

Q. Zu et al. (Eds.): HCC 2021, LNCS 13795, pp. 107–118, 2022.
https://doi.org/10.1007/978-3-031-23741-6_10

In any recommendation algorithm, recommendation is accompanied by scoring prediction of unknown items, and recommendation of items with highly predictive scores. In collaborative filtering algorithms, finding similar users or items is critical to system performance. Various similarity calculation methods, such as Pearson correlation coefficient or cosine similarity, are widely used in recommendation systems. These methods use user ratings for a given item to calculate similarity. In fact, most commercial systems maintain a large number of products, and users can only rate a few products. Therefore, the user-item scoring matrix that the algorithm can use is extremely sparse [2]. This kind of data sparseness is used in collaborative filtering research. A very challenging problem because it usually produces untrustworthy similarities. In addition, many businesses will hire a group of people to give very high ratings to their products for profit, which leads to the algorithm to analyze the priority of this product incorrectly and recommend it to more users, that is, the robustness of the algorithm [3]. In order to solve the above problems, many new similarity models have been developed, such as constrained Pearson correlation coefficients and fuzzy-based similarity models. In addition to the similarity itself, the study found that people are more willing to trust the ratings of users they trust. Researchers propose a measure of the reliability of users' trust relationships to obtain more credible rating predictions. Although the introduction of trust information has improved the recommendation effect to a certain extent, the existing trust model is still not sufficient for mining user information.

In order to solve the above problems, this paper proposes a new collaborative filtering recommendation algorithm based on user entropy and implicit trust to solve the two main problems in traditional collaborative filtering: data sparsity and robustness. In most memory-based collaborative filtering algorithms, similarity calculations are essentially determined by the aggregation of absolute rating differences. For example, Pearson similarity and other consistency measures are calculated by the absolute difference between two users' absolute scores or deviations from their respective average scores. We combine information entropy to consider using the relative difference between user ratings to introduce user rating consistency, and use the "small world" theory to evaluate the trust between users. The results show that the information entropy of the relative rating difference between two users captures additional coherent information compared to only considering the absolute rating difference of the individual. In addition, a prediction model that integrates user entropy and trust can effectively improve the accuracy of score prediction. Therefore, we propose a trust calculation method that integrates user entropy. Our contributions are as follows:

1. We proposed a new entropy-based similarity to improve the performance of traditional similarity. Different from the comparison of absolute score differences, we consider the relative score differences of users to enhance the consistency calculation.
2. We use the "small world" theory to build a user trust transfer chain, and fully tap all the trust relationships of users.
3. Integrate user entropy and trust relationship to obtain a comprehensive trust degree, and select neighbors according to the comprehensive trust degree to improve the accuracy of prediction.

2 Related Research

The recommendation system selects user neighborhoods based on similarity measures. Common similarity measures include Pearson correlation coefficient and cosine similarity. These similarity measures are derived from two users' ratings of common items. However, a large number of items are maintained in a system, resulting in a very sparse user-item rating matrix, and traditional similarity measures will produce unreliable similarity.

In order to solve the above-mentioned traditional problems, Natarajan et al. [4] proposed a new similarity measure called LOD similarity, which is a combination of improvised PCC+ similarity PICSS that is used to discover semantically similar items of a target item to expand item-factor vector in the matrix factorization process to improve accuracy. Lee [5] incorporated a weight into the existing similarity measures. This weight is usually defined as a function of the number of items co-rated by two users. However, this approach is surely based on the assumption that two users with more common items would demonstrate higher similarity between their ratings. Feng et el. [7] introduced the Pearson correlation coefficient and the FP-growth association rule algorithm to accurately select the participating experts in the historical project similar to the scale of the project to be reviewed, and combine the experts to calculate and obtain the expert group with the highest fit. In Zhu et al. [7], an extended concept of Jaccard index is designed and exploited to measure similarity. This idea combines the numerical relevance of the ratings with non-numerical information mainly to improve the current memory-based prediction times. Some recent studies have adopted the concept of entropy proposed by Shannon [8] as a new method that reflects the calculation from user ratings to similarity. Lee S [9] et al. proposed a method aims to reflect the global rating behaviors of users on an item, which utilizes information entropy of ratings for each item and incorporates it into the conventional similarity measures. However, the measure they proposed significantly outperforms the traditional similarity measures in terms of both prediction and recommendation qualities with a small-scaled sparse dataset. Wang et el. [10] proposed a new information entropy-driven user similarity measure model which is proposed to measure the relative difference between ratings and a Manhattan distance-based model is developed to address the fat tail problem by estimating the alternative active user average rating to provides better recommendations.

Although information entropy is used in the collaborative filtering recommendation system for similarity calculation, it solves the sparsity of data and also improves the accuracy of prediction, but the information entropy does not completely represent the relationship between users. Many scholars have begun to study the behavior of users, and integrate social network information to dig out trust information between users and find the potential relationship between trust information and the recommendation system to improve the accuracy of recommendation. Jiang et al. [11] proposed a slope one algorithm based on an improved fusion of user trust data and user similarity. The algorithm uses the helpfulness attribute in the Amazon data set as the trust rate to determine trust data, and solves the low accuracy of the traditional slope one algorithm. Rate and distrust data issues. Duricic et al. [12] In order to solve the problem of cold start users, they proposed to use a measurement method in network science, namely regular equivalence, and apply it to the trust network to generate a similarity matrix for selecting k nearest neighbors. Make recommendations. Alejandro et al. [13] studied the degree to which user similarity is essential for obtaining high-quality item recommendations, and proposed to select neighbors for recommendation based on the degree of overlap between user preferences and target user preferences. Wang et al. [14] believed that if two users show similar preferences or personality characteristics, the trust between them should be high. To this end, they proposed to calculate trust-enhanced user similarity in user-based collaborative filtering based on network representation learning. That is, user preferences with enhanced trust are merged into potential POIs with geographic and temporal influences for POI recommendation. Wang et el. Tong et el. [15] incorporated additional information into the recommendation process such as explicit trust scores that are assigned by users to others or implicit trust relationships that result from social connections between users to form a very sparse trust network to generate recommendations for users.

Although the calculation of information entropy in the similarity in the CF system has been proven to improve the accuracy of the system in many ways, the entropy has nothing to do with the previous similarity measures and trust. Therefore, determining the relative weight and combination of entropy and trust is another important factor of injection performance.

3 Proposed Trust Measure

The recommendation system analyzes the user's historical scoring behavior and item characteristics, mines the user's preferences, trains a recommendation model, and obtains predictions of ratings and recommendations. In the process of training the model, whether the data set matches the recommended model is an important factor that affects the prediction results. However, a recommendation system maintains a large number of items, and a user may only rate a small number of items. Therefore, the user-item rating data set is very sparse, resulting in unreliable prediction results. According to the research on trust mechanism and social network, this paper proposes a trust recommendation algorithm that integrates user entropy in order to solve the data sparse problem of collaborative filtering algorithm. Implicit Trust User Nearest Neighbor Recommendation (I-TNNRec), through mining the implicit trust relationship in the data set, and applying the obtained trust information to the nearest neighbor algorithm, so as to achieve the effect of improving the accuracy of scoring and recommendation prediction.

3.1 User Entropy

Each user has his own scoring habits, which means that users' ratings are usually focused on a specific average attitude. The closer the ratings of two users to an item are, the more similar the two users are. This article believes that it is necessary to additionally consider the relative difference and absolute difference of the scoring deviation. For items scored by two users, if the absolute difference in the score deviation is large, but rarely occurs on a few items, the similarity should not be significantly affected. In contrast, if most items always have differences, the similarity should be smaller. For example, in Table 1, using the Pearson correlation coefficient to calculate the similarity between user1 and user2, the result is 0.471. Change the first score of user2 from 5 to 1, and then use the Pearson correlation coefficient to calculate the similarity between use1 and user2 and the result is 0. Obviously, when there is a score that is completely different from the average score distribution, although the Pearson correlation coefficient cannot correctly determine whether two users are similar, it can provide more discriminative information to determine whether user preferences are similar. Intuitively speaking, users rarely give ratings to some items, and do not provide enough information to distinguish them from other items. In contrast, if a user maintains a score difference with other users, we can easily distinguish him/her from other users. This is the motivation to use the information entropy of the relative difference in the ratings of the items by users to measure the similarity of two users instead of assigning different weights to the absolute difference.

Table 1. Ratings of user1 and user 2

User1	User2	User2+	User1	User2	User2+
5	5	⟹1	4	4	4
5	5	5	4	4	4
5	5	5	4	4	4
5	5	5	4	4	4
4	5	5	4	4	4
4	3	3	4	4	4
5	3	3	5	5	5

The concept of information entropy was proposed by Claude E. Shannon, which represents the probability of a certain specific information. Information entropy solves the problem of quantitative measurement of information. Let X be a discrete random variable, corresponding to it is the set of all possible outputs, defined as the symbol set. x is the output of a random variable. P(x) represents the output probability function. The greater the uncertainty of the variable, the greater the entropy, and the greater the amount of information needed to analyze it. The entropy function on P is defined as follows.

$$H(P) = -\sum_{x=1}^{X} p(x) \log P(x) \tag{1}$$

By definition of P(x), we can easily obtain:

1. For any P(x), we have $0 \leq P(x) \leq 1$.
2. We have $\sum_{x \in X} P(x) = 1$.
3. $P(x) \log P(x) = 0$, when $P(x) = 0$.

For users u and v, the common items are represented as $\{(r_{u,i}, r_{v,i})\}$ and $i \in \{1 \ldots N\}$. N is the number of items that users u and v rated in common. The respective average rating is $\overline{r_u}$ and $\overline{r_v}$, and the deviation from mean rating is $r_{u,i} - \overline{r_u}$. The absolute difference between two deviations is denoted as $\Delta d_i = |(r_{u,i} - \overline{r_u}) - (r_{v,i} - \overline{r_v})|$. We can obtain a serial normalized ratio on all common items, given Δd represents the sum of all differences that $\Delta d = \sum_{i \in N} \Delta d_i$

$$P_i = \frac{\Delta d_i}{\Delta d} \tag{2}$$

Then, P_i can be seen as probability function of a random variable. Furthermore, we can use information entropy to measure the disorder of this variable. The greater the disorder of this variable, the less similarity we consider there to be.

$$H = -\sum_{i \in N} P_i log_2 P_i \tag{3}$$

Lastly, we define the entropy-driven user relevance as

$$Sim_{u,v}^{Entropy} = 1 - \frac{H}{log_2 N} = 1 - (\sum (-\frac{\Delta d_i}{\Delta d} log_2 \frac{\Delta d_i}{\Delta d})/log_2 N) \tag{4}$$

3.2 Comprehensive Trust Calculation

3.2.1 Normalize Rating Data

Because the rating scales of different users are inconsistent, it is very likely that two users with the same hobbies will have a relatively large difference in the similarity of the user ratings obtained. For example, a user who is very dissatisfied with an item has a score of 1 and a user who is very satisfied with a score of 5, which is the same as a user who scores 4 points on an item or another user who scores 3 points on this item. However, the similarity obtained by the two users must be different. Therefore, this paper uses subjective score normalization to process the scores of each user uniformly, and eliminate the lack of accuracy in the measurement of similarity due to different user subjective score scales.

The user-item matrix is E [m, n], where m represents the number of users and n represents the number of items. $r_{i,j}$ is the rating given by user i onto item j.

1. The average rating, denoted by $\overline{r_i}$, is defined as follows.

$$\overline{r_i} = \frac{\sum_{j=1}^{n} r_{i,j}}{n} \tag{5}$$

Reset the scoring range of each user, so that the average of the sum of the minimum scores of all users is used as the lower limit of the scoring range, and the average of the sum of the maximum scores of all users is the upper limit of the scoring range. The calculation formula is as follows.

$$[\frac{\sum_{i=1}^{m} min(r_{i,1}, r_{i,2}, \ldots, r_{i,m})}{m}, \frac{\sum_{i=1}^{m} max(r_{i,1}, r_{i,2}, \ldots, r_{i,m})}{m}] \tag{6}$$

The calculation method of the average value of this interval is as follows.

$$k = \frac{\frac{\sum_{i=1}^{m} \min(r_{i,1}, r_{i,2}, \ldots, r_{i,m})}{m} + \frac{\sum_{i=1}^{m} \max(r_{i,1}, r_{i,2}, \ldots, r_{i,m})}{m}}{2} \tag{7}$$

2. Use the normalized calculation formula to get $r'_{u,i}$, is defined as follows.

$$r'_{i,j} = \frac{k * r_{i,j}}{\overline{r_i}} \tag{8}$$

where $\frac{k}{\overline{r_i}}$ is the normalization coefficient. Combine (1) and (4) can get formula (5),

$$r'_i = \frac{\sum_{j=1}^{n} r'_{i,j}}{n} = \frac{\sum_{j=1}^{n} \frac{k*r_{i,j}}{\overline{r_i}}}{n} = \left(\frac{k}{\overline{r_i}}\right)\left(\frac{\sum_{j=1}^{n} r_{i,j}}{n}\right) \tag{9}$$

It can be seen that through the above conversion, the converted $\overline{r'_1} = \overline{r'_2} = \ldots = \overline{r'_m} = k$, the user's value coordinate system has been unified, effectively reducing the measurement deviation of similarity between users.

3.2.2 Trust Calculation

The core idea value of trust calculation uses the common scoring items among users to compare the scoring difference of users. If the common item scores of users are similar, it indicates that the two users have similar interests in the item, which means that there is greater implicit trust between users. This paper uses the fast prediction method to simply and quickly calculate the score of the target user. The calculation formula is as follows.

$$P^f_{ui} = \overline{r_u} + (r'_{v,i} - \overline{r_v}) \tag{10}$$

where P^f_{ui} is the common scoring item score of the target user predicted by the reference user v. The difference in preference between the target user and the reference user for the unified item can be determined by comparing the p of the target user with the actual score. The calculation formula is as follows.

$$S_{u->v} = 1 - \frac{\sum_{i \in |I_u \cap I_v|} (P^f_{ui} - r'_{u,i})}{|I_u \cap I_v|} \tag{11}$$

we also introduces the Pearson correlation coefficient to determine the credibility of user interest difference calculation. Pearson calculation formula is as follows.

$$Pearson_{u->v} = \frac{\sum_{i \in |I_u \cap I_v|} (r_{u,i} - \overline{r_u})(r_{v,i} - \overline{r_v})}{\sqrt{\sum_{i \in |I_u \cap I_v|} (r_{u,i} - \overline{r_u})^2} \sqrt{\sum_{i \in |I_u \cap I_v|} (r_{v,i} - \overline{r_v})^2}} \tag{12}$$

So the trust between users is as follows.

$$IUT_{u->v} = S_{u->v} * Pearson_{u->v} \tag{13}$$

In some cases, because $I_u \cap I_v$ is an empty set, the value of $S_{u \to v}$ cannot be calculated, resulting in missing iut among ranger users. In order to improve the sparsity of trust data and ensure the recommendation effect. This paper decides to calculate indirect user trust. Selecting the intermediate user is to calculate the trust degree between s and user u and user v. We stipulates that only one hop can reach a pair of users who can calculate the trust degree.

3.2.3 Combine User Trust and User Entropy

Because the degree of trust between users can be comprehensively considered from the two aspects of user rating distribution characteristics and differences in common project interests. Therefore, the definition of comprehensive user trust is as follows.

$$AIUT_{u \to v} = IUT_{u \to v} * (1 - Sim_{u,v}^{Entropy}) \tag{14}$$

3.3 Calculating Predicted Rating

After obtaining the similarity of the active user and the average rating, we can calculate the predicted rating by using the weighted sum of deviation from the average rating of similar neighbors. The equation to predict the rating of user u for item i is shown in

$$pred_{u,i} = \overline{r_u} + \frac{\sum_{v \in Neighbors} (r_{v,i} - \overline{r_v}) * AIUT_{u \to v}}{\sum_{v \in Neighbors} |AIUT_{u \to v}|} \tag{15}$$

where *Neighbors* is the set of users selected through comprehensive trust.

4 Experiment

4.1 Data Set

This experiment uses the MovieLens rating set published by GroupLens, a social computing research group at the University of Minnesota. This data set has stable benchmark data sets of different sizes. In this experiment, a 100k data set is used, which includes 943 MovieLens users' 100,000 ratings data for 1682 movies, and the rating range is 1–5. The lowest score is 1 point, and the highest score is 5 points. The higher the user score for a movie, the more the user likes the movie.

This experiment generates a standard user-item rating data set according to a certain format, and divides it into a training set and a test set. The ratio of the training set to the test set is 4:1.

4.2 Experiment Design

The evaluation of the recommendation system is also very important for the research of the recommendation system.We can conduct a comprehensive evaluation of the recommendation system through multiple indicators. The main evaluation indicators are MAE, RMSE, Precision, and Recall.

MAE mainly calculates the average absolute error between the predicted score and the actual score in the test data set. The smaller the MAE, the more accurate the forecast, and thus better recommendations can be made. The calculation formula of MAE is as follows.

$$MAE = \frac{\sum_{i \in N} |P_i - r_i|}{N} \tag{16}$$

More stringent than MAE is the root mean square error (RMSE), which increases the penalty (square penalty) for inaccurate prediction scores, so the evaluation requirements for the system are higher. The smaller the RMSE, the more accurate the prediction, which constitutes a better recommendation list. The calculation formula of MAE is as follows.

$$RMSE = \sqrt{\frac{\sum_{i \in N} (P_i - r_i)^2}{N}} \tag{17}$$

The simple understanding of the accuracy rate is whether the recommendation system recommends the item of interest to the user, that is, how accurate the recommendation result is. The accuracy rate is the quotient of counting the number of users actually like in the recommended results and the total number of recommended results, and the specific definition is as follows.

$$\Pr ecision = \frac{N_{rl}}{N_r} \tag{18}$$

Recall, in popular terms, is how many accurate results are recommended. The specific definitions are as follows.

$$Recall = \frac{N_{rl}}{N_{all}} \tag{19}$$

4.3 Experiment Result

This paper compares the values of MAE, RMSE, Precision, Recall to analyze the proposed collaborative filtering algorithm that combine user trust and user entropy (I-TNNRec) and the traditional user-based nearest neighbor recommendation algorithm with Pearson correlation coefficient (UserCF(PCC)) and with Jaccard similarity (UserCF(Jaccard)). In order to verify the effectiveness of the algorithm, this paper selects neighborhood sets of different sizes for users to verify the prediction accuracy of I-TNNRec and UserCF on different neighborhood sets.

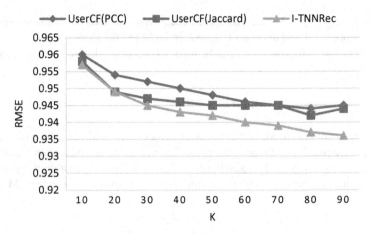

Fig. 1. RMSE value under different number of nearest neighbor users.

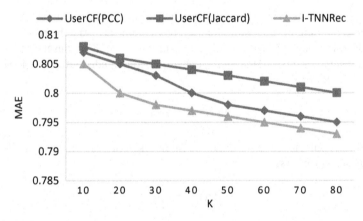

Fig. 2. MAE value under different number of nearest neighbor users.

From Fig. 1 and Fig. 2, with the increase of the number of nearest neighbors, the RMSE and MAE values of all algorithms tend to decrease and gradually flatten. The calculation method of trust degree based on user entropy proposed in this paper has a more obvious downward trend, which shows that the prediction accuracy of our algorithm is better than baseline algorithm.

Figure 3 and Fig. 4 show the changes of Precision and Recall indexes of the I-TNNRec and the traditional UserCF using different similarity measures with the nearest neighbor K. It can be seen that the I-TNNRec has no obvious advantages when the number of nearest neighbors is not very large. With the gradual increase of the number of nearest neighbors, the Recall and Precision have better performance.

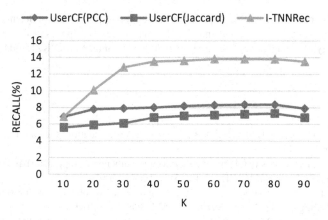

Fig. 3. Recall under different number of nearest neighbor users.

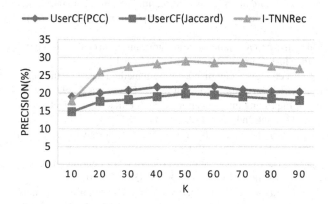

Fig. 4. Precision under different number of nearest neighbor users.

5 Conclusion

This paper proposes a trust calculation method that integrates user entropy. Firstly, PCC cannot accurately measure the similarity of users according to the special ratings of users. The I-TNNRec introduces user entropy weighted PCC similarity to improve the accuracy of PCC. Secondly, we establish a user trust model, transfer trust information between users through the "small world" theory and user preferences, fully mine the trust relationship between users, and establish a trust network, which solves the problem of data sparseness. Finally, the weighted PCC similarity and trust network are combined to select trusted neighbors, which reduces the proportion of "pseudo-neighbors" in the nearest neighbors, and improves the accuracy of prediction and the quality of recommendations. In the future, we will consider establishing a trust network through social networks and user attributes, etc., to solve the the user's cold start problem.

Acknowledgments. The paper is supported in part by the National Natural Science Foundation of China under Grant No. 61672022 and No. U1904186, Key Disciplines of Computer Science and Technology of Shanghai Polytechnic University under Grant No. XXKZD1604.

References

1. Das, D., Sahoo, L., Datta, S.: A survey on recommendation system. Int. J. Comput. Appl.**160**(7) (2017)
2. Qi, L., et al.: Data-sparsity tolerant web service recommendation approach based on improved collaborative filtering. IEICE Trans. Inf. Syst. **100**(9), 2092–2099 (2017)
3. Turk, A.M., Bilge, A.: Robustness analysis of multi-criteria collaborative filtering algorithms against shilling attacks. Expert Syst. Appl. **115**, 386–402 (2019)
4. Natarajan, S., et al.: Resolving data sparsity and cold start problem in collaborative filtering recommender system using linked open data. Expert Syst. Appl. **149**, 113248 (2020)
5. Lee, S.: Improving jaccard index for measuring similarity in collaborative filtering. In: International Conference on Information Science and Applications, pp. 799–806. Springer, Singapore (2017)
6. Feng, W., et al.: An expert recommendation algorithm based on Pearson correlation coefficient and FP-growth. Clust. Comput. **22**(3), 7401–7412 (2019)
7. Zhu, B., et al.: An efficient recommender system method based on the numerical relevances and the non-numerical structures of the ratings. IEEE Access **6**, 49935–49954 (2018)
8. Song, M., et al.: Improving the evaluation of cross efficiencies: a method based on Shannon entropy weight. Comput. Ind. Eng. **112**, 99–106 (2017)
9. Lee, S.: Using entropy for similarity measures in collaborative filtering. J. Ambient. Intell. Humaniz. Comput. **11**(1), 363–374 (2020)
10. Wang, W., Zhang, G., Lu, J.: Collaborative filtering with entropy-driven user similarity in recommender systems. Int. J. Intell. Syst. **30**(8), 854–870 (2015)
11. Jiang, L., et al.: A trust-based collaborative filtering algorithm for E-commerce recommendation system. J. Ambient. Intell. Humaniz. Comput. **10**(8), 3023–3034 (2019)
12. Duricic, T., et al.: Trust-based collaborative filtering: tackling the cold start problem using regular equivalence. In: Proceedings of the 12th ACM Conference on Recommender Systems, pp. 446–450 (2018)
13. Bellogín, A., Castells, P., Cantador, I.: Improving memory-based collaborative filtering by neighbour selection based on user preference overlap. In: Proceedings of the 10th Conference on Open Research Areas in Information Retrieval, pp. 145–148 (2013)
14. Wang, W., et al.: Trust-enhanced collaborative filtering for personalized point of interests recommendation. IEEE Trans. Industr. Inf. **16**(9), 6124–6132 (2019)
15. Tong, C., et al.: TimeTrustSVD: a collaborative filtering model integrating time, trust and rating information. Futur. Gener. Comput. Syst. **93**, 933–941 (2019)
16. Bedi, P., Gautam, A., Bansal, S., Bhatia, D.: Weighted bipartite graph model for recommender system using entropy based similarity measure. In: Thampi, S.M., Mitra, S., Mukhopadhyay, J., Li, K.-C., James, A.P., Berretti, S. (eds.) Intelligent Systems Technologies and Applications, pp. 163–173. Springer International Publishing, Cham (2018). https://doi.org/10.1007/978-3-319-68385-0_14

A Pedestrian Detection Method Based on Improved ResNet for Container Terminal

Zheng Shen[1], Wenxiang Wu[1], Shuaiya Sun[2(✉)], and Kan Hu[3]

[1] Ningbo Special Equipment Inspection and Research Institute,
Ningbo 315100, China
[2] School of Logistics Engineering, Wuhan University of Technology,
Wuhan 430063, China
shuaiyasun@163.com
[3] Wuhan Onew Technology Co., Ltd., Wuhan 430223, China

Abstract. Pedestrian detection in the scene of automated container terminal can bring massive benefits to improving operation safety of the terminal. However, pedestrian detection in container terminal environment exists small pedestrian target size, extreme foregroung-background class imbalance problems. To solve these problems, this paper proposes a one-stage pedestrian detection model based on the improved ResNet. For small target pedestrian detection, we introduce the Channel attention module and spatial attention module to ResNet, enhancing the network's attention to small target pedestrians. Moreover, the feature pyramid network is added to achieve semantic fusion of different scales to enhance the detection of small-scale targets. Finally, the focal loss function is employed as the loss function to suppress the weight influence of simple samples and relieve the problem of extreme foregroung-background class imbalance. The experimental results on the virtual container terminal pedestrian dataset show that the average accuracy of the model is 74.3%, which is 3.9% higher than that of ResNet. The detection accuracy is also improved by comparing with traditional pedestrian detection models. In addition, the effectiveness of the model is verified on Caltech and COCO2017 datasets.

Keywords: Pedestrian detection model · Automated container terminal · ResNet · Attention mechanism

1 Preface

As an important transportation hub and the window of international trade, the port plays an irreplaceable role in "The Belt and Road" strategy of China. Container transportation is currently one of the fundamental modes of marine transportation, but there are potential security hazards during the operation process of the container terminal: High-level automatically, large size of the machines and three-dimensional space cross operations, which not only cause serious casualties and property losses to the port enterprises, but also creates negative impacts on

Q. Zu et al. (Eds.): HCC 2021, LNCS 13795, pp. 119–132, 2022.
https://doi.org/10.1007/978-3-031-23741-6_11

society and economy. The application of pedestrian detection in the automated container terminal can detect the pedestrians in the equipment area accurately and timely, which can trigger the risk warning system, so that the safety accident is reduced. Therefore, the study of pedestrian detection under the operating environment of automated container terminals has important practical significance and application value.

Pedestrian detection is an important branch of object detection, with the rapid development of Deep Learning (DL), DL based detection methods have been widely utilized in pedestrian detection. DL models are different from traditional feature learning and feature extraction algorithms [1], as they don't need designed feature extractors because they can extract features automatically. Convolutional neural networks are often used for feature extraction in the field of computer vision, which applies a multi-layer convolutional structure to extract feature information at different scales of the input image. In 2012, Alex and Hinton et al. proposed AlexNet [2], which consists of five convolutional layers with three fully-connected layers, and won the ImageNet large-scale image classification competition, achieving an accuracy rate of 90%. AlexNet applied the ReLU activation function in convolutional neural networks for the first time and also used GPUs for computing acceleration, which laid the foundation for the application of convolutional neural networks in object detection. Afterwards, researchers focus on the accuracy and gradient disappearance problem of convolutional neural network image classification tasks from the aspects of layer deepening, parallel convolution and residual connection. Therefore, network structures such as VGG [3], GoogLeNet [4], and ResNet [5,6] are proposed by researchers. The gradual deepening of layers of ResNet proved that after solving the gradient disappearance issue, the increasing of convolutional layers has a very obvious effect on the performance of the algorithm.

The convolutional neural network R-CNN [7] proposed by Girshick et al. pioneered the introduction of convolutional neural networks into the field of object detection and showed excellent performance in the field of pedestrian detection. However, the SVM algorithm and the bounding box regression module slow down the model's detection speed, and the detection time for a picture is about 5 s on average, which can't meet the need for immediacy, thus this method can't be applied in industrial fields. To solve the above problems, Fast R-CNN [8] and Faster R-CNN [9] put all modules of the algorithm running on GPU, and also make the speed of bounding box generation and detection significantly improved by adding region proposal network (RPN). One-stage object detection algorithms such as YOLO [10] and SSD [11] were proposed to further increase the detection speed and reduce the complexity, which has been widely used in the fields of autonomous driving and vehicle safety [12,13]. Although pedestrian detection has been widely used in the fields such as autonomous driving and vehicle safety, the research applying it in the fields of automated container terminals is rare, because of incidental feature loss during feature extraction and the foreground-background class imbalance caused by the huge size of container terminal operations equipment and the small scale of pedestrians compared with the background. In order to solve the above problems, an improved ResNet based one-stage pedestrian detection model is proposed in this paper. In this model, ResNet is used as the backbone for feature extraction, and by using Convolutional Block Attention Module [14] to obtain global information, highlight local target features and improve the feature extraction effect, the model solves the problems of limited receptive field. To strengthen the detection effect of the small object, the idea of multi-scale fusion is utilized in this model: Feature Pyramid Networks [15] are connected with the improved ResNet to abstract and fuse the multiscale feature information. Focal Loss function is chosen as the loss function [16,17], addressing the foreground-background class imbalance.

2   ResNet Network

As ResNet addresses the gradient disappearance problem arising from increasing network depth of traditional convolutional neural network during training, it has been widely applied in machine vision, and the architecture of which is shown as Fig. 1.

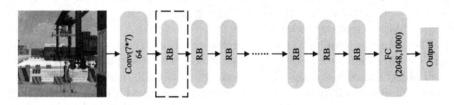

Fig. 1. The network structure of ResNet.

In pedestrian detection, there are problems such as continuous change of pedestrian walking status, and pedestrians overlap, thus the ordinary convolutional neural network can't extract deep features in the image well. ResNet can obtain the characteristics of each layer of multiple models, and by using skip connection, unhindered information flow between residual blocks is allowed, which helps to learn deep features better. Besides, the number of parameters in the network can be reduced, and the detection is more real-time. Therefore, this paper uses ResNet as the backbone network for feature extraction.

ResNet consists of multiple successive stacks of Residual Blocks (RB). A residual block consists of one or more convolutional layers, in which the adjacent layers are directly connected by skip connection. Take the residual block in ResNet50 as an example, as shown in Fig. 2, the input image firstly passes through three convolutional layers, this is then added with the original input as the input of the next convolutional layer. The residual block structure is employed in ResNet to achieve the transfer of the features from the bottom to the top layer, which effectively alleviates the network degradation of deep networks.

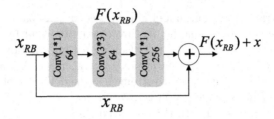

Fig. 2. Residual block structure in ResNet50.

3   Improved Pedestrian Detection Model for ResNet

As described above, ResNet solves the issues including gradient disappearance and gradient explosion caused as the depth of the deep network increases. Meanwhile, by fusing the features of different layers, ResNet can effectively defect the obscured pedestrians. However, as ResNet has a limited receptive field, it fails to gain the global information of images, thus the features are ignored easily, leading to the insufficient detection accuracy. Therefore, in this paper, we improve ResNet to strengthen the learning of target features by introducing the convolutional block attention module.

The monitoring equipment in the container terminal environment is far away from the operation site, resulting in a small scale of target pedestrians, and the small objects have less pixel information, which is easily lost in the process of under-sampling. This paper uses feature pyramid network in the model, being able to fuse feature maps with strong semantic information at low resolution and feature maps with weak semantic information but rich spatial information at high resolution with less computational effort, so that the feature maps of each scale have strong semantic information.

In this paper, we propose a one-stage pedestrian detection model based on the improved ResNet network for small target pedestrian detection in automated container terminal operation environment, and its framework is shown in Fig. 3.

The network structure of the model is divided into three main parts.

(1) An improved convolutional module. Which focuses on features containing pedestrians by adding a channel attention module and a spatial attention module to the ResNet to obtain global information while enabling the ResNet to ignore irrelevant information and focus on key information.
(2) Feature Pyramid Network. Connecting the feature pyramid network structure after the backbone network to strengthen the detection ability of small targets and improve the accuracy of pedestrian detection by extracting multi-scale feature information for fusion.
(3) For the imbalance of foreground-background class of pedestrian detection in the automated container terminal environment, the Focal Loss function is selected as the loss function, and the cross-entropy loss is dynamically adjusted according to the confidence level to solve the sample imbalance.

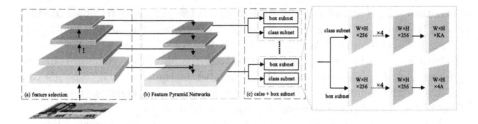

Fig. 3. Network structure of the detection method.

3.1 Improved ResNet Network

Although the ResNet can extract rich semantic information from images, the convolutional operation has a significant drawback that its receptive field is limited, i.e., it works only on local scope and thus may miss the information such as small target pedestrians, thus the attention mechanism is introduced into the model to obtain the global information of the image to make the network focus on important information. As the structure of the improved feature extraction module shown in Fig. 4, the channel attention module and the spatial attention module are added after the first convolutional layer as well as the last convolutional layer of the ResNet.

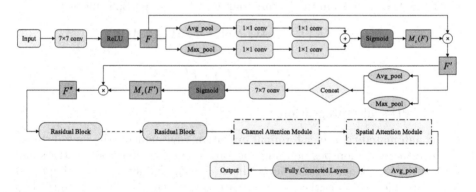

Fig. 4. Structure of the feature extraction module.

In the channel attention module, the input feature maps F are pooled by global maximization and global average pooling based on width and height respectively, then the pooled results are fed into the multi-layer perceptron for convolution. Finally, the features output from the multi-layer perceptron are summed up element by element, and the final channel attention feature map $M_c(F)$ is generated by the Sigmoid activation function, as shown in Eq. (1).

$$M_c(F) = \sigma(MLP(AvgPool(F)) + MLP((MaxPool(F)))) \tag{1}$$

From the channel attention input and output of the channel attentional module, it can be seen that F has three dimensions of information: height, width, and channel. And the output $M_c(F)$ is a $1 \times 1 \times C$ tensor (C is equal to the number of channels), and it can be seen that this tensor is obtained by compressing the information of height and width. Each number in the tensor corresponds to a channel of the input feature map F and represents the weight of this channel. This tensor represents the importance of each channel in F.

The input features F' of the spatial attention module are generated by multiplying this channel attention feature map and the input feature map element by element, as shown in Eq. (2).

$$F' = M_c(F) \times F \tag{2}$$

The spatial attention module is similar to the channel attention module, the input features F' are firstly pooled by the channel-based global max pooling and the global average pooling severally, then the results are combined based on the channels, and these are next reduced to one channel by a convolution. Then the spatial attention feature map $M_s(F')$ is generated by Sigmoid activation function. Finally, this feature is multiplied element by element with the input features of this module to get the final generated feature , and the calculation process is shown in Eqs. (3) and (4). The reason why the spatial attention module performs maximum pooling and average pooling operations in the channel dimension is that pooling operations in the channel dimension can effectively highlight those regions in the feature map that have important information.

$$M_s\left(F'\right) = \sigma\left(f^{7\times7}\left(\left[\text{AvgPool}\left(F'\right) \circ \text{MaxPool}\left(F'\right)\right]\right)\right) \tag{3}$$

$$F'' = M_s\left(F'\right) \times F' \tag{4}$$

3.2   Multi-scale Integration

In the automated container terminal operation environment, the long distance between the detection position and the yard crane location leads to the small scale of the target pedestrians, shown in the Fig. 5. And although the improved ResNet is able to extract the semantic features of the images, it leads to the loss of detailed information after convolutional pooling. Therefore, once the last layer of feature map of the improved ResNet is utilized directly for object detection, the detection performance of small target pedestrians is not good.

For the problem of small pedestrian targets in the container terminal, we add a feature pyramid network after the improved ResNet for multi-scale fusion of features. The last four layers of features extracted from the improved ResNet are sequentially noted as C2, C3, C4, and C5, and the coarsest resolution mapping P5 is generated by a 1×1 convolution layer at the highest layer C5, followed by 2 times up-sampling in turn. Although the spatial location of the generated feature maps is coarser, there are stronger semantic features that produce features of higher resolution. Then the feature maps of the same spatial size are fused

Fig. 5. A small target example in container terminal environment.

by lateral concatenation, i.e., P5 with 2 times up-sampling process is summed with C4 with 1×1 convolution, producing P4, similarly P3 and P2. Finally, a convolution operation with a convolution kernel of 3×3 and a step size of 1 is performed on the fused features (P2, P3, P4, P5) to eliminate the confounding effect of up-sampling.

As shown in Fig. 6, P2, P3, P4, P5 with the same spatial dimensions as C2, C3, C4, C5 can be obtained after the above procedures. Pyramid feature network enhances the detection accuracy of small targets and the position accuracy of the deep features by fusing features of different depth to increase the semantic features in the shallow layer.

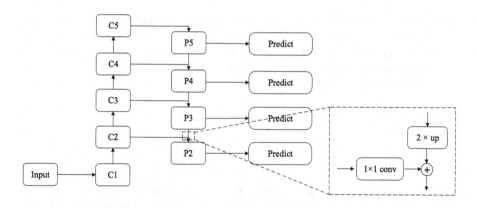

Fig. 6. Feature pyramid networks.

3.3 Loss Function

The pedestrian detection in the automated container terminal environment is a small target detection problem with the serious foreground-background class imbalance of the image, i.e., the proportion of the background is much larger than the target, so the negative samples are much more than the positive samples when calculating the loss function value, leading to low accuracy. This is because simple negative samples will play a major contribution to the loss value and will dominate the update direction of the gradient, thus making it difficult for the network to learn useful features to classify the target accurately. The simple negative samples refer to the negative samples that easy to classify and are not on the transition region between foreground and background.

In order to reduce the influence of simple samples on detection results, this paper use Focus Loss as the loss function in the network. Focus Loss is improved on the basis of the cross-entropy loss function.

$$FL_{(p_t)} = -\alpha_t (1 - p_t)^\gamma \log (p_t) \tag{5}$$

p_t is the classification probability of different categories; α_t denotes the positive sample weight factor, which takes the value between 0 and 1; $1 - \alpha_t$ denotes the negative sample weight factor; γ is a number greater than 0. From the formula, whether foreground or background, $(1 - p_t)^\gamma$ becomes smaller when the probability of a sample increases, i.e., simple samples can be suppressed by $(1 - p_t)^\gamma$. Using this loss function to reduce the weights of simple samples, the model can be trained to focus more on the hard-to-classify samples.

In many experiments, the cross-entropy loss function is adopted as weighted sum of the confidence loss (conf). As shown in Eq. (6).

$$L_{conf}(x, c) = - \sum_{i \in Pos}^{N} x_{ij}^p \log (\hat{c}_i^p) - \sum_{i \in Ne.g.} \log (\hat{c}_i^0) \tag{6}$$

From Eq. (6), it can be seen that the error of confidence includes positive sample error and negative sample error. In order to solve the problem of positive and negative sample imbalance, this paper introduces the Focal Loss function instead of the cross-entropy loss function as the new confidence loss function, which can be obtained according to Eq. (7).

$$
\begin{aligned}
FL_{\text{conf}} &= \sum_{i \in Pos} FL(p_i) + \sum_{i \in Neg} FL(p_i) \\
&= - \sum_{i \in Pos} (1 - p_i)^r \log (p_i) - \sum_{i \in Neg} (1 - p_i)^r \log (p_i)
\end{aligned} \tag{7}
$$

In Eq. (7), p_i is the probability that the first sample is predicted to be positive or negative, and γ is the modifiable factor. When $\gamma = 0$, Focal Loss is the traditional cross-entropy loss function, γ can effectively adjust the weights of hard samples and reduce the foreground-background class imbalance.

4   Experiment

4.1   Experimental Environment and Data Set Introduction

The experimental environment parameters are shown in Table 1.

Table 1. Experimental environment parameters.

Name	Parameter
Operating system	Ubuntu 18.04
Video card	NVIDIA RTX TITAN
Video memory	96G
CPU	Intel Xeon E5-2678 v3
Framework	Pytorch 1.7.1

Deep learning requires learning features from numerous datasets, and if the datasets are not representative, it is difficult to learn the features needed, thus the experiments use pedestrian videos in an automated container terminal operation environment, and then clip the videos into images frame by frame, 80% of the dataset with 2529 images and 6291 pedestrians is used as the training set; the 20% with 483 images and 483 pedestrians is used as the test set, and some test set images have no pedestrians.

The task of pedestrian detection is using rectangular boxes to mark the pedestrians and label the category information, where the rectangular box is confirmed by four parameters, including the coordinate values of the top left corner of the rectangular box, the length and the width of the rectangle. In the experiments we use labelme software as the image annotation tool to generate the annotation files in json format, and as this paper aims at pedestrian detection, the category information only contains the pedestrian, represented by people, and finally all the annotation files are converted into json format and saved.

4.2 Pedestrian Detection Result

The detection results of the improved ResNet pedestrian detection model on the dataset are shown in Fig. 7. From Fig. 7, it can be seen that the model can accurately identify and localize the target pedestrians in the automated container terminal operation scenario, even when the pedestrian's scale is very small, pedestrians in the image overlap or appear suddenly.

(a) small target   (b) overlapping targets   (c) sudden target

Fig. 7. The pedestrian detection results in container terminal environment.

4.3 Analysis and Comparison of Experimental Results

For the evaluation of results, the Average Precision (AP), Average Precision with an IoU of 50% (AP50) and Average Precision with an IoU of 75% (AP75) were used as evaluation metrics. The average precision is calculated as Eq. (8), where T_p indicates true positive; F_p indicates false positive.

$$AP = \frac{T_p}{F_p + T_p} \qquad (8)$$

Among many backbone networks such as VGG, ResNet, GoogleNet, etc., ResNet has the deepest network structure and extracts complex and diverse features, and the residual connections simplify the network learning objectives and avoid gradient dissipation to a certain extent. Other networks have shallow depth, relatively simple extracted features, and low detection accuracy, therefore, ResNet is chosen as the backbone network. In this paper, we debug the learning rate, the number of iterations, the γ and α_t parameters in the loss function during the training process. According to the experiments, it is found that the learning rate is 0.005 and the batch_size is 44 when the number of GPUs is 4. Using ResNet as the backbone network and setting the maximum number of iterations as 10000, when the attention module is added, the maximum number of iterations should be increased accordingly. The effect of different values on the precision are shown in Table 2.

Table 2. Experimental results of different values.

γ	AP (%)	AP50 (%)	AP75 (%)
1	71.7	97.8	87.3
1.5	73.2	**98.9**	88.2
2	74.2	**98.9**	88.5
2.5	**74.3**	98.8	**89.7**
3	74.2	**98.9**	88.6
3.5	73.9	**98.9**	88.6

It can be seen that the precision is highest when $\gamma = 2.5$. This is due to the fact that in the container terminal operation environment, the proportion of the background in the data set is much larger than the detection target, which leads to more simple negative samples, and taking larger values can give less weight to the background, and instead the detection target has more weight in the loss function, making the model more focused on the detection target and improving the detection accuracy.

The comparison experiments were conducted on the container terminal environment dataset with different depths of ResNet as the backbone network, and the different evaluation results are shown in Fig. 8.

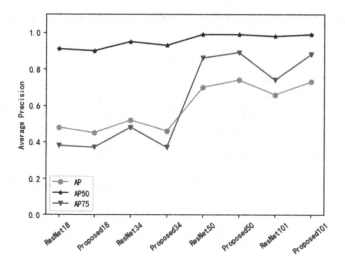

Fig. 8. Experimental results of ResNet at different depths on container terminal dataset.

From Fig. 8, it can be seen that with the deepening of the backbone network layers, all three metrics, AP, AP50 and AP75, gradually improve, with AP50 showing a relatively small improvement and AP75 showing the largest improvement. It can be seen that the deeper of the backbone network, the higher the detection precision, and the backbone network has less influence on the detection task of true positive and more influence on the regression task of rectangular boxes. The detection effect is highest when the number of layers is 50. According to the experimental results, when the backbone network is ResNet50, the average precision reaches 70.4% and the average precision of the proposed model reaches 74.3%. In comparison, it is found that the average precision of pedestrian detection results is significantly improved by 3.9% after adding the attention module to the ResNet50 network.

In order to verify the effectiveness of the network, this article selects SSD300, SSD512 and YOLOV3 for experimental comparisons on the container terminal environment dataset, and the results are shown in Table 3. It can be seen that compared with the other four models, the proposed model in this paper has the best performance on AP and AP75, as for AP50 the proposed model is consistent with SSD300 and ranks only second to the ResNet50 model. Overall, our model outperforms the other models in the box regression.

Table 4 shows the detection results of the proposed model along with SSD512, SSD300, YOLOV3 and ResNet50 models on the Caltech dataset. The results show that the AP value of the detection results of this paper's model reaches 68.0%, which is 6% higher than that of ResNet50, and is higher than that of SSD512 model by 6.7% and YOLOV3 model by 9.4%. In the AP75, this model outperforms other models by 9.5%, 19.8%, 10.7%, and 8.9% respectively, which shows that it is effective in detecting data with IoU above 0.75.

Table 3. Detection results of different models on container terminal environment dataset.

	AP (%)	AP50 (%)	AP75 (%)
SSD512	68.1	98.6	86.1
SSD300	67.3	98.8	48.7
YOLOV3	54.7	96.9	53.1
ResNet50	70.4	**99.9**	85.8
Proposed	**74.3**	98.8	**89.7**

Table 4. Detection results of different models on Caltech dataset.

	AP (%)	AP50 (%)	AP75 (%)
SSD512	62.2	91.6	72.4
SSD300	56.4	88.5	62.1
YOLOV3	59.5	92.3	70.2
ResNet50	62.9	92.8	73.0
Proposed	**68.9**	**95.2**	**81.9**

Table 5 shows the detection results of this paper's model (Proposed) with SSD512, SSD300, YOLOV3 and ResNet50 models on the COCO2017 dataset. In terms of AP and AP75, this model is higher than the other four models, and in terms of AP50, it is slightly lower than YOLOV3 and SSD300. Overall, the detection results of this model are better than the other models.

Table 5. Detection results of different models on COCO2017 dataset.

	AP (%)	AP50 (%)	AP75 (%)
SSD512	20.2	38.6	19.6
SSD300	22.3	40.4	22.3
YOLOV3	21.4	**44.4**	18.2
ResNet50	21.0	36.9	21.2
Proposed	**23.7**	40.3	**24.2**

5   Conclusion

In order to realize the danger warning based on pedestrian detection, ensure the normal operation of automated container terminals and safeguard the lives of personnel, this paper investigates the pedestrian detection problem in this environment, and proposes a one-stage pedestrian detection model based on an improved ResNet network for these problems, such as small target detection and extreme foreground-background class imbalance. The model uses the improved convolutional module as the backbone network to extract image features, and by adding the channel attention module and spatial attention module to the ResNet network, the negative impact of redundant information is eliminated while acquiring the global information of the image, and the representation capability of the features is further enhanced to solve the problem of limited perceptual field of the ResNet network. And the feature pyramid network is connected after the improved ResNet network to do feature multi-scale fusion, fusing contextual information at different scales helps to improve the detection performance, promote the detection accuracy of small target pedestrians. Finally, for the imbalance of the dataset, we use focal loss as the loss function, and design appropriate weighting parameters to solve the problem of extreme foreground-background class imbalance. It is found through experiments that the pedestrian detection model with improved ResNet not only improves the accuracy on the pedestrian dataset of automated container terminals, but also outperforms traditional methods on other publicly available datasets.

References

1. Vaillant, R., Monrocq, C., Le Cun, Y.: Original approach for the localisation of objects in images. IEE Proc.-Vis. Image Signal Process. **141**(4), 245–250 (1994)
2. Krizhevsky, A., Sutskever, I., Hinton, G.E.: ImageNet classification with deep convolutional neural networks. Adv. Neural. Inf. Process. Syst. **25**, 1097–1105 (2012)
3. Simonyan, K., Zisserman, A.: Very deep convolutional networks for large-scale image recognition. In: International Conference on Learning Representations (2015)
4. Szegedy, C., Liu, W., Jia, Y., et al.: Going deeper with convolutions. In: CVPR, pp. 1–9 (2015)
5. He, K., Zhang, X., Ren, S., et al.: Deep residual learning for image recognition. In: CVPR, pp. 770–778 (2016)
6. Haque, M.F., Lim, H.Y., Kang, D.S.: Object detection based on VGG with ResNet network. In: ICEIC, pp. 1–3 (2019)
7. Girshick, R., Donahue, J., Darrell, T., et al.: Rich feature hierarchies for accurate object detection and semantic segmentation. In: CVPR, pp. 580–587 (2014)
8. Girshick, R.: Fast R-CNN. In: ICCV, pp. 1440–1448 (2015)
9. Ren, S., He, K., Girshick, R., et al.: Faster R-CNN: towards real-time object detection with region proposal networks. In: NIPS, pp. 91–99 (2015)
10. Redmon, J., Divvala, S., et al.: You only look once: unified, real-time object detection. In: CVPR, pp. 779–788 (2015)
11. Liu, W., et al.: SSD: single shot multibox detector. In: Leibe, B., Matas, J., Sebe, N., Welling, M. (eds.) ECCV 2016. LNCS, vol. 9905, pp. 21–37. Springer, Cham (2016). https://doi.org/10.1007/978-3-319-46448-0_2
12. Sun, P., Boukerche, A.: Challenges and potential solutions for designing a practical pedestrian detection framework for supporting autonomous driving. In: MobiWac, pp. 75–82 (2020)
13. Karg, M., Scharfenberger, C.: Deep learning-based pedestrian detection for automated driving: achievements and future challenges. In: Pedrycz, W., Chen, S.-M. (eds.) Development and Analysis of Deep Learning Architectures. SCI, vol. 867, pp. 117–143. Springer, Cham (2020). https://doi.org/10.1007/978-3-030-31764-5_5

14. Woo, S., Park, J., Lee, J.-Y., Kweon, I.S.: CBAM: convolutional block attention module. In: Ferrari, V., Hebert, M., Sminchisescu, C., Weiss, Y. (eds.) ECCV 2018. LNCS, vol. 11211, pp. 3–19. Springer, Cham (2018). https://doi.org/10.1007/978-3-030-01234-2_1
15. Lin, T.Y., Dollár, P., Girshick, R., et al.: Feature pyramid networks for object detection. In: Proceedings of IEEE Conference on Computer Vision and Pattern Recognition, pp. 936–944 (2017)
16. Lin, T., Goyal, P., Girshick, R., et al.: Focal loss for dense object detection. IEEE Trans. Pattern Anal. Mach. Intell. **42**(2), 318–327 (2020)
17. Hoang, T.M., Nguyen, P.H., et al.: Deep RetinaNet-based detection and classification of road markings by visible light camera sensors. Sensors **19**(2), 281 (2019)

Detection of Advertising Users Based on K-SMOTE and Ensemble Learning

Zihan Qiu, Zekai Zhou, Yongxu Long, Chang Ji, Jianguo Li[✉], and Yong Tang

South China Normal University, Guangzhou 510630, Guangdong, China
{hhhqzh,longyongxu}@m.scnu.edu.cn, gumpye@163.com

Abstract. Aiming at the problem of the unbalanced advertising user data of social networks leading to unsatisfactory prediction results, we propose a prediction model for advertising users based on the combination among K-Means, synthetic minority oversampling Technique (SMOTE), and Ensemble Learning. On the basis of the real user data provided by Scholat, we analyzed the data and extracted many key features from it to draw a portrait of advertising users. Our algorithm first clusters the minority class, and then processes the continuous and discrete features of each sample separately through the improved SMOTE to synthesize new minority samples, and finally constructs an integrated classifier using the ensemble learning. This method effectively avoids the problems of blurred positive and negative class boundaries caused by SMOTE and the inability of SMOTE to process discrete features. Meanwhile, ensemble learning enables the classifier to get more reasonable results and reduce overall errors. The experimental results show that our method improves the quality of the generated minority class samples and significantly improves the prediction performance of advertising users.

Keywords: Social network · Unbalanced datasets · User classification · SMOTE · K-Means · Ensemble learning

1 Introduction

Scholat[1], an online academic information service platform, is one of the most influential platforms in the domestic academic circle and one of the most representative academic social network platforms in China. With both the number of users and word-of-mouth increasing, Scholat has gradually become a hotbed for advertising users to make profits. The advertising users in social networks have attracted a wide of researchers' attention. After extracting users' basic information, behavioral, and social characteristics, researchers use traditional classification algorithms to detect advertising users effectively. However, the number of advertising users is much smaller than normal users', which results in most of the user datasets being unbalanced in the current social network.

SMOTE is a synthetic minority over-sampling technique proposed by Chawla et al. [1] in 2002. It uses minority samples and neighboring samples to generate new ones.

---

[1] https://www.scholat.com.

Q. Zu et al. (Eds.): HCC 2021, LNCS 13795, pp. 133–145, 2022.
https://doi.org/10.1007/978-3-031-23741-6_12

However, the algorithm has several shortcomings. First, it is blind in selecting neighbor samples. Second, it is impossible to overcome the data distribution problem of unbalanced datasets. Third, SMOTE cannot process discrete features. Therefore, we propose an improved K-SMOTE algorithm that generates more aggregated and high-quality samples compared to SMOTE. First, we use K-means to cluster the samples of the minority class and find the center of each cluster. Then for each sample in the cluster, we generate new samples by linearly interpolating the continuous features of the samples with the features corresponding to the clustering centers, while using the discrete data with the highest frequency of occurrence in the K-nearest neighbor samples as the values of the discrete features of the new samples.

Ensemble learning algorithm constructs and combines multiple base classifiers to complete the learning task. The generalization abilities of ensemble classifiers are usually stronger than a single classifier.

According to the above analysis, we propose an improved K-SMOTE algorithm that generates more aggregated and high-quality samples compared to SMOTE. Combine K-SMOTE with ensemble learning, we construct an integrated learning model for junk advertising user detection. The construct experiment on the Scholat dataset shows that our algorithm improves the quality of the synthesis of minority samples and has a better effect on advertising user detection than SMOTE. Several UCI public datasets[2], which are kinds of open-source data sets proposed by the University of California, Irvine, and suitable for pattern recognition as well as machine learning, are chosen to verify the correctness of our model's proposed algorithm. The results show that the model has a great effect on the binary classification of unbalanced data.

2   Related Work

At present, the research on the detection of abnormal users in social networks is mainly to extract the characteristics of advertising users. They classify users based on their characteristics to determine whether they are normal or spam users. The main researches in China include: Xixian Peng et al. [2] used metrology methods to perform statistical analysis on user characteristics, used decision tree analysis, correlation analysis, and association to mine user characteristics. Xiangfei Meng et al. [3] constructed a feature system of spam advertising users based on the causes of spam advertising users in social networks, and used C4.5 decision tree to classify users. The main researches in Other countries include: By capturing the ratio of the number of followers to the number of following, the ratio of URLs contained in tweets, and the similarity of information, G Stringhini et al. [4] established a user behavior model and selected random forest algorithms to predict effectively. According to the analysis of the characteristics of Youtube users, Fabrico et al. [5] used Support Vector Machine (SVM) to analyze effective methods for identifying advertising users.

For the problem of data imbalance, Chawla et al. [1] proposed the Synthetic Minority Over-sampling Technique (SMOTE) to make the dataset balanced. However, the synthesized samples may destroy the original distribution and blur the positive and negative

---

[2] http://archive.ics.uci.edu/ml/index.php.

sample boundaries. And SMOTE cannot process discrete features. Therefore, Hui Han et al. [6] proposed the Borderline-Smote algorithm, which only considers the minority samples distributed near the classification boundary, it solves the problem of generating sample overlap better. But how to determine the boundary samples scientifically needs to be further solved.

Sanchez et al. [7] proposed a cluster-based oversampling algorithm. This algorithm can effectively avoid the generation of boundary samples. Barua et al. [8] combined the clustering algorithm with SMOTE to identify sample classes using the clustering algorithm, and then SMOTE is used for linear interpolation. Douzas et al. [9] proposed a simple and effective oversampling method based on k-means and SMOTE, which can avoid noise and effectively improve the imbalance.

The ensemble learning algorithm is an effective way to solve the weak learning problem. It integrates several weaker learning machines into a powerful hybrid learning machine with better performance than a single learning machine and improves the accuracy of classification algorithms. Currently, the classical ensemble learning algorithms are Boosting, Bagging, Random Forest, etc. Ruan et al. [10] proposed an effective learning model for user classification based on ensemble learning. This model demonstrated the feasibility that ensemble learning substantially improves classification accuracy.

According to the above solutions, we find that most scholars using the improved SMOTE do not reduce the imbalance between and within-sample categories at the same time. The problem that SMOTE cannot process discrete features still exists. Therefore, we propose an advertising user detection model based on the combination of K-SMOTE and ensemble learning, which can improve the detection performance of minority class samples and help social network platforms effectively identify advertising users.

3 Datasets and Features

3.1 Dataset of Scholat

The dataset for the experiment is collected from the time of the establishment of Scholat to 23:59 on January 4, 2021, and the total number of users in Scholat is 142,833. We remove some users such as one-time users and banned users and marks the filtered dataset manually. Finally, we extract 1631 active users and 30 junk advertising users for experiments.

3.2 Feature Analysis and Extraction

User Basic Information Characteristics
Is there any URLs. Through observations, the advertising users in Scholat often insert URLs into the basic information to publish malicious information or advertising information. Therefore, whether there is a URL in the basic information is an effective feature to predict advertising users. We use regular expressions to find out whether there is a URL in the basic personal information and mark the basic attributes.

The proportion of Arabic numerals. Advertising users have an obvious feature when disseminating advertisements. They will insert contact information such as QQ number, WeChat ID, and mobile phone number into any information they can modify. These messages generally do not appear as complete information, but rather inserts other characters into the contact information or uses Chinese numbers to represent. Besides, some URLs also contain numeric features. Therefore, the proportion of Arabic numerals in the basic information is an effective feature to predict advertising users.

Whether it is an authenticated user. This feature is a mark for users in Scholat who have real information, real avatar, complete profile, complete academic information, and a publicly visible personal homepage. It is used to measure the authority of users.

User Relationship Characteristics

The ratio of followers to followings. For most normal users, the gap between the number of followers and the number of fans is very small, while advertising users follow a large number of normal users to get more attention, which will cause a large gap between the number of followers and the number of fans.

The ratio of followers to friends. This feature indicates the degree of recognition of the user to its followers.

The ratio of followings to friends. This feature indicates the degree of recognition of the user to its followings.

User Behavior Characteristics

The ratio of successful invitations. It means the ratio of the number of successful user invitations to the number of initiated invitations. For normal users, the invitee usually responds to the invitation they send, and the chance of successful invitations is higher. However, advertising users use this function to send advertising information to many mailboxes, and the chance of successful invitations is lower or even zero.

4   Proposed Model

The method proposed in this paper employs K-Means algorithm in conjunction with the SMOTE algorithm in order to rebalance skewed data sets. It reduces the generation of boundary samples and maintains the distribution of original samples through over-sampling within the region of each cluster while achieving the processing of discrete features. We also utilize Ensemble Learning that can reduce the information loss of the classifier and improve the performance of the classification algorithm.

4.1   K-SMOTE Algorithm

SMOTE is a technique for over-sampling and synthesizing a few samples. Its main idea is to calculate the distance between each sample x in the minority class and all samples based on the Euclidean distance and get the K nearest neighbor. Next, according to the sampling magnification N, several samples are selected from the K nearest neighbor, denoted as x_n. Finally, every sample x_n is performed random linear subtraction with the minority sample X to constructed new samples.

$$x_{new} = x + rand(0, 1) * (x_n - x) \tag{1}$$

x_{new} represents the newly generated sample, rand(0,1) represents the random number between the interval (0,1), x represents the selected minority sample, x_n. Represents the neighboring sample selected among the K nearest neighboring samples of x.

However, the classic SMOTE algorithm has some problems: First, SMOTE selects minority samples randomly, which is likely to cause the generative samples to be unbalanced at the end and to be incompatible with the distribution of the original sample set. Second, if the minority sample is at the boundary of the minority class. The generative samples are likely to be closer to the majority class, which may marginalize the sample distribution and cause the classification model unable to distinguish the boundary between positive and negative samples, thus increasing the difficulty of classification. Third, the new sample, constructed by random linear subtraction with the K nearest neighbor of the selected sample, only contains continuous feature values, while discrete features generally have their special physical meaning or represent a certain category, and the values can only be integers, so SMOTE cannot process discrete features.

According to the above analysis, we propose an algorithm based on K-Means and the basic ideas of SOMTE, which combines the traditional classification model and ensemble learning to predict the advertising users of Scholat. Specific procedures are as follows:

1. Use K-Means to get K cluster centers $[K_1, K_2, \ldots, K_k]$ and samples corresponding to each center.
2. Use the ratio of the majority class to the minority class as the sampling rate N, and construct the new samples according to N.
3. For each minority sample x in each cluster, calculate the new sample's feature with that cluster center according to steps 4 or 5.
4. For the discrete feature, we use the value with the highest frequency of this feature in the k-nearest neighbor samples to replace it.
5. For the continuous feature, it is constructed according to the following formula:

$$x_{new,j} = K_{i,j} + rand(0, 1) * (x_j - K_{i,j}), i = 1, 2, \ldots, k \qquad (2)$$

$x_{new,j}$ represents the jth eigenvalue of the new sample, $K_{i,j}$ represents the jth eigenvalue of the ith cluster center, rand(0,1) represents the random number between the interval (0,1), x_j represents the jth eigenvalue of the original sample with K_i as the center.

In the improved algorithm, we cluster the dataset and generate new samples based on clusters, which can make them lie in the clusters and effectively prevent changes in the distribution characteristics of the dataset. The formula for generating the eigenvalues of new samples in the KM-SMOTE algorithm is modified so that the new samples are located between the cluster center and the original sample, which can reduce the appearance of boundary data. For the discrete feature, we use the value with the highest frequency of this feature in the K-nearest neighbor samples to replace it, which can solve the drawback that the SMOTE algorithm cannot process discrete features.

4.2 Combined with Ensemble Learning

We combine the new minority class dataset, obtained by oversampling the minority classes with the KM-SOMTE algorithm, into a balanced or near-balanced dataset with the majority class dataset. The integrated samples are randomly divided into several new training subsets, and each training subset is used to train a base classifier, and finally, we synthesize all classifiers to obtain an ensemble learning classifier. The number of base classifiers chosen in this paper is 10. The ensemble method adopted is the voting method, that is, select the result that appears the most times in basic classifiers as the final result of the ensemble learning classifier. Due to each basic classifier has certain differences, they have different classification boundaries, which means that they will make different mistakes in decision-making. Ensemble learning can get a more reasonable boundary and achieve a better classification result.

5 Experiment

5.1 Datasets

As mentioned above, we choose 1631 active users and 30 advertising users in Scholat to analyse the classification effect of the proposed model. To verify the generalization ability of the K-SMOTE, we select three unbalanced datasets of Yeast, Segment and Bankmarketing-master derived from the UCI machine learning database for experiment. Among them, the BankMarketing-master and Scholat datasets are unbalanced dichotomous datasets, and the Yeast and Segment datasets are unbalanced multiclassification datasets. For the multiclassification datasets, we label the smallest number of classes as the minority class and merge other samples into the majority class. For all datasets, we normalize each feature. In this experiment, we used seventy percent of the dataset as the training set and thirty percent as the test set. Specific description is shown in Table 1.

Table 1. List of unbalanced datasets.

Dataset	Samples	Feature	Minority samples	Majority samples	Unbalanced ratio
Scholat	1661	11	30	1631	1.84%
Yeast	1485	9	52	1433	3.63%
BankMarketing-master	45307	921	5091	40216	12.66%
Segment	2310	19	300	2010	14.93%

5.2 Evaluation Indicators

For unbalanced datasets, traditional classifier performance evaluation metrics may be flawed, so it is important to choose appropriate evaluation metrics for classifiers with unbalanced datasets. For unbalanced datasets, traditional classifier performance evaluation metrics may be flawed, so it is important to choose appropriate evaluation metrics for classifiers with unbalanced datasets. Among the evaluation Indicators of classifier, the common metrics is Average Precision, which is used to measure how good or bad a model is in each category. Average Precision is the area under the curve drawn by Recall and Precision. However, in an unbalanced dataset, it is more biased towards the majority class. For example, for an unbalanced sample, the classification model is trained to classify the data into majority samples. If all the samples are classified as majority samples, the model has a high precision and recall for the majority class but 0 for the minority class. Therefore, the Average Precision is not applicable to evaluate the imbalance problem. In this paper, G-mean, F1-score and AUC are used to evaluate the imbalance.

The geometric mean score (G-mean) has a great reference value when the data is unbalanced. It is the square root of the accuracy in both types of samples. If the model predicts the two kinds of samples with relatively high accuracy, then the value of the G-mean will be large. Therefore, it can evaluate the prediction performance of the model reasonably on unbalanced datasets.

$$\text{Recall} = \frac{TP}{TP + TN} \tag{3}$$

$$\text{Specificity} = \frac{TN}{TN + FP} \tag{4}$$

$$\text{G} - \text{mean} = \sqrt{Recall * Specificity} \tag{5}$$

The F1-score is also used to evaluate classification problems. It is the harmonic mean of precision and recall. It is used to maximize the degree of evaluation of individual class performance and therefore can be used to measure the classification performance of a classifier on minority class samples. The better the classifier, the greater the F1-score. The β in the formula is a parameter that usually takes the value of 1.

$$\text{Precision} = \frac{TP}{TP + FP} \tag{6}$$

$$\text{F1} - \text{score} = \frac{1 + \beta^2 * \text{Precision} * \text{Recall}}{\beta^2 * \text{Precision} + \text{Recall}} \tag{7}$$

The receiver operating characteristic curve (ROC) and Area Under Curve (AUC). ROC is a very effective metric to evaluate dichotomous models, where the horizontal coordinate is the proportion of misclassified negative class samples to all negative class samples, and the vertical coordinate is the proportion of correctly classified positive class samples to the total samples. AUC is the area value between ROC and the horizontal coordinate, and the area closer to 1 corresponds to the higher truthfulness of the model.

5.3 Experiment Settings

In the experiment, we use three algorithms to conduct contrast experiments, including SMOTE, K-SMOTE, and K-SMOTE + Ensemble Learning. To test the effectiveness of these algorithms under different classifiers, after oversampling the dataset, the training set is divided into ten subsets. Two different classifiers C4.5 decision tree and SVM are used as basic classifiers to classify the dataset and then get ten base classifiers. Finally, the ten base classifiers are constructed into one integrated classifier using ensemble learning, and three evaluation metrics, G-mean, F1-score, and AUC, are calculated based on the classification results for evaluation.

The proposed K-SMOTE utilizes the K-Means algorithm for clustering the minority class samples. The choice of the number of clusters K for the minority class samples is very important, and it affects the accuracy of the algorithm. In response to this problem, we use the sum of the squared errors (SSE) and Silhouette Coefficient to select K. As K continues to increase, the divided clusters will be more refined, thus the degree of aggregation will gradually increase and SSE of all samples will gradually decrease. When K is less than the true value of clusters, the degree of aggregation of each cluster will greatly increase with the increase of K, so the decline in SSE will be large. However, when K reaches the true value, SSE tends to flatten with the continuous increase of K. At this time, the relationship between SSE and Silhouette Coefficient is the shape of the elbow, and the value corresponding to this elbow is the optimal value of K. According to this method, the number of clusters K in the Scholat dataset is determined to be 4, 3 for Yeast dataset, and 5 for BankMarketing-master and Segment dataset.

For the processing of discrete features, the K-SMOTE algorithm uses the number of k-nearest neighbors of the samples, where the k is the same as that of SMOTE. In this paper, the nearest neighbor k is set to 5 according to the method recommended in the original implementation of SMOTE [1]. Meanwhile, the value of β in the evaluation indicator F-measure is set as 1.

5.4 Experimental Results and Analysis

Using the Scholat dataset, it is possible to illustrate how K-SMOTE can improve the results attained by SMOTE. As can be seen from Fig. 1 (a), the original dataset has four to five distinct, with slightly noisy, clusters. We observe that the minority samples generated through SMOTE have a greater chance of appearing within majority clusters or directly at the class boundaries and SMOTE may change the distribution characteristics of the original dataset. In contrast, K-SMOTE avoids generating data outside of minority clusters and reduces the generation of class boundary data. The experimental results show that the method is easy to achieve inter- and intra-class balance while reducing noise generation.

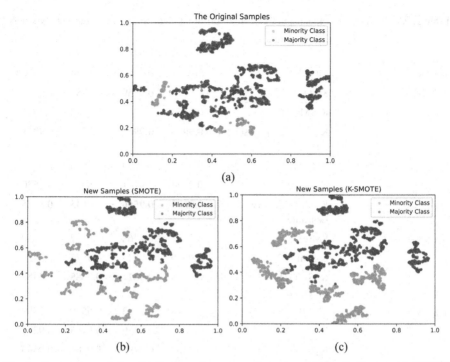

Fig. 1. Comparison of the distribution of new samples generated by the improved SMOTE algorithm

Table 2 shows the comparison of the G-mean and F1-score results for different algorithms using C4.5 decision trees and SVM. When using the C4.5 decision tree, although the G-mean and F1-score of K-SMOTE in the Scholat dataset are slightly smaller than those of SMOTE, K-SMOTE outperforms SMOTE in the other datasets. When using the SVM, the G-mean and F1-score of K-SMOTE in the Yeast dataset are also slightly smaller than those of SMOTE, but K-SMOTE outperforms SMOTE in the other datasets. However, K-SMOTE combined with Ensemble Learning performs the best among the three algorithms in both C4.5 decision tree and SVM, with a significant improvement in both F1-score and G-mean. This is because Ensemble Learning accomplishes the learning task by constructing and combining multiple learners. It can obtain significantly better generalization performance than a single learner, and also reduces overall errors, achieving better classification results. The Experimental results show that our method enables the classifier to achieve higher accuracy in predicting both advertising users and normal users.

To further reflect the classification effect of the models, we use the ROC curve and AUC to evaluate the generalization capability of the proposed method in this paper. The ROC curve for the Scholat dataset, Yeast dataset, Segment dataset, and BankMarketing-master dataset is shown in Figs. 2 and 3.

Table 2. Comparison of G-mean and F1-score of different algorithms under different classifiers.

		C4.5 decision tree		SVM	
Dataset	Model	G-mean	F1-score	G-mean	F1-score
Scholat	SMOTE	0.9730	0.9759	0.9781	0.9794
	K-SMOTE	0.9664	0.9703	0.9878	0.9881
	K_SMOTE + Ensemble Learning	**0.9960**	**0.9960**	**0.9921**	**0.9921**
Yeast	SMOTE	0.9013	0.8999	0.8612	0.8571
	K-SMOTE	0.9184	0.9161	0.8567	0.8530
	K_SMOTE + Ensemble Learning	**0.9572**	**0.9566**	**0.8645**	**0.8735**
Segment	SMOTE	0.9751	0.9768	0.9837	0.9849
	K-SMOTE	**0.9819**	0.9823	0.9875	0.9880
	K_SMOTE + Ensemble Learning	0.9818	**0.9824**	**0.9885**	**0.9888**
BankMarketing-master	SMOTE	0.7618	0.8313	0.6590	0.7859
	K-SMOTE	0.9402	0.9459	0.9165	0.9275
	K_SMOTE + Ensemble Learning	**0.9434**	**0.9497**	**0.9180**	**0.9303**

As seen in Fig. 2 (a) and Fig. 2 (b), on both the Scholat and Segment datasets, the ROC curves for K-SOMTE + Ensemble Learning are closest to the upper left corner whether using C4.5 decision tree or SVM. The ROC curves of K-SOMTE + Ensemble Learning in the Scholat dataset are more distinct from the other algorithms, with the AUC values as high as 0.996 and 0.992. The ROC curves for the Segment dataset are relatively close to those of other algorithms, but the AUC values for K-SOMTE + Ensemble Learning are as high as 0.982 and 0.989 under the two classifiers.

From Fig. 3 (a) and Fig. 3 (b), it shows that for both Yeast dataset and BankMarketing-master dataset, the ROC curves of K-SOMTE + Ensemble Learning are closest to the upper left corner compared to the other two methods, and both of them have better AUC values. Meanwhile, it also shows that the K-SOMTE + Ensemble Learning algorithm performs better than the SVM in the C4.5 decision tree. The above fully illustrate that the proposed method in this paper has strong generalization ability. It can improve the validity of the data generated through oversampling and enhance the classification accuracy of the classifier.

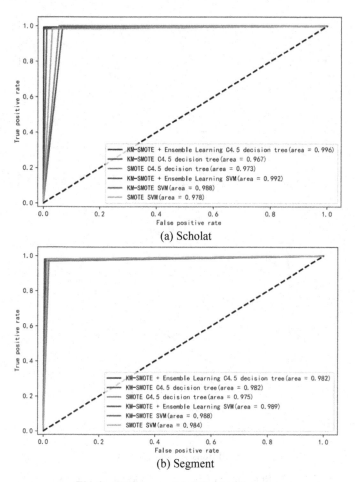

(a) Scholat

(b) Segment

Fig. 2. ROC curve of Scholat and Segment

6   Conclusion

This paper constructs a feature system containing basic user information, relationship features, and behavioral features based on the user information of Scholat. In order to deal with the flaws of SMOTE on unbalanced datasets, we propose a junk advertising user detection model based on improved SMOTE combined with K-Means and ensemble learning. Using real user data from Scholat, the experiment demonstrates our model can effectively solve the shortcomings of SMOTE, and using ensemble learning can effectively reduce the overall error. Our model enables better detection of advertising users and has powerful generalization capabilities. The K-Somte algorithm proposed in this paper can not only generate higher quality samples in the user dataset of Scholat but also allows samples of users with undesirable behaviors such as posting advertising messages to be learned repeatedly, which makes the classifier to better identify advertising users. This algorithm also gets better results on other public datasets than SMOTE.

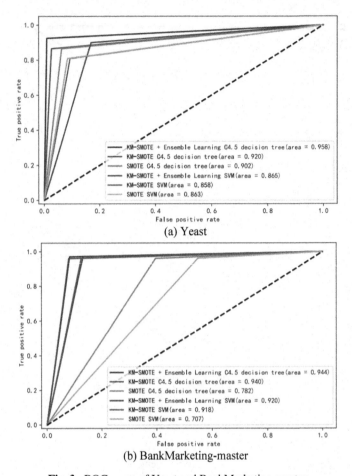

(a) Yeast

(b) BankMarketing-master

Fig. 3. ROC curve of Yeast and BankMarketing-master

In the future, we will further study the behavior of the advertising user, consider the correlation between user behavior and spamming to build a profile of the user with more characteristics. We will consider the influence of noise and other factors on the synthesized new sample, and improve the accuracy and rationality of the synthesized sample. There are also some major disadvantages of using synthetic generative method, such as bias in the generated data, which may not faithfully reflect the real-life data, and we will make an in-depth research of the disadvantages of SMOTE.

Acknowledgements. We thank the anonymous reviewers for their insightful comments. This work was supported by National Natural Science Foundation of China under grant number U1811263, by National Natural Science Foundation of China under grant number 6177221.

References

1. Chawla, N.V., Bowyer, K.W., Hall, L.O., Kegelmeyer, W.P.: Smote: Synthetic minority over-sampling technique. J. Artif. Intell. Res. **16**(1), 321–357 (2002)
2. Xixian, P., Qinghua, Z., Xuan, L.: Research on behavior characteristics and classification of micro-blog. Inf. Sci. **033**(001), 69–75 (2015)
3. Meng, X., Xu, L., Wang, S.: Spam analysis and detection of social network based on sina weibo. Sci. Technol. **000**(015), 125–127 (2014)
4. Stringhini, G., Kruegel, C., Vigna, G.: Detecting spammers on social networks. In: Twenty-Sixth Annual Computer Security Applications Conference, ACSAC 2010, Austin, Texas, USA, 6–10 December 2010 (2010)
5. Benevenuto, F., Rodrigues, T., Almeida, V., Almeida, J.M., Gonçalves, M.: Detecting spammers and content promoters in online video social networks. In: IEEE (2009)
6. Hui, H., Wang, W.Y., Mao, B.H.: Borderline-smote: A new over-sampling method in imbalanced data sets learning. In: Proceedings of the 2005 international conference on Advances in Intelligent Computing - Volume Part I (2005)
7. Sánchez, A.I., Morales, E.F., Gonzalez, J.A.: Synthetic oversampling of instances using clustering. Int. J. Artif. Intell. Tools **22**(02), 1350008 (2013). https://doi.org/10.1142/S02182130 13500085
8. Barua, S., Islam, M.M., Yao, X., Murase, K.: MWMOTE--majority weighted minority over-sampling technique for imbalanced data set learning. IEEE Trans. Knowl. Data Eng. **26**(2), 405–425 (2014). https://doi.org/10.1109/TKDE.2012.232
9. Douzas, G., Bacao, F., Last, F.: Improving imbalanced learning through a heuristic oversampling method based on k-means and SMOTE. Inf. Sci. **465**, 1–20 (2018). https://doi.org/10.1016/j.ins.2018.06.056
10. Ruan, Q., Qingfeng, W., Wang, Y., Liu, X., Miao, F.: Effective learning model of user classification based on ensemble learning algorithms. Computing **101**(6), 531–545 (2018). https://doi.org/10.1007/s00607-018-0688-4

Quantitative Relationship Between Achievement Motivation and Game Behavior Based on Structural Equation Model

Haiyan Zhou[1,2], Tingshao Zhu[1,2(✉)], and Nan Zhao[1,2]

[1] Institute of Psychology, Chinese Academy of Sciences, Beijing, China
tszhu@psych.ac.cn

[2] Department of Psychology, University of Chinese Academy of Sciences, Beijing, China

Abstract. Considering that achievement motivation is an important variable to explain human behavior, the characteristics of online games can potentially stimulate motivation in some people. The online game Dota 2 has such characteristics as widespread popularity, high and varied complexity and openly accessible data on its participants' behavior. For the first time, in focusing on the specific behavior and achievement motivation of college students who have played the online game Dota 2, this study utilized a quantitative methodology to study the relationship between them. Based on the achievement motivation scale and structural equation model, this study found that the overall achievement motivation of college students is weak, and reached the conclusion that the total achievement motivation is negative which is obviously different from the previous researches. Achievement motivation has significant influence on online game behavior, and it has both direct and indirect effect on the core behavior of players.

Keywords: College students · Achievement motivation · Game behavior · The online game Dota 2 · Structural equation model

1 Introduction

Since entering the new century, with the rapid development of science and technology, mobile Internet technology has achieved rapid development, and the e-sports industry has also developed at a speed far beyond ordinary people's imagination. College students have become the main constituents of the e-sports market, especially the Internet e-sports market.

Achievement Motivation refers to the motivation of individuals to pursue the things they consider valuable and to achieve an expected goal, that is, to set high standards for themselves and strive to achieve the success of activities (Wei Wang et al. 2013). It is one of the most important motives among many psychological motives. With the continuous development of social economy, all circles of society pay attention to and study the psychological motivation and health of college students with achievement motivation as the breakthrough point.

Q. Zu et al. (Eds.): HCC 2021, LNCS 13795, pp. 146–152, 2022.
https://doi.org/10.1007/978-3-031-23741-6_13

Given that "achievement motivation and other game motivations are important variables to explain game behaviors" (Jing Zhou 2019), and "the characteristics of online games themselves determine that they can better stimulate the achievement motivation of most people" (Shuguo Jiao et al. 2010), and that popularity, complexity and openness of the online game's behavior data, the study is the first to focus on the specific behavior of "Dota 2" that is a kind of Multiplayer Online Battle Arena (MOBA) and achievement motivation of college gamers, in order to determine the influence mechanism and degree of achievement motivation on game behavior.

2 Literature Review

The term achievement motivation originated from the concept of achievement need theory proposed by Murray (1938). The real use of the term achievement motivation and its systematic elaboration is the book Social Achievement by McClelland (1961). Later, different scholars defined achievement motivation based on their own research contents. With the development of time and the deepening of research, the definition of achievement motivation in the academic world tends to be increasingly integrated.

The measurement of achievement motivation has experienced a development process from scratch, from extensive to accurate, from single to multiple. There are currently three main methods to measure achievement motivation: apperception test, self-reported questionnaire and integration of the two methods. Among the three methods, method of self-reported questionnaire is the most commonly used. There are many self-reported questionnaires, and Achievement Motivation Scale (AMS) proposed by Gjesme et al. (1970) has the greatest influence.

Since "It can satisfy the psychological needs of game players and enable them to experience more autonomy and decision-making power in the game environment", and "game players like to seek virtual entertainment experience, and the virtual environment of online games provides them with a physiological and cognitive stimulating experience", many scholars use online game behavior to study psychological behavior including achievement motivation. Bartle (1996) from the University of Essex in the UK and Yee (2006; 2014) from Stanford University in the US were the first scholars to establish a system of psychological motivation based on online game behavior. Based on foreign scholars' research, Chinese scholars also tried to study the relationship between game players' behavior and achievement motivation through game behavior, especially MOBAs, and draw a series of positive conclusions.

According to the literature review, there are many studies on college students' achievement motivation and game behavior (especially online game behavior) respectively, but there are few literatures that combine the two. Based on the game behavior data of college students who engage in "Dota 2" online and the corresponding achievement motivation questionnaire data, this study will analyze the relationship between the two, in order to provide quantitative analysis support for defining the psychological state of this specific group and its influencing factors.

3 Data Acquisition and Preprocessing

In this study, hundreds of "Dota2" game players were invited to participate in the completion of AMS through online and offline methods such as game forums, "Dota2" post bar and acquaintance recommendation. Considering the invited players' proficiency in the game and their educational background, 292 college students were selected as the research objects. At the same time, this paper obtains the game behaviour data of "Dota 2" by crawler software. Statistics show that the average age of the subjects is 23.95 years old and the standard deviation is 2.37 years old. Among them, 280 are male, accounting for 95.89%.

According to the design principles of Gjesme and Nygard (1970), the 30 questions listed in AMS can be divided into two categories. Namely, motivation to pursue success (MS) and motivation to avoid failure (MF). The total score of achievement motivation (M) can be obtained by subtracting MF from MS. According to the calculation, the highest score of achievement motivation of 292 college players is 23, and the lowest score is −41, with an average of −1.613.

The study obtained a total of 150 game behavior characteristics of college students who participated in the online game "Dota2". Based on the quality of the acquired data, this study eliminated some of the behavioral indicators of the aforementioned 150 game behaviors that could not be used. This process include eliminating indicators that do not get a value, eliminating most of the indicators of 0, and removing derivative indicators. After basic data processing, there are 40 remaining behavioral indicators that can be quantified at a higher order.

4 Econometric Analysis

Structural Equation Modelling (SEM) is a statistical method used to analyse the relationship between variables based on the covariance matrix of variables, so it is also called covariance structural model. Structural equation model is the combination of confirmatory factor model and causal model (latent variable). The former is called measurement model, and the corresponding equation is called measurement equation, which describes the relationship between latent variable and index. The latter is called the latent variable model, also known as the mechanism model, and the corresponding equation is called the structural equation, which describes the relationship between the latent variables.

Structural equation model includes measurement equation, structural equation and model hypothesis. In the most general case, both exogenous and endogenous variables in the causal model are latent variables, and both exogenous and endogenous variables have measurement equations.

The model is as follows:

Measurement equation: $y = \Lambda y \eta + \varepsilon$; $x = \Lambda x \xi + \delta$

Structure equation: $\eta = B\eta + \Gamma \xi + \zeta$

Considering the structural equation model has handle multiple dependent variables at the same time, allow contain dependent and independent variables and measurement error, at the same time as the factor structure and the measurement model of factor relations, and allow greater flexibility, and estimate the entire model fitting degree, etc., many scholars in the analysis cannot accurately and directly measure the relationship between the variables choice when using the model.

The purpose of this study is to identify and quantify the influence of achievement motivation on various game behaviours. Considering the characteristics of structural equation model, many scholars choose to use this model when analyzing the relationship between variables that cannot be accurately and directly measured. Therefore, this study chooses to use structural equation model to construct a quantitative relationship model between game behavior and achievement motivation.

This study summarizes game behaviors into three types of specific behaviors, namely "participating behavior", "killing behavior" and "purchase and use of props". Combined with the integrity of data and the correlation of indicators, three indicators (J1, J2 and J3 respectively), including the total duration of matches, the total number of team battles and the number of operations per minute, were selected as the observation variables of the latent variable "participation behavior". Four indicators (K1, K2, K3 and K4 respectively), including the number of player's counterkill, the number of player's kills, the number of multiple kills and the maximum damage value, were used as the observation variables of the latent variable "killing behavior". Three indicators (P1, P2 and P3 respectively), such as purchase quantity of equipment, number of control symbols and use times of active props, were used as the observation variables of the latent variable "prop purchase and use". At the same time, this study chose to directly calculate two achievement motivation indicators as the observation variables of the latent variable "achievement motivation". Considering that Linnenbrink et al. (2000); Yang Dan et al. (2016); Zhou Jing et al. (2019) and other scholars defined the relationship between psychological motivation and behavioral process as the former influencing the latter, in the process of studying achievement motivation and game behavior, this study also assumes that the former is the main factor affecting the latter.

Before formally constructing the structural equation model between achievement motivation and game behavior, this study conducted factor analysis on the observed variables corresponding to each latent variable. The KMO and Bartlett test results of factor analysis (see Table 1 for specific results) showed that the KMO values of the four groups of observed variables were all greater than 0.5, meeting the prerequisite requirements of factor analysis, and the data passed the Bartlett sphericity test ($P <$ 0.001), indicating that the four groups of data were suitable for factor analysis, i.e., the measurement relationship was of high quality.

Table 1. KMO and Bartlett tests of observed variables corresponding to different latent variables

Statistics latent variable		M	Participative behavior	Kill behavior	Purchase and use of props
Statistics observed variables		MS and MF	J1 - J3	K1 - K4	P1 - P3
KMO		0.5	0.672	0.578	0.662
Bartlett sphericity test	Approximate chi squa	77.323	836.975	572.088	163.171
	df	1	3	6	3
	p	0.000	0.000	0.000	0.000

Based on the determination of latent variables, observed variables, and their relationships/paths, the structural equation model (see Fig. 1) was established.

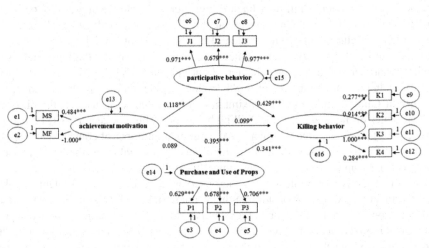

Fig. 1. Structural equation model of achievement motivation and game behavior

By adjusting the influence relation and covariance relation, the path coefficient between each latent variable and the load coefficient between observation variable and latent variable are finally obtained (see Fig. 1 for specific coefficients). The fitting index of the model (see Table 2) and the p-values of each regression coefficient (see Fig. 1) show that the overall fitting effect of the model is relatively ideal, and the regression coefficient is basically significant, indicating that it is reasonable to use structural equation model to quantitatively analyse the influence of achievement motivation on game behavior.

Table 2. Model fitting index values summary table

Statistics common indicators	χ^2/df	GFI	RMSEA	RMR	CFI	NFI
Statistics judgment criteria	<3	>0.9	<0.10	<0.05	>0.9	>0.9
Value	2.541	0.943	0.071	0.059	0.969	0.949

According to the structural equation model, the influence effect data between variables can be further sorted out (Table 3). It can be seen from Fig. 1 and Table 3 that the influence effect data between the three types of game behaviors are significantly higher than that of between achievement motivation and game behaviors. The direct effect of achievement motivation on participating behavior and killing behavior is higher than the direct effect on purchase and use of props, and the significance is higher. Achievement motivation has direct and indirect effects on killing behavior, and the total effect is higher. The relationship among the three kinds of game behaviors shows a one-way trend, and the influence of each other is very significant, among which the killing behavior is the "core" of the three kinds of game behaviors.

Table 3. Analysis table of effects among variables in structural equation model

Relationship between variables	Direct effect	Indirect effect	Total effect
Achievement motivation → participation behavior	0.118	–	0.118
Achievement motivation → killing behavior	0.099	0.097	0.196
Achievement motivation → purchase and use of props	0.089	0.047	0.136
Participation behavior → killing behavior	0.429	0.135	0.564
Participation behavior → purchase and use of props	0.395	–	0.395
Purchase and use of props → killing behavior	0.341	–	0.341

5 Conclusions

Firstly, a special conclusion is that the achievement motivation of "Dota2" college gamers is weak, not only the willingness to avoid failure is not high, but also the willingness to pursue success is not high. The total achievement motivation is actually negative, which is obviously different from the conclusion of other scholars' research on college students' achievement motivation.

Secondly, achievement motivation has a positive effect on all three kinds of game behaviors. Among them, the influence of achievement motivation on participation behavior only includes direct effect, but its size is the largest in the direct effect of achievement motivation on the three kinds of game behaviors. The effect of achievement motivation on killing behavior includes both direct effect and indirect effect (the proportion is 50.51% and 49.49% respectively), and the total effect size is the largest among the three types of game behavior. Achievement motivation has both direct and indirect effects on item purchase and use, but the direct effect is not significant. In addition, there are also significant effects among the three kinds of game behaviors, but the influence direction is relatively single, that is, participation directly affects killing behavior, or indirectly affects killing behavior through item purchase and use. These results not only show that "achievement motivation is an important reason for players to trigger game behavior and feel satisfied", but also show that killing behavior is the core behavior of the game, and the sense of accomplishment of game players is mainly reflected by killing behavior.

References

Wang, W., et al.: Personality Psychology, p. 79. People's Medical Publishing House, Shelton (2013)

Zhou, J.: Study on game behavior and motivation of KG players: a case study of Wuhan university students. Zhongnan University of Economics and Law (2019)

Jiao, S., et al.: Social motivation analysis of online games, pp. 121–122. Bridge of Century (2010)

Murray, H.A.: Explorations in Personality. Ford University Press, New York (1938)

McClelland, D.C.: The Achieving Society. Van Nostrand Reinhold (1961)

Gjesme, T., et al.: Achievement-related motives: theoretical considerations and construction of a measuring instrument. University of Oslo (1970)

Bartle, R.: Hearts, clubs, diamonds, spades: players who suit MUDs. J. MUD Res. 1(1), 19 (1996)

Yee, N.: Motivations for play in online games. Cyberpsychol. Behav. 9(6), 772–775 (2006)

Yee, N.: The Proteus Paradox: How Online Games and Virtual Worlds Change Us-and How They Don't. Yale University Press, New Haven (2014)

Linnenbrink, A., et al.: Multiple Pathways to Learning and Achievement: The Role of Goal Orientation in Fostering Adaptive Motivation, Affect, and Cognition, Intrinsic and Extrinsic Motivation, pp. 195–227. Academic Press, Pittsburgh (2000)

Yang, D., et al.: The relationship between achievement motivation and learning burnout in college students: the mediating role of hope. China J. Health Psychol. 24, 255–259 (2016)

Dictionary-Based Classical Chinese Word Segmentation and Its Application on Imperial Edicts of Jin Dynasties

Huan Xiong[1,2], Gengxuan Wu[3], Shujie Xue[3], Hua Li[3], and Tingshao Zhu[1,2(✉)]

[1] Institute of Psychology, Chinese Academy of Sciences, Beijing, China
tszhu@psych.ac.cn
[2] Department of Psychology, University of Chinese Academy of Sciences, Beijing, China
[3] Institute of Qilu Culture, Shandong Normal University, Jinan, China

Abstract. Big data technology can play a significant role in exploring and analyzing classical Chinese literature and in enhancing our understanding and promotion of traditional culture. Analyzing psycholinguistic words used in ancient people's self-expression texts is a good way to understand their psychological state. Based on the classical Chinese segmentation methods used by such dictionaries as CCI-Dict and CC-LIWC, this paper proposed a word segmentation algorithm that can better cover the ancient Chinese vocabulary used in imperial edicts. We used this algorithm to calculate the psycholinguistic words in imperial edicts of the Western and Eastern Jin Dynasties (265–420). We firstly collected 613 edicts from 18 emperors of the Western and Eastern Jin Dynasties, with a total word count of more than 45,000. After being analyzed and calculated by the dictionary-based classical Chinese word segmentation algorithm, all these words were divided into 78 categories of psycholinguistic words. By comparing the frequencies of such word categories in imperial edicts of the Western Jin (265–317) and the Eastern Jin (317–420), we found significant differences in the following five word categories: personal pronouns (p = 0.027), modal particles (p = 0.034), social process words (p = 0.016), difference words (p = 0.016), and time words (p = 0.043). Based on differences in these five categories, we analyzed the psychological changes of the Western Jin and Eastern Jin emperors. This paper thereby verified the applicability and feasibility of the dictionary-based classical Chinese word segmentation algorithm.

Keywords: Classical Chinese word segmentation · Imperial edicts · Psycholinguistic · Word frequency analysis

1 Introduction

Analyzing psycholinguistic words used in ancient people's self-expression texts is good way to understand their psychological state. Although many studies have made psychological analysis of ancient people, most of them used such research methods as expert evaluation and manual reading of ancient literature. Such methods confine studies to

Q. Zu et al. (Eds.): HCC 2021, LNCS 13795, pp. 153–160, 2022.
https://doi.org/10.1007/978-3-031-23741-6_14

a small number of cases, making it hard to see the whole picture. Given that, it is of vital importance to use big data technology in such studies as it can expand the research scope. This can facilitate our understanding and promotion of the traditional culture.

The first step for analyzing classical Chinese texts with big data technology is to work out a word segmentation method. About word segmentation research, Xue [1] first proposed to model Chinese word segmentation as a sequence annotation task, and determine the boundary of word segmentation by assigning a segmentation label to each character in a sentence; Then Low [2] proposed to use the maximum entropy model to process the sequence annotation task of Chinese word segmentation; Tseng [3] introduced conditional random fields into the study of Chinese word segmentation; Yan S [4] proposed an ancient Chinese model based on Conditional Random Field (CRF); Wang XY [5] combined CRFs model with dictionary for ancient Chinese word segmentation; Qian ZY [6] took CHU CI as the word segmentation object and annotated it with Hidden Markov Model (HMM); Li XY [7] carried out new words discovery based on mutual information and information entropy, and combined with dictionary information for word segmentation of ancient books HAN SHU; Fan MR [8] put forward CC-LIWC ancient Chinese dictionary, which provides an objective way for psychosemantic analysis of ancient Chinese texts; On this basis, Xing FG [9] proposed a CCDict word segmentation method based on word segmentation dictionary, so as to better include CC-LIWC words.

This paper optimized the word segmentation methods used in two classical Chinese word dictionaries of CCIDict and CC-LIWC as follows: ① expanding the labelled word segmentation data by supplementing a large number of classical Chinese corpora including emperors' edicts, letters, self-narratives and self-evaluation materials; ② training polysemous word vectors to address disambiguation of polysemous words; ③ correcting errors and simplifying redundancies. We then applied this new algorithm to analyze the frequencies of psycholinguistic words in the imperial edicts of the Western and Eastern Jin Dynasties, in an effort to test its applicability.

Imperial edicts convey the political ideas and intentions of the supreme ruling class and represent the will of the supreme rulers rather than emotionless official documents. For example, the *Rescript for Penitence* shows how an emperor made self-reflection and self-criticism; the *Rescript for Amnesty* shows the clemency and charity of the ruling class. Given that, this paper proposed this new word segmentation algorithm that can better cover different categories of words in the imperial edicts. Any text is a mirror of the psychological state of its writer and its language style tells the writer's personality, emotions and social relations. Language style analysis can tell a lot about the changes in a person's personality and emotions [10]. In return, personality, emotions and social relations can take part in shaping a person's language style. This paper selected the imperial edicts of the Western and Eastern Jin Dynasties as the research object, since both the dynasties were ruled by the Sima family and the ruling family went through great psychological changes following the first mass migration of Han people in Chinese history. The ruling family fell from "enjoying the supreme position above all" during the Western Jin to "sharing the actual authority with the Wang family from Langya" during the Eastern Jin. This paper verified such psychological changes by analyzing the word frequency differences of these imperial edicts with the dictionary-based classical Chinese word segmentation algorithm.

2   Methods

2.1   Data Collection

Quan Jin Wen, compiled by Yan Kejun during the Qing Dynasty, includes imperial edicts of the Western and Eastern Jin Dynasties. We accessed the electronic version of this book from an ancient script website (www.zhonghuadiancang.com), from which we collected 613 imperial edicts of 18 emperors (including 3 queen regents) as the corpus of this research.

Writers of Western Jin imperial edicts lived in the north, while those of Eastern Jin's lived in the south. The latter is the continuation of the Sima family of the Western Jin, including those who personally experienced the southward migration and their offspring.

2.2   Data Processing

Though the CCIDict is a basic dictionary of classical Chinese, we cannot affirm that it included a comprehensive vocabulary of imperial edicts. To supplement it, we extracted new words from a large number of imperial edicts, letters, self-narratives and self-evaluation materials by combining the methods of the n-gram model, mutual information, information entropy, and word position probability. This paper implemented a distributed-Trie through Spark RDD, which improved analysis efficiency. Figure 1 shows the process of the classical Chinese word segmentation algorithm.

Input: basic dictionary: CCIDict, Original corpus: s=[s_1,...,s_n], Minimum word length: min_wl, Maximum word length: max_wl, Minimum word frequency: min_wf, Minimum mutual information entropy threshold: min_pmi, Minimum information entropy threshold: min_en.
Output: Candidate words set: C_S (u).
    1: **procedure** DISCOVERY(gram^T)   ◁ New word discovery process
    2: Calculate position probability based on the CCIDict
    3: Load the original corpus s into the memory in the form of RDD, construct a Trie from the entire corpus according to max_wl and calculate the word frequency of the gram, broadcast the built Trie to other computing nodes, reducing the communication overhead in the calculation. Calculate the word frequency tree gram^T.
    4: **while** gram^T **do**   ◁ Traverse all gram^T units
    5: Compute mutual information
    6: Calculate the left information entropy and the right information entropy
    7: **end while**
    8: Filter out qualified words according to min_wl, max_wl, min_wf, min_pmi, min_en. Generate C_S(U).
    9: **return** C_S(U)   ◁ Candidate words set
    10: **end procedure**

Fig. 1. Process of the dictionary-based classical Chinese word segmentation algorithm

2.3 Data Analysis

The analysis method and process of this paper are as follows:

(1) **Grouping.** This paper divided the 613 imperial edicts collected into two groups: – those written by Western Jin emperors (Group A) and those written by Eastern Jin emperors (Group B), to make a comparative study of psycholinguistic words used in these two groups.
(2) **Word segmentation**. Using the dictionary-based classical Chinese word segmentation algorithm, this paper read all the words of the two groups in the text form of TXT, then selected and divided the words with psychological meanings into different categories aligned with the categories used in the CC-LIWC dictionary.
(3) **Statistical indicators**. Basic statistical indicators used by this paper include TCC (Total Chinese character Count), TWC (Total Word Count), LWC (LIWC Word Count), LCR (LIWC Cover Rate, see Eq. 1).

$$LCR = \frac{LWC}{TWC} \tag{1}$$

The words were divided into 78 categories. Each category is calculated in terms of basic statistical indicators, word frequency and proportion.
(4) **Significant difference test**. Wilcoxon nonparametric test was used to test the significant differences between the two groups.
(5) **Psycholinguistic analysis.** We selected five categories of words with significant differences for psycholinguistic analysis, including personal pronouns, modal particles, social process words, difference words, and time words.

3 Results

The basic statistical results are shown in Table 1.

Table 1. Results of basic statistical indicators

Group	Number of writers	Number of edicts	TCC	TWC	LWC	LCR
Group A: Western Jin emperors (incl. 1 queen regent)	5	339	24487	17029	11726	0.6886
Group B: Eastern Jin emperors (incl. 2 queen regent)	13	274	21347	15001	10309	0.6872

Using the dictionary-based classical Chinese word segmentation algorithm, we calculated the frequencies of 78 categories of words with psychological meanings of Group A and Group B respectively. Since one set of data presents a normal distribution and the other set presents a non-normal distribution, we conducted a Wilcoxon nonparametric statistical test of the 78 categories of words to calculate how significant the differences between the two sets of data are.

From the significant difference test, we obtained five word categories with significant results (p-value <0.05).

Table 2. List of word categories with significant differences

Category	M		SD		p value
	Group A	Group B	Group A	Group B	
ppron	0.017	0.008	0.007	0.006	0.027*
modal-par	0.038	0.061	0.014	0.020	0.034*
social	0.107	0.148	0.018	0.055	0.016*
differ	0.017	0.027	0.005	0.011	0.016*
time	0.037	0.055	0.006	0.033	0.043*

Note: Each number was rounded up to three decimal places, *P <0.05

As shown in Table 2, these five word categories are personal pronouns (ppron), modal particles (modal-par), social process words (social), difference words (differ), and time words (time). Figure 2 shows the mean frequency differences of these five categories: a positive number indicates that Group B is higher than Group A, and a negative number indicates that Group B is lower than Group A. As we can see in Fig. 2, of the five categories, the frequency of personal pronouns is much lower in Group B than in Group A while the frequencies of the other four categories are much lower in Group A than in Group B.

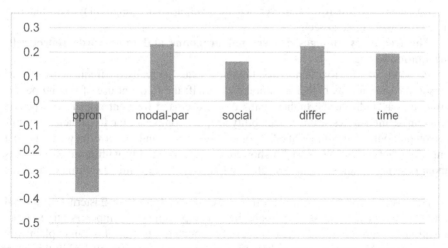

Fig. 2. Mean frequency differences in word categories with significant difference between Group A and Group B

Personal pronouns include first-person singular and plural, second-person singular and plural, and third-person singular and plural. Since there is no first-person plural or second-person plural in imperial edicts, this paper presents in Fig. 3 the frequencies of the other four types of personal pronouns, namely first-person singular (I), second-person singular (you), third-person singular (she, he) and third-person plural (they). As displayed in Fig. 3, Group B is higher than Group A in terms of the frequency of first-person singular; the two groups share a similar frequency of second-person singular; as for the frequencies of third-person singular and plural, Group B is smaller than Group A.

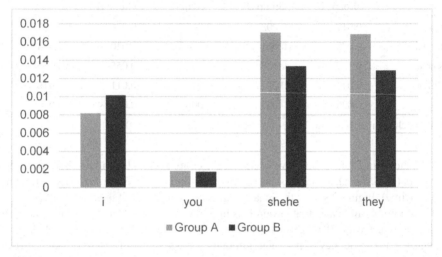

Fig. 3. Mean frequency differences in personal pronouns between Group A and Group B

Based on the above results, we verified the psychological changes of the Jin emperors in the following three aspects.

The frequency changes of personal pronouns and time words reflect self-orientation changes.

Pronouns are a mirror of one's psychological state. Generally, the frequent use of first-person pronoun means higher attention on oneself; the frequent use of second-person pronoun may indicate the higher status of the user; the frequent use of third-person pronouns demonstrates stronger sociability [10]. By comparing the frequencies of third-person pronouns in the imperial edicts of the Western Jin and Eastern Jin, we found that imperial edicts of the Western Jin showed stronger sociability with more expressions about power and status, which was closely linked with the political environment at the time.

However, the first-person pronoun is more frequently used in Eastern Jin imperial edicts, which means the ruling class at the time represented by emperors turned more attention on themselves than their Western Jin counterparts did. This can explain why many Eastern Jin emperors loved literature and were rather accomplished in this field.

The more frequent use of time words in Eastern Jin imperial edicts confirms this self-orientation, since time words are deemed "self-focused" due to their reference to the personal opinions of the user [11]. In short, Eastern Jin emperors who were cornered to the south were more self-focused than their Western Jin counterparts who governed both the north and the south.

The frequency changes of social process words mirror changes in social relations and social impacts.

Social process words include those representing friendship, family and human [8], which reflect the psychological features of users in social interaction. According to the result that social process words are more frequently used in Eastern Jin imperial edicts than in Western Jin ones, we can say that the Eastern Jin ruling class had different social differentiation and coordination. Considering the social background at the time and historical researches on this period, we can see the link between frequency changes of social process words and changes in the ruling class's social relations and social impacts.

The Eastern Jin regime is said to be "jointly ruled by the Wang and Sima families". This expression not only vividly depicts the unusual monarch-subject relationship between the brothers Wang Dao and Wang Dun (leading figures of the Wang family) and Sima Rui (the first emperor of the Eastern Jin), but also highlights that the social impact of ministers overwhelmed that of their king during the Eastern Jin [12]. Such a shared-ruling regime enabled the Eastern Jin to last over a century, far longer than the Western Jin.

The higher frequency of modal particles and difference words reflects stronger subjective and conflicting orientation.

According to some researches, modal particles indicate to what extent a writer wants to interact with readers regarding a topic in a subjective manner. In other words, writers want to use modal particles to realize coordinated cognition and interaction with their readers [13]. The more frequent use of modal particles in Eastern Jin imperial edicts means that Eastern Jin emperors were more subjective and interactive than their Western Jin counterparts.

Subjectivity is always accompanied by inner conflict, so the frequency of difference words is as significant as that of modal particles. Difference words are usually used for adversative transition and negation to express logical thinking. They show a stronger conflicting orientation [14]. Therefore, we can say that the imperial edicts of the Eastern Jin showed more subjectivity and conflicting orientation, which is consistent with the historical situation of the Eastern Jin and historians' evaluation of that dynasty.

4 Conclusions

This paper made an experimental study of the dictionary-based classical Chinese word segmentation algorithm which can better cover the vocabulary of ancient Chinese imperial edicts. We used this algorithm to analyze the psychological changes of emperors of the Jin Dynasties following the first mass migration of Han people in Chinese history from the perspective of psycholinguistics. According to the results, imperial edicts of the Western Jin and Eastern Jin show significant differences in the frequencies of personal pronouns, modal particles, social process words, difference words and time words. Such different writing styles reflect the different social backgrounds of the two dynasties. Echoing the situation at the time, we can see that Eastern Jin emperors were more self-focused, subjective and conflicting than their Western Jin counterparts and experienced different social relations and social impacts.

Through this research, this paper verified the efficiency and accuracy of the dictionary-based classical Chinese word segmentation algorithm and its applicability in the psycholinguistic study of classical Chinese texts. In addition, using imperial edicts to analyze the psychological changes of the ruling class of the Jin Dynasties, this paper provides a unique and representative perspective for studying the psychological impacts of the first mass southward migration of Han people in Chinese history. However, it should be noted that imperial edicts are not an unrestricted expression of personal will, so they cannot fully show the psycholinguistic differences. As the psycholinguistic research of imperial edicts can reflect the psychological changes of emperors, we can apply the same approach to study the psychological changes of other groups of people of the same period, in an effort to enrich studies on the social and psychological changes of this period.

References

1. Xue, N.: Chinese word segmentation as character tagging. Int. J. Comput. Linguistics Chinese Language Process. **8**(1), 29–48 (2003)
2. Low, J.K.: A maxiumun entropy approach to Chinese word segmentation. In: Proceedings of the Fourth SIGHAN Workshop on Chinese Language Processing, pp. 161–164, Jeju Island, Korea (2005)
3. Tseng, H.: A conditional random field word segmenter for Sighan Bakeoff 2005. In: Proceedings of the Fourth SIGHAN Workshop on Chinese Language Processing, Jeju Island, Korea, pp. 168–171 (2005)
4. Yan, S.: Research on ancient Chinese word segmentation and annotation model based on CR. Jiangsu Sci. Technol. Inf. **485**(8), 14–16 (2016)
5. Wang, X.Y.: Automatic word segmentation of Medieval Chinese based on CRFs and dictionary information. Data Anal. Knowl. Discovery 1(5) (2017)
6. Qian, Z.Y.: Research on automatic word segmentation and annotation of CHU CI based on HMM. Libr. Inf. Serv. (4), 105–110 (2014)
7. Li, X.Y.: Research on word segmentation of ancient books based on new word discovery and dictionary. Softw. Guide **18**(4), 66–69 (2019)
8. Fan, M.R.: Critical technology in ancient Chinese psychological semantic analysis based on LIWC. Master Dissertation, University of Chinese Academy of Sciences (2020)
9. Xing, F.G., Zhu, T.S.: Research on classical Chinese dictionary construction and word segmentation technology based on large-scale corpus. J. Chin. Inf. Process. (2021)
10. Pennebaker, J.W.: The Secret Life of Pronouns. China Machine Press, Beijing (2018)
11. Prior, A.N.: Papers on Time and Tense. Oxford University Press, Oxford (2003)
12. He, L.Q.: The causes, roots and lessons of the pattern of "strong officials and weak masters" under the gate politics of the Eastern Jin Dynasty. Leadership Sci. (23), 3 (2020)
13. Wang, J.: The functional model of modal particles. J. Chin. Linguist. (2016)
14. Zhao, X.: Frege's thought of "Negation" – from the perspective of sentence schema. Acad. Res. (2021)

Visualization Analysis of Hot Event Propagation Topic Map

Weidong Huang[✉], Yuan Wang, Jieyun Huang, and Xiaoxiang Cheng

Nanjing University of Posts and Telecommunications, Nanjing 210000, China
huangwd@njupt.edu.c

Abstract. With the rapid development of online social media platforms, online public opinion is becoming more and more complex. False news will not only reduce the credibility of the media, affect people's value orientation, but also combat related industries. On the basis of combing the relevant theories of knowledge map and social network public opinion event topic map, this paper takes the hot event of 'Rumors of illegal soaking antibacterial agent for Wuming fertile orange' as an example, selects the data of related topics on Sina Weibo, extracts the entity and relationship of the topic map, and constructs the topic map construction process model. Neo4j is used to construct the topic map of hot events and analyze the evolution of public opinion, so as to provide suggestions for public opinion control.

Keywords: Topic map · Network public opinion · Visual analysis

1 Introduction

With the high popularity of the Internet, the network public opinion is complicated. False news not only makes the credibility of the media decline, has a negative impact on people's value orientation, but also causes a major blow to the directly related industries. The analysis of the characteristics of public opinion propagation network and the role of Internet users in these events can achieve regulatory or cooperative relations with these key users in similar events, so as to control and guide similar public opinion events in the future. Therefore, taking the hot event of 'Rumors of illegal soaking antibacterial agent for Wuming fertile orange' as an example, a visual public opinion propagation network is constructed based on the propagation topic map, which is used to analyze the key users and propagation paths in the propagation network, and make suggestions for rumor management and public opinion guidance.

2 Related Research

The knowledge map was first proposed by Google in 2012 and applied to search engines. The knowledge map aims to describe various entities or concepts that exist in the world. Each entity or concept is identified by a globally unique ID, each attribute is used to describe the internal characteristics of an entity, and relationships are used to connect two entities and describe the association between them. Entities are the basic units in the knowledge map, which are represented as nodes in the knowledge map. Attributes are used to describe the characteristics of the entity, and relationships describe the connections between entities [1]. Several typical general knowledge maps include language knowledge maps, common sense knowledge maps and encyclopedia knowledge maps [2], and then gradually refined to the research of knowledge maps in specific fields, such as geography, medicine, e-commerce and other fields.

Some researchers put forward the concept of topic map based on knowledge map. The essence of topic map is a knowledge base that stores topics and their logical relations. Many researchers apply topic maps to the fields of digital resources [3] and subject research [4], aiming to improve the efficiency of resource retrieval and provide visual information. Grasping the dietary lifestyle type and the dessert cafe selection attribute type, Mi [5] proposes a recommendation system based on the topic map keyword extraction technique and wide deep learning. Zhou [6] uses probabilistic topic models to build knowledge maps for songs and users in the music market, and applies them to the visual analysis of the music market. Visual analysis based on topic maps has also been applied to the field of online public opinion research. Yang [7] proposes a topic map based on geographic information features and topic features, aiming to provides important information to event prediction, source detection, and news propagation. On the basis of previous studies, a topic map is constructed in this paper to visually analyze the propagation process of hot events, and puts forward suggestions for public opinion management.

3 Problem Analysis and Model Construction

In the topic map, the entity is the user node, and the relationship is the edge between entities, which is the comment relationship and forwarding relationship in social media [8]. Based on the analysis of user influence and communication efficiency in the process of public opinion event communication, this paper constructs the topic map construction process model, as shown in Fig. 1:

(1) Data collection. The publishing user name, publishing time, content, comments, forwarding, and comments of all microblogs under relevant topics are collected.
(2) Construct entities. Use users as entity nodes [9].
(3) Construct relationships. Use comments and forwarding relationships between user nodes as directed edges to connect entities [10].
(4) Public opinion evolution analysis and public opinion propagation analysis.

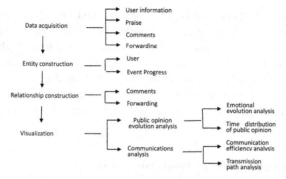

Fig. 1. The topic map construction process model.

4 Visualization Analysis of Hot Event Based on the Topic Map

The hot event studied in this paper is a typical food safety public opinion event 'Rumors of illegal soaking antibacterial agent for Wuming fertile orange'. In this study, the following three aspects are tried to solve: 1) using propagation topic map to find important users in the dissemination of public opinion; 2) visual analysis of the propagation path between user nodes; 3) visual analysis of the propagation graph to provide suggestions for public opinion control.

4.1 Data Collection and Preprocessing

We crawled 7553 pieces of Weibo data on related topic. The whole event is divided into three stages, that is the initial stage of the outbreak of public opinion, the progress of the survey, and the survey results stage. According to the stage division, we divide the entities into event progress and user nodes.

4.2 Analysis of Hot Event Propagation Based on User Influence

The importance of entity nodes in the propagation topic map is calculated by PageRank algorithm, and the results are shown in Table 1.

Table 1. Ranking of node importance.

No	Name	Score
1	The Paper	666.4833981
2	China News Network	204.8546445
3	China Three Agriculture Release	81.11720154
4	Zhu Yi	44.48248564
5	Vegetable Shi Jun	41.23017859

As the mainstream media, 'China News Network' and the government official micro-blog 'China Three Agriculture Release' are authoritative and highly trusted. In addition, the node importance of the earliest anti-rumor we-media is relatively high, which reflects the role that we media cannot be ignored in the process of anti-rumor. In the process of public opinion guidance, it is not only necessary to make use of the influence of mainstream media, but also call on the media with great influence to crack down on rumors, and the users with great influence to forward, so as to speed up the process of crack down on rumors.

4.3 Analysis of Public Opinion Propagation Node

The nodes whose number of likes, comments or forwarding is more than 100 are defined as the main node, and the remaining users are defined as commodes (common nodes). Comments and forwarding constitute the relationship between nodes. We set the main node to blue and the ordinary node to green. In the connection between the main nodes, red represents forwarding relationship, yellow represents comment relationship. The arrow points in the direction of information dissemination. The number of nodes in the query results is controlled at 1000, and the visualization results of the topic graph are shown in Fig. 2.

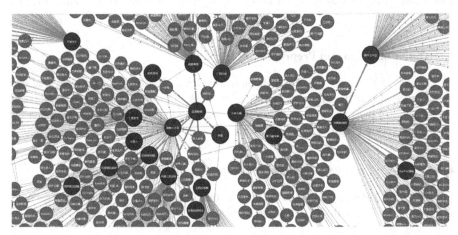

Fig. 2. Topic map of rumors of illegal soaking antibacterial agent for Wuming fertile orange. (Color figure online)

It can be seen from Fig. 2 that the topic map of online rumors in the process of hot events propagation is a directed network diagram, in which the key nodes have a strong influence. The nodes of 'The Papers' as the first rumor are closely related to other main nodes, and the propagation of ordinary user node messages is greatly affected by the main node.

User Propagation Path Analysis. The propagation efficiency is related to the propagation path length between user nodes. By calculating the shortest propagation path and the average propagation path length, the propagation of the source node can be analyzed based on the spread of the node. Call the gds.alpha.shortestPath.stream module in neo4j to calculate the shortest path length from 'The Papers' to 'Cat Monster in the Bird's Nest'. The results are shown in Table 2.

The calculation formula of the average path length is shown in Formula 1:

$$L = \frac{1}{\frac{1}{2}N(N-1)} \sum_{i \geq j} d_{ij} \tag{1}$$

where N is the number of all nodes, d_{ij} is the shortest path length from node i to node j.

Table 2. The shortest path length.

No.	Name	Cost
1	The Paper	0
2	Vegetable Shi Jun	1
3	Ka Deng Ren	2
4	Qing leaves for Chang'an	3
5	He Zhe_	4

The average path length between the source information node 's surging news' and the main nodes is 0.55. The short average path indicates that the speed of information propagation is fast, the centrality of source nodes is very high, and the nodes between networks are dense. There are three main reasons for the short propagation path and dense nodes: 1) The theme of rumors is food safety, which touches people's sensitive nerves and triggers the fierce reaction of Internet users, making the spread faster and wider; 2) As a big V of millions of fans, 's surging news' has great influence; 3) The speed of refuting rumors is fast, which effectively prevents the event from continuing to ferment.

Node Analysis. Figure 3 show the important nodes of three different stages in the process of spreading and anti-rumor.

At the beginning of the event, 'The Papers' is the primary node of communication, and the number of forwarding, comment and praise of the other important nodes are much less than those of 'The Papers'. It can be judged that the rumor information obtained by most users is directly from 'The Papers'.

In the investigation progress stage, the number of main nodes increased. We-media has carried out science popularization and rumor suppression spontaneously. However, they are mostly researchers in related fields, while Internet users as fans are selective attention to different areas of we-media, so we-media influence is limited. Compared with the tens of thousands of likes of 'The Papers' in the first stage, it can be seen that the influence of rumor refutation of we-media in this stage is far from enough to reverse the rumors.

At the stage of the investigation results, the official micro-blogs of government ministries and mainstream news media accounted for half of the important nodes, and the numbers of likes, comments and forwarding are several times larger than the relevant micro-blogs of we-media and other micro-blogs of the same phase. Different from the we-media, whether to follow the news has little correlation with the user's interest preferences. The news media has a large user base, which can gain widespread attention.

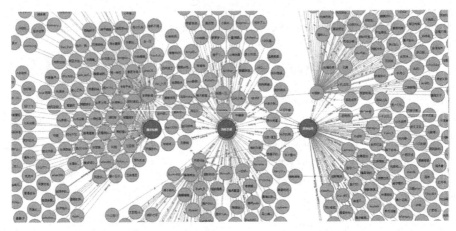

Fig. 3. User distribution map at different stages.

5   Conclusion

This paper constructs the propagation topic map for the event of 'Rumors of illegal soaking antibacterial agent for Wuming fertile orange', and analyzes the influence of nodes and the evolution of public opinion. Based on the above research, the following suggestions on rumor governance and public opinion guidance are put forward: 1) The official media respond to public opinion events in time. Making full use of the initial discussion heat to refute rumors is helpful to expand the spread scope and influence of microblog, and a timely response can prevent the further spread of negative emotions and greater losses. 2) Make full use of the official information release platform, improve self-information dissemination system. The mainstream media are authoritative, reliable and influential. The response of official media to negative public opinion events can speed up the process of anti-rumors and strengthen the guidance of public opinion. 3) Make full use of the influence of we-media. We-media often question the unreasonable parts of rumors based on professional knowledge. Their response speed is faster than the official response, which can shorten the time to refute rumors.

Acknowledgement. Work described in this paper was funded by the National Natural Science Foundation of China under Grant No.71671093, and Jiangsu Provincial Graduate Research and Innovation Program No.KYCX20_0832.

References

1. Xu, Shi, Quan, et al.: https://mp.weixin.qq.com/s/bhk6iZdphif74HJlyUZOBQ. Last accessed 5 Jan 2020
2. Jun, Z.: Knowledge Graph. Higher Education Press, Beijing (2018)
3. Liu, J., Fang, R.: Research on the visualization of Nanyin characteristic resources based on topic maps. In: 3rd International Workshop on Materials Engineering and Computer Sciences (IWMECS), pp. 358–362. ACSR-Advances in Comptuer Science Research, Jinan (2018)
4. Marrone, M., Linnenluecke, M.: Interdisciplinary research maps: a new technique for visualizing research topics. PLOS ONE **15**(11) (2020)
5. Mi, Y., Moon, S., Ryu, G.: A topic map keyword extraction technique using dietary dessert cafe selection attributes and a recommendation system based on wide deep learning. Soc. Converg. Knowl. Trans. **9**(2), 11–24 (2021)
6. Zhou, J., Fan, Y., Zhang, J.: Generating knowledge maps for songs and users in music market with probabilistic topic model. In: 5th IEEE International Conference on Big Data Computing Service and Applications, pp. 83–92. IEEE Computer Soc, San Francisco (2019)
7. Yang, H.: Learning topic map from large scale social media data. In: 29th World Wide Web Conference (WWW), pp. 279–283. Assoc Computing Machinery, Taipei (2020)
8. Zheng, H.: Research on the Construction Method of Character Graph Based on Microblog. Xihua University, Chengdu (2017)
9. Li, D., Zhang, Y., et al.: Overview of entity relation extraction methods. Comput. Res. Dev. **57**(07), 1424–1448 (2020)
10. Wang, C., Xu, J., Zhang, Y.: Summary of entity relation extraction. Comput. Eng. Appl. **56**(12), 25–36 (2020)

Communication

Pilot Reuse Joint Partial APs in Cell-Free Massive MIMO System

Xingyu He[(✉)] and Yang Liu

Beijing University of Posts and Telecommunications, Beijing, China
{hexingyu,ly}@bupt.edu.cn

Abstract. In this paper, we propose a pilot reuse scheme based on partial access points (APs) for the performance of the uplink link level. Considering the interaction between pilot reuse and channel gain, this scheme proposes the concept of minimizing the sum of the normalized errors of the estimated channel between the user and selected APs and suppress intral channel interference of user groups using non-orthogonal pilots. The scheme's performance is reflected and analyzed by the uplink rate, and the simulation results show that the proposed scheme has achieved remarkable results compared with the existing schemes.

Keywords: Cell-Free Massive MIMO · MMSE combing · Pilot contamination · AP selection · Channel estimation

1 Introduction

Cell-free Massive MIMO (multiple input multiple output, MIMO) as a distributed Massive MIMO system is composed of a central processing unit (CPU) and multiple access points (APs) [1]. The high computational capability of the CPU and the better anti-shadowing attenuation performance of distributed access points make Cell-free Massive MIMO more competitive. In cell-free massive MIMO systems, the importance of the accuracy channel estimation lies in the fact that the system utilizes the estimated channel state information rather than the assumed one [2]. A lot of research focus on how to minimize the influence of the channel estimation error and use the receiving vector to select and amplify the required signal from the received signal. [3] Proposed that the combined vector with minimizes the mean square error processing is more beneficial to improve the system link-level performance than the maximum ratio (MR) processing. Although minimum mean-squared error (MMSE) combing is much more computation-complex than maximum ratio (MR) processing, it is no longer challenging to use minimum mean-squared error (MMSE) combing vector to process information by sending pilot information and data information collected from AP to CPU with high computing power through the return link.

In addition, [1–3] believes that the channel state of the user will only behave well in local-range distributed access points. In contrast, out-of-locality APs will

Q. Zu et al. (Eds.): HCC 2021, LNCS 13795, pp. 171–182, 2022.
https://doi.org/10.1007/978-3-031-23741-6_16

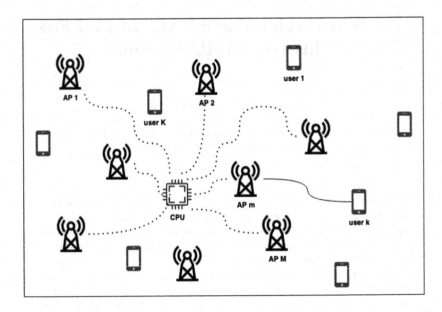

Fig. 1. Cell-Free Massive MIMO system

behave poorly in system link performance. [4] proposes a series of options for selecting partial access points to serve every user, as opposed to having every user served every access point, [5,6] when capacity limitations and hardware damage are considered for backhaul loads in the system.

In the cell-free system training phase, the channel estimation error is exacerbated by the fact that we can not guarantee that the pilots owned by each user are orthogonal when the coherence interval allocated to pilot signals is much shorter than the number of users. The clustering method proposed in [7] avoids intra-cluster interference by ensuring that the user size in each cluster is less than the number of orthogonal pilots. Still, it cannot guarantee that the orthogonal pilots are fully utilized, and the out-cluster interference will be worse when adjacent users outside between clusters have the same pilot. [8] results in the reduction of pilot contamination to enlarge spatial separation between the two users. It means that pilot reuse time is only once, which requires a large amount of pilot resource overhead in the cell Free system with many users. [9] proposes to consider the minimum correlation between non-orthogonal users, which depends heavily on selecting the first batch of users, and the correlation between subsequent sets of iterative users is not considered.

In this paper, we propose a pilot reuse scheme to improve system link performance and use the method of receiving a combination vector with the minimum mean square error between selected access points to maximize the mutual information between channels [10]. The main contributions of this paper are as follows:

- We propose MMSE receive combining with channel state information (CSI) of partial selected APs and apply it to deduce achievable SE expressions.

- The proposed user group schedule is motivated by pilot resource overhead and channel interference between adjacent users. We ensure that pilot resources are fully utilized, and intra-cluster interference is suppressed to improve the uplink performance of users.
- The proposed pilot reuse scheme aims to suppress out-cluster interference. The simulation results show that the proposed pilot reuse scheme is superior to other tasks.

The rest of this paper is organized as follows. Section 2 describes the system model and spectral efficiency. In Sect. 3, the proposed user schedule scheme and pilot reuse scheme are introduced in detail. Simulation results are shown in Sect. 4. In Sect. 5, the conclusion of this paper is presented.

2   System Model and Spectral Efficiency

2.1   Channel Estimation

We consider a Cell-free Massive MIMO system with M two-dimensional uniformly distributed Aps and K randomly distributed users, operating in time division duplex (TDD) mode. Each single-antenna user is served by more than one N-antenna equipped Aps and the amount of Aps is more than the number of users($M >> K$). The central processing unit (CPU) exchanges the network information with all APs via fronthaul networks with finite capacity and capable of error-free operation [1]. The channel $\mathbf{h}_{m,k}$ for every $m = 1,..,M, k = 1,...,K$ is associated to the spatial correlation matrix $\mathbf{R}_{m,k}$ [3] and is denoted as:

$$\mathbf{R}_{m,k} = \mathrm{E}\{\mathbf{h}_{m,k}\mathbf{h}_{m,k}^{\mathrm{H}}\} \tag{1}$$

the diagonal elements of $\mathbf{R}_{m,k} \in C^{N \times N}$ mean the large-scale fading $\beta_{m,k}$, and the off-diagonal ones describe the correlation among channels.

In the uplink training phase, pilot sequences are the uplink training sequences used for channel estimation. L imited by the length of coherence interval for the uplink training channel, there are not enough pilots for each user, so that several users assign the same pilot. We denote $\boldsymbol{\eta} = \{\boldsymbol{\eta}_1, \boldsymbol{\eta}_2, ..., \boldsymbol{\eta}_{\tau_p}\}$ as the set of all users, where $\boldsymbol{\eta}_\tau$ is the set of users allocated by the τ-th pilot sequence. And we consider that pilot signals designed as mutually orthogonal pilot sequences are regularly assigned to K users, and the normalized form of pilot sequences with the length of τ_p and set the pilot sequence allocated to the k-th user as $\sqrt{\tau_p}\varphi_{i_k}, i_k \in \{1, ..., \tau_p\}$ is the subscript representing the pilot sequence allocated by the kth user.

$$\varphi_{i_k}^{H}\varphi_{i_j} = \begin{cases} 1, j \in \eta_\tau \\ 0, j \notin \eta_\tau \end{cases} \tag{2}$$

In the process of uplink training transmission, each access point will receive the pilot signals sent by K users at the same time, so the pilot signal matrix received at the m-th access point $\mathbf{Y}_m^{\mathrm{p}} \in C^{N \times \tau_p}$ can be expressed as:

$$\mathbf{Y}_m^{\mathrm{p}} = \sum_{k=1}^{K} \sqrt{\rho_k \tau_p}\mathbf{h}_{m,k}\varphi_{i_k}^{H} + \mathbf{N}_m \tag{3}$$

where $N_m \in C^{N \times \tau_p}$ is the gaussian noise matrix and its components are independent identically distributed complex Gaussian random variables. And ρ_k is the transmit power of the k-th user. In order to obtain the estimated channel between the k-th user and the m-th access point, we need to use φ_{i_k} to despread the matrix Y_m^p received by the m-th access point to obtain the processed pilot signal vector $y_{m,k}^p$.

$$
\begin{aligned}
y_{m,k}^p &= \frac{1}{\sqrt{\rho_k \tau_p}} Y_m^p \varphi_{i_k} \\
&= \sqrt{\tau_p \rho_k} \sum_{k=1}^{K} \mathbf{h}_{m,k} \varphi_{i_k}^H \varphi_{i_k} + \mathbf{n}_m \varphi_{i_k} \\
&= \sqrt{\tau_p \rho_k} \sum_{k' \in \eta_\tau} \mathbf{h}_{m,k'} + \eta_m
\end{aligned}
\tag{4}
$$

By using MMSE estimation, the channel estimation between the k-th user and the m-th AP, is given by:

$$
\hat{\mathbf{h}}_{m,k} = \sqrt{\tau_p \rho_k} \mathbf{R}_{m,k} \Big(\sum_{k' \in \eta_\tau} \tau_p p_{k'} \mathbf{R}_{m,k} + I_N \Big)^{-1} y_{m,k}^{\tau_p}
\tag{5}
$$

With the imperfect estimates, the channel estimation error cannot be ignored. We can denote the channel estimate error as $\tilde{\mathbf{h}}_{m,k} = \mathbf{h}_{m,k} - \hat{\mathbf{h}}_{m,k}$. The covariance error matrix is:

$$
e_{m,k} = \mathrm{E}\{(\mathbf{h}_{m,k} - \hat{\mathbf{h}}_{m,k})(\mathbf{h}_{m,k} - \hat{\mathbf{h}}_{m,k})^H\}
\tag{6}
$$

2.2   Uplink Data Transmission and Spectral Efficiency

In the uplink data transmission, all users synchronously transmit the data signal to the Aps. Thus, the received signal at the m-th AP is given by:

$$
y_m^{\tau_d} = \sum_{k=1}^{K} \sqrt{\rho_k} \mathbf{h}_{m,k} \mathbf{s}_k + \mathbf{n}_m
\tag{7}
$$

where $\mathbf{s}_k$ is the data signal of the k-th user, $\mathrm{E}\{|\mathbf{s}_k|^2\} = 1$, ρ_k is the data power of the k-th users, and the additive noise $\mathbf{n}_m \sim \mathcal{CN}(0, \sigma^2 I)$ is independent.

It is recommended to select a subset of APs for the k-th user [4]. The m-th Ap belonging to the set of $\boldsymbol{m}_k$ sends $y_m^{\tau_d}$ to the CPU via networks, and CPU forms $\mathbf{v}_{m,k}$ by the channel estimation information to process the signal from APs and obtain the estimation of the data signal. The processing signal of the k-th user at the CPU can be expressed as:

$$
\begin{aligned}
r_{d,k} &= \sum_{m \in \boldsymbol{m}_k} \mathbf{v}_{m,k}^H y_m^{\tau_d} = \sqrt{\rho_k} \sum_{m \in \boldsymbol{m}_k} \mathbf{v}_{m,k}^H \mathbf{h}_{m,k} \mathbf{s}_k \\
&+ \sum_{k' \neq k}^{K} \sqrt{\rho_{k'}} \sum_{m \in \boldsymbol{m}_{k'}} \mathbf{v}_{m,k'}^H \mathbf{h}_{m,k'} \mathbf{s}_{k'} + \sum_{m \in \boldsymbol{m}_k} \mathbf{v}_{m,k}^H \mathbf{n}_m
\end{aligned}
\tag{8}
$$

Then, the spectral efficiency of the k-th user using the combining vector is given as:

$$\text{SE}_k = (1 - \lambda)\text{E}\{\log_2(1 + \frac{\rho_k|\sum_{m\in m_k} \mathbf{v}_{k,m}^H \hat{\mathbf{h}}_{k,m}|^2}{\psi_i + \psi_e + \psi_n})\} \tag{9}$$

where λ, the proportion of the pilot in the coherence interval, is denoted as τ_p/τ_c, ψ_i, ψ_e and ψ_n respectively the interference caused by the undesired signal, the uncertainty caused by channel errors and the noise result. They can be defined as:

$$\psi_i = \sum_{k'\neq k}^K \rho_k | \sum_{m\in m_k} \mathbf{v}_{m,k}^H \hat{\mathbf{h}}_{m,k'}|^2 = \rho_k \sum_{k'\neq k}^K |\mathbf{v}_k^H \hat{\mathbf{h}}_{k'}|^2$$

$$\psi_e = \rho_k \sum_{k=1}^K \sum_{m\in m_k} \mathbf{v}_{m,k}^H e_{m,k} \mathbf{v}_{m,k} = \rho_k \sum_{k=1}^K \mathbf{v}_k^H e_k \mathbf{v}_k \tag{10}$$

$$\psi_n = \sigma^2 \sum_{m\in m_k} \mathbf{v}_{m,k}^H \mathbf{v}_{m,k} = \sigma^2 \mathbf{v}_k^H \mathbf{v}_k$$

2.3 Partial AP Selected MMSE Combining (PAS-MMSE)

We consider that the combing vector of the k-th user with PAS-MMSE can be $\mathbf{v}_k^{MMSE} = \rho_k \mathbf{HC}^{-1}\hat{\mathbf{h}}_k$, where

$$\mathbf{HC} = \sum_{k=1}^K \rho_k \hat{\mathbf{h}}_k \hat{\mathbf{h}}_k^H + \sum_{k=1}^K \rho_k e_k + \sigma^2 \mathbf{I}_{NKL} \tag{11}$$

where $\hat{\mathbf{h}}_k \in C^{NKL\times 1}$ only Combines with the estimated channel $\hat{\mathbf{h}}_{m,k}, m \in m_k$, $e_k \in C^{NKL\times NKL}$ is the block-diagonal combined matrix with $e_{m,k}, m \in m_k$.

3 Pilot Resource Allocation for Cell-free System

In the Cell-free Massive MIMO system, two key factors affecting channel estimation accuracy are channel gain and reused pilots. Channel estimation between the user and APs could get terrible, especially if others assigned the user-owned pilot has better channel gain. So, we consider the combined effect of AP selection and pilot reuse on the quality of cell-free communications and propose a partial AP-based pilot allocation scheme. The main strategies of the method are divided into the following key points:

Key point 1: We try to cluster the users suitable for orthogonal pilots into the same group and ensure that K users are pressed into n_c user groups, each containing τ_p users. Let $\boldsymbol{\lambda} = \{\boldsymbol{\lambda}_1, ..., \boldsymbol{\lambda}_{n_c}\}$ denote the set of all user groups and $\boldsymbol{\lambda}_n$ represents the set of the n-th group users. The K-means algorithm, a suitable approach to govern the pilot allocation process, aims to divide k elements into n clusters according to a certain strategy. We rely on K-means algorithm and the metric of $\mathbf{loc}^{ue}$ named the set of user positions to obtain user groups and their corresponding centroid and consider $\mathbf{ctr} = \{ctr_1, ..., ctr_{n_c}\}$ as the centroid set, where the centroid of n-th user group is ctr_n and take Euclidean distance as the similarity and distance criterion:

$$d_n = \sum_{x_i \in \lambda_n} ||x_i - ctr_n||^2 \tag{12}$$

where x_i is the i-th user's coordinate value. The goal is to obtain the minimum sum of squares of distances:

$$\text{minimize} \sum_{n=1}^{n_c} \sum_{x_i \in \lambda_n} ||x_i - ctr_n||^2 \tag{13}$$

since the clustering algorithms does not guarantee any of the resulting clusters from having a number of users equivalent to τ_p, our approach is to remove redundant users or fill in absent users in the user groups. By rolling out absent users into adjacent user groups or filling nearby users into the absent one, we make sure that the user size of each group does not exceed τ_p. The key steps of this strategy are as follows:

1)We determine the user groups by utilizing the centroid set. Specific search criteria are as follows:

$$n \leftarrow \arg\max_{n \in n_c} \{|ctr_c - ctr_n|\} \tag{14}$$

where ctr_n represent the m-th cluster center, and ctr_c is the local center. Once the user group is selected, it can no longer be chosen.

2) Adjust the size of the user group. We denote the user size of η_n as us_n and the dependent one η_n as $us_{n,d}$.

If us_n is less than τ_p, we consider preferentially moving outsize-cluster users that are close to the user set and get the distance of all users in the dependent user group to the n-th centroid. The distance is given by:

$$dt_k^{in} = |loc_k - ctr_n| \tag{15}$$

where k is the k-th user in the dependent one, then the distances are ordered according to their magnitude. The sorted result is given by:

$$\mathbf{dt}^{in} = \{dt_1^{in}, ..., dt_{us_{n,d}}^{in}\}(dt_1^{in} < ... < dt_{us_{n,d}}^{in}) \tag{16}$$

Pull $\mathbf{U}_{abs}$ named the users corresponding to the first $\tau_p - us_n$ element in the set $\mathbf{dt}$ from η_m into η_n.

If us_n exceeds τ_p, although the edge users of the user set are best pushed out of the user set, part of they are not suitable to belong to other clusters. We should get the distance of all users in η_n to the m-th centroid. The distance is given by:

$$dt_k^{out} = \frac{|loc_k - ctr_n|}{\min_{ctr_m \in \mathbf{ctr} \backslash ctr_n} |loc_k - ctr_m|} \tag{17}$$

where k is the k-th user in η_n. Then, the distances are ordered according to their magnitude. The sorted result is given by:

$$\mathbf{dt}^{out} = \{dt_1^{out}, ..., dt_{us_n}^{out}\}(dt_1^{out} < ... < dt_{us_n}^{out}) \tag{18}$$

push $\mathbf{U}_{red}$ named as the users corresponding to the first $us_n - \tau_p$ elements in the set $\mathbf{dt}$ from η_n into η_m. This process is performed until all user obtain pilot and the proposed algorithm is given in Algorithm 1.

Input: the coordinate set of area users $\mathbf{loc}^{ue}$ and the orthogonal pilot number $\mathbf{n}_c$;

Output: the cluster result set $\lambda_1, \lambda_2, ..., \lambda_{n_c}$;

step 1: Initialize category and result set $\boldsymbol{\lambda}$;

step 2: The remaining step of the algorithm is to group users;

step 3: it will be based on the coordinate set $\mathbf{loc}^{ue}$ and the number of current classification categories n_c perform a kmeans clustering to obtain the cluster center set $\mathbf{ctr}$;

step 4: Calculate the geometric distance from each cluster center to the region center, and find the corresponding clustering result set λ_n according to the maximum geometric distance from the region center ctr_c;

step 5–14: Different adjustment strategies are implemented according to the number of users in the clustering result set λ_n;

step 15: If the adjustment is not completed, return to step 2, otherwise end the process.

Key point 2: This point concentrates on pilot assignment. We know that channel estimation in (2) is affected by channel gain and pilot reuse. Taking two factors into account, we propose partial-AP based pilot reuse scheme. To select partial APs with substantial channel gain for k-th user, we define the scheduled-AP set for the k-th user as follows:

$$\underset{\mathbf{m}_k \subset \{1,...,M\}}{\text{maximize}} \sum_{m \in \mathbf{m}_k} \text{tr}(\mathbf{R}_{m,k}) \tag{19}$$

Relying on $\mathbf{m}_k$, we define the sum of the normalized channel estimation errors of the k-th user as follows:

$$\zeta_k = \sum_{m \in \mathbf{m}_k} \zeta_{m,k} \tag{20}$$

$$\zeta_{m,k} = \text{tr}(e_{m,k}\mathbf{R}_{m,k}^{-1}) \tag{21}$$

where

$$e_{m,k} = \mathbf{R}_{m,k} - \mathbf{R}_{m,k}(\sum_{k' \in \eta_\tau} \tau_p p_{k'} \mathbf{R}_{m,k} + \mathbf{I}_N)^{-1}\mathbf{R}_{m,k} \tag{22}$$

We firstly select $\boldsymbol{\lambda}_n, \forall n \in \mathbf{n}_c$ and users in $\boldsymbol{\lambda}_n$ can be randomly assigned to $\boldsymbol{\eta}_\tau$, $\tau = 1, .., \tau_p$ respectively due that $\boldsymbol{\eta}_\tau = \emptyset, \forall \tau$. Next, we solve the pilot allocation of other user groups one by one. Our main purpose is to make interior interference that affects channel estimation accuracy as small as possible. ζ_k will be different

---

Algorithm 1. Push Or Pull User Schedule Algorithm (POP-USA)

Input: n_c, loc^{ue}
Output: $\lambda_1, \lambda_2, ..., \lambda_{n_c}$
  1: **Initalize** $\boldsymbol{\lambda}$
  2: **for** $n = 1 \rightarrow (n_c - 1)$ **do**
  3:     $[\mathbf{index}, \mathbf{ctr}] = kmeans(n, \mathbf{loc}^{ue})$, the initial user-cluster set and the centroid set
  4:     Find $n \leftarrow \arg\max\limits_{n \in \mathbf{n}_c}\{|ctr_c - ctr_n|\}$, the group number by utilizing the centroid set
  5:     Set $\mathbf{n}_c \backslash n \rightarrow \mathbf{n}_c$, get rid of n in $\mathbf{n}_c$
  6:     Find λ_n from $\mathbf{index}$, the n-th user group
  7:     **if** $us_n < \tau_p$ **then**
  8:         Obtain dt_k^{in} by the formula (13), generate $\mathbf{dt}^{in}$ in ascending order
  9:         Pull $\mathbf{U}_{abs}$ into λ_n
 10:     **end if**
 11:     **if** $us_n > \tau_p$ **then**
 12:         Obtain dt_k^{out} by the formula (15), generate $\mathbf{dt}^{out}$ in ascending order
 13:         Push $\mathbf{U}_{red}$ out of λ_n
 14:     **end if**
 15: **end for**

---

if the k-th user are selected into different $\boldsymbol{\eta}_\tau$, so our goal is to find $\boldsymbol{\eta}_\tau$ that minimizes ζ_k. The selective criterion is applied as follows:

$$\tau \leftarrow \arg\min_{\tau \in \tau_p} [\zeta_k(\tau)] \tag{23}$$

After the k-th user finds the appropriate one, update the k-th user into $\boldsymbol{\eta}_\tau$. This process is performed until all users obtain pilot, and we give the proposed algorithm in Algorithm 2.

Input: the cluster result set λ, the spatial correlation matrix R and the coordinate set of area users $\mathbf{loc}^{ue}$;
Output: The pilot allocation set $\eta_1, \eta_2, ..., \eta_{\tau_p}$;
Step 1: Initialize the pilot allocation set $\boldsymbol{\eta}$;
Step 2: Randomly select user group $\lambda_{n`}, \forall n` \in \mathbf{n}_c$ to allocate pilots;
Step 3: Assign pilots to the remaining user groups in turn;
Step 4–6: Define the available pilot set $\tau_p = \{1, ..., \tau_p\}$ and perform pilot allocation for users in the group according to (23);
Step 7: Update pilot result set η_τ and available pilot set τ_p;
Step 8: If the pilot allocation in the group is not completed, return to step 4, otherwise go on the next step;
Step 9: If the assigned tasks are not completed, return to step 3, otherwise end the process.

Algorithm 2. Partial AP based Pilot Reuse Algorithm (PAB-PR)

Input: loc^{ue}, R, λ
Output: $\eta_1, \eta_2, ..., \eta_{\tau_p}$;
  1: **Initalize η**
  2: Randomly assign τ_p orthogonal pilots to the users of $\lambda_{n'}, \forall n' \in \mathbf{n}_c$, set
     $\lambda \backslash \{\lambda_{n'}\} \rightarrow \lambda$
  3: **for** $n \in \mathbf{n}_c \backslash \{n'\}$ **do**
  4:     Define $\tau_p = \{1, ..., \tau_p\}$
  5:     **for** $k \in \lambda_n$ **do**
  6:         Find $\tau \leftarrow \arg\min_{\tau \in \tau_p}[\zeta_k(\tau)]$, the subscript of users set for the non-
     orthogonal pilot
  7:         Set $\eta_\tau \cup k \rightarrow \eta_\tau, \tau_p \backslash \tau \rightarrow \tau_p$
  8:     **end for**
  9: **end for**

---

4 Simulation and Numerical Analysis

This section evaluates the performance of the proposed PAB-PR scheme in the uplink cell-free massive MIMO network.100 APs with 4 antennas are two-dimensional deployed in a 1×1 km squared coverage area. The channel coherence blocks contain $\tau_c = 200$ time samples. We consider that channel model matches well with the 3GPP Urban Microcell model [2]. The large-scale fading coefficient between the k-th user and the m-th Ap can be expressed in dB as:

$$\beta_{m,k}[\text{dB}] = \gamma - 10\alpha \log_{10}\left(\frac{d_{m,k}}{1km}\right) + F_{m,k} \qquad (24)$$

where dkl is the distance between the k-th user and the m-th Ap(computed as the one in [2]) and $F_{mk} \mathcal{N}(0, 4^2)$ is the shadow fading. The channel bandwidth W = 20 MHZ and the per-user transmit power $p_k = 100$ mW.

The points with the same color in the Fig. 1 represent the users assigned to the same group, and Fig. 1a shows the result of user grouping obtained by K-means and Fig. 1b represents the user grouping result obtained by using POP-USA algorithms. Comparing a and b in Fig. 1, we can find that POP-USA algorithms not only has significant effect on the adjustment of user grouping but also achieves uniformity which K-means algorithm can do. Figure 2 shows the average up linking spectrum rates for users with three different pilot allocation schemes. We can see that the uplink rates of these methods are close to the rates of all selected Aps when we selectively allocate 60 Aps to serve each user, which is consistent with the reality under the action of AP selection and it indicates that an AP with channel ill-conditioned is not suitable for users to improve uplink performance and the pilot reuse scheme outperforms the other two pilot allocation schemes. Simulation results show that the proposed pilot frequency allocation algorithm is effective. Figure 3 show the cumulative distribution of per-user uplink SE for different k. Results show our pilot reuse scheme does well, especially the uplink

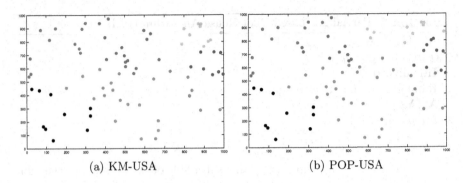

(a) KM-USA   (b) POP-USA

Fig. 2. The comparison of clusterization for users. Here, $M = 80, \tau_p = 10$. Circle markers represent users and colors identify the distinct user group. (color figure online)

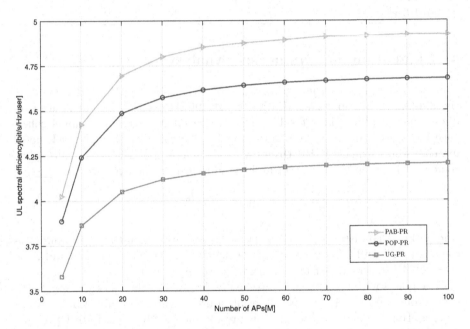

Fig. 3. The average UL SE of different pilot reuse scheme versus the number of selected APs with $M = 100, K = 80$

SE exceeding $2\,bit/s/Hz$. When k doubles, that is, the inter-user interference increases, the SE attenuation of PAB-PR is less, indicating that our scheme has stronger pilot control ability (Fig. 4).

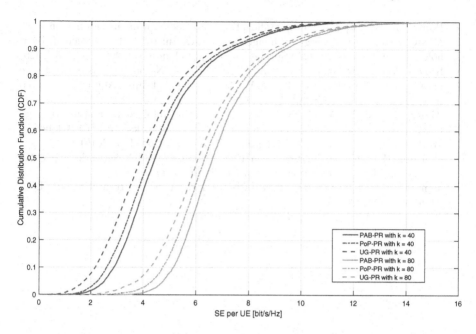

Fig. 4. The cumulative distribution (CDF) of the per-user SE with $\tau_p = 10, KL = 60$

5   Conclusions

In this paper, we designed a pilot reuse scheme with selected Aps for Cell-free Massive MIMO system. Taking advantage of the distributed Aps' characteristics, we form a receive vector based on partial user-friendly pilots and consider them into pilot reuse analysis and analyze the impact of three different pilot allocation schemes on the system performance. Numerical results show that our scheme is superior to the other two schemes.

References

1. Ngo, H.Q., Ashikhmin, A., Yang, H., Larsson, E.G., Marzetta, T.L.: Cell-free massive MIMO versus small cells. IEEE Trans. Wireless Commun. **16**(3), 1834–1850 (2017)
2. Mai, T.C., Ngo, H.Q., Egan, M., Duong, T.Q.: Pilot power control for cell-free massive MIMO. IEEE Trans. Veh. Technol. **67**(11), 11264–11268 (2018)
3. Björnson, E., Sanguinetti, L.: Making cell-free massive MIMO competitive with MMSE processing and centralized implementation. IEEE Trans. Wireless Commun. **19**(1), 77–90 (2020)
4. Buzzi, S., Andrea, C.D.: Cell-free massive MIMO: user-centric approach. IEEE Wirel. Commun. Lett. **6**(6), 706–709 (2017)
5. Ngo, H.Q., Tran, L., Duong, T.Q., Matthaiou, M., Larsson, E.G.: On the total energy efficiency of cell-free massive MIMO. IEEE Trans. Green Commun. Netw. **2**(1), 25–39 (2018)

6. Hamdi, R., Qaraqe, M.: Power allocation and cooperation in cell-free massive MIMO systems with energy exchange capabilities. In: IEEE 91st Vehicular Technology Conference (VTC2020-Spring), Antwerp, Belgium, vol. 2020, pp. 1–5 (2020)
7. Riera-Palou, F., Femenias, G., Armada, A.G., Poérez-Neira, A.: Clustered cell-free massive MIMO. In: IEEE Globecom Workshops (GC Wkshps), Abu Dhabi, United Arab Emirates, vol. 2018, pp. 1–6 (2018)
8. Akbar, N., Yan, S., Yang, N., Yuan, J.: Mitigating pilot contamination through location-aware pilot assignment in massive MIMO networks. In: IEEE Globecom Workshops (GC Wkshps), Washington, DC, vol. 2016, pp. 1–6 (2016)
9. Björnson, E., Hoydis, J., Sanguinetti, L.: Massive MIMO Networks: Spectral, Energy, and Hardware Efficiency. Now Publishers, Delft (2017)
10. Jain, A.K.: Data clustering: 50 years beyond K-means. Pattern Recognit. Lett. **31**(8), 651–666 (2010)

Multi-task Allocation Under Multiple Constraints in Mobile Crowdsensing

Jin Liu[1], Wenan Tan[1,2]([⊠]), Zhejun Liang[1], and Kai Ding[1]

[1] Nanjing University of Aeronautics and Astronautics, Nanjing 211106, China
wtan@foxmail.com
[2] Shanghai Polytechnic University, Shanghai 201209, China

Abstract. Task allocation is a key technology in the research of mobile crowdsensing. The previous research only focused on single-task allocation, and seldom considered the monopoly nature of tasks, quality requirements, and the constraint relationship between tasks. This paper comprehensively considers the above factors and designs a multi-task allocation scheme for mobile crowdsensing to maximize the profit of the service platform. First, divide the tasks into monopoly tasks and non-monopoly tasks, and judge whether they will be executed according to the profit that monopoly tasks can bring to the platform; For non-monopoly tasks, an efficient allocation plan is designed based on genetic algorithm and greedy algorithm; Secondly, considering the quality requirements of tasks and the constraint relationship between tasks, comparing the existing classic task allocation schemes, simulation experiments verify that the proposed algorithm has better effects in terms of platform profit and task coverage.

Keywords: Mobile crowdsensing · Multi-task allocation · Monopoly task · Quality constraint · Task constrain

1 Introduction

In recent years, Mobile Crowdsensing (MCS) [6] has become a popular paradigm by borrowing a large number of people to extensively collect information. Unlike traditional sensor networks that require a large number of dedicated sensors, users in MCS can use mobile smart terminal devices (mobile phones, tablets, smart wearable devices, etc.) to collect data consciously or unconsciously. These mobile smart terminals not only have powerful functions such as storage and communication, but also are equipped with a variety of sensors, such as cameras, microphones, GPS modules, gyroscopes, and temperature sensors. Therefore, many complex and large-scale tasks that are difficult to be completed by one user alone can be broken down into many subtasks, which are allocated to

Supported by the National Natural Science Foundation of China (61672022, U1904186), Shanghai Second Polytechnic University Key Discipline Electronic Information Special Master Program Project (XXKZD1604).

multiple users equipped with mobile intelligent terminal devices to jointly complete them. Compared with traditional methods, MCS has many advantages such as flexible deployment, multi-source perception of data heterogeneity, wide and uniform coverage, and high scalability and multi-function. Therefore, MCS systems are widely used in various fields such as smart cities, smart transportation, environmental monitoring, noise detection, privacy protection, public safety, and smart medical [1,2,7,8,11,14,17].

Most of the existing MCS applications are composed of three parts: task requester, MCS platform, and task executor [5]. In the MCS system, task allocation is a core module, and the main purpose of task allocation is to find the optimal allocation plan to achieve optimization goals such as the shortest task completion time, the largest platform benefits, and full coverage of tasks. At present, many scholars have researched the MCS system, and have proposed some task allocation algorithms and incentive algorithms [5,12,13,19,20].

However, task allocation is an NP-hard problem. Many scholars use greedy algorithm to solve the approximate solution of the problem [3,13,16,22]. This paper uses genetic algorithm based on the greedy algorithm. Because only using greedy algorithm may fall into the local optimum, combined with genetic algorithm can effectively avoid the local optimum problem, and better realize the global search. Inspired by the literature [18], this paper divides the task set into two categories, one is monopoly tasks (MT), that is, tasks that only one person can complete; The other is non-monopoly tasks (NMT), that is, tasks that can be completed by multiple people. Since there is only one executor of a monopoly task, the quotation may be falsely high and unreal. The solution for this type of task in [18] is to directly delete it from the task set. This article has improved the scheme and judged the reasonableness of the commission of the monopoly task performer. If it is reasonable, the task will still be executed, otherwise, the task will be deleted. This will greatly improve task coverage. Many current studies do not consider the quality constraints of the tasks. For example, literature [13] only considers the time constraints between tasks but does not consider the quality constraints. Tasks and tasks are not independent and unrelated, so the constraint relationship between tasks should be considered when assigning. For example, literature [9,10] only considers the quality requirements of tasks and does not consider the constraint relationship between tasks. Given the above problems, this paper proposes non-monopoly tasks allocation (NMTA) and monopoly tasks allocation (MTA) respectively for NMT and MT allocation algorithms. The contributions of this article are as follows:

- Divide tasks into monopoly tasks and non-monopoly tasks, and evaluate monopoly tasks instead of directly deleting them, which can effectively increase platform profit and task coverage;
- Consider the relationship between tasks instead of dividing them independently. Combining the advantages of greedy algorithm and genetic algorithm, output task assignment sequence to maximize platform profit;
- Assign the tasks that can be completed to the performer, taking into account his capabilities, to ensure the quality of the tasks completed.

2   Related Work

There have been many studies on single task assignment. For example, Tan et al. [15] proposed the EBRA (Experience-Based incentive mechanism using Reverse Auction) algorithm. In each round of auction, the candidate with the lowest commission is selected from the set of candidates to assign tasks. However, only relying on the lowest commission for task allocation may have problems such as vicious competition or low task quality; Literature [4] designed a Bayesian asynchronous task selection algorithm, considering the distributed task selection problem of heterogeneous users with different initial locations, destinations, costs, and speeds. But these tasks mainly consider single-task assignments.

To improve the efficiency of the MCS service platform and fully develop the potential of the executors, multitasking has now become the main research direction. The purpose of the multi-task allocation strategy proposed by Wang et al. [16] is to maximize the overall benefits of the platform, and meet the minimum quality requirements of each task, and measure its quality requirements through space-time coverage. When the space-time coverage of the task is lower than the threshold, it is considered that it does not contribute to the overall benefit. Both literature [16] and literature [19] fully consider the temporal and spatial factors of task allocation but do not study the relationship constraint relationship between tasks. To improve the allocation algorithm, many scholars will add some heuristic algorithms based on the greedy algorithm to avoid the algorithm from falling into the local optimum. For example, Li et al. [13] and Xing et al. [19] both use greedy algorithms and genetic algorithms for task assignment, aiming at maximizing platform benefits and minimizing perceived costs respectively; Yan et al. [21] introduced an ant colony optimization algorithm with a recommendation function to improve the problem-solving performance. At present, the factors considered in the current research are further increasing, and time and space factors [13, 16], quality constraints [9], time constraints [13, 20], and the relationship between tasks and tasks [23] will be considered.

Some researches screen tasks before task assignment and delete some tasks that do not meet the conditions. For example, Zhang et al. [18] aimed at non-monopolistic tasks because the performers of such tasks may ask for inflated commissions. To avoid this situation, the literature [18] removes monopolistic tasks. Literature [15] also adopted this approach. However, deleting all monopoly tasks may cause some tasks that could be completed cannot be completed, which will harm the interests of the platform and is irresponsible to the task requester. Therefore, this article will add a judgment link to the authenticity of the commission of the monopoly task performer, and delete the untrue tasks instead of all monopoly tasks.

3   Problem Definition

Definition 1 (task set): The task set $T = \{t_1, t_2, \ldots, t_N\}$ is composed of N tasks issued by the requester, and each task has its minimum quality requirement

$Q = \{q_1, q_2, \ldots, q_N\}$, and the requester will give the corresponding reward $V = \{v_1, v_2, \ldots, v_N\}$ for the task after the task is completed. For example: q_1 is the minimum quality required by the task t_1, and the requester pays platform reward v_1 after t_1 is completed.

Definition 2 (executor set): M executors form an executor set $W = \{w_1, w_2, \ldots, w_M\}$. The quality set that the executor can achieve is $Q' = \{q'_1, q'_2, \ldots, q'_M\}$. The executor can perform multiple tasks. These tasks form a task subset $\Phi_i = \{\phi_{i1}, \phi_{i2}, \ldots, \phi_{ij}\} \subseteq T$, where ϕ_{ij} means that the executor i completes the jth task of the corresponding task set. After the task is completed, the quality assessment and commission settlement will be carried out. After quality evaluation, the corresponding quality set $Q_i^* = \{q_{i1}, q_{i2}, \ldots, q_{ij}\}$ is obtained, where q_{ij} represents the quality of the executor i completing the task j; the corresponding commission set is $R_i = \{r_{i,1}, r_{i,2}, \ldots, r_{i,j}\}$, where $r_{i,j}$ represents the commission obtained after the executor i completes the task j . The quality set Q_i^* is averaged to obtain the quality q'_i (show in formula 1) that can be achieved by the executor i. Only when $q'_i \geq q_j$ the executor i can perform the task j.

$$q'_i = \frac{\sum_{j=1}^{|Q_i^*|} q_{ij}}{|Q_i^*|} \tag{1}$$

Definition 3 (MCS system): MCS system consists of three parts: requester, service platform, and executor. The requester submits the task request to the platform, and the platform distributes the task to the executor. After the executor completes the task, he submits the data to the platform and gets the corresponding commission. The requester will give the platform corresponding compensation after the task is completed. The platform profit is the difference between the reward received by the platform and the commission given by the platform to the executor, and the platform will get its corresponding share of profit for each completed task.

   In this paper, we use $profit$ to denote the total profit received by the platform, and p_i to denote the profit received by the platform after the completion of task. For example, the platform assigns the task t_i to the executor w_j, and when the task t_i is completed, the platform receives the reward v_i from the task requester, and the platform also gives the executor the commission $r_{i,j}$. The profit p_i brought to the platform by task t_i completion is shown in formula 2.

$$p_i = v_i - r_{i,j} \tag{2}$$

The total profit obtained by the platform is shown in formula 3. x_i is binary 0 or 1, and when $x_i = 1$, it means that task t_i is completed.

$$profit = \sum_{i=1}^{N} x_i \, p_i \tag{3}$$

Constraint 1: Each task can only be executed by one executor at most. As shown in formula 4. Where $z_{i,k}$ represents binary 0 or 1. There are M executors in total. When $z_{i,k} = 1$, it means that task i has been executed.

$$\sum_{k=1}^{M} z_{i,k} \leq 1 \tag{4}$$

Constraint 2: The constraint relationship between tasks. Tasks are not independent, and there are certain spatial, temporal, or logical constraints between them. In this paper, the task execution priority is measured by the task depth value. The smaller the depth value, the higher the execution priority. $deep_i$ represents the depth value of the task t_i. As shown in Fig. 1, $deep_1 = deep_4 = 1$, $deep_2 = deep_5 = deep_6 = 2$, $deep_3 = deep_7 = 3$, because $deep_1 < deep_2 < deep_3, t_1 \rightarrow t_2 \rightarrow t_3$ is a legal task sequence; in the same way, because $deep_3 > deep_5 > deep_4$, $t_3 \rightarrow t_4 \rightarrow t_5$ is an illegal task sequence.

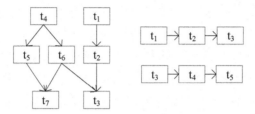

Fig. 1. The left is the task relationship diagram, the upper right is a legal sequence, and the lower right is an illegal sequence

Constraint 3: Task quality constraints. Only when the quality of the executor can complete the task is greater than or equal to the required quality of the task, the task may be assigned to the executor, otherwise it cannot be assigned to the executor.

4   MTA Framework and NMTA Framework

4.1   MTA Framework

The task division algorithm is Algorithm 1, the quality achieved by the executor is compared with the quality required by the task. The tasks that can be achieved by two or more executors are incorporated into the NMT set, and the MT that can be completed by only one person is returned to the task and the corresponding executor.

Literature [18] mentioned that the executor of monopoly tasks can ask for an arbitrarily high commission, so all monopoly tasks are deleted. This paper adds a link to evaluate the authenticity of commissions, leaving monopoly tasks with reasonable commissions, or deleting them. The monopoly task is allocated as in Algorithm 2. Tasks whose profit is lower than the expected profit of the platform will be deleted. In Algorithm 2, α is used to represent the profit rate. If the execution of the monopoly task can bring the lowest expected profit to the platform, then the task will be retained. According to the literature [10], this paper will provide additional rewards to the performer.

Algorithm 1. Task Set Partition

Input: task set T, worker set W, worker can reach quality set q, tasks require quality set Q;

Output: non-monopoly task set NMT, monopoly task and worker pair MT−W;

1: **Initialize:** $NMT \leftarrow \emptyset$, $MT\text{-}W \leftarrow \emptyset$;
2: **for** each $t_i \in T$ **do**
3:    $num \leftarrow 0$;
4:    **for** each $w_j \in W$ **do**
5:       **if** $(q_j \geq q_i')$ **then**
6:          $num \leftarrow num+1$;
7:          $w_i \leftarrow w_j$;
8:       **end if**
9:    **end for**
10:    **if** $num==1$ **then**
11:       $MT\text{-}W \leftarrow MT\text{-}W \cup \{w_i, t_i\}$;
12:    **else**
13:       $NMT \leftarrow NMT \cup \{t_i\}$;
14:    **end if**
15:    $T \leftarrow T\backslash\{t_i\}$;
16: **end for**

4.2   NMTA Framework

NMTA is based on greedy algorithm combined with genetic algorithm for task assignment.

Chromosome Coding and Fitness Function. NMTA uses character encoding, and each chromosome represents a task allocation plan. As shown in Fig. 2, C_i and C_j respectively represent two chromosomes in the population, the task is the gene on the chromosome, and the chromosome subscript represents the executor; The set of tasks to be completed by each executor is a gene fragment. For example, tasks t_6, t_8 to be completed by executor w_3 on C_j form a gene fragment; The sequence of genes represents the task assignment order of the executor. For example, the task order assigned to executor w_1 on C_i is $t_3 \rightarrow t_2 \rightarrow t_4$. The fitness function is calculated as shown in formula 5. The higher the fitness of the chromosome, the higher the profit obtained by the platform.

$$fitness(C_i) = profit = \sum_{i=1}^{N} x_i \, p_i \qquad (5)$$

Population Initialization. The population initialization is shown in Algorithm 3. The size of the population is *size*. First, find a set of candidate executors W that meet the quality constraints for each task, and randomly select an executor from W to assign tasks to him until all tasks are allocated. Then find the corresponding task set for each executor and add chromosome C, and then merge C into the population P.

Algorithm 2. Monopoly Task Allocation Mechanism

Input: Monopoly task-worker pair set MT−W, worker commission set C,worker can reach quality set q,payment of platfrom V,earning rate α;

Output: commission of worker c;

1: **for** each $w_i \in$ MT-W **do**
2:    **if** $c_{i,j} > \alpha v_j$ **then**
3:        *abortive auction of the task t_j*;
4:    **else**
5:        $c_{i,j} \leftarrow \min\{(q_i/q'_j)c_{i,j}, \ \alpha v_j\}$;
6:    **end if**
7: **end for**
8: *return c*;

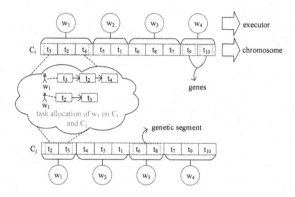

Fig. 2. Chromosome coding

Select Operation. Those with high individual fitness are more likely to be selected, and vice versa. This paper selects N chromosomes from the population to form the set of parent individuals. First, sort the fitness of all chromosomes from large to small, and select the top $M(M > N)$ chromosomes to retain excellent individuals. To avoid the convergence speed caused by prematurity, the result will fall into the local optimum, this paper will use the roulette wheel selection algorithm to select $N - M$ chromosomes from the remaining chromosomes.

Cross Operation. The purpose of the crossover operation is to preserve the excellent gene fragments in the chromosomes so that they can be passed on to the next generation. In this paper, two chromosomes are randomly selected from the parental individuals, the corresponding gene fragments are compared, and the gene fragments with greater fitness are passed on to the offspring. As shown in Fig. 3.

Mutation Operation. The mutation operation can increase the diversity of the population. The mutation operation in this article is to randomly select two

---

Algorithm 3. Population Initialization

Input: Non−monopoly task set NMT, worker set W, population size;

Output: population P;

 1: **Initialize:** $C \leftarrow \emptyset$, $W^* \leftarrow W$, $T^* \leftarrow NMT$, $W' \leftarrow \emptyset$, $P \leftarrow \emptyset$, iteration counter
    $num \leftarrow 0$;

 2: **while** $num < size$ **do**

 3:     **for** each $t_j \in T^*$ **do**

 4:         **for** each $w_i \in W^*$ **do**

 5:             **if** $q_i > q'_j$ **then**

 6:                 $W' \leftarrow W' \cup \{w_i\}$;

 7:             **end if**

 8:         **end for**

 9:         *randomly select a worker* $w \in W'$;

10:         *allocate* t_j *to* w;

11:     **end for**

12:     $C \leftarrow$ *find the corresponding task set for each worker*;

13:     $P \leftarrow P \cup C$;

14:     $num \leftarrow num + 1$;

15: **end while**

16: *return P*;

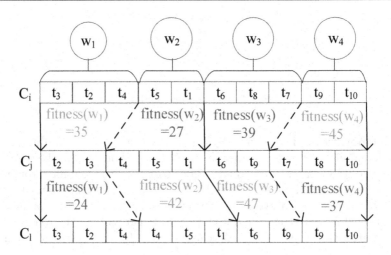

Fig. 3. Cross operation

points on the chromosome to exchange the genes corresponding to these two points, that is, to exchange the tasks corresponding to these two points.

Legalization Operation. In this paper, the chromosomes that meet constraint 1, constraint 2, and constraint 3 at the same time are called legal chromosomes. And the chromosome that violates constraint 1, constraint 2, or constraint 3 is called an illegal chromosome.

After crossover and mutation operations, chromosomes may become illegal chromosomes. Because the tasks t_4, t_9 in the chromosome C_l in Fig. 3 are repeatedly assigned to violate constraint 1, C_l is an illegal chromosome. This article legalizes illegal chromosomes and turns them into legal chromosomes. The legalization operation is shown in Algorithm 4.

In Algorithm 4, when constraint 3 is violated, the task is deleted from the gene fragment; When constraint 1 is violated, the task depth in the gene fragment is arranged in ascending order to adjust the task sequence; When constraint 2 is violated, the fitness values of all gene fragments containing repetitive tasks will be compared, the gene fragment with the greatest fitness will be retained, and the repetitive task will be deleted from the remaining gene fragments. As shown in Fig. 3, after the crossover operation, t_7 and t_8 do not appear in the offspring. This paper will collect the unassigned tasks, and then randomly select an unassigned task and assign it to the executor who meets the constraints.

5 Simulation Experiment and Analysis

In this paper, mobile crowdsensing multi-task allocation is proposed to maximize the benefits of the platform, comprehensively consider the task quality constraints and the constraint relationship between tasks. For monopoly tasks and non-monopoly tasks, two allocation schemes of MTA and NMTA are proposed respectively. In the simulation experiment, this paper regards the sum of the benefits of MTA and NMTA as the total benefits of the platform and the sum of the tasks assigned by MTA and NMTA as the total tasks assigned. In this paper, MTA and NMTA are collectively referred to as MTA-NMTA. Zhang et al. [18] proposed a multi-task allocation scheme IMC-SM(Incentive Mechanism for Crowdsourcing in the Single-requester Multiple-bid) and Tan et al. [15] proposed that EBRA that uses a greedy algorithm to achieve task allocation will delete monopoly tasks before task allocation. This paper compares the MTA-NMTA algorithm with IMC-SM [18] and EBRA [15].

Every time a task is completed, the platform will get a profit, so the actual amount of tasks completed will directly affect the platform's profit. Therefore, this paper will compare the task coverage and platform profit of the three algorithms. The task coverage rate ($task\_coverage$) is shown in formula 6. The number of tasks completed is n, and the number of tasks submitted by the requester is N.

$$task\_coverage = \frac{n}{N} \tag{6}$$

Algorithm 4. Legalization Operation

Input: an illegal chromosome C, worker set W, non−monopoly task set NMT;
Output: a legal chromosome C';
1: **Initialize:** $C' \leftarrow C$;
2: **for** each genetic segment $C'_{(w_i)}, w_i \in W$ **do**
3:      **if** the quality q_i of worker w_i can achieve is less than the required quality q'_j of the task t_j assigned to w_i **then**
4:          $C'_{(w_i)} \leftarrow$ *delete the task t_j from the genetic segment $C'_{(w_i)}$;*
5:      **end if**
6:      **if** the sequence of multiple tasks assigned to worker w_i violates constraint 1 **then**
7:          $C'_{(w_i)} \leftarrow$ *sort the task depth in ascending order in genetic segment $C'_{(w_i)}$;*
8:      **end if**
9: **end for**
10: **for** each task $t_j \in NMT$ **do**
11:     $C^* \leftarrow$ *all genetic segments containing task t_j;*
12:     $C^*_{best} \leftarrow$ *the maximum fitness value of the gentic segment in C^*;*
13:     **for** each genetic segment in $C^* \backslash C^*_{best}$ **do**
14:         *delete task t_j*
15:     **end for**
16: **end for**
17: $UT \leftarrow$ *the tasks that unallocated task;*
18: **while** $UT \neq \emptyset$ **do**
19:     *select a task t from UT randomly;*
20:     $C''_{(w)} \leftarrow$ *slelct a worker w, add task t to the end of task sequence $C'_{(w)}$;*
21:     **if** $C''_{(w)}$ meets constraint 1 & constraint 2 & constraint 3 **then**
22:         $C'_{(w)} \leftarrow C''_{(w)}$;
23:     **end if**
24:     $UT \leftarrow UT \backslash \{t\}$;
25: **end while**
26: *return C';*

5.1 The Impact of Changes in the Number of Users on Algorithm Performance

This paper sets the task $N = 40$, and the relationship between the number of users and platform profit is shown in Fig. 4. We can conclude that the platform profit obtained by the MTA-NMTA algorithm will be much higher than that of EBRA and IMC-SM. The first is that the MTA-NMTA proposed in this paper will retain monopoly tasks that can bring greater benefits to the platform, while EBRA and IMC-SM will delete all monopoly tasks, resulting in lower platform profit. Secondly, the MTA-NMATA algorithm combines the greedy algorithm based on the genetic algorithm, which can find the optimal solution under comprehensive consideration of multiple constraints, while EBRA and IMC-SM only use the greedy algorithm to easily fall into the local optimal solution.

The relationship between the number of users and task coverage is shown in Fig. 5. We can conclude that the task coverage rate obtained by the MTA-NMTA algorithm will be much higher than that of EBRA and IMC-SM. This is because MTA-NMTA will retain monopoly tasks that can bring greater benefits to the platform. As can be seen from Fig. 5, the low coverage of the task at the beginning is due to the low number of performers at the beginning and the limited number of executors with strong ability. Therefore, there are more monopoly tasks, but with the increase of executors, many tasks can be well allocated. Therefore, when the number of performers reaches 10, the task coverage of MTA-NMTA will exceed 90%. When it reaches 15 people, the task coverage of MTA-NMTA will stabilize above 95%.

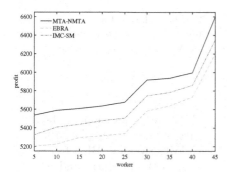
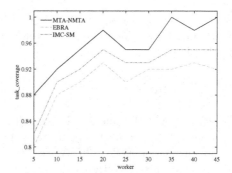

Fig. 4. The relationship between the total amount of tasks and platform profit, N = 40

Fig. 5. The relationship between the total number of tasks and the coverage of tasks, N = 40

5.2 The Impact of Changes in the Number of Tasks on Algorithm Performance

This paper sets the executor $M = 20$, and the relationship between the number of tasks and platform profit is shown in Fig. 6. As the tasks completed increase, the platform's profit has shown an upward trend. However, because the MTA-NMTA algorithm will jump out of the local optimum and the task coverage is greater than EBRA and IMC-SM, the platform profit of the MTA-NMTA algorithm will be higher than the other two algorithms.

The relationship between the number of tasks and task coverage is shown in Fig. 7 At first, the number of tasks was small, which led to a larger proportion of monopoly tasks, so the task coverage of EBRA and IMC-SM algorithms was low. Because MTA-NMTA does not delete all monopoly tasks, the task coverage of MTA-NMTA is much higher than that of EBRA and IMC-SM. As the number of tasks increases, the proportion of monopoly tasks decreases, and the task coverage of EBRA and IMC-SM algorithms begins to rise. It can be seen from Fig. 7 that the task coverage of the MTA-NMTA algorithm is higher than that of EBRA and IMC-SM.

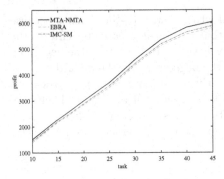
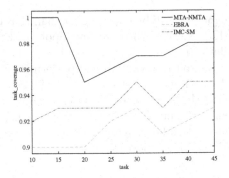

Fig. 6. The relationship between the total amount of tasks and platform profit, M = 20

Fig. 7. The relationship between the total number of tasks and the coverage of tasks, M = 20

6   Conclusion

In this paper, MTA and NMTA algorithms are designed for monopoly and non-monopoly tasks, respectively, from the perspective of maximizing platform profits. In this paper, MTA-NMTA is compared with IMC-SM and EBRA to demonstrate that this algorithm can bring more profit to the platform and achieve higher task coverage. The experimental results are in accordance with our expectation because this paper preserves the preferential choice for monopolistic tasks and effectively finds the approximate optimal solution for non-monopolistic tasks by combining genetic algorithm and greedy algorithm. In practice, there are not only simple atomic tasks (tasks completed by only one person), but also complex tasks (tasks that require the collaboration of multiple people), and in the future we will add complex task assignments to make our algorithm more realistic.

References

1. Alemdar, H., Ersoy, C.: Wireless sensor networks for healthcare: a survey. Comput. Netw. **54**(15), 2688–2710 (2010)
2. Cerotti, D., Distefano, S., et al.: A crowd-cooperative approach for intelligent transportation systems. IEEE Trans. Intell. Transp. Syst. **18**(6), 1529–1539 (2017)
3. Cheng, R., Xiao, M.: Greedy task assignment algorithm for collaborative crowdsensing. J. Chin. Comput. Syst. **38**(5), 1039–1043 (2017)
4. Cheung, M., Hou, F., Huang, J., et al.: Distributed time-sensitive task selection in mobile crowdsensing. IEEE Trans. Mob. Comput. **20**(6), 2172–2185 (2021)
5. Fang, W., Zhou, Z., Sun, S.: Research on task assignment for mobile crowd sensing. Appl. Res. Comput. **35**(11), 3206–3212 (2018)
6. Ganti, R., Ye, F., Lei, H.: Mobile crowdsensing: current state and future challenges. IEEE Commun. Mag. **49**(11), 32–39 (2011)
7. Goncalves, A., Silva, C., Morreale, P., et al.: Crowdsourcing for public safety. In: Proceedings of the 8th Annual IEEE Systems Conference, pp. 50–56 (2014)

8. Hachem, S., Mallet, V., et al.: Monitoring noise pollution using the urban civics middleware. In: Proceedings of the first International Conference on Big Data Computing Service and Applications, pp. 52–61 (2015)
9. Han, K., Huang, H., Luo, J.: Quality-aware pricing for mobile crowdsensing. IEEE/ACM Trans. Netw. **26**(4), 1728–1741 (2018)
10. Jin, H., Su, L., Chen, D., et al.: Quality of information aware incentive mechanisms for mobile crowd sensing systems. In: Proceedings of the 16th ACM International Symposium on Mobile Ad Hoc Networking, pp. 167–176 (2015)
11. Kong, X., Liu, X., et al.: Mobile crowdsourcing in smart cities: technologies, applications, and future challenges. IEEE Internet Things J. **6**(5), 8095–8113 (2019)
12. Li, Q., Cao, H., Wang, S.: A reputation-based multi-user task selection incentive mechanism for crowdsensing. IEEE Access **8**, 74887–74900 (2020)
13. Li, X., Zhang, X.: Multi-task allocation under time constraints in mobile crowdsensing. IEEE Trans. Mob. Comput. **20**(4), 1494–1510 (2021)
14. Marjovi, A., Arfire, A., Martinoli, A.: High resolution air pollution maps in urban environments using mobile sensor networks. In: Proceedings of the 11th International Conference on Distributed Computing in Sensor Systems, pp. 11–20 (2015)
15. Tan, W., Jiang, Z.: A novel experience-based incentive mechanism for mobile crowdsensing system. In: Proceedings of the First International Conference on Artificial Intelligence, Information Processing and Cloud Computing, pp. 170–176 (2019)
16. Wang, J., Wang, Y., et al.: Multi-task allocation in mobile crowd sensing with individual task quality assurance. IEEE Trans. Mob. Comput. **17**(9), 2101–2113 (2018)
17. Wang, L., Yang, D., et al.: Location privacy-preserving task allocation for mobile crowdsensing with differential geo-obfuscation. In: Proceedings of the 26th International Conference on World Wide Web, pp. 627–636 (2017)
18. Xiang, Z., Xue, G., Yu, R., et al.: Truthful incentive mechanisms for crowdsourcing. In: Proceedings of the 34th IEEE Conference on Computer Communications, pp. 2830–2838 (2015)
19. Xing, Q., Sun, X., Yuan, C.: Assignment mechanism for spatial tasks in mobile crowd sensing. Appl. Res. Comput. **37**(3), 868–871 (2020)
20. Xu, J., Xiang, J., Yang, D.: Incentive mechanisms for time window dependent tasks in mobile crowdsensing. IEEE Trans. Wireless Commun. **14**(11), 6353–6364 (2015)
21. Yan, Z., Xing, L., Chen, Y.: Ant colony algorithm with recommendation of task allocation problems. Comput. Integr. Manuf. Syst. **19**(9), 2220–2228 (2013)
22. Zhao, L., Tan, W., et al.: Crowd-based cooperative task allocation via multicriteria optimization and decision-making. IEEE Syst. J. **14**(3), 3904–3915 (2020)
23. Zhong, Q., Xie, T., Chen, H.: Task matching and scheduling by using genetic algorithms. J. Comput. Res. Dev. **37**(10), 46–52 (2000)

Optimization of Kalman Filter Indoor Positioning Method Fusing WiFi and PDR

Yanling Lu[1,2], Shiqi Luo[1], Zhenxuan Yao[1], Junfen Zhou[1], Shenchuan Lu[3], and Jingwen Li[1,2(✉)]

[1] College of Geomatics and Geoinformation, Guilin University of Technology, Guilin 541004, China
lijw@glut.edu.cn
[2] Guangxi Key Laboratory of Spatial Information and Geomatics, Guilin 541004, China
[3] School of Information and Communication, Guilin University of Electronic Technology, Guilin 541004, China

Abstract. With the increase of people's work activities indoors, indoor positioning technology has become a hot spot in the field of positioning technology. The current mainstream indoor positioning includes WiFi, infrared, Bluetooth, ultra-wideband, ZigBee, RFID and ultrasonic technologies, each of which has its own advantages, but there are also certain shortcomings. The paper is based on WiFi localization technology, incorporating Pedestrian Dead Reckoning (PDR) localization technique and extending Kalman filter algorithm to solve the fused data. The experiments prove that the positioning error of the fused WiFi and PDR indoor positioning methods is smaller than that of the two technologies alone. The maximum error of the combined positioning method is 1.9532 m, the minimum error is 0.4727 m, and the mean error value is 0.8491 m. Compared with the two separate positioning methods, the accuracy of the Kalman filtered indoor positioning method fusing WiFi and PDR improved by 42.57% relative to PDR accuracy and 31.1% relative to WiFi accuracy, thus verifying the effectiveness of the Kalman filtered indoor positioning accuracy improvement by fusing WiFi and PDR.

Keywords: WiFi · PDR · Kalman filter

With the continuous improvement of people's quality and standard of living, life and work are active indoors, especially due to the epidemic situation, indoor positioning is widely used in public health, catering and other fields [1–3]. According to data, the money flow for indoor positioning went from $900 million in 2014 to $7.11 billion in 2017, and the market amount is also rising and is expected to reach $40.99 billion by 2022[4]. As a result, indoor positioning has become a popular research topic today. Currently, WiFi positioning technology is widely used in daily life due to its wide range of transmission signals, good positioning accuracy and low development cost [5–7]. WiFi fingerprint positioning system developed by Google can control the accuracy within 5m, and is used in many large indoor places in North America [8]. Into the "13th Five-Year Plan" period, China in-depth research and development in the field of indoor positioning, which includes WiFi positioning technology research and development. However,

Q. Zu et al. (Eds.): HCC 2021, LNCS 13795, pp. 196–207, 2022.
https://doi.org/10.1007/978-3-031-23741-6_18

the WiFi positioning method has certain drawbacks, such as interference from obstacles leading to deviations in the accuracy of positioning results. In contemporary mobile smart devices are equipped with inertial sensors, including accelerometers, gyroscopes, etc., through which the user's displacement state can be determined, called pedestrian trajectory projection (PDR) [9–11]. Based on PDR to obtain information about direction, speed, angle and other position information in the device, small cost, simple equipment, and independent of the environment. It can be seen that it is difficult to make a break-through in the accuracy of a single indoor positioning technology, and it has become an urgent problem to explore a higher accuracy positioning technology through fusion improvement research [12–14].

Therefore, this paper integrates WiFi and PDR for indoor localization method improvement. The Kalman filter algorithm is extended to correct the errors caused by the positioning results of PDR by using WiFi, and the Kalman filter is fused to process the positioning data of WiFi and PDR, so as to improve the accuracy of indoor positioning.

1 Kalman Filtered Indoor Localization Method by Fusing WiFi and PDR

1.1 WiFi Technology

WiFi localization based on fingerprint matching can effectively reduce the error of multi-path effect generated by indoor multi-obstacle complex structure, which mainly includes two stages of offline training and online matching [15, 16]. In the offline training phase, the area to be measured is divided equally, the signal intensity values of each sampling point are collected, the information of the obtained sequence values is saved and a database is established [17]. The database contains the sampling point location information and the fingerprint information of each AP access point, such as the WiFi fingerprint at the i-th reference point (RPi) is:

$$FW_i = \{(x_i, y_i), (ssid_{i,1}, rssi_{i,1}), (ssid_{i,2}, rssi_{i,2}), \cdots (ssid_{i,mj}, rssi_{i,mj})\} \quad (1)$$

(x_i, y_i) denotes the position coordinates of the point RPi; ssidi, mj and rssii, mj are the service set identification and signal strength of the AP nodes received at point RPi, respectively, and mj is the number of AP nodes received at point RPi.

In the online localization stage, the RSSI values of the sampling points are matched against the fingerprint library and solved using the K-neighborhood algorithm. Specifically, the information of the reference point RPs in the range to be tested is collated, and the position information of each fingerprint reference point in the training set is denoted as (XRP, YRP).

$$\begin{bmatrix} P(A_1 O_1 | Pt_i) & \cdots & P(A_n O_1 | Pt_i) \\ \vdots & \ddots & \vdots \\ P(A_1 O_V | Pt_i) & \cdots & P(A_n O_V | Pt_i) \end{bmatrix} \quad (2)$$

where, A is the signal strength of an AP point of the positioning system; O is the position characteristic data; Pt is the position information of a point of the RSS. According to the K-neighborhood algorithm, K location fingerprint information in the offline data that are similar to the actual target points are selected to compare the actual location coordinates.

1.2 PDR Positioning Technology

In PDR, the initial position of the pedestrian is known, and the direction and number of steps the pedestrian walks in a given time is estimated using inertial sensors such as speed sensors, gyroscopes and magnetism to derive its indoor trail [18]. This is shown in Fig. 1.

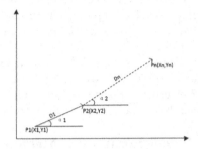

Fig. 1. Pedestrian dead reckoning model

Take the first step, the pedestrian P_1 time point coordinates (x_1, y_1), along the direction to move the distance D_1 to $P_2(x_2, y_2)$, Continuing with the next step, walk along the direction to the next location point, followed by the projected equation from $P_1(x_1, y_1)$ to $P_2(x_2, y_2)$ as [19]:

$$\begin{cases} x_2 = x_1 + D_1 \cos \alpha_1 \\ y_2 = y_1 + D_1 \sin \alpha_1 \end{cases} \tag{3}$$

From this, the P_n points can be extrapolated to obtain the coordinates of each walk. Given that pedestrians rely on the swing of their legs to generate periodic states such as step frequency and acceleration while walking, the pedestrian posture information can be estimated over a period of time by extrapolating the state of pedestrian walking according to the periodicity rule [20].

1.3 Extended Kalman Filtering Indoor Positioning Algorithm

Kalman filtering is a state-recursive algorithm, which needs to be extended for the utilization of nonlinearity. The initial values are input, a round-robin algorithm is performed on the initial values, and the error is corrected to obtain the filtered optimization results. The Extendend Kalman Filter (EKF) is a linearization of a nonlinear system using Taylor series so that the linear Kalman filter can be applied to the system [21]. The equation of state for the following nonlinear system and the equation of measurement.

$$\begin{cases} X(k) = f[X(k-1), W(k-1)] \\ Y(k) = h[X(k), V(k)] \end{cases} \tag{4}$$

$f[\alpha]$ and $h[\beta]$ are nonlinear vector functions. $X(k)$ indicates the state quantity, $Y(k)$ Indicates volume measurement, $W(k)$ indicates the system noise, $V(k)$ denotes the measurement noise sequence, $W(k)$ and $V(k)$ denote white noise with zero mean and uncorrelated. The Taylor series expansion is applied to generate a linearized system of equations, and the estimates are solved according to the general Kalman filter cycle to extend the Kalman filter prediction stage:

1) State vector prediction equation

$$\hat{X}_k = f_k(\hat{X}_{k-1}) \tag{5}$$

2) State transfer matrix

$$F_k \approx \frac{\partial(F_k X_{k-1})}{\partial X}\bigg|_{X=X_{k/k-1}} \tag{6}$$

3) Prediction variance array

$$C_{k/k-1} = F_{k/k-1} C_{k/k-1} F_{k/k-1}^T + T_{k-1} Q_{k-1} T_{k-1}^T \tag{7}$$

4) Perform extended Kalman filtering and update the stage gain matrix

$$K_k = C_{k/k-1} H_k^T \left(H_k C_{k/k-1} H_k^T + R_k \right)^{-1} \tag{8}$$

5) Estimation of state variables

$$\hat{X}_k = \hat{X}_{k/k-1} + K_k \left(Y_k - \hat{Y}_{k/k-1} \right) \tag{9}$$

6) Updated state variance array

$$C_k = (I - K_k H_k) C_{k/k-1} \tag{10}$$

The EKF with recursive filtering is implemented by linearization function to algorithmically correct WiFi positioning information and obtain more accurate WiFi positioning information, set the initial value of PDR as the initial value of WiFi positioning, input the measured PDR step and direction information as the state information, and set the increments of WiFi initial coordinates and PDR heading angle as the measurement information of EKF [22]. The modeling is done by pedestrian walking information as the following equation:

$$X_x = \begin{bmatrix} x_k \\ y_k \\ \theta_k \end{bmatrix} = \begin{bmatrix} x_{k-1} + s \times \cos(\theta_{k-1}) \\ y_{k-1} + s \times \sin(\theta_{k-1}) \\ \theta_k \end{bmatrix} + W_{k-1} \tag{11}$$

(x_k, y_k) is the position of the pedestrian at moment k, the coordinates of the first step of the pedestrian are the positioning coordinates of WiFi, θ_k is the directional angle of the pedestrian at moment k, W_{k-1} is system noise, s is the step size at moment k.Measure the time of each step of PDR, obtain WiFi positioning coordinates and PDR directional angle increments, The variables of WiFi positioning data and PDR positioning data are the equation input parameters of the EKF measurement, the measurement equation is shown below:

$$
Z_k = \begin{bmatrix} x_k \\ y_k \\ \theta_k \\ \Delta\theta_k \end{bmatrix} = \begin{bmatrix} x_k \\ y_k \\ \theta_{k-1} + \Delta\theta_k \\ \theta_k - \theta_{k-1} \end{bmatrix} + V_K \tag{12}
$$

(x_k, y_k) is the coordinates of WiFi at the moment of pedestrian k, $\Delta\theta_k$ is the change in directional angle of the pedestrian at moment k, θ_k, θ_{k-1} denote the directional angles of the pedestrian at moment k and moment k − 1 respectively, V_K is a systematic observation of noise.

Thus, the steps of WiFi and PDR fusion are briefly summarized as follows: first initialize the coordinate position of the pedestrian, apply Eq. (11) to calculate the predicted value of the pedestrian state vector [23], Eq. (12) to calculate the WiFi position information for the current step and the state increment information such as the PDR direction, and then apply the first-order linearized state equation to solve the state transfer matrix Eq. to calculate the PDR state vector, which is used to predict the variance array equation, calculate the gain matrix equation, and solve the PDR state estimation

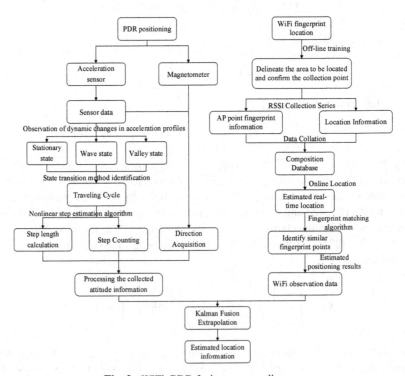

Fig. 2. WiFi, PDR fusion process diagram

value equation. Finally, the current pedestrian state is predicted by estimating the variance array. The final output of the location information of Xk is obtained through the continuous recursive state update. This is shown in Fig. 2.

2 Experiments and Results

2.1 Experimental Environment and Operation

The experimental site is on the first floor of Building 8, Guilin University of Electronic Technology. The site has a good signal environment and a relatively open view, few external interference conditions are conducive to WiFi data acquisition, and there are no more metal devices to affect the calibration of the PDR device.

The experimental hardware equipment is AP signal base station, which is fixed by intelligent mobile devices at multiple points to release signals for testing. The software has an apk installation package based on Android studio, which is downloaded to an Android smartphone to run the Sensor Sense program.

1) The route planning for the experimental area is designed as a rectangular area of 12.63 m in length and 10 m in width. The WiFi base station signals are arranged to each corner location, with AP1 arranged as the origin (0, 0) and the other base station points as AP2 (10, 0), AP3 (10, 12.63), and AP4 (0, 12.63), respectively. This is shown in Fig. 3 below.

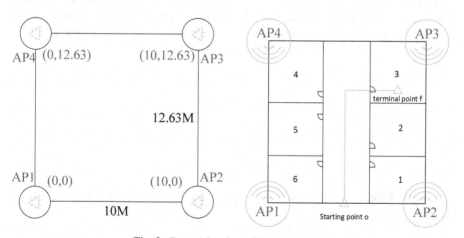

Fig. 3. Route planning of the experiment

2) Collects the RSSI value for each AP access point. The experimental area is divided into six regions, and the smart mobile device is held to collect the signal characteristic values of the six regions, combined with the device's own sensors to measure the state of the experimenter's walking, including pedestrian acceleration, step count, direction and other state information.

3) The collected RSSI equivalents are integrated to create a fingerprint library, that is, RSSI generates corresponding data information to complete the offline training phase.
4) In the online training phase, the experimenter locates the initial location to move from, matches that location with the offline data collected by the computer service therein, and then forms a trajectory roadmap to complete WiFi localization.
5) Set the step size of the initial position of the pedestrian and use the sensor to measure the state data of the tester. Using the initial position O (0, 5) of WiFi positioning as the initial position of PDR positioning, set the coordinate value, measure the initial step length of the experimenter roughly at 45cm, walk from the starting point O, make a turn, stop at the point F in zone 3, travel 15m, walk 30 steps, and store the collected information.
6) Using the offline training data, the location information of the experimenter in the online training phase is estimated and WiFi individual localization is performed. The WiFi data and the sensor data on the smart mobile device are input into the computer for processing, fitted by MATLAB, combined with PDR positioning, corrected using WiFi positioning data, and the two are combined and compared for accuracy. The location information after fusion is obtained.

2.2   Data Acquisition and Processing

The collected data include RSSI value information of WiFi positioning and walking status information of PDR pedestrians. Install and download WIRELESSMON for WiFi positioning RSSI acquisition, Using the equipment comes with inertial sensors and sensor recording program Sensor Sense, the experimenter mounted on the leg to do

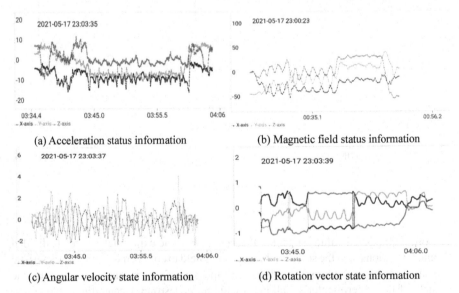

(a) Acceleration status information   (b) Magnetic field status information

(c) Angular velocity state information   (d) Rotation vector state information

Fig. 4. Data collection results of mobile phone sensors

walking motion state recording data, and the data will be analyzed. The four status messages are shown in Fig. 4.

With the operation of two devices, it may lead to an increase in error due to jitter when a single pedestrian walks under the same path. When using inertial navigation devices, you can also choose to use a single sensor connected to a computer or cell phone USB for experiments. Here a 9-axis posture sensor connected to a computer is used to demonstrate the acquisition test.

The WiFi signal characteristic values are collected according to six regions, written into an Excel table and organized into txt, while the tested walking state data are input and organized from a cell phone connected to a computer USB, also generating a txt text format to facilitate later solving. The txt text format of both data was generated as shown in Table 1 and Table 2 below.

Table 1. Partially collection status information of the PDR

Ay/g	Az/g	Wx/(deg·s^{-1})	Wy/(deg·s^{-1})	Wz/(deg·s^{-1})	AngleX/deg	AngleY/deg
−0.9863	1.9614	−0.2441	2.5635	0.5493	−26.911	1.4557
−0.9746	1.9404	−2.3193	0.2441	−2.3193	−27.0978	1.5051
−0.9702	1.9424	−2.1362	−1.77	−1.8311	−27.2296	1.2305
−0.9883	1.9209	−1.77	−5.0049	−6.958	−27.4329	0.7141
−0.9087	1.9102	−6.8359	6.4697	−0.6714	−27.7789	0.3625

Table 2. Partially collected information of WiFi signal strength

X	Y	AP1	AP2	AP3	AP4
10	0	−62	−41	−71	−61
10	7	−56	−68	−58	−63
10	12	−68	−74	−28	−58
0	12	−62	−73	−69	−58
0	7	−52	−71	−65	−62
0	0	−28	−70	−72	−54

The WiFi and PDR data are examined and integrated, and generated in the form of csv files, which are analyzed on MATLAB and solved using the extended Kalman filter algorithm to generate localization results.

2.3   Analysis of Results

The PDR localization is first experimented by planning the path. Start from the starting point O, walk 10 m, then turn right to area 3 and walk about 4m to stop at point F. Mark the coordinates of the walk, using external sensors for travel status measurements, acceleration, angular velocity and directional status vectors are measured, and the measured data are entered into an Excel spreadsheet for integration. The useful data were extracted for integration and imported into MATLAB software for localization analysis to generate a trajectory map, as shown in Fig. 5.

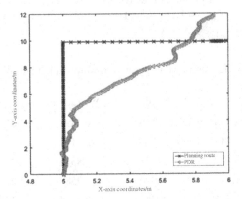

Fig. 5. Positioning trajectory diagram of PDR

By placing AP signal base station points at each of the four corner points in the experimental area. Off-line training phase for RSSI value acquisition, with information on the relationship between the location of the acquisition points as shown in Fig. 6; In the online localization stage, the matching algorithm model is applied to solve the data and input fingerprint features to derive the corresponding location information, as shown in Fig. 7.

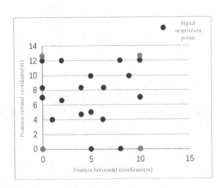

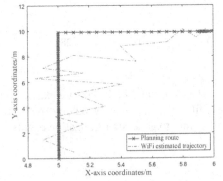

Fig. 6. Location distribution map of collection points and AP base station points

Fig. 7. Positioning trajectory diagram of WiFi

The first set of PDR localization and the second set of WiFi fingerprint localization are fused by Kalman filtering model to generate the effect map. As shown in Fig. 8, where the blue line is the actual planned route, the yellow line is the WiFi positioning estimated trajectory, the red line indicates the PDR positioning trajectory route, and the purple indicates the fused trajectory effect.

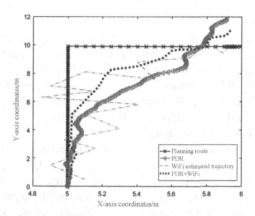

Fig. 8. Comparison chart of three sets of trajectory routes

The comparison shows that the PDR positioning has a high accuracy in a short period of time, but the change of time causes the cumulative error of PDR positioning to increase continuously and shift, in which the maximum error reaches 3.2632 m. Using WiFi fingerprint positioning, the collected data may be affected by various factors such as multipath effect or interference from other electronic devices, and the positioning effect shows a jump discrete distribution with large randomness, and the maximum error reaches 2.8350m. The extended Kalman filter fusion WiFi and PDR localization is closer to the planned route, and although there are errors, the relative accuracy has improved, with a minimum error of 0.4727 m. The details are shown in Table 3.

Table 3. Comparison of the error data of PDR, WiFi and the combination of the two positioning

Positioning method	Mean value of error /m	Minimum Error /m	Maximum Error /m
PDR	1.4785	0.9611	3.2632
WiFi	0.2324	0.6861	2.8350
WiFi&PDR	0.8491	0.4727	1.9532

As can be seen from the table, the average error of PDR positioning is 1.4785m, the average error of WiFi positioning is 1.2324 m, the maximum error of the positioning method based on the fusion of the two is 1.9532 m, the minimum error is 0.4727 m, and the average error value is 0.8491 m. Compared with the two separate positioning methods, the Kalman filtered indoor positioning method incorporating PDR and WiFi has improved in accuracy by 42.57% compared to the PDR separate positioning method and 31.1% compared to the WiFi positioning method, this further confirms the effectiveness of the Kalman filter indoor localization method of fused PDR and WiFi technology in locating indoor pedestrian information.

3 Conclusion

Today's indoor positioning technology has been closely related to people's lives, but each technology has certain shortcomings, and it is difficult to improve the accuracy of a single positioning technology due to space and time constraints. For this reason, the fusion method of multiple positioning techniques has become a hot topic of indoor positioning research nowadays. This paper proposes a combined WIFI and PDR fusion positioning method, and establishes both online and offline databases to achieve further high-precision autonomous positioning.

The experimental verification shows that the average error of PDR positioning is 1.4785 m, and the average error of WIFI positioning is 1.2324 m. The average error value is only 0.8491 m with the introduction of the extended Kalman filter model, which effectively improves the positioning accuracy by using the paper's proposed PDR technique that integrates the more prevalent WIFI and easy operation. By exploring the accuracy differences between single and fused positioning techniques, it is verified that multi-sensor fusion can build a more reliable and accurate indoor positioning method.

Funded Projects National Natural Science Foundation of China (41961063); Guangxi Natural Science Foundation – innovative Research Team Project (2019GXNSFGA245001).

References

1. Mazhar, F., Khan, M.G., Sällberg, B.: Precise indoor positioning using UWB: a review of methods, algorithms and implementations. Wireless Pers Commun. **97**, 4467–4491 (2017)
2. Bi, J.: Study on optimization problem of Wi-Fi/PDR indoor hybrid positioning on smartphone. Acta Geodaetica et Cartographica Sinica **50**(10), 1416 (2017)
3. Yuting, Z., Jing, C.: Indoor fusion positioning technology using EKF and PF. Chin. J. Sens. Actuators **33**(02), 245–251 (2020)
4. Mianhe, L.: The research on high-precision indoor positioning technology based on LFMCW. Sch. Electron. Eng. (2016)
5. Chen, G., Ma, H., Zeng, Q.: The design of an indoor high-precision multi-source wireless positioning system in B5G environment. Phys. Commun. **43**, 101232 (2020)
6. Zhang, G., Sun, X., Ren, J., Lu, W.: Research on improved indoor positioning algorithm based on WiFi–pedestrian dead reckoning. Int. J. Distrib. Sens. Netw. **15**(5) (2019)
7. Chen, J., Song, S., Yu, H.: An indoor multi-source fusion positioning approach based on PDR/MM/WiFi. AEU – Int. J. Electron. Commun. **135**, 153733 (2021)
8. Chang, Q., van de Velde, S., Wang, W., Li, Q., Hou, H., Heidi, S.: Wi-Fi Fingerprint Positioning Updated by Pedestrian Dead Reckoning for Mobile Phone Indoor Localization. Springer, Berlin Heidelberg (2015)
9. Jianqiang, S., Junna, S., Huli, S.: PDR-assisted UWB for indoor non-line-of-sight positioning. Chin. J. Sens. Actuators **33**(05), 711–717 (2020)

10. Song, Y., Yu, W., Cheng, C., Wang, L.: Research onindoor positioning based on fusion of WiFi, PDR and geomagnetism. Microelectron. Comput. **35**(6), 60–64, 68 (2018)
11. Li, M., Wang, S., Tan, D.: Research on the fusion method of the initial position of indoor location based on WiFi/PDR. J. Geodesy Geodyn. **39**(6), 602–606 (2019)
12. Jung, S.H., Moon, B.C., Han, D.: Unsupervised learning for crowdsourced indoor localization in wireless networks. IEEE Trans. Mobile Comput. **15**(11), 2892–2906 (2016). https://doi.org/10.1109/TMC.2015.2506585
13. Hu, Z., Liu, J., Huang, G., Tao, Q.: Integration of WiFi, laser, and map for robot indoor localization. J. Electron. Inf. Technol. **43**(8), 2308–2316 (2021)
14. Wang, H., Gao, K., Lyu, H.: Survey of high-precision localization and the prospect of future evolution. J. Commun. **42**(7), 198–210 (2021)
15. Linsheng, Z., Hongpeng, W., Jingtai, L.: An indoor localization method based on Wi-Fi fingerprint in the human-robot shared environment. Robot **41**(3), 404–413 (2019)
16. Binzi, H., Bo, Q.: Hybrid filtering algorithm for INS/GPS integrated navigation. Electron. Technol. Softw. Eng. **24**, 75–77 (2018)
17. Zhou, R., Lu, X., Lu, S., Li, Z.-Q.: Fused indoor localization based on particle filtering and map matching. J. Univ. Electron. Sci. Technol. China **47**(3), 415–420 (2018)
18. Liyang, Z., Chaoyuan, C., Rujing, W.: Method of pedestrian indoor positioning based on real-time step-size matching. Comput. Syst. Appl. **26**(04), 236–240 (2017)
19. Tong, W., Xin, L.: Localization and mapping of visual travel aids assisted by IMU/GPS integrated navigation. Process Autom. Instrum. **40**(01), 45–49 (2018)
20. Jinzhong, M., et al.: Research on intelligent application of indoor location service. Sci. Surveying Mapp. **46**(06), 1–8 (2021)
21. Wu, Y., Zhu, H.B., Du, Q.X., Tang, S.-M.: A survey of the research status of pedestrian dead reckoning systems based on inertial sensors. Int. J. Autom. Comput. **6**(01), 65–83 (2019)
22. Liu, Q., Guan, W., Li, S., Wang, F.: Indoor WiFi-PDR fusion location algorithm based on extended Kalman Filter. Comput. Eng. **45**(04), 66–71+77 (2019)
23. Tong, H., Xin, N., Su, X., Chen, T., Wu, J.: A robust PDR/UWB integrated indoor localization approach for pedestrians in harsh environments. Sensors **20**(1), 1–20 (2019)

Constructing an UAV Network with Relative Positioning

Yun Wang[1,2(✉)] and Daihai Tian[1,2]

[1] Southeast University, Nanjing, Jiangsu, China
ywang_cse@seu.edu.cn
[2] Key Lab of Computer Network and Information Integration, Ministry of Education, Nanjing, China

Abstract. In some emergency scenarios, UAV relay network is often used to provide temporary communications services. Different from the absolute position information, this paper proposes a deployment scheme of UAV network which is based on the relative position information. As a dynamic scheme, it contains several strategies for the deployment, retrieval, and topology control. Compared with other two schemes based on the absolute position information, greedy-based scheme and genetic algorithm-based scheme, the network based on our scheme achieves 90% and 70% of the coverage performance of them respectively and significantly outperforms those two static schemes in robustness and load balancing.

Keywords: UAV · Relay network · Deployment · Relative positioning

1 Introduction

In scenarios such as emergency rescue, battlefield environment, and polar exploration, it is usually necessary to build temporary communication network. Mobile ad-hoc network (MANET) [1] provides a feasible solution to this problem. Due to the restrictions of deployment environment, using unmanned aerial vehicle (UAV) to build the communication network [2] is a good option. As the relay nodes, UAVs have more advantages in terms of speed and moving space compared with the nodes on the ground, and can quickly reach the designated locations due to the high mobility and flexibility. The communication between the UAV and the nodes within its coverage can be hardly interfered by the terrain and obstacles, which guarantees the higher communication quality and efficiency.

In most cases, the controller can determine the position of UAVs in the network before the deployment with the absolute position information provided by the satellite positioning system. However, it will be a great challenge for the deployment of the UAV relay network when the satellite positioning system is unavailable. Thus, it has become a significant issue to develop a deployment solution for UAV network without the satellite positioning system.

© The Author(s), under exclusive license to Springer Nature Switzerland AG 2022
Q. Zu et al. (Eds.): HCC 2021, LNCS 13795, pp. 208–218, 2022.
https://doi.org/10.1007/978-3-031-23741-6_19

There are severe challenges of constructing an UAV network without absolute positioning system. One is that the relative position information only contains the distance between the UAVs and their change, without angle or absolute direction information, which greatly increases the construction difficulty of the network topology. The other is that it is necessary to maintain the connectivity of the network while covering all nodes on the ground, and the number of UAVs ought to be minimized.

Considering the challenges mentioned, this paper proposes an equilateral triangle topology generation scheme. It supports on-demand deployment of an UAV and the tracking coverage of the nodes based on the relative position information. This paper aims to realize the deployment of UAV based on the relative position information. As a dynamic scheme, it contains a series of algorithms and strategies such as the deployment, retrieval and topology control. Compared with the other two static schemes, i.e. greedy-based scheme (Greedy) and genetic algorithm-based scheme (GA), which are based on the absolute location information, the network based on our scheme achieved 90% and 70% of the coverage performance of them respectively and significantly outperforms them in robustness and load balancing.

The rest of this paper is organized as follows. Section 2 introduces the related work. In Sect. 3, the problem is defined and the system hypothesis is provided at first. Then, the proposed scheme in detail is described. The evaluation of the scheme is set in Sect. 4. Sect. 5 is the conclusion.

2 Related Work

At present, there are two kinds of methods to deploy an UAV relay network, i.e. the methods based on the absolute position information and the methods based on the relative position information. The former obtains the absolute position information of all nodes before the deployment, while the latter needs to gather the relative position information during the deployment process. Most of the existing research focuses on the former [3–5]. Ibrah et al. [6] proposed a deployment scheme for UAV network based on simulated annealing, which is applied in emergency communication scenarios. The scheme effectively simplifies the time complexity and guarantee the accuracy of the solution. Reina et al. [7] proposed a multi-layout multi-subpopulation genetic algorithm (MLMPGA) to solve the problem of optimal coverage in UAV network, which uses different subpopulations to evolve in different layouts, and carries out multi-objective deployment based on the weighted fitness function. Zhang et al. [8] studied two kinds of deployment problems of UAV, namely, the minimization of maximum deployment delay among all UAVs considering fairness (Min-max) and the minimization of total deployment delay considering efficiency (Min-sum). Kalantari et al. [9] developed a heuristic algorithm based on particle swarm optimization, and the algorithm sub-optimally finds the minimum number of UAVs and their locations to serve all the users in a particular region with different user densities. Liu et al. [10] introduced the reinforcement learning in the process of the deployment to maximize the sum mean opinion score (MOS) of ground users. In the above research, it is assumed that the coordinates of the UAVs and the ground users are known.

In some research, the position of the ground users is not necessary. Wang et al. Reference [11] proposed an adaptive UAV assisted communication network deployment scheme, in which the UAV adaptively adjusts its direction and distance to provide services for users moving randomly in the target area. The UAV does not need to acquire the location of the user in real time, but chooses its direction by flying to the area with the largest number of users in the cell. Zhao et al. [12] respectively discussed two opposite situations. One is how to use the least amount of UAVs to provide on-demand coverage for terminals given the number and location of terminals. The other is how to optimize the deployment of a given number of drones to maximize their coverage. And a heuristic search algorithm was used to solve the first problem while an algorithm based on a virtual force field is applied in the second problem.

3   The Proposed Approach

3.1   Problem Definition

The deployment of the UAV network only relies on the relative position information between the UAV and the beacon or other UAVs. During the deployment process, each UAV needs to continuously collect the relative position information, and adjust the direction through the change of the position, so as to make the right decision. After arriving at the deployment location, the UAV needs to exchange the topology information and the coverage information of ground nodes with other UAVs in the network to judge the effectiveness of the deployment. In addition, considering the change of the position of the nodes on the ground, the UAV network ought to catch the change and adjust the topology in time. When the temporary communication is finished, all UAVs in the network should be retrieved.

3.2   Assumptions

In order to simplify the problem, there are some assumptions including: (i) the communication channel of the UAV is the ideal channel, and the distance between UAVs can be measured by receiving signal strength indicator (RSSI) accurately; (ii) all the UAVs in the network fly at the same altitude; (iii) all the nodes are equipped with the ad-hoc network communication protocols, and the communication between nodes does not interfere with each other; and (iv) the endurance of the UAV is not considered.

3.3   The Proposed Scheme

Our proposed scheme is to construct the UAV network based on the relative positioning. The equilateral triangle structure is chosen because it is easier for the UAVs to construct the layout of the equilateral triangle than other polygons in the absence of the absolute location information, and the equilateral triangle structure has an excellent property that for any one of its sides (or angles), the remaining sides (or angles) have perfect symmetry which is not available to any other polygons. The symmetry is benefit to simplify the design of the strategy.

Considering the characteristics of the scenarios that need the UAV relay network for temporary communication, it is unrealistic to control the flight of UAVs by the control center on the ground. On the one hand, the size of the UAV is small but the communication distance is large, so it is difficult to observe the situation to make operations when the UAV needs to be deployed far away. On the other hand, due to the distance limitation of the remote control device, the UAV cannot be recovered after flying far away from start in the absence of the satellite positioning system. Therefore, the capabilities of the autonomous control and decision are necessary for the UAVs.

During the process of flying, UAV obtains the following four kinds of information from the surroundings to achieve the intelligent deployment.

(i)   Global network topology (GNT). Each UAV in the network maintains a copy of the global topology information stored in an adjacency list and can determine the position in the network according to the neighbor node list and the equilateral triangle unit structure of the network.

(ii) Coverage situation of the nodes on the ground (CSON). It records the coverage relationship between each UAV and the nodes within its coverage range.

(iii) Collection of the UAV-edges need to be deployed (COE). In the UAV network, two deployed UAVs within communication range construct an UAV-edge as the endpoints. An UAV-edge will be considered as an edge need to be deployed if it only belongs to one equilateral triangle structure rather than two and it has not been attempted to be deployed.

(iv) Collection of the paths to the edge need to be deployed (COP). The collection contains the path from the initial position to all the UAV-edges need to be deployed. The position change of the UAV is represented by the UAV-edge it is on, as a result, each path is composed of multiple UAV-edges.

The scheme contains four phases, i.e., initialization phase which deploys the initial UAVs, deployment phase which locate all the UAVs in the network, topology control phase which controls the UAV network topology maintaining the connectivity and coverage, and the retrieval phase which releases all the UAVs.

Initialization Phase. Initialization phase is to deploy the initial UAVs according to the location of the nodes on the ground marked by the beacon. There are three situations in the deployment of the initial UAVs. In the first situation, as shown in Fig. 1 (a), the coverage could be completed by only one UAV. Second, the coverage is completed when two initial UAVs are deployed at the maximum communication distance as shown in Fig. 1 (b). In Fig. 1 (c), the third situation is that three initial UAVs are arranged as an equilateral triangle structure, but there are still some uncovered nodes on the ground. The solutions for the first two situations are straight-forward. The following content of this paper mainly focus on the third situation, in which the subsequent UAVs could start deploying from the midpoint between the two initial UAVs. Any practical application is a mixture of the three situations.

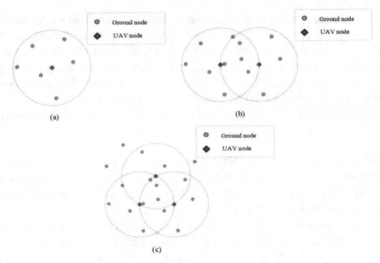

Fig. 1. Initial situation

Deployment of an UAV Network. The deployment strategy of the UAV network is described as follow:

(i)   Arrives at the initial position, the midpoint between the two initial UAVs, joins the network, and obtains the GNT, CSON, COE, COP from the neighbor nodes.

(ii) Extracts an UAV-edge from the COE as the destination, and broadcasts to the other UAVs to update their COE.

(iii) Finds the path from the initial position to the destination from the COP and reaches the destination under the guidance of the flight-control strategy. If it does not start off from the initial position, finds the shortest path from the current edge to the destination by the path-searching algorithm.

(iv) After reaching the destination, carries out the deployment operation to construct the new equilateral triangle structure according to the flight-control strategy and detects whether there are new nodes on the ground being covered.

(v)   If there are no new nodes being covered, the current deployment is fail. Therefore, returns to the midpoint of the corresponding UAV-edge according to the flight-control strategy and jumps to (2).

(vi) If there are some new nodes being covered, the current deployment is successful. Therefore, updates the COE using the COE updating strategy, adds the path from the initial position to the newly constructed UAV-edge into the COP, and broadcasts to the other UAVs to update the GNT, CSON, COE, COP.

(vii) When the COE is empty, the coverage of the current node group on the ground is completed. Otherwise, continues to the deployment process of the next UAV according to the steps as above.

In some cases, there are multiple node groups on the ground which are far away from each other, as shown in Fig. 2. Although the two node groups have completed the deployment of the relay network respectively, there are no links for them to communicate with each other. The situation is not acceptable because messages from one UAV in one network cannot reach the other UAV in the other network. In other words, the UAVs cannot work together as a whole. This problem cannot be solved by the UAVs themselves. The UAVs need to be guided by the ground control. Therefore, the mobile beacons on the ground is introduced, which have the ability to reach from one node group to another relying on the results of the terrain exploration. In order to connect the two networks, mobile beacon moves from the edge of the source network to the target network along the path represented by the dashed line in Fig. 2. Whenever the beacon moves to reach the maximum communication radius of the UAV, it will stop in place and release an UAV to keep hovering to connect with the source network. When the beacon reaches below the target network, a communication link composed of multiple UAVs could be constructed between the source network and the target network.

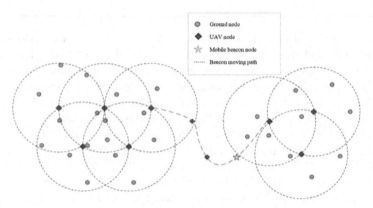

Fig. 2. Deployment for multiple node groups

In addition, the deployment strategy of the UAV network described above cannot success without the assistant of the path-searching algorithm and the updating strategy of the COE, which will be introduced in the following sections.

When the current deployment of the UAV is fail, it needs to reach the next position to deploy along the path obtained by the path-searching algorithm. In the deployment strategy of the UAV network, UAV always moves from the midpoint of one UAV-edge to another. The first step of the path-searching algorithm is to transform the topology of the network into the connected graph consisted of the midpoint of the UAV-edges, in which the midpoints of the two edges belonging to the same triangle structure are connected. Then, the BFS algorithm is used to find the shortest path between the source point (the source UAV-edge) and the target point (the target UAV-edge).

Algorithm Path-searching

Input: The adjacency list storing the topology of the
network: NList. Source point of the UAV: $node_s$
Target point of the UAV: $node_d$
Output: The shortest path between the source point and the target point.
1.   EList ← {}   // adjacency list to store the connected graph of the midpoints
2.   **for** $node_i$ in NList:
3.   Obtain the neighbor list of $node_i$: neighborList

4.   **for** $neighbor_i$, $neighbor_j$ in neighborList :
5.   **if** $neighbor_i$ is the neighbor of $neighbor_j$:
6.   Record the connectivity of the three midpoints of the edges constructed by
                 $node_i$, $neighbor_i$ and $neighbor_j$ in EList.
7.   **end if**
8.   **end for**
9.   **end for**
10.   Using BFS to find the shortest path from $node_s$ to $node_d$.

When an UAV is deployed successfully, the waiting-for-deployment edge set of the
UAV should be updated. This is because once the UAV is deployed, the relationship
between the UAV and some other nodes are determined. It means there are some new
UAV-edges being constructed and some old UAV-edges being deleted to update the
COE. The waiting-for-deployment edge set is the basis for further deployment. This
is the updating strategy. As shown in Fig. 3, the number of the neighbors of the UAV,
denoted by N, ranges from two to five in different situations. In Fig. 3 (a), NA and NB
should be added in COE, and AB should be deleted. In Fig. 3 (b), NA and NC should be
added in COE, and AB and BC should be deleted. In Fig. 3 (c), NA and ND should be
added in COE, and AB, BC and CD should be deleted. In Fig. 3 (d), NA and NE should
be added in COE, and AB, BC, CD and CD should be deleted.

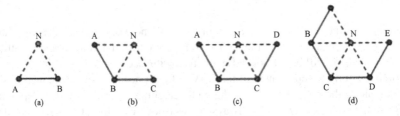

Fig. 3. Updating of COE

Topology Control of an UAV Network. In order to meet the mission requirements, the nodes on the ground may move out of the area covered by the UAV network. In this case, the UAV network needs to adjust the topology to track and cover the nodes in time.

For the UAV in the network which lost a node, the edge has to track and cover the node again after the deployment constructed by itself. Thus, the current UAV will add the deployment edges containing itself in the COE again and broadcast to the other UAVs to update the relative information. The retrievable UAV in the network will find the path from the current position to the new edge added in the COE and carry out the deployment. In the network, an UAV that does not cover any nodes is considered as the retrievable UAV, when the edges constructed by it are not in the only path for other UAVs to reach any edges in the network. If there are multiple retrievable UAVs in the network, the priority of dispatching is determined by the ID of UAV. And if there are no retrievable UAVs in the network, the ground control center will be notified to deploy more UAVs to finish the work. A distributed protocol is proposed to realize the function above by installing it on each UAV node.

Retrieval of an UAV Network. When the temporary communication is over, all the UAVs in the network should be recovered. In fact, the retrieval process of the UAV is the reverse execution of the deployment process.

4   Experimental Analysis

In order to evaluate the performance of our scheme, two other schemes based on the absolute position information are modified and implemented: greedy-based scheme (Greedy) and genetic algorithm-based scheme (GA), in which the global position information of all nodes participating in the schemes has been obtained before the deployment. On the contrary, the relative position information used in our scheme needs to be gathered during the deployment process of UAV. In fact, GA can get close to the theoretical optimal solution in terms of the number of UAVs.

4.1   Coverage Performance

The coverage performance of the network topology is denoted by the number of UAVs in the network when ensuring the connectivity of the network and the coverage of the nodes on the ground.

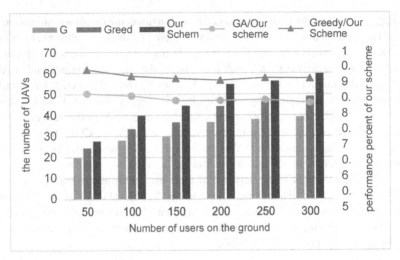

Fig. 4. Coverage performance

As shown in Fig. 4, the vertical axis on the left is the number of the UAVs and the axis on the right is the ratio of the performance of our scheme and the other two schemes. Although the coverage performance of our scheme is not as good as that of Greedy and GA, it reaches the 90% and 70% of them respectively, which proves the effectiveness of our scheme. The reason of the performance difference is that in our scheme the triangle frame is used to construct rather than the circle frame. The area of a triangle is smaller than that of a circle if the distance from the center to the vertex in a triangle equals the radius of a circle.

4.2 Robustness

In the network, the more neighbors the node has, the closer the connection between the node and the network, the higher the robustness of the local topology, and the stronger the communication ability. In Fig. 5, the average number of neighbors of nodes is compared. The figure manifests that with the increase of the number of nodes on the ground, the network deployed based on our scheme has the most average number of neighbors, followed by Greedy and GA. Although GA needs the least number of UAVs to form the communication network, the cost is the reduction in the robustness of the network topology.

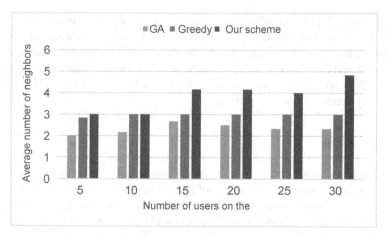

Fig. 5. Average number of neighbors

4.3 Load balance

The UAV relay network is constructed to provide the communication service for the users on the ground. There are mainly two user access policies: nearest-priority and minimum-priority. The former is to access to the nearest UAV preferentially and the latter is to access to the UAV with the minimum number of users preferentially. The more users a UAV connects to, the heavier load it has. The variance of the user number of each UAV is used to measure the load balancing degree of the network.

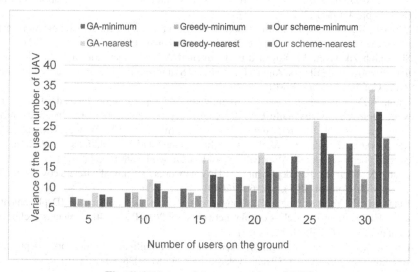

Fig. 6. Variance of the user number of UAV

As shown in Fig. 6, regardless of the user access strategy, the network based on our scheme has the smallest variance of the number of users accessing, which indicates that the network based on our scheme has the best load balancing performance compared with the GA and Greedy. In addition, it can be seen that the user access policies have the impact on the load balancing performance of the network, in which the minimum-priority is obviously better than nearest-priority.

5 Conclusion

In this paper, a scheme based on the relative position information is proposed, which realizes the deployment, topology control and retrieval of UAV. Experimental results show that the network constructed based on our scheme achieves 90% of the coverage performance of the Greedy and 70% of the GA. And in robustness and load balancing, it is significantly better than those two static schemes. Our further work will focus on the topology modification when the network deployment is destroyed due to node failure or the target is moved away.

References

1. Cai, R.J., Li, X.J., Chong, P.: An evolutionary self-cooperative trust scheme against routing disruptions in MANETs. IEEE Trans. Mob. Comput. **18**(1), 42–55 (2019)
2. Liu, D., et al.: Self-organizing relay selection in UAV communication networks: a matching game perspective. IEEE Wirel. Commun. **26**(6), 102–110 (2019)
3. Yang, L., Yao, H., Zhang, X., Wang, J., Liu, Y.: Multi-UAV deployment for MEC enhanced IoT networks. In: 2020 IEEE/CIC International Conference on Communications in China (ICCC), pp. 436-441 (2020).
4. Valiulahi, I., Masouros, C.: Multi-UAV deployment for throughput maximization in the presence of co-channel interference. IEEE Internet Things J. **8**(5), 3605–3618 (2021)
5. Shabanighazikelayeh, M, Koyuncu E.: Optimal UAV deployment for rate maximization in IoT networks. In: IEEE 31st Annual International Symposium on Personal, Indoor and Mobile Radio Communications, PIMRC (2020)
6. Ibrah, A.D., Chuang, L., Na, L., Meng-yuan, Z.: Optimization method of relay network deployment using multi-UAV for emergency communication. In: 2nd International Conference on Data Mining, Communications and Information Technology, DMCIT (2018)
7. Reina, D.G., Tawfik, H., Toral, S.L.: Multi-subpopulation evolutionary algorithms for coverage deployment of UAV-networks. Ad Hoc Networks **68**, 16–32 (2018)
8. Zhang, X., Duan, L.: Fast deployment of UAV networks for optimal wireless coverage. IEEE Trans. Mob. Comput. **18**(3), 588–601 (2019)
9. Kalantari, E., Yanikomeroglu, H., Yongacoglu, A.: On the number and 3D placement of drone base stations in wireless cellular networks. In: 2016 IEEE 84th Vehicular Technology Conference (VTC-Fall). IEEE (2017)
10. Liu, X., Liu, Y., Chen, Y.: Reinforcement learning in multiple-UAV networks: deployment and movement design. IEEE Trans. Veh. Technol. **68**(8), 8036–8049 (2019)
11. Wang, Z., Duan, L., Zhang, R.: Adaptive deployment for UAV-aided communication networks. IEEE Trans. Wireless Commun. **18**(9), 4531–4543 (2019)
12. Zhao, H., Wang, H., Wu, W., Wei, J.: Deployment algorithms for UAV airborne networks toward on-demand coverage. IEEE J. Sel. Areas Commun. **36**(9), 2015–2031 (2018)

Resource Allocation for Multi-service NOMA System Based on Deep Reinforcement Learning

Zhenyu Zhang[1], Weijun Zheng[2], Weiping Shao[3], Yong Zhang[1]([✉]), and Da Guo[1]

[1] School of Electronic Engineering, Beijing University of Posts and Telecommunication, Beijing 100876, People's Republic of China
{zhangzhenyucad,Yongzhang,guoda}@bupt.edu.cn
[2] Jiaxing Power Supply Company, State Grid Zhejiang Electric Power Co.ltd Jiaxing, Zhejiang, People's Republic of China
zhengweijun@zj.sgcc.com.cn
[3] Department of Science and Technology Information, State Grid Zhejiang Electric Power Co.ltd Hangzhou, Zhejiang, People's Republic of China
shao_weiping@zj.sgcc.com.cn

Abstract. In this paper, a resource allocation algorithm based on deep reinforcement learning (DRL) is proposed to solve the problem of co-existing enhanced mobile broadband (eMBB) slices and ultrareliable low latency communication (URLLC) slices based on Non-orthogonal Multiple Access (NOMA) in downlink network scenarios. Double Deep Q network (DDQN) is designed to output subcarrier and power allocation simultaneously. In addition, expert data is added in the training process to accelerate network convergence, and our goal is to optimize the spectral efficiency of the system. Simulation results show that compared with the baseline based on heuristic joint user pairing and power allocation algorithm [1] and Orthogonal Multiple Access (OMA), proposed algorithm can achieve higher spectral efficiency and ensure isolation between slices.

Keywords: Deep reinforcement learning · Network slicing · Resource allocation

1 Intoduction

With the rapid development of the 5th generation communication technology, the number of terminal users has increased sharply, and the standards and requirements for mobile devices have also increased. In order to avoid the exhaustion of spectrum resources and meet the needs of various services, network slice resource allocation methods based on NOMA are developing rapidly. At present, NOMA technology has been widely used. NOMA technology is introduced in V2V Scenario with scarce resources and large amounts of vehicles to improve spectral efficiency [2]. The orthogonal characteristics between channels of NOMA technology can achieve physical isolation between tenants [3]. NOMA improves the throughput of access networks [4]. In order to meet various business requirements,

Q. Zu et al. (Eds.): HCC 2021, LNCS 13795, pp. 219–231, 2022.
https://doi.org/10.1007/978-3-031-23741-6_20

a scenario combining network slicing and NOMA technology was constructed. It was proved in [5,6] that slicing based on NOMA technology significantly improved performance compared with orthogonal slicing technology.

The problem of resource allocation based on NOMA technology has been studied extensively. In order to solve the resource allocation problem of multi-carrier cellular network, a heuristic scheme is proposed to select the user with the lowest hunger index for pairing, and then the sub-carrier and power joint allocation is carried out [7]. The goal is to maximize the system capacity under the constraint of general proportional user fairness. In the fog network combined with NOMA network scenario, a subchannel matching scheme based on bilateral users is proposed for subchannel allocation. In the power allocation part, a distributed iterative power allocation algorithm based on pricing is proposed [8]. A heuristic joint user pairing and power allocation algorithm is proposed in cellular network scenarios where eMBB slices and URLLC slices coexist [1]. As the problem [1]to be solved is similar to that in this paper, the heuristic joint user pairing and power distribution algorithm are used as the baseline algorithm in the experimental part to compare with proposed algorithm.

Reinforcement learning algorithms are used to solve decision-making problems and obtain optimal strategies through continuous interaction with the environment. In order to solve complex control problems, deep reinforcement learning combines reinforcement learning with deep learning to learn control strategies from high-dimensional raw data. The basic idea of deep reinforcement learning is to use deep learning to automatically learn abstract features of large-scale input data, and then use reinforcement learning based on deep learning feature representation to learn and optimize problem solving strategies. Deep reinforcement learning has become more and more widely used in solving resource allocation problems in communication and network fields [3,9]. Since most resource allocation problems are non-mixed integer nonlinear programming (MINLP) problems, it is difficult to solve, while reinforcement learning can gain experience through constant trial and error, and gradually learn the optimal decision, so as to solve the target problem. In this paper, we also solve the problem of resource allocation through deep reinforcement learning.

This paper studies the resource allocation problem of multi-service network slice based on NOMA technology. In the multi-service network slice where eMBB slice and URLLC slice coexist, we ensure the isolation between different network slices and meet different network slice requirements, and the goal is to maximize the overall spectral efficiency of the system. We propose a resource allocation algorithm based on DDQN to solve both power allocation and subcarrier allocation problems. Simulation results show that compared with baseline algorithm and OMA scheme, our proposed scheme can achieve higher spectral efficiency.

2   System Model and Problem Formulation

2.1   System Model

Consider the downlink NOMA cellular network, which contains a base station(BS) and N users, and the physical resources of the base station are virtualized into eMBB network slices and URLLC network slices. The system model is shown in Fig. 1. Slices that provides the eMBB service for N_1 users are called K_1 slice, and slices that provides the URLLC service for N_2 users are called K_2 slice. NOMA is used for reuse between users, and the receiver uses Successive Interference Cancellation (SIC) for demodulation. Considering SIC complexity, two users are paired together and occupy a subcarrier simultaneously. The system has M subcarriers, and the bandwidth of each subcarrier is B. Because the two services are isolated from each other, there is no pairing between users of two different services.

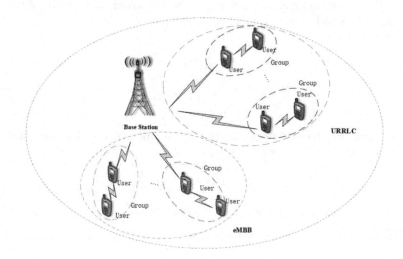

Fig. 1. System Model

If the number of users is odd, there must be a single user occupying a subcarrier and the user occupies all the power resources of the subcarrier. In the case that the number of users is even, the total transmitting power of the base station is P_{tot}, and two users are multiplexed on the sub-channel k . Then, on the sub-channel k, the signal received by user n from the base station is as follows:

$$y_{k,n} = h_{k,n} \sum_{n=1}^{2} \sqrt{x_{k,n}\alpha_{k,n}P}S_{k,n} + N_n \tag{1}$$

Where $x_{k,n}$ is 1, it indicates that user n is allocated to subchannel k; otherwise, it is 0. N_n represents channel additive Gaussian white noise . $\alpha_{k,n}$ is the power allocation coefficient of user n on the subchannel k, and $\sum_{n=1}^{N} \alpha_{k,n} = 1$. $h_{k,n}$ represents the channel gain coefficient between the user and BS

Assuming that the channel gain $h_{k,1}$ of the first user in the pair of two users on the subcarrier k is higher than that $h_{k,2}$ of the second user. In NOMA, the sender will use the power multiplexing technology to distribute power to different users. In general, users with high channel gain will allocate less power resources, while users with low channel gain will allocate more power resources. In order to ensure that SIC can decode correctly, it is necessary to set a threshold of power difference between the first user and the second user on the subcarrier k, so the power constraint of SIC in decoding the second user is shown in Eq. (2).

$$\alpha_2 P_{tot}|h_{k,n}|^2 - \alpha_1 P_{tot}|h_{k,n}|^2 \geq \psi \tag{2}$$

In NOMA user group, users with high channel gain will give interference to users with low channel gain. Therefore, on the subcarrier k, the SINR of the first user and the second user $\gamma_{k,1}, \gamma_{k,2}$ is respectively:

$$\gamma_{k,1} = \frac{|h_{k,1}|^2 \alpha_1 P_{tot}}{N} \tag{3}$$

$$\gamma_{k,2} = \frac{|h_{k,2}|^2 \alpha_2 P_{tot}}{|h_{k,2}|^2 \alpha_1 P_{tot} + N} \tag{4}$$

According to Shannon formula, the throughput of the first user and the second user on the subcarrier k are $R_{k,1}$ and $R_{k,2}$:

$$R_{k,1} = B \times \log(1+\gamma_{k,1}) \tag{5}$$

$$R_{k,1} = B \times \log(1+\gamma_{k,2}) \tag{6}$$

The spectral efficiency of the system is:

$$\eta = \frac{R}{K \times B} = \frac{1}{K} \sum_{n=1}^{N} \log(1 + \gamma_n) \tag{7}$$

In this paper, the service requirements of eMBB scenarios are expressed as constraints on user rates:

$$R_n \geq R_{\min}, \forall k \in K_1, n = 1, 2, \ldots, N_1 \tag{8}$$

Where R_n represents the rate of the user n associated with the eMBB slice, and $R_{\min}$ represents the minimum rate required by the user associated with the eMBB slice.

For URLLC slices, the latency per user should be below the specified threshold. Secondary users associated with URLLC slices should be subject to the following constraints:

$$\Pr\{D_j \geq D_j^{\max}\} = e^{-(R_j - d_j^{\max})D_j^{\max}} \leq \varepsilon, \forall k \in K_2, j = 1, 2, \ldots, N_2 \tag{9}$$

Where D_j represents the delay of the user j associated with URLLC slice. $D_j^{\max}$ represents the maximum delay requirement of the user j associated with URLLC slice, and $d_j^{\max}$ represents the maximum data arrival rate of the user j . ε limits the probability that the user delay is higher than the required delay.

2.2   Problem Formulation

This paper focuses on maximizing the spectral efficiency of the system. Therefore, the objective of our optimization is Eq. (10).

$$\max \eta \tag{10a}$$

$$st:$$

$$C1: \sum_{n=1}^{N} \alpha_{k,n} = 1, \forall k \in K, n \in N, \tag{10b}$$

$$C2: \sum_{n \in N} x_{k,n} \leq 2, \forall k \in K \tag{10c}$$

$$C3: x_{k,n} \in \{0,1\}, \forall k \in K, n \in N \tag{10d}$$

$$C4: \alpha_2 P |h_{k,1}|^2 - \alpha_1 P |h_{k,1}|^2 \geq \psi, \forall k = 1, ...K, \tag{10e}$$

$$C5: R_{k,n} \geq R_{\min}, \forall k \in K_1, n \in N_1, \tag{10f}$$

$$C6: \Pr\{D_j \geq D_j^{\max}\} = e^{-(R_j - d_j^{\max}) D_j^{\max}} \leq \varepsilon, \forall k \in K_2, n \in N_2 \tag{10g}$$

$C1$ indicates that the sum of power allocation factors of each user is 1, and $C2$ and $C3$ limit the maximum number of users that can be reused in each channel. $C4$ is to ensure valid SIC that can be decoded normally. $C5$ and $C6$ ensure minimal service requirements for URLLC and eMbb scenarios.

This optimization problem is a mixed integer nonlinear programming (MINLP) problem, which is difficult to solve. In this paper, the optimization problem is decomposed into two sub-problems: subcarrier allocation and power allocation. The reinforcement learning method will be introduced below to solve this problem.

3   Resource Allocation Based on Deep Reinforcement Learning

In this paper, a DRL Resource Allocation algorithm based on DDQN is proposed to model the resource allocation problem as a reinforcement learning task. DDQN is an algorithm for solving discrete problems in deep reinforcement learning, and uses neural network to approximate Q value (action value function). In the decision-making process of DDQN, the state is taken as the input of neural network, and the Q value of each action is obtained through neural network analysis and calculation, and then the action corresponding to the maximum Q value is selected to execute. DDQN reduces the deviation caused by data correlation and alleviates the overestimation problem through two key technologies of experience pool playback and target network. The specific framework of the algorithm is shown in Fig. 2. In the reinforcement learning task, *State*, *Action* and *Reward* are defined as follows:

State: The agent's state is defined as the user's SINR, $s_t = \{\gamma_1(t), \gamma_2(t), \cdots, \gamma_N(t)\}$ where $t = \{1, 2, \cdots, T_{\max}\}$, and $T_{\max}$ represents the maximum episode set.

Action: The action of agent consists of two parts $a_t = \{a_1(t), a_2(t)\}$. Action 1 represents the subcarrier allocation of users. Since eMbb slice users and URLLC slice users are isolated, the subcarrier allocation of the two slice users is carried out respectively.

$$a_1(t) = \{x_{URLLC}(t), x_{eMbb}(t)\} \tag{11}$$

$$x_{URLLC}(t) = \{x_1^{URLLC}(t)x_2^{URLLC}(t), ...x_{N_1}^{URLLC}(t)\} \tag{12}$$

$$x_{eMbb}(t) = \{x_1^{eMbb}(t)x_2^{eMbb}(t), ...x_{N_2}^{eMbb}(t)\} \tag{13}$$

Action 2 indicates the power allocation.

$$a_2(t) = \{\alpha_1(t), \alpha_2(t), ...\alpha_N(t)\} \tag{14}$$

Where x_n^{URLLC}, x_n^{eMbb} indicates that user n is allocated to a specific subchannel. Since the output of DDQN algorithm is discrete value, the transmitted power of users is divided into 20 discrete power distribution factors on average, and the specific power allocated by corresponding users is expressed in Equation (15).

$$P_n \in \{0, \frac{P_{tot}}{19}, \frac{2P_{tot}}{19}, ..., P_{tot}\} \tag{15}$$

Reward: Since the state space and action space of the entire network are extremely large, if only the actions and states that meet the constraints are rewarded, and the rewards for those that do not meet the constraints are set to 0, the problem of sparse rewards will be caused, and it is difficult for the agent to learn. Therefore, in this paper, the common reward method is modified, we set internal reward and external reward. Internal reward is to meet the constraints of the reward, and external reward is to reward the overall goal.

1. Internal reward
   (1) Rewards for subcarrier constraints:

$$r_t^{u,int} = \omega^{u,int} \Gamma(C2) \tag{16}$$

   Meet $C2$, $\Gamma(C2) = 0$; Otherwise $\Gamma(C2) = 1$, $\omega^{u,int} < 0$
   (2) Rewards for power constraints:

$$r_{m,t}^{p,int} = \omega_I^{p,int} \Gamma(C4) + \omega_{II}^{p,int} \left(\sum_{i=1}^{N_1} (R_i - R_{min}) \right) + \omega_{III}^{p,int} \left(\sum_{i=1}^{N_2} (D_{min} - D_i) \right) \tag{17}$$

   Meet $C4$, $\Gamma(C4) = 0$; Otherwise $\Gamma(C4) = 1$, $\omega_I^{p,int} < 0$, $\omega_{II}^{p,int} > 0$, $\omega_{III}^{p,int} > 0$

2. External reward

$$r_t^{u,jo} = \omega^{u,jo} \sum_{m=1}^{N} R_m, \omega^{u,jo} < 0 \tag{18}$$

Immediate rewards for the environment are defined as:

$$r(t) = r_t^{u,int} + r_{m,t}^{p,int} + r_t^{u,jo} \qquad (19)$$

The goal of reinforcement learning is to maximize long-term cumulative rewards, not immediate rewards. Therefore, the cumulative discount reward function is constructed:

$$R_t = r_{t+1} + \gamma r_{t+2} + \gamma^2 r_{t+3} + \cdots = \sum_{k=0}^{n} \gamma^k r_{t+k+1} \qquad (20)$$

Here $\gamma \in [0,1]$ is the discount rate, which shows how important future rewards are compared to current rewards.

The action value function $Q_\pi(s_t, a_t)$ in reinforcement learning is defined as:

$$Q_\pi(s_t, a_t) = E[R_t | s_t, a_t] \qquad (21)$$

Where s_t is the state, a_t is the action.

Q network is used to approximate the action value function $Q(s_t, a_t; \omega)$ in DDQN. Choose the action with the highest score in each decision to maximize the ultimate reward.

$$a_t = \arg\max_{a_t \in \alpha} Q(s_t, a_t; \omega) \qquad (22)$$

Where A represents the action space that the agent can take, that is, all schemes for subcarriers and power distribution. ω indicates the parameter of the neural network Q network.

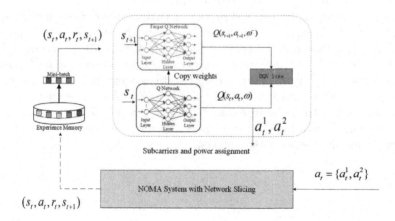

Fig. 2. DRL resource allocation algorithm based on DDQN

Target Q network and Q network have the same structure, but parameter updates are different. DDQN algorithm trains neural network through TD learning algorithm. Target Q network can obtain the action value corresponding to the next state, and through Temporal Difference (TD), it can be deduced that:

$$Q(s_t, a_t; \omega) \approx r_t + \gamma \max Q(s_{t+1}, a; \omega^-) \tag{23}$$

The difference between the left and right is used as the loss in the neural network, and the loss function form of DDQN can be obtained, as shown in Equation (15).

$$J(\omega) = \frac{1}{m} \sum_{j=1}^{m} [r_j + \gamma \max Q(s_{j+1}, a_j; \omega^-) - Q(s_j, a_j^1; \omega)]^2 \tag{24}$$

Exploration is also an essential step when choosing actions based on state. With the $\varepsilon - greedy$ greedy strategy adopted, the agent has the ε probability to explore new actions by using random functions, and has the $1 - \varepsilon$ probability to output the action with the highest score by Q network. Because the action space of the network is too large and there are many restrictions on actions with high rewards, it is very easy to generate data with small rewards stored in the experience pool in the random exploration of greedy strategy, such as: generating a subcarrier occupied by three users of the data. When the agent learns, it is difficult to converge to the optimal allocation scheme. Therefore, some expert high score data should be added to the experience pool before the agent learns. For example, the data that meets all constraints should be generated and stored in the experience pool. It has been proved in experiments that this scheme can make the agent converge to the optimal scheme faster.

Then we introduce the detailed process of DRL resource allocation algorithm based on DDQN. First, some expert high score data are added into the experience pool. And then initialize the agent state s_t which is SINR of the user. DQN algorithm adopts $\varepsilon - greedy$ greedy strategy to output action $a_t = \{a_1(t), a_2(t)\}$. Through Equations (4) and (19), the next state of agent and immediate reward can be solved. The quad under each episode is stored in the experience pool. In episodes higher than the threshold,the agent starts to learn, sampling minibatch size quads from the experience pool to train Q network, and then target Q network updates network parameters.

Algorithm 1. Resource Allocation Algorithm For Joint User Pairing And Power Allocation Based On DDQN

1: Initialize Q Network $Q(s_t, a_t; \omega)$ of the codebook assignment DDQN unit with weights ω.
2: Initialize Target Q Network $Q(s_t, a_t; \omega^-)$ with initial weights $\omega^- = \omega$.
3: Initialize the maximum episode $T_{\max}$, replay memory block D, agent network parameter update threshold φ
4: Initialize the agent state s_t
5: Add some expert high score data to the experience pool
6: **for** $t = 1, 2, \cdots, T_{\max}$ **do**
7:    DDQN unit selects action a_t following the $\varepsilon - greedy$ policy.
8:    Input $a_t = \{a_t^1, a_t^2\}$ and calculate the next state s_{t+1} according to formula (4).
9:    Store tuple (s_t, r_t, a_t, s_{t+1}) in memory block D.
10:    $s_t = s_{t+1}$
11:    **while** $t > \varphi$ **do**
12:       Sample a random mini-batch of N tuples (s_t, r_t, a_t, s_{t+1}) from D.
13:       For the DDQN unit, update its weights by minimizing the loss function (19).
14:       Update target Q Network weights ω^- of the DDQN unit by copying ω
15:    **end while**
16: **end for**

---

4   Simulation Results and Analysis

4.1   Simulation Results

In the model, users are randomly distributed in a (100 m, 100 m) two-dimensional space. There are 16 channels in the system, and the maximum number of reusable users in each channel is 2. Path loss formula is $L(d) = 37 + 30 \log(d)$, where $d(km)$ is the distance between the base station and the user. The total transmitting power of the base station P_{tot} is 46 dbm, and the noise power σ^2 is $1e^{-7}$. The minimum rate required by the user associated with eMBB slice R_{min} is 0.1 Mbps, and the maximum delay required by the user associated with URLLC slice D^{max} is 10 ms.

Table 1. Parameters of simulation.

Parameter	Value
T_{max}	4000
ε-greedy	0.1
Discount rate γ	0.995
Activation function	Relu
Optimizer	Adam
Threshold for agent network parameter update φ	3300

All the networks in the algorithm framework are composed of four layers: an input layer, a hidden layer composed of 128 neurons, a hidden layer composed of 64 neurons and an output layer. We set batchsize to 128. The specific network parameters are shown in Table 1. First of all, the purpose of the first experiment is to find an appropriate learning rate so that the algorithm can quickly converge and obtain the highest reward value. In the scenario of $N = 32$, $N_1 = 16$, $N_2 = 16$, $M = 16$, three learning rates are selected: $lr = 0.01, 0.001, 0.00001$. A point on each curve in the experiment was the average of reward under 30 episodes. It can be seen from Fig. 3 that setting too large a learning rate leads to the algorithm falling into the local optimal value, while setting a small learning rate and setting a middle learning rate can both converge to a higher reward value, but the curve of setting a middle learning rate converges faster than that of setting a small learning rate. Therefore, it is the optimal learning rate setting value that we seek. All experiments below will be trained at this learning rate.

The second experiment is to compare the spectral efficiency changes of the proposed algorithm, baseline algorithm [1] and the scheme using OMA under different base station transmitting powers. Figure 4 shows that as the transmitting power of the base station increases, the spectral efficiency of the corresponding curves of the three schemes also increases. And it is easy to see that in all power scenarios, the spectral efficiency of the system can be higher by using the algorithm proposed in this paper than the other two schemes.

The third experiment is to compare the spectral efficiency of the three algorithms applied by different number of users. Figure 5 shows that as the number of users increases, the spectral efficiency of the three curves decreases continuously.

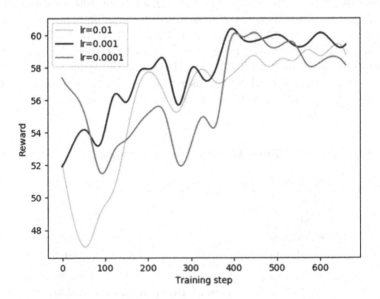

Fig. 3. Comparison of performance under different learning rates

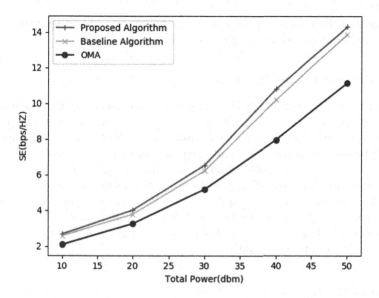

Fig. 4. System SE versus base station power

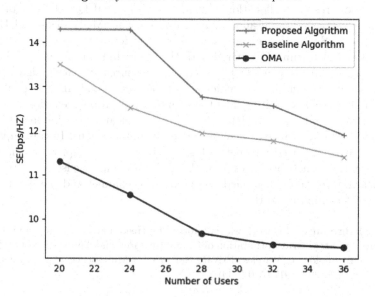

Fig. 5. System SE versus the number of user

This is because the total transmitting power of the base station is determined. As the number of users increases, each user is allocated less and less power, which directly leads to the decrease of the spectral efficiency of the system. However, it can be seen from the figure that compared with the other two algorithms, with the increase of users, the curve of the algorithm proposed in this paper can still maintain high spectral efficiency. Compared with the other two schemes, the algorithm proposed in this paper can access more users.

4.2 Advantages and Disadvantages

Compared with the heuristic joint user pairing and power distribution algorithm [1], the proposed algorithm can achieve higher spectral efficiency under different number of users and different transmitting power of base station. Moreover, NOMA technology is introduced into the system, and multiple users occupy one channel. Compared with the scheme using OMA, the proposed algorithm significantly improves spectral efficiency. However, the disadvantage of the proposed algorithm lies in that DDQN algorithm is used to solve the problem in discrete scenes, while the power distribution problem is in continuous scenes. Discretization of power will lead to exponential growth of agent's action space and affect the convergence rate of the model.

5   Conclusion

We propose a resource allocation algorithm based on DDQN. This algorithm is used to solve the resource allocation problem when eMBB slices and URLLC slices coexist. Simulation experiments prove the feasibility and correctness of the proposed algorithm. Compared with the algorithms proposed by OMA and baseline algorithm [1], the DDQN-based DRL resource allocation algorithm significantly improves the spectral efficiency of the system and ensures the isolation between slices. 5G is divided into three main application scenarios: Enhanced Mobile Broadband (eMBB); URLLC (Ultra-reliableand Low Latency Communications); MMTC (Massive MachineType Communication). In this paper, two scenarios are virtualized into network slices. In the next step, we virtualize the three scenarios as network slices. In addition to ensuring slice isolation, reinforcement learning method is applied to explore the channel and power allocation scheme of downlink network.

Acknowledgment. This work was supported by Headquarters Science and Technology Project of State Grid Corporation of China: Research and Application of Optimized Evolution Technology of Wireless Private Network for Multi-service Ubiquitous Access (Grant No. 5700-202019174A-0-0-00).

References

1. Bao, J., Zheng, W.J., Shao, W., Ma, T., Qie, W., Zhang, Y.: Joint user pairing and power allocation in multi-slicing NOMA system. J. China Univ. Posts Telecommun. **28**(3), 28–35 (2021)
2. Xu, Y., Gu, X.: Resource allocation for NOMA-based V2V system. In: 2018 International Conference on Network Infrastructure and Digital Content (IC-NIDC) (2018)

3. Sinaie, M., Ng, D.W.K., Jorswieck, E.A.: Resource allocation in NOMA virtualized wireless networks under statistical delay constraints. Wirel. Commun. Lett. IEEE **7**(6), 954–957 (2018)
4. Jang, G., Lee, C., Kim, N., Kang, W., Cho, S.: Throughput maximization for uplink IoT NOMA systems with efficient resource allocation. In: 2020 International Conference on Information and Communication Technology Convergence (ICTC) (2020)
5. Sun, G., Zemuy, G.T., Xiong, K.: Dynamic reservation and deep reinforcement learning based autonomous resource management for wireless virtual networks. In: 2018 IEEE 37th International Performance Computing and Communications Conference (IPCCC) (2019)
6. Zhang, Y., Kang, C., Teng, Y., Li, S., Zheng, W., Fang, J.: Deep reinforcement learning framework for joint resource allocation in heterogeneous networks. In: 2019 IEEE 90th Vehicular Technology Conference (VTC2019-Fall) (2019)
7. Wang, C.L., Hung, C.W.: Proportional-fairness resource allocation for a downlink multicarrier NOMA system. In: 2020 14th International Conference on Signal Processing and Communication Systems (ICSPCS) (2020)
8. Wen, X., Zhang, H., Zhang, H., Fang, F.: Interference pricing resource allocation and user-subchannel matching for NOMA hierarchy fog networks. IEEE J. Sel. Top. Sign. Proces. **13**(3), 467–479 (2019)
9. Wei, Y., Yu, F. R., Mei, S., Zhu, H.: User scheduling and resource allocation in HetNets with hybrid energy supply: An actor-critic reinforcement learning approach. IEEE Trans. Wirel. Commun. (2017)

5G Resource Sharing Scheme and Consensus Algorithm Based on Blockchain

Siyuan Sun[1,2], Xiaojun Jin[1(✉)], Ligang Ren[2], Dong Tian[2], and Yifei Wei[1]

[1] Beijing University of Posts and Telecommunications, Beijing 100876, China
jinxiaojun@bupt.edu.cn

[2] China United Network Communications Co., Ltd., Beijing Branch, Beijing 100052, China

Abstract. One of the outstanding features of 5G is the powerful resource sharing ability to cope with the increasing content demand and data usage, especially in 5G IoT scenarios. However, due to data attacks, sharing resources in mobile networks is extremely vulnerable to serious data leakage risks and security threats. Blockchain has the characteristics of decentralization, security, non-tamperability, and incentive mechanism, which enables this emerging disruptive technology to provide innovative solutions to the challenges in 5G networks. This paper combines resource sharing in 5G with blockchain technology, proposes a blockchain-based 5G resource sharing architecture, provides incentives for resource sharing between nodes, and considers the latency issue in 5G, and proposes BFT-PoS consensus algorithm, which combined PBFT and PoS, improves the efficiency of the consensus algorithm and is verified by simulation.

Keywords: 5G · Blockchain · Resource sharing · PBFT · PoS

1 Introduction

Fifth-generation (5G) wireless networks are about to be deployed globally. 5G technology aims to support diversified vertical applications by connecting heterogeneous devices and machines, and has been significantly improved in terms of high-quality services, increased network capacity, and enhanced system throughput [1]. Different from traditional wireless networks, 5G and other networks are particularly focused on providing decentralization, security, privacy protection and ubiquitous services [2]. Since 5G and higher versions operate at high frequencies (i.e. millimeter waves) above 30 GHz, the signal transmission distance is shorter. Covering 4G equivalent areas requires denser and more complex heterogeneous network infrastructure, resulting in higher infrastructure management costs. Therefore, 5G and later applications still face many challenges, including security threats, privacy vulnerabilities, management automation, lack of incentive mechanisms, etc. [3]. 5G and higher versions require substantial capital investment in network infrastructure. The shared infrastructure approach can reduce the

Q. Zu et al. (Eds.): HCC 2021, LNCS 13795, pp. 232–241, 2022.
https://doi.org/10.1007/978-3-031-23741-6_21

cost burden of network deployment. Users may not agree to share their resources without compensation or incentives for corresponding costs (such as energy costs). Therefore, it is necessary to establish an incentive mechanism to promote sustainable resource sharing in 5G and beyond [4, 5]. For example, due to complex interference management and real-time protocols, there is currently no motivation for dynamic spectrum sharing [6]. Without proper financial compensation, rational and self-interested users may not agree to the sharing of spectrum resources.

Blockchain is an emerging disruptive technology that can provide innovative solutions to effectively solve the challenges in 5G networks. Blockchain mainly refers to the basic technology of cryptocurrency Bitcoin [7]. The core idea of blockchain is decentralization. This means that the blockchain does not store any of its databases in a central location. Instead, the blockchain is copied and spread through a network of participants (i.e., computers).

Blockchain has inherent characteristics such as security, automation, privacy protection, availability, and capitalization. These features are due to the fact that the blockchain is designed to be a distributed and shared ledger, storing records in a tamper-proof and immutable manner. In fact, it can enhance data integrity protection and protect privacy through encryption technology. In addition, its security can support smart contracts to verify and execute transactions in an automated manner. A comprehensive audit of all events and data changes makes the application transparent so that all users can use the records. Therefore, blockchain is a promising platform that can promote 5G and trust beyond the network without relying on TTP (a trusted third party) [1].

The current blockchain performance and scalability are limited, which hinders the application of blockchain in 5G and beyond. Because the blockchain needs a lot of bandwidth resources in the consensus process [3], the consensus algorithm of the blockchain has become a bottleneck of system efficiency.

2 Related Work

The consensus algorithm is the core of the blockchain, and the most widely used consensus algorithm is PoW, such as the Nakamoto consensus protocol. Although the Nakamoto consensus protocol effectively prevents the double-spending attack problem, the algorithm will cause a lot of energy waste, and the protocol also encounters some performance bottlenecks. The PoS algorithm avoids the energy consumption caused by the mining process and is considered to be the mainstream algorithm in the future. But PoS also faces problems such as easy forks and N@S attacks. In addition, many researchers have tried to replace the Nakamoto consensus with the classic BFT protocol [8]. The BFT protocol can ensure the safe operation of distributed computing systems in the presence of malicious nodes. Decades of studies have shown that the BFT protocol performs well in terms of flexibility and performance [9]. However, the BFT protocol is traditionally studied in a closed environment, and the number of participants and their identities need to be known. Blockchain prefers open membership and can even keep in touch with thousands of participants. In addition, the deployment of the blockchain to the wide area network requires a consensus to set higher variability to accommodate communication delays. Designing consensus in the context of blockchain is much more difficult than the closed setting of traditional distributed systems. The development of more efficient consensus protocols will play an important role in the development of blockchain.

[10] studies the consensus propagation problem in the PoS-based alliance blockchain network, and strikes a balance between the delay in the propagation process and the transaction fees provided by blockchain users. [11] proposed a new blockchain-based contract settlement protocol, which uses PBFT and an improved PoS two-phase consensus algorithm to ensure the security, energy and time efficiency of the system. [12] proposed a Robust Proof of Stake (RPOS) consensus protocol based on PoS. RPoS selects data to write nodes based on the currency balance, and other nodes accept new data to maintain the consistency of the ledger. In the comparison part, RPoS is more energy-efficient than PoW, faster than PoS, and more robust to PoS-related attacks such as Nothing-at-Stake (N@S) attacks and coin age accumulation attacks. [13] proposed a consensus protocol called Extended PoS (e-PoS), which solves the limitations of PoW and PoS, and realizes decentralization, energy saving and fair mining in the blockchain system. At present, there is no document that proposes a blockchain consensus algorithm suitable for 5G scenarios, and the corresponding methods for different resource sharing are also different. Specific solutions can be solved by designing different smart contracts and identity authentication methods. This paper proposes a general incentive Mechanism is a consensus mechanism that is suitable for the combination of PBFT and PoS in 5G scenarios. The main contribution of this paper:

1) Propose a three-tier architecture for 5G resource sharing based on blockchain.
2) Propose a consensus algorithm that combines PBFT and PoS suitable for 5G blockchain systems to provide incentives for nodes participating in resource sharing and improve efficiency.
3) The performance of the consensus algorithm is analyzed, and the experiment proves that the algorithm proposed in this paper has improved efficiency compared with the traditional PBFT.

3   System Architecture

The blockchain-based 5G resource sharing architecture is shown in the Fig. 1:

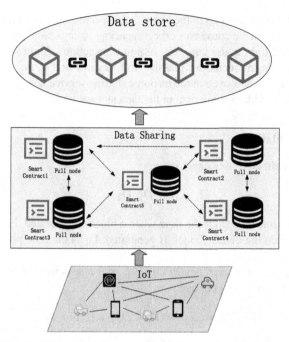

Fig. 1. 5G resource sharing architecture based on blockchain

The structure is divided into three layers from bottom to top:

1) **Internet of things data collection layer**: Providing massive IoT data. Collect raw data of different types (videos, pictures, texts, etc.) from different sources such as social networks, mobile devices, Internet of Things devices, wearable devices, etc. These data can be collected and managed by existing applications, or they can be collected and managed by developing innovative applications that depend on the type of data source.

2) **Resource sharing service layer**: Provide resource sharing services, including consensus algorithms and incentive mechanisms. Resource sharing between nodes will be spread in the form of transactions. Specific resource sharing can be spectrum resources, Internet of Things data resources, and so on. The business logic of different resource sharing is different, such as spectrum resource sharing, Internet of Things data sharing, etc. Therefore, different smart contracts can be designed to realize different resource sharing services, such as different smart contracts as shown in the figure. The specific resource sharing logic is beyond the scope of this paper. Both full nodes and light nodes can initiate resource sharing transactions, and the system provides tokens as incentives for nodes participating in packaging blocks and sharing resources.

3) **Data storage layer**: Store data to the blockchain. The data is stored in the blockchain, so that the data can be stored securely and immutably, and 5G resource sharing transactions can be traced.

This paper divides the nodes in the blockchain into full nodes and light nodes, where full nodes participate in the consensus process, package transactions, and can also submit transactions, while light nodes can only submit transactions. Light nodes mainly exist in the IoT device layer, including massive IoT devices and terminals such as smart phones. Full nodes are deployed in the resource sharing service layer, execute consensus algorithms, and store blockchain data in the data storage layer.

3.1 Stake Calculation

The time series defined in this paper is:

$$T = \{D_0, D_1, D_2, ...\} \tag{1}$$

The adjacent time interval is the time when a block is generated. For example, D_0 is the time point when the genesis block is generated, D_1 is the time point when the first block is generated, and so on.

In Peer-to-peer crypto-currency(PPC) [14], coin age is used for stake calculation. The calculation formula for coin age is:

$$coin\_age_t = coin * (D_t - D_{t-1}) + coin\_age_{t-1} \tag{2}$$

Among them, PPC reduces the difficulty of mining by accumulating the coin age. The more the coin age, the lower the mining difficulty, and the coin age will be cleared after the block is mined. The mining process of the blockchain needs to calculate a hash value that meets a certain range of conditions. The PoS calculation for PPC is:

$$hash(cur\_blockheader) < T \arg et * coin\_age_t \tag{3}$$

hash(cur_blockheader) represents the hash value of the current block header, Target represents the target threshold, and coin_age$_t$ represents the coin age at time t. The problem with this kind of stake calculation is that a node can accumulate currency age offline for a long time, and then go offline again after digging a block to obtain considerable benefits. Obviously, if a large number of nodes do this, it will threaten the security of the entire system.

This paper improves the calculation method of coin age, and reduces the risk of coin age accumulation attacks by adding a decay factor. The reward in this paper is represented by "token", and the concept of "coin age" is abstracted as stake. The improved calculation method for stake is:

$$stake_{i,t} = (token * (D_t - D_{t-1}) + stake_{i-1,t-1}) * e^{\delta*(t-T_i)} \tag{4}$$

Among them, stake$_{i,t}$ is the stake of node i at time t, δ is the attenuation coefficient, and T_i is the time when node i participated in the package block last time. Nodes participating in the packaging block will get a fixed reward in each block, and light nodes participating in the transaction will get a partial reward. The specific reward is determined by the specific logic in the smart contract.

3.2 BFT-PoS Consensus Process

The BFT-PoS consensus algorithm process is as follows and showed in Fig. 2:

Step1: select the block-producing node according to the election algorithm. Since some nodes may be offline and no block is generated when the node produces a block, the longest waiting time T_{max} of a node is set. If the block is not received over T_{max}, the system automatically executes the election algorithm to select the next block node.

Step 2: Enter the pre-prepare stage, the block-producing node generates a block, broadcasts the message < < pre-prepare,view, signature,digest >,block > to other candidate nodes, digest is the summary of the message, and view is the current view. Signature is the digital signature of the node.

Step 3: Enter the prepare phase. After the replica node receives the pre-preparation message, it checks that the message is legal. If the verification passes, it sends a prepare message < prepare,view, signature,digest,id > to other nodes, with its own id information.At the same time, it receives prepare information from other nodes. The node that receives the prepare message also checks the message legitimacy of the message. After the verification is passed, the preparation message is written into the message log, and at least 2/3 of the nodes have been verified. Before entering the prepare state.

Step 4: Enter the commit & view-change stage and broadcast a commit message to tell other nodes that the current block is in the ready state in view v. If at least 2/3 of the commit messages passed by the nodes are collected, it means that the block is passed and a consensus is reached on the block generated by the current master node. At the same time, enter the view-change to execute the node election algorithm, and the block will be generated by the next accounting node. If no block is generated after T_{max}, skip the current block node, enter the view-change stage, and re-select the accounting node.

Step 5: Repeat the pre-prepare, prepare and commit and view-change processes according to the above process, until the kth node completes the block generation task, forming a temporary blockchain, which is broadcast by the first block generation node to all followers Node, finally complete an epoch. If other nodes exceed T_{max} and do not receive the message from the first node, the second node will broadcast the temporary blockchain to other nodes. In Fig. 3 node n2 failed to become the last block-producing node in the epoch because it was offline after n1 produce the block, and doesn't completed the block generation task.

Step 6: Enter the Broadcast Blockchain stage: other nodes do not receive the message of n2 within T_{max}, execute the view-change process, and select n0 as the master node. At this time, n0 is online and serves as the master node to send the temporary blockchain to Other full nodes that did not participate in this epoch.

Step 7: Enter the reply stage: All nodes that have not participated in the consensus will execute the reply process after receiving the temporary blockchain. First, verify the legitimacy of the temporary blockchain, and make sure that the temporary blockchain produces blocks in the correct order. After verifying the signature information in a block, send a reply message to other nodes. All nodes will reach a consensus on this temporary block chain after receiving more than 2/3 of the reply messages from nodes not participating in the block generation and add it to the local blockchain.

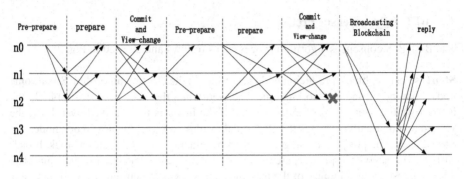

Fig. 2. BFT-PoS consensus process of one epoch

The node n2 in the block generation queue has not completed the block generation task because it is offline, so it will not receive the reward token. This is also a penalty for offline nodes. At the same time, its stake will be cleared like other nodes participating in this epoch.

3.3 Consensus Efficiency Analysis

The block propagation time is determined by the transmission delay on each link and the transaction verification time of each node. For a block of size s, the transmission delay is:

$$\tau_p(s) = \frac{s}{\gamma c} \tag{5}$$

where γ is a parameter related to the network scale, and c is the average effective channel capacity of each link. At the same time, since verifying a transaction requires a certain amount of calculation, the block verification time can be modeled as a linear function

$$\tau_v(s) = \beta s \tag{6}$$

where β is a parameter determined by the network size and the average verification speed of each node. Then, the average time for a block of size s to propagate on the network is:

$$\tau(s) = \tau_p(s) + \tau_v(s) = \frac{s}{\gamma c} + \beta s \tag{7}$$

The occurrence rate of non-packed blocks due to propagation delay or node offline follows a Poisson process with an average rate of 1/T. Therefore, the probability that the node does not produce a valid block of size s is:

$$\Pr(s) = 1 - e^{-\tau(s)/T}$$
$$= 1 - e^{-(\frac{s}{\gamma c} + \beta s_i)/T} \tag{8}$$

The expected number of blocks in an epoch is:

$$blockNumber = [k * (1 - \Pr(s)]$$
$$= [k * e^{-(\frac{s}{\gamma c} + \beta s_i)/T}]$$

(9)

where $[\cdot]$ means rounding down.

Then the time to complete an epoch in the BFT-PoS consensus is:

$$T_{epoch} = (1 - \Pr(s)) * \eta * k^2 * \tau(s)$$
$$+ \Pr(s)*k * T_{max} + T_{election}$$
$$= e^{-(\frac{s}{\gamma c} + \beta s_i)/T} * \eta*k^2 * (\frac{s}{\gamma c} + \beta s)$$
$$+ (1 - e^{-(\frac{s}{\gamma c} + \beta s_i)/T}) * k * T_{max} + T_{election}$$

(10)

Among them, η is a communication complexity parameter, and $\eta*k2*\tau(s)$ represents the time spent in the propagation process of a block with a block size of s.

The TPS of the blockchain architecture in this paper is:

$$TPS = \frac{blockNumber * block_{size}}{Tx_{size} * T_{epoch}}$$
$$= \frac{[k * e^{-(\frac{s}{\gamma c} + \beta s_i)/T}]*s}{Tx_{size} * (e^{-(\frac{s}{\gamma c} + \beta s_i)/T} * \eta*k * (\frac{s}{\gamma c} + \beta s_i) + (1 - e^{-(\frac{s}{\gamma c} + \beta s_i)/T}) * k * T_{max} + T_{election})}$$

(11)

After each epoch, the node calculates the stake of each node. If the node is offline and does not participate in this consensus, the stake of the node will also be cleared to zero, and will not receive block rewards, so the node will tend to stay online for a long time.

4 Simulation

This section compares the performance of the BFT-PoS algorithm proposed in this paper with the PBFT algorithm in the traditional consortium chain. The setting parameters are as follows: blocksize = 10MB, tx_size = 0.2kb, effective channel capacity C = 50kbps, $\beta = 0.00005$, $\gamma = 50$, Telection = 0.1s, $\eta = 0.3$, Poisson distribution parameter T = 100, corresponding node offline rate 0.39, $T_{max} = 2s$, block producing node ratio $\mu = 0.5$, that is, half of all nodes participate in producing block.

1). The time spent and tps in each epoch varies with the number of nodes.

Compare the time spent in each epoch of the two algorithms with the number of nodes, as shown in Fig. 3, The comparison of TPS between BFT-PoS and PBFT under different numbers of nodes is shown in the Fig. 4.

It can be seen from the Fig. 3 that the efficiency of the BFT-PoS algorithm to generate the same number of blocks is much higher than that of PBFT.It can be seen from Fig. 4 that the tps of the BFT-PoS algorithm is much higher than that of the PBFT algorithm.

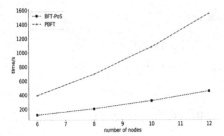

Fig. 3. Delay comparison of BFT-PoS and PBFT

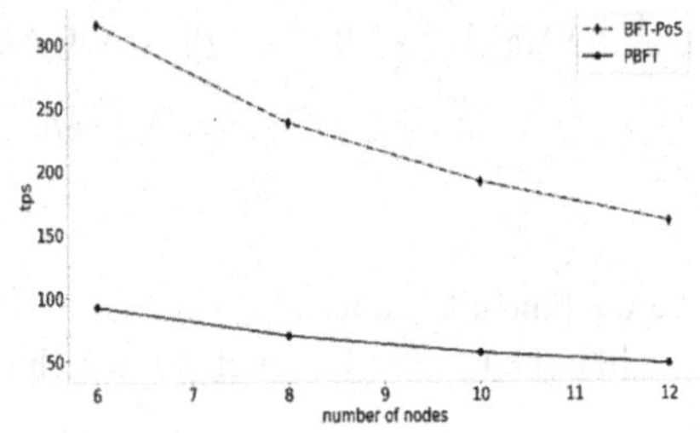

Fig. 4. Tps comparison of BFT-PoS and PBFT

2). Comparison of epoch time and tps of the two algorithms under different block generation ratio μ:

This section changes the block generation ratio parameter μ to compare the algorithm performance.μ is respectively taken as 0.7, 0.4, 0.2, the epoch time comparison of BFT-PoS and PBFT under different μ are shown in Fig. 5, the comparison of tps under different μ is shown in Fig. 6

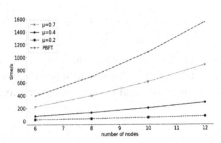
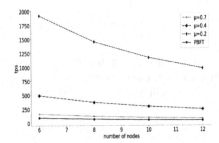

Fig. 5. Delay comparison between BFT-PoS and PBFT under different offline rates

Fig. 6. Comparison of tps between BFT-PoS and PBFT under different offline rates

It can be seen from Fig. 5 that as μ decreases, the time of each epoch will also decrease, and the closer μ is to 1, the closer the curve is to the epoch delay curve of PBFT. It can be seen from Fig. 6 that the smaller the μ, the higher the tps, and the higher the consensus efficiency. But the value of μ is not as high as possible. Too few block nodes may cause the system to tend to be centralized, so μ can be a compromise choice in actual situations, such as 0.4.

5 Conclusion

This paper first introduces the meaning of resource sharing in the 5G scenario, the lack of incentives, and the lack of motivation for users to share data. It proposes an innovative solution based on the emerging technology of blockchain, and designs the third resource sharing based on blockchain. Layer architecture, and proposed a hybrid consensus mechanism of PBFT and PoS, which provides incentives for nodes participating in resource sharing, and improves the consensus efficiency, so that it can better meet the low-latency requirements of 5G. This paper does not design a specific incentive mechanism. Shared data can be spectrum, Internet of Things data, etc. When nodes share different data, they get different incentives. These can be designed with different smart contracts and identity authentication protocols,which is also a research direction in the future.

Acknowledgment. This work supported by the research project of China Unicom: Research on the Core Technology of SMS Capability Platform Based on "5G Message + Blockchain".

References

1. Nguyen, D.C., Pathirana, P.N., Ding, M., Seneviratne, A.: Blockchain for 5G and beyond networks: a state of the art survey. J. Netw. Comput. Appl. **166**, 102693 (2020)
2. Chaer, A., Salah, K., Lima, C., Ray, P.P., Sheltami, T.: Blockchain for 5g: Opportunities and challenges. In: 2019 IEEE Globecom Workshops(GC Wkshps), pp. 1–6 (2019)
3. Yue, K., et al.: A survey of decentralizing applications via Blockchain: the 5G and beyond perspective. IEEE Commun. Surveys Tutorials **23**, 2191–2217 (2021)
4. Wei, Y., Ng, J.S., Xiong, Z., Niyato, D., Yang, Q.: Incentive mechanism design for resource sharing in collaborative edge learning. arXiv e-prints (2020)
5. Gao, J., Zhao, L., Shen, X.: Network utility maximization based on an incentive mechanism for truthful reporting of local information. IEEE Trans. Veh. Technol. **67**(8), 7523–7537 (2018)
6. Maksymyuk, T., et al.: Blockchain-empowered framework for decentralized network management in 6G. IEEE Commun. Mag. **58**(9), 86–92 (2020)
7. Nakamoto, S.: Bitcoin: A peer-to-peer electronic cash system. Decentralized Bus. Rev. 21260 (2008)
8. Golan Gueta, G., et al.: SBFT: a scalable and decentralized trust infrastructure. In: 2019 49th Annual IEEE/IFIP International Conference on Dependable Systems and Networks (DSN), pp. 568–580 (2019)
9. Vukolić, M.: The quest for scalable blockchain fabric: proof-of-work vs. BFT replication. In: Camenisch, J., Kesdoğan, D. (eds.) iNetSec 2015. LNCS, vol. 9591, pp. 112–125. Springer, Cham (2016). https://doi.org/10.1007/978-3-319-39028-4_9
10. Kang, J., Xiong, Z., Niyato, D., Wang, P., Ye, D., Kim, D.I.: Incentivizing consensus propagation in proof-of-stake based consortium blockchain networks. IEEE Wirel. Commun. Lett. **8**, 157–160 (2019)
11. Masaud, T.M., Warner, J., El-Saadany, E.F.: A blockchain-enabled decentralized energy trading mechanism for islanded networked microgrids. IEEE Access **8**, 211291–211302 (2020)
12. Li, A., Wei, X., He, Z.: Robust proof of stake: a new consensus protocol for sustainable blockchain systems. Sustainability **12**(7), 2824 (2020)
13. Saad M, Qin Z, Ren K, Nyang, D., Mohaisen, D.: e-PoS: Making Proof-of-Stake Decentralized and Fair. arXiv preprint arXiv:2101.00330 (2021)
14. King, S., Nadal, S.: Ppcoin: Peer-to-peer crypto-currency with proof-of-stake. Inform. Secur.: An Int. J. **47**(1), 109–121 (2020)

5G Message Log Credit Management and Verification System Based on Blockchain

Siyuan Sun[1,2], Jiazheng Yu[1(✉)], Zikui Lu[1], Ligang Ren[2], and Yifei Wei[1]

[1] Beijing University of Posts and Telecommunications, Beijing 100876, China
416883000@qq.com
[2] China United Network Communications Co., Ltd., Beijing Branch, Beijing 100052, China

Abstract. With the development of the Internet and 5G era, RCS (Rich Communication Suite) based on native SMS interface is developing at a high speed, which will develop a multi-functional service to provide users with picture, audio, video and other forms of interaction. In this context, frequent messaging between users or interaction between users and third-party enterprises will produce a large number of RCS logs. These logs play a very important role in the credit granting of electronic vouchers and the traceability of message source documents. This paper proposes a 5G message log credit management and verification system based on blockchain. Under the background of traditional 5G message service, combined with blockchain technology and distributed storage, it realizes the decentralization, trust and tamper resistant ability of RCS logs, so that users can trace and authenticate RCS logs. The paper also proves the feasibility of the scheme, and analyze its good retrieval efficiency and throughput requirements through experiments.

Keywords: RCS logs · 5G · Blockchain · Distributed storage · Traceability

1 Introduction

1.1 Background

In 2020, major operators and more than a dozen other terminal manufacturers collectively announced their support for 5G business, which actually refers to RCS business. RCS (Rich Communication Suite), which can also be understood as multimedia communication.

In 5G communication network, the RCS log is an attractive target of network attack. The transmission of RCS messages is facing the problem of network log authentication. Traditional log storage system lacks tamper proof function. If the 5G network system is attacked, the contents of the message log will be maliciously tampered with. The integrity of data cannot be protected, and the rights and interests of users will be infringed. It is tricky to identify attacks or prevent such failures because data integrity depends too much on the system itself [1].

Q. Zu et al. (Eds.): HCC 2021, LNCS 13795, pp. 242–251, 2022.
https://doi.org/10.1007/978-3-031-23741-6_22

1.2   Related Work

With the development of the Internet, methods to solve the phenomenon of data forgery and tampering have long existed. One of the modern popular verification technologies is the secure hash algorithm, which is used as a means to verify the content or attributes of electronic data; The source code management system git generates a SHA-1 signature for a "commit" and uses it to track the entire source code life cycle. In addition, many authentication service platforms also provide integrity control for uploaded data. For example, literature [2] provides a repository for electronic documents and ensures their integrity. The main disadvantage of these services is their centrality and the need to trust third-party central institutions.

At present, in the research on RCS log and blockchain, literature [3] proves the feasibility of blockchain technology in 5G background; Literature [4] constructs a blockchain log storage system based on removable storage devices, but does not give a clear system model; Literature [5] created a double chain structure based on fabric, one of which is the log chain and the other is the supervision chain, which is responsible for recording the state changes on the log chain and can achieve data integrity [6]. However, in the 5G scenario, the RCS log is too large to store all log information on the chain.

1.3   Paper Work

The first chapter introduces the current background and related work. In the second chapter, combined with fast indexable blockchain technology and distributed storage under the chain, 5G message log credit management and verification system are proposed based on blockchain. The system uses the distributed database under the chain to store the credit documents, stores the hash value of the message log and the credit documents on the blockchain, extracts the keywords in the log, establishes an inverted index, and speeds up the query process on the chain. In the third chapter, the paper conducts experimental tests, simulate the throughput and index performance of the system, and analyze the cost. The fourth chapter summarizes the article and gives the conclusion.

2   5G Message Log Credit Management and Verification System

2.1   System Architecture

In this paper, the whole 5G scene is divided into three entities: user, 5G message center and RCS log management system. The RCS log management system is composed of log processing module, blockchain and distributed database. Figure 1 shows the architecture of this article:

User. Individuals or enterprises in 5G network are collectively referred to as users. They can manually select whether credit is required for all RCS messages generated. The credit documents can be traced and tamper proof through the system. At the same time, it also needs to pay a certain fee according to the size of the credit documents.

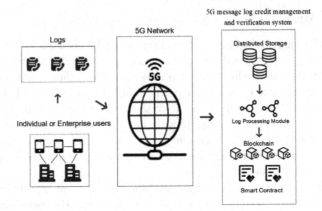

Fig. 1. System architecture diagram

5G Message Center. 5G message center generally refers to the traditional 5G network maintained by operators. The 5G message center will always generate RCS logs according to the messages sent and received by users, and store the contents (text or multimedia files) contained in the messages in the message center.

The RCS log contains Table 1 field information:

Table 1. RCS log field description

Number	Field
1	LogID
2	ServiceType
3	Sender_uid
4	Reciver_uid
5	Timestamp
6	Credit_Identification
7	MessageID
8	Size
9	Type
10	Filepath

Message Log Credit Management and Verification System. The system consists of log processing module, distributed database and blockchain. The log processing module is responsible for parsing and processing the RCS log of 5G message center, managing credit documents and completing distributed storage and query; Establish an index and call the smart contract of the blockchain to complete the interaction with the data on the chain.

2.2 Index

This paper uses searchable encryption technology to realize ciphertext retrieval of credit data. The user obtains the hash value of the private key and message sequence number, constructs a unique key, and then gives the credit documents to the distributed database as value. Then, the log processing module saves the message sequence number and data digest in the blockchain, and establishes an inverted index structure at the head of the block according to the keyword group in the log. Before the message digest is chained, it is necessary to expand the field of the block header and add an inverted index based on keywords.

First, the keyword fields in the RCS log, such as, *reciveID*, *SenderID*, timestamp, service, etc., are used to form a keyword set:

$$K = (K_1, K_2, K_3, K_4, \cdots, K_n) \tag{1}$$

For each K_i, Extract the digest containing the keyword and insert it into the index as a list. The digest list corresponding to keywords K_i is F_{ij}:

$$F_{K1} \to \left(F_{K1,1}, F_{K1,2}, F_{K1,3}, \cdots, F_{K1,n}\right)$$
$$F_{K2} \to \left(F_{K2,1}, F_{K2,2}, F_{K2,3}, \cdots, F_{K2,n}\right)$$
$$\cdots$$
$$F_{Kn} \to \left(F_{Kn,1}, F_{Kn,2}, F_{Kn,3}, \cdots, F_{Kn,n}\right)$$

The index is established based on this, as shown in Fig. 2:

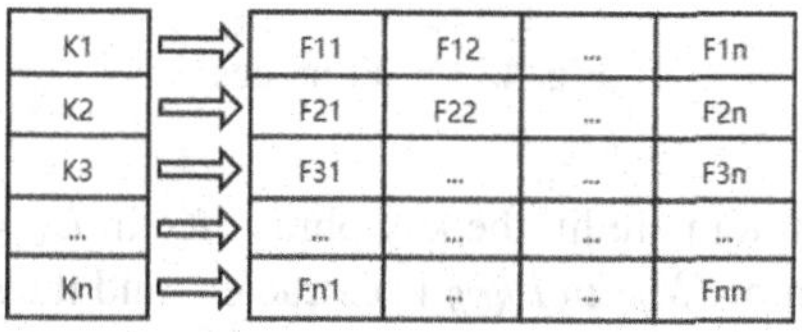

K1	⇒	F11	F12	...	F1n
K2	⇒	F21	F22	...	F2n
K3	⇒	F31	...	...	F3n
...	⇒	...	...	...	...
Kn	⇒	Fn1	...	...	Fnn

Fig. 2. Inverted index

In this paper, a field extension is made in the block header to store the inverted index of the RCS log after processing. The transaction in the block body is the message sequence number and message digest. Figure 3 shows the block structure diagram:

2.3 Credit Process Model

All RCS logs generated by 5G message center will be handed over to the log management system for processing. The credit flow chart of the system is shown in Fig. 4:

Step 1. After receiving L_{RCS}, the log processing module determines whether the corresponding message needs credit according to the *credit identidication* field.

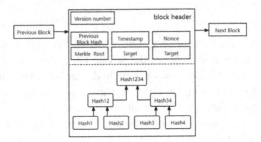

Fig. 3. Block header

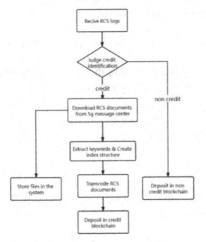

Fig. 4. Credit process

Step 2. For messages without credit, the key phrase K_R in L_{RCS} is directly extracted as the key, the message number M_{id} in L_{RCS} is extracted, and the source file is used as the value stored on the untrusted chain.

$$Key_{incredit} \rightarrow K_R$$
$$Value_{incredit} \rightarrow M_{id} + \text{Hasher}(L_{RCS})$$

Step 3. For credit messages, extract M_{id} and credit documents path F_{url}, send a request to the north interface of 5G message center, and obtain the corresponding credit documents F_{RCS}:

$$Resquest \rightarrow M_{id} + F_{url}$$
$$Response \rightarrow F_{RCS}$$

Step 4. The user calculates the combination of private key and M_{id} according to the system security parameters λ, calculates the hash value, and uses it as a key, the RCS log and credit documents are stored in the distributed database as values.

$$Key_{Database} \rightarrow Hasher(PK + M_{id})$$
$$Value_{Database} \rightarrow F_{RCS}$$

Step 5. Extract K_R in the log, establish the inverted index according to the index structure of Sect. 3.2, and expand the block header field. F_{RCS} is transcoded and hashed by H264 [11].

Step 6. Store M_{id} and encrypted digest on trusted blockchain. Among them, φ Is the transcoding coefficient, f is the offset determined by the encoder, Q_s is the quantization step.

$$Key_{credit} \rightarrow K_R$$
$$Z_{out} = \left(\varphi \frac{F_{RCS}}{Q_s} + f \right) \qquad (2)$$
$$Value_{credit} \rightarrow M_{id} + \text{Hasher}(L_{RCS} + Z_{out})$$

2.4 Integrity Verification

The system can verify the data integrity of the retrieved messages. Figure 5 shows the schematic diagram of data integrity verification.

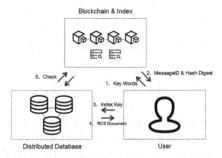

Fig. 5. Integrity verification

Step 1. The user enters the query keyword combination K_R. Query the blockchain according to the inverted index.

Step 2. The system obtains the keyword combination entered by the user, queries the corresponding block in the blockchain according to the timestamp, and then lists the message sequence number and digest list that the user wants to query according to the inverted index:

$$Encry_{verify1} list = (F_{R,1}, F_{R,2}, F_{R,3}, \cdots, F_{R,n})$$
$$M_{ID} list = (M_1, M_2, M_3, \cdots, M_n)$$

Step 3. The user selects M_{ID} with the highest weight from the list and uses its own private key and specific hash function to find the index value:

$$Index = Hasher(PK + M_{ID})$$

Step 4. Index L_{RCS} and F_{RCS} in the distributed database.

Step 5. The hash value $Encry_{verify2}$ encoded by the log source file and the credit documents is calculated and compared with the message digest $Encry_{verify1}$ on the blockchain. If it is consistent, the retrieved log data has not been maliciously tampered with; Otherwise, the data has been maliciously tampered with.

$$Encry_{verify2} = \text{Hasher}\left(L_{RCS} + \left(\varphi \frac{F_{RCS}}{Q_s} + f\right)\right) \qquad (3)$$

2.5 Energy Consumption Model

In the 5G network energy consumption, the energy consumption of base station equipment accounts for more than 80% of the total energy consumption [8]. This paper divides the base station power consumption model into three parts: P_{trans}: amplification, P_{static}: static and $P_{n,r}$: dynamic. Static consumption is mainly used for circuit operation of the system, and dynamic consumption is mainly used for information processing of all nodes. The specific formula is as follows:

$$P_{all} = \sum_{n=1}^{N} P_{n,sum} \qquad (4)$$

$$P_{n,sum} = \mu P_{n,trans} + P_{static} + \sum_{r=1}^{R_n} P_{n,r} \qquad (5)$$

$$P_{n,r} = \left(\gamma P_{n,mt} \sum_{m=1}^{M} D_n + P_{n,e}\right) e^{\delta} \qquad (6)$$

P_{all} is the total power of all base stations in 5G network. $P_{n,sum}$ is the total power of base station n. $P_{n,mt}$ is additional power consumed by the repair unit to tamper with the data. $P_{n,e}$ is rated power required for the dynamic operations. R_n is the number of dynamic power consumption nodes to be processed. N is the total number of base stations. M is the total amount of data; D_n is network data. μ is the set magnification factor; γ is the network security factor; δ is the network transmission parameter.

In traditional networks, due to the risk of data tampering, the loss power of the network is bound to increase. After using blockchain γ Approaching 0 can reduce network energy consumption, reduce maintenance cost and enhance network security.

3   System Experimental Analysis

3.1   Safety Analysis

In this scheme, PBFT algorithm is used to complete the consensus process of data blocks. Assuming that $n = |T_R|$ is the number of nodes participating in the consensus, T_R is the consensus node set. PBFT provides fault tolerance of $f = \frac{(n-1)}{3}$. Where, f represents the number of malicious nodes.

In order to prove the security of the system, this paper assumes that all formula nodes of the system network are divided into three sets:

$$T_R = T_1 \vee T_2 \vee F \qquad (7)$$

$$T_1 \wedge T_2 = \emptyset \tag{8}$$

T_1, T_2 are trusted node sets and F is a collection of untrusted nodes. If a malicious node wants to destroy the consensus process, it can only communicate with T_1 reach a consensus, then release the new block without informing T_1 with T_2. This process must meet:

$$|T_1| + |F| \geq n - f \tag{9}$$

$$|T_2| + |F| \geq n - f \tag{10}$$

The worst case of the system is $|F| = f$, the above inequality is simplified as:

$$n \leq 3f \tag{11}$$

PBFT cannot perform malicious destruction within the allowable range of fault tolerance.

3.2 Performance Analysis

In order to verify the 5G message log credit management and verification system proposed in this paper, we develop log chain based on Python language. The blockchain is deployed in the cloud environment, and the system adopts Ubuntu 18.04, an alliance chain with 5 nodes; At the same time, the distributed database adopts Hadoop file storage system, and a pseudo distributed cluster environment is built on the server. We tested the TPS performance of the system when the number of order nodes is different. The results are shown in Fig. 6:

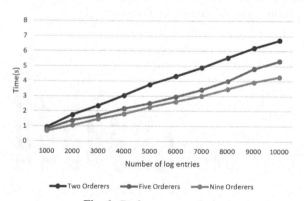

Fig. 6. Performance analysis

In order to verify that the scheme in this paper can not only ensure the normal process and data integrity, but also ensure the function and retrieval efficiency of keyword index. At the same time, the off-chain retrieval performance of inverted index used in the scheme is tested. Under the log scale of 100000 levels, the efficiency comparison of keyword retrieval using forward ordinary index, inverted index and non-index is tested, as shown in Fig. 7:

Compared with forward index, inverted index is slightly less efficient, but in acceptable range, inverted index can provide keyword ambiguous query and increase user experience.

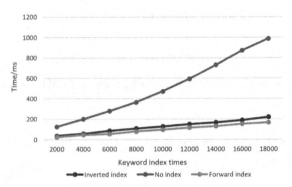

Fig. 7. Index performance analysis

3.3 Cost Analysis

Regardless of the transmission loss caused by network expansion, according to the experience of base station construction, it is assumed that the normal rated power of macro base station is 3500 W [9]. Under the standard data scale, the cost of repairing a macro base station data is 5000 yuan per month [10]. Figure 8 shows the cost budget with network security factor of 0.03 and 0.05 respectively:

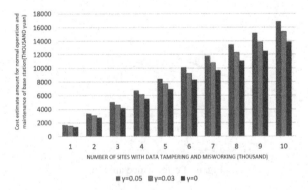

Fig. 8. Cost analysis

4 Conclusion

In order to solve the problem that RCS logs and credit documents face the risk of tampering in the network scenario of 5G message communication, a 5G message log credit management and verification system based on blockchain is proposed in this paper. Through fast indexable blockchain technology and distributed storage, it provides traceability and tamper proof ability for RCS logs. And it provides users with an interface for data integrity verification. At the business level, the system receives the whole business process log of users' 5G messages to realize the data analysis and transcoding of multimodal 5G messages. Users can credit the content of 5G messages on the platform, form the electronic deposit certificate of user credit documents, generate data summary according to the data on blockchain, and call the blockchain smart contract for query and uplink operation. In addition, the inverted index is added to the block to provide an interface for user keyword query and improve the retrieval performance. In the future, we will consider retrieval and business processes more comprehensively to improve the efficiency of the system as much as possible.

Acknowledgment. This work was supported by the research project of China Unicom: Research on the Core Technology of SMS Capability Platform Based on "5G Message + Blockchain".

References

1. Sookhak, M., et al.: Remote data auditing in cloud computing environments: a survey. Taxonomy open issues. ACM Comput. Surv. **47**(4), 65:1–65:34 (2015)
2. Chen, X., Hu, X., Li, Y., Gao, X., Li, D.: A blockchain based access authentication scheme of energy internet. In: 2018 2nd IEEE Conference on Energy Internet and Energy System Integration (EI2), pp. 1–9 (2018). https://doi.org/10.1109/EI2.2018.8582570
3. Fedorov, I.R., Pimenov, A.V., Panin, G.A., et al.: Blockchain in 5G networks: performance evaluation of private blockchain. In: 2021 Wave Electronics and its Application in Information and Telecommunication Systems (WECONF), pp. 1–4. IEEE (2021)
4. Lee, G., Son, M., Choi, N., et al.: Blockchain based removable storage device log management system. In: 2020 22nd International Conference on Advanced Communication Technology (ICACT), pp. 276–279. IEEE (2020)
5. Schaefer, C., Edman, C.: Transparent logging with hyperledger fabric. In: 2019 IEEE International Conference on Blockchain and Cryptocurrency (ICBC), pp. 65–69. IEEE (2019)
6. Lu, Y.: The blockchain: state-of-the-art and research challenges. J. Ind. Inf. Integr. **15**, 80–90 (2019)
7. Nunez, J.L., Chouliaras, V.A.: High-performance arithmetic coding VLSI macro for the H264 video compression standard. IEEE Trans. Consum. Electron. **51**(1), 144–151 (2005). https://doi.org/10.1109/TCE.2005.1405712
8. Che, Y.L., Duan, L., Zhang, R.: Dynamic base station operation in large-scale green cellular networks. IEEE J. Sel. Areas Commun. **34**(12), 3127–3141 (2016)
9. Ma, J., et al.: Blockchain and northbound data trusted storage. In: 2020 IEEE 3rd International Conference on Electronic Information and Communication Technology (ICEICT), pp. 135–138 (2020). https://doi.org/10.1109/ICEICT51264.2020.9334176
10. Renga, D., Al Haj Hassan, H., Meo, M., Nuaymi, L.: Energy management and base station on/off switching in green mobile networks for offering ancillary services. IEEE Trans. Green Commun. Netw. **2**(3), 868–880 (2018). https://doi.org/10.1109/TGCN.2018.2821097

A Graph-Based Service Composition Method for Science and Technology Resources

Zhuo Tian[1], Changyou Zhang[1(✉)], Jiaojiao Xiao[1], and Shubin Liang[2]

[1] Laboratory of Parallel Software and Computational Science, Institute of Software Chinese Academy of Sciences, Beijing, People's Republic of China
changyou@iscas.ac.cn
[2] Beijing Information Science and Technology University, Beijing, People's Republic of China

Abstract. Science and technology resources can be regarded as web services on the Internet, in order to realize the reuse of science and technology resources, the industry provides services for Internet users in multiple web service methods. In order to reuse of the web services, multiple web services need to be combined according to certain rules and business logic to solve the problem of limited functions of a single web service. The web service composition algorithm focuses on finding a service composition scheme with the best service quality. A single service composition scheme cannot cope with the dynamic changes of the network environment in real time, such as service failures. This paper proposes a graph-based service composition method, which uses the service dependency graph to establish the relationship between services, and combines the functional and non-functional attributes of the service. In the service selection stage, a formula for calculating the matching degree between the service and the target parameters is proposed to evaluate the current matching degree between the service and the target parameters, and the service with the best matching degree is selected.

Keywords: Web services · Service composition · Graph · Matching degree

1 Introduction

With the widespread application of service-oriented architecture and the continuous development of service technology, service computing has been applied to various fields of the Internet platform. Service computing puts forward the concepts of service quality, software as a service, etc., and leads to service management related issues such as service interaction, service composition, and service recommendation [1–3]. Then, how to effectively combine various services distributed on the Internet and realize the close integration and collaboration between services has become a research hotspot in industry [4–6]. At present, most service composition strategies only consider the static characteristics of services [7], but do not consider the operating characteristics of service instances under the microservice architecture. How to monitor and manage the real-time processing capabilities of microservices and dynamically update microservice paths to achieve efficient application execution efficiency is a hot research topic today [8, 9]. This

Q. Zu et al. (Eds.): HCC 2021, LNCS 13795, pp. 252–258, 2022.
https://doi.org/10.1007/978-3-031-23741-6_23

paper proposes a graph-based service composition method, which effectively improves the reuse rate of services in the microservice platform and improves the search efficiency of service composition.

2 Graph Planning Algorithm

In the service composition solution problem, the research of intelligent planning and scheduling has now become the mainstream solution method. The research on intelligent planning and scheduling problems mainly includes partial order algorithm, total order algorithm, hierarchical task network (HTN), graph planning and other research directions. The graph planning method was first proposed by Blum et al. [10] to describe the task planning problem by using a graph structure. This method transforms the task planning problem into a planning problem that can be solved by searching, and makes a new breakthrough in the field of task planning. Graph planning algorithms are concise, easy to describe, and extensible.

The graph planning method transforms the task planning problem into a problem of searching the target state from the initial goal in the planning graph. The planning graph is composed of special nodes and edges. In the planning diagram, nodes are state nodes, and edges include no-operation edges, delete effect edges, add effect edges, and precondition edges. The graph planning method is composed of two parts: the construction of the proposition layer and the construction of the action layer. The initial proposition layer is constructed from the initial state, which is the state layer, and all the actions that can be called by the initial state are added to form the action layer, adding different edges for each action. Through different actions to transform to get the second proposition layer, and so on, until all the target states appear in the existing state node.

3 Graph-Based Service Composition Problem Modeling

When a single service cannot satisfy a user's request, it is necessary to select and combine related services from many services in the service library to solve the user's request. The problem of service composition (Service Composition) refers to how to find the services related to the user's request and effectively combine them to solve the user's request after a given user request.

Generally, a web service contains two parameter sets, an input parameter set and an output parameter set. The input parameter set corresponds to the request in the SOAP message format; the output parameter set corresponds to the response in the SOAP message format. Here we consider the problem of service composition as a service composition under Web services. Assume that when calling a Web service, the user can provide all the input parameters required by the service. In this way, the Web service will return all output parameters as the return value. Therefore, a Web service w can be defined as:

$$w = \left(w^i, w^o \right)$$

Among them, the input parameter set $w^i = (I_1, I_2, \ldots)$, and the output parameter set $w^o = (O_1, O_2, \ldots)$.

Given a request $r = (r^i, r^o)$, where r^i refers to the requested input parameter set, and r^o refers to the requested target parameter set. If a single service w such as $w^i \subseteq r^i$ and $w^o \supseteq r^o$ can be found in the service library, such a problem is called service discovery.

In general, a single service cannot satisfy a user's request, and only a combination of several related services can find a set of services that satisfy the request. The final set of services should meet these two conditions: the initial service satisfies $w^i \subseteq r^i$, and the target service satisfies $w^o \supseteq r^o$. Therefore, the service composition problem is: given a request, how to solve the Web service composition sequence that can meet the conditions.

The graph planning method is introduced above. In the service composition problem, the planning and solving problem of service composition can be transformed into the STRIPS quadruple model of the planning problem:

$$\Pi = \left\langle P, W, r^i, r^o \right\rangle$$

Among them, P refers to the parameter set. W refers to a collection of Web services. r^i refers to the initial input parameters of the request, with $r^i \subseteq P$. r^o refers to the requested target output parameter, which has $r^o \subseteq P$.

In this model, the state refers to the parameter set P, and the action refers to the invocation of the service. The set P is changed by invoking the reachable service through the current state. Until $r^o \subseteq P$, the search process stops. In the design of the quadruple model Π, the state space in the search process is defined as follows:

$$\Psi = \langle S, s_0, S_G, \Omega(.), f, c \rangle$$

The state s refers to the current set of parameters in the process of searching for the Web service. S is a set of states s, there are $s \in S$.

The initial state s_0 refers to the set of requested input parameters, which satisfies $s_0 \in S$, $s_0 = r^i$.

S_G refers to the target state after the end of the search Web service process, which satisfies $S_G \in S$, $S_G \supseteq r^o$.

$\Omega(s)$ refers to the set W of Web services that can be called when the current state is s. Therefore, there is a service $w \in \Omega(s)$ if and only if the input parameter of the service w is $w^i \subseteq s$.

f refers to the mapping from one state s to another state s'. The mapping rule is $f(w, s) = s'$, where $w \in \Omega(s)$, and the state $s' = s \cup w^o$.

c refers to the cost of invoking the service w (cost). The cost can be either the QoS attribute of the service or the path length in the figure.

Under the definition of this state space, the final solution to the service composition problem is transformed from a series of service invocation sequences $(w_1, w_2, \ldots, w_n)$ to a series of state change sequences $(s_1, s_2, \ldots, s_{n+1})$. In the state sequence, $s_{i+1} = f(w_i, s_i)$.

Based on the definition of this state space, the service composition problem can be formally defined as follows:

Suppose there is currently a request r, the input parameter set of r is r^i, and the output parameter set of r is r^o. The service composition problem refers to finding a certain set of service sequences $(w_1, w_2, \ldots, w_n)$ to use:

w_i can be called in sequence from 1 to n;

$$\left(r^i \cup w_1^o \cup \ldots \cup w_n^o \right) \supseteq r^o;$$

The total cost of calling the service $\sum_{i=1}^{n} c(w_i)$ is the smallest.

4   Service Diagram

The service relationship graph is a data structure that allows you to visually view the relationship between services. This section will describe how to map the service set W to the service relationship graph $G = (V, E)$. A single service w of the service set W can represent a single node. The directed edges between nodes can represent the matching relationship between services. The definition of service matching relationship will be given below.

Assume that an existing parameter set is currently given. Under the existing parameter set, the service w_1 can be called, but the service w_2 cannot be called. In this case, the Web service can be called after the service w_1 is completed, so there are the following two relationships between w_1 and w_2:

If $w_1^o \supseteq w_2^i$, it is called service w_1 exactly matches service w_2.

If $w_1^o \not\supseteq w_2^i$ and $w_1^o \cap w_2^i \neq \emptyset$, it is called service w_1 partial matching service w_2.

According to the definition of the matching relationship above, we can map the service w_1 completely or partially to the service w_2 as a directed edge w_1, w_2 from the nodes w_1 to w_2 in the service composition graph.

In the service relationship graph, nodes are service nodes or request nodes, and edges are complete or partial matching relationships between nodes. The input parameter set and the input parameter set requested by the user are used as the starting point and the ending point, respectively. In this way, the service composition problem can be transformed into finding the least costly path from the start point to the end point in the graph. As shown in the service relationship diagram shown in Fig. 1, it can be seen from the figure that, due to the partial and complete matching between services, it is not easy to search for the combined service path in the service relationship diagram. Therefore, the utilization diagram planning appears. The service plan generated by the method.

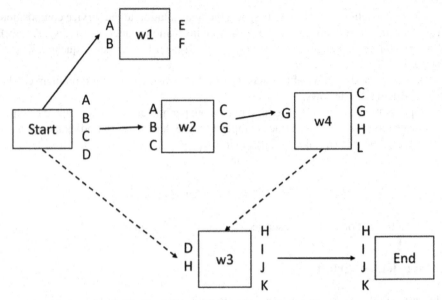

Fig. 1. Service relationship graph example

5 Service Planning Diagram

The service planning graph $G_s(V_s, E_s)$ refers to the state $s_i \in S$ in the search process as the node $i \in V_s$, and E_s as the set of directed edges between nodes. If there is a directed edge $(i, j) \in E_s$, it means that there is a mapping relationship between the state s_i corresponding to node i and the state s_j corresponding to node j, $f(w, s_i) = s_j$ and $w \in \Omega(s_i)$. In this way, the weight of the edge (i, j) is the cost $c(w)$ required to call the service w. In the planning representation of the service composition problem, calling the service represents the addition effect of the action, and there is no delete effect or recurring effect of the action in the problem.

After constructing the service planning graph $G_s(V_s, E_s)$, the search for the combined service is transformed into the search for the path from the initial state to the target state. When calling a service in the service portfolio diagram, it is necessary to consider whether the existing parameters support calling this service. When searching for a service in the state node graph, you only need to search for an edged path.

The example of the service state diagram shown in Fig. 2, s_0 is the initial state of the service composition problem, that is, the requested input parameters. Starting from the current existing parameters, service w_1 and service w_2 can be called. By calling different services, the state includes The new parameters are transferred to different nodes, and the current callable services are continuously searched to obtain new parameters. And so on, until it enters the target state, which is the nodes s_4 and s_7 in the figure.

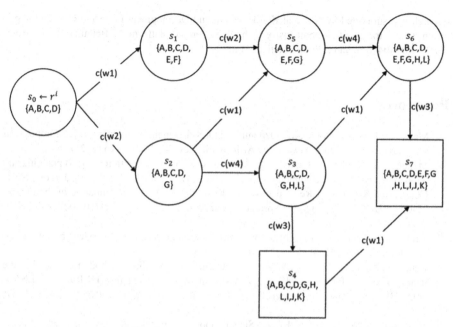

Fig. 2. Service planning graph example

It can be seen from Fig. 2 that the shortest path from the initial state to the target state is: s_0, s_2, s_3, s_4. When the scale of the combination problem becomes larger and the combination method becomes more complicated, the state node diagram will also become more complicated. Moreover, it can be seen from the state diagram that the complexity of service composition does not lie in the service itself, but in the number of parameters. Because the state in the search process is a collection of existing parameters, the complexity of the search problem will increase rapidly with the increase in the number of parameters.

6   Conclusion

This paper proposes a graph-based service composition method, which stores the service data in the form of a graph, and uses the shortest path method of the graph in the service composition to solve the search problem of composite services. The service search is transformed into finding the shortest path according to an edged path. The complex business logic functions in the system can be realized by selecting and combining existing services. At the same time, under the dynamic changes of the network environment, the performance of different service instances of the same function is also different. Therefore, the research work of this article is about the existing services under the microservice system architecture. The graph-based service composition method for science and technology resources is very important.

Acknowledgement. The authors would like to express their thanks to the editors and experts who participated in the review of the paper for their valuable suggestions and comments. This research was supported by National Key Research and Development Project—R&D and application demonstration of comprehensive technology service platform for Beibu Gulf city group (2018YFB1404404), and Beijing Practical Training Project.

References

1. Masdari, M., Nozad Bonab, M., Ozdemir, S.: QoS-driven metaheuristic service composition schemes: a comprehensive overview. Artif. Intell. Rev. **54**, 3749–3816 (2021)
2. Medema, M., Kaldeli, E., Lazovik, A.: Automated service composition using AI planning and beyond. In: Aiello, M., Bouguettaya, A., Tamburri, D.A., van den Heuvel, W.-J. (eds.) Next-Gen Digital Services. A Retrospective and Roadmap for Service Computing of the Future. LNCS, vol. 12521, pp. 16–32. Springer, Cham (2021). https://doi.org/10.1007/978-3-030-73203-5_2
3. Valderas, P., Torres, V., Pelechano, V.: Towards the composition of services by end-users. Bus. Inf. Syst. Eng. **62**(4), 305–321 (2020)
4. Lou, Q., Zhang, S.-Z., Song, W.W.: Combination of evaluation methods for assessing the quality of service for express delivery industry. In: Wang, J., et al. (eds.) WISE 2015. LNCS, vol. 9419, pp. 414–425. Springer, Cham (2015). https://doi.org/10.1007/978-3-319-26187-4_39
5. Viriyasitavat, W., Xu, L.D., Bi, Z., Sapsomboon, A.: Blockchain-based business process management (BPM) framework for service composition in Industry 4.0. J. Intell. Manuf. **31**(7), 1737–1748 (2020)
6. Dara, N., Emadi, S.: Enriching web services tags to improve data-driven web services composition. J. Web Eng. **20**(2), 327–358 (2021)
7. Xu, L., Sun, Q., Xu, B., Zhang, W.: Statically detect data races for WS-BPEL web services by constraint solver. In: ICWS 2016, pp. 476–483 (2016)
8. Taherkordi, A., Eliassen, F., Mcdonald, M., Horn, G.: Context-driven and real-time provisioning of data-centric IoT services in the cloud. ACM Trans. Internet Techn. **19**(1), 7:1–7:24 (2019)
9. Michael, M., Llorca, J., Tulino, A.M.: Approximation algorithms for the optimal distribution of real-time stream-processing services. In: ICC 2019, pp. 1–7 (2019)
10. Blum, A.L., Furst, M.L.: Fast planning through planning graph analysis. Artif. Intell. **90**(1–2), 281–300 (1997). https://doi.org/10.1016/S0004-3702(96)00047-1

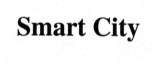
Smart City

Optimization of Energy Transaction Strategy Between Microgrids Based on MADDPG

Haiwei Zhang[1]($\boxtimes$), Weijun Zheng[2], Ding Chen[2], Jinghui Fang[2], and Yifei Wei[1]

[1] School of Electronic Engineering, Beijing University of Posts and Telecommunications, Beijing, China
{zhanghaiwei,weiyifei}@bupt.edu.cn

[2] Jiaxing Power Supply Company, State Grid Zhejiang Electric Power Co. Ltd., Jiaxing, China
{zhengweijun,chending,fangjinghui}@zj.sgcc.com

Abstract. In recent years, with the deepening of power system architecture adjustment and market-oriented reform, smart microgrid has become the main development direction of power grid architecture. In order to meet the higher requirements of decentralization, autonomy, intelligence and marketization in the process of power grid reform, digital technologies such as artificial intelligence and block chain should be introduced as the key support. In view of the consistency between the technical characteristics of block chain and the development demand of power grid, a power trading system model based on alliance chain is proposed. In order to realize the power balance and maximize the benefits of the microgrid within the power grid, a trading strategy optimization scheme based on MADDPG algorithm is proposed. The experimental results show that the algorithm can help microgrids to formulate the trading strategy which is most in line with the overall benefits of the grid and maximize the total revenue of the system. The performance of this algorithm is better than DDPG algorithm and random trading method.

Keywords: Microgrid · Power system architecture · Blockchain · Trading strategies · Multi-agent reinforcement learning

1 Introduction

With the rapid development of new digital information technologies such as big data, artificial intelligence and block chain, the power system architecture has undergone profound changes. As an important component unit of smart grid, microgrid is a low-voltage distribution network composed of various distributed generation, storage devices and response loads [1]. By setting up multiple interconnected MGs in the main power grid, the efficiency and reliability of distribution network can be improved, various distributed energy can be effectively integrated, and the utilization rate of renewable energy can be improved [2].

Q. Zu et al. (Eds.): HCC 2021, LNCS 13795, pp. 261–271, 2022.
https://doi.org/10.1007/978-3-031-23741-6_24

As a decentralized digital technology, blockchain can realize the common mainte-nance, safe storage and efficient sharing of power grid data, and is one of the technical support to promote the transformation of power system [3]. With the deepening of the market-oriented reform of electricity trading, the traditional centralized sales model has been broken. Point-to-point energy trading between microgrids is a good option to improve the utilization of renewable energy and reduce energy costs.

In recent years, there have been many studies on P2P energy trading, many of which use blockchain technology to build trading platforms and store critical data. Literature [4] proposes a multi-point energy trading framework based on blockchain to realize multi-settlement market. Literature [5] proposed an energy trading mechanism based on blockchain smart contract technology to realize P2P energy trading between producers and consumers. A P2P energy trading algorithm between MGs based on DQN is proposed in [6]. In reference [7], a DQN-based MG energy trading scheme was designed to reduce MG's dependence on the main power grid.

Considering the uncertainty of renewable energy generation and power load, the power trading decision problem is described as a Markov decision process, and then solved by MADDPG algorithm. At the same time, in order to ensure the integrity of P2P energy transaction data, block chain technology is used to record relevant energy data. The main contributions are summarized as follows:

(1) Design a microgrid P2P transaction model based on block chain and consider relevant physical constraints.
(2) The joint optimization problem of power trading strategies under various physical constraints is defined and solved by MADDPG algorithm.
(3) Simulation experiments prove the effectiveness and accuracy of the proposed algo-rithm. Compared with random trading, the proposed algorithm can formulate the most suitable trading strategy for users and reduce costs.

The remaining parts are arranged as follows: The second section presents the system model and problem definition. In the third section, a P2P energy trading algorithm based on MADDPG is proposed. The fourth section verifies the effectiveness of the algorithm by analyzing the simulation results, and the last section summarizes.

2   System Model and Problem Definition

The architecture of blockchain-based smart grid is shown in Fig. 1, which includes N microgrids (MG) and a main grid. The MGs mainly through renewable energy generation to meet its own internal energy demand, but sometimes it also needs to trade electricity through the trading platform to balance power demand.

The user client sends a transaction request to the trusted node in the network. The transaction information forms an tamper proof record on the blockchain according to the consensus process, and carries out actual power transmission.

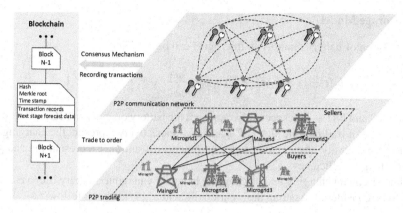

Fig. 1. Power transaction system architecture of smart grid based on block chain

2.1 Trading Model

A time slot trading model is proposed, and the duration of each time slot is 1 h. The blockchain platform uses smart contracts to count the information of all transaction participants, and the smart contracts will automatically determine which party will be the first to announce the information based on the comparison of expected transaction electricity between buyers and sellers.

The transaction can be divided into two situations. One is that the supply exceeds the demand. In this case, the sellers shall first announce the information such as selling price, selling quantity, then the electricity buyers shall make the decision. The other is that the supply is less than the demand, the buyers to announce the information first.

The price of energy in a blockchain-based peer-to-peer marketplace is dynamic. The energy transaction price is set as follows:

$$\rho_{grid}^- < \rho_{ij} < \rho_{grid}^+ \tag{1}$$

where, ρ_{grid}^- represents the unit price of MGs selling power to the main grid, ρ_{grid}^+ represents the unit price of MGs buying power from the main grid, and ρ_{ij} is the unit price of transactions between MGs.

When the purchase or sale of electricity is decided between the MGs participating in the transaction, the actual cost or income of the transaction can be obtained:

$$P_{ij} = C_{ij}\rho_{ij} \tag{2}$$

C_{ij} is the electric quantity traded between MGi and MGj.

If MG's needs cannot be met by trading with other MGs, it needs to trade with the main grid. Thus, the total cost or income of MG can be obtained as:

$$Q_i = \sum_{j=1, and j \neq i}^{N} P_{ij} - C_i^+ \rho_{grid}^+ + C_i^- \rho_{grid}^- \tag{3}$$

C_i^+ and C_i^- represents the energy purchased and sold by MGI to the main grid respectively.

2.2 Storage Model

The variation of battery quantity in microgrid can be modeled as:

$$b_i(t+1) = b_i(t) + E_{ch}\eta_{ch} - \frac{E_{dis}}{\eta_{dis}}, \quad 0 < \eta_{ch}, \eta_{dis} < 1 \tag{4}$$

where $b_i(t)$ and $b_i(t+1)$ respectively represent the battery quantity of MGi at the beginning and end of trading time slot T; E_{ch} and E_{dis} respectively represent the charging and discharging quantity of energy storage equipment; η_{ch} and η_{dis} represent the charging and discharging efficiency.

Since frequent charging and discharging behavior can reduce battery life, wear costs need to be considered. Assume the wear coefficient $c_\omega(\$/kWh)$ as follows:

$$c_\omega = \frac{C_{rep}}{S_b Q_b \sqrt{\eta_{rt}}} \tag{5}$$

where C_{rep} represents the replacement cost of the battery, S_b represents the capacity of the battery, Q_b represents the service life of the battery, and η_{rt} represents the round-trip efficiency.

2.3 Transmission Model

Transmission of electrical energy through power transmission lines results in power loss, so it is necessary to model the loss:

$$r_{ij}(t) = p_{ij}(t) - k_{ij}d_{ij}p_{ij}^2(t) \tag{6}$$

where $p_{ij}(t)$ is the average received or emitted power, $r_{ij}(t)$ is the actual received power of the receiver, k_{ij} is the loss constant of the power transmission line, and d_{ij} is the length of the power transmission line between MGi and MGj.

It is assumed that the power transmission stability of MG is divided into four grades A, B, C and D according to the historical transmission status. Each microgrid has different standards for power stability, so there are requirements for transactions as follows.

$$S_{sell} \geq S_{buy} \tag{7}$$

S_{sell} is the power transmission stability rating of the power seller, and S_{buy} is the minimum stability requirement of the power buyer.

2.4 Energy Balance Model

In order to achieve the balance of power supply and demand in microgrid. Set the average load power required by MGi to be $l_i(t)$ during trading period t. The following formula can be obtained:

$$\beta = G_i(t) + \sum_{j=1,j\neq i}^{N} r_{ij}(t) + r_{ig}(t) + O_i(t) - l_i(t) - I_i(t) \tag{8}$$

where, β represents the numerical expression of power supply and demand imbalance degree, and when $\beta = 0$, it represents the balance of power supply and demand. $G_i(t)$ represents the renewable energy power generation power in MGi, $r_{ig}(t)$ represents the incoming or outgoing power of the power transaction between MGi and the main grid. $O_i(t)$ represents the discharge power of the energy storage device in MGi, and $I_i(t)$ represents the charging power of MGi to the energy storage device.

2.5 Utility Model

The purpose of each MG is to maximize its own utility in a long-term range. The utility function is mainly composed of four parts, namely, the expenditure or income of electricity transaction with other MGs $u_i^1(t)$, the expenditure or income of electricity transaction with the main grid $u_i^2(t)$, the wear cost caused by frequent charge and discharge of energy storage equipment $u_i^3(t)$. And virtual penalties for energy transactions that do not meet energy balance requirements $u_i^4(t)$.

The utility function $u_i(t)$ of MGi can be obtained as follow:

$$u_i(t) = u_i^1(t) + u_i^2(t) - u_i^3(t) - u_i^4(t) \tag{9}$$

$$u_i^1(t) + u_i^2(t) = Q_i \tag{10}$$

$$u_i^3(t) = c_\omega d_i(t) \tag{11}$$

$$u_i^4(t) = C_p|\beta| \tag{12}$$

where $d_i(t)$ is the total amount of charge and discharge of batteries in the trading period t. C_p is the penalty coefficient. In order to maximize the utility function, each MG needs to make and select the optimal trading decision.

3 Proposed Solution

In order to obtain the optimal trading strategy for each MG, the optimization problem described in Sect. 2 can be transformed into a multi-agent extension of Markov decision [8]. Therefore, the MADDPG algorithm is proposed to learn the optimal strategy of each MG.

3.1 DRL Model for Multi-agent Game

In order to maximize the reward, cooperation between MGS is required to make decisions. The states, action spaces and rewards of N agents are defined as follows:

State: The state of a single microgrid in each transaction period can be divided into two parts, namely public state and local state.

$$o_{i,t} = (P_t, C_t, G_t, D_{i,t}, b_{i,t}, g_{i,t}, l_{i,t}) \tag{13}$$

The $P_t = \{p_{1,t}, \cdots p_{M,t}\}$, $C_t = \{c_{1,t}, \cdots c_{M,t}\}$, $G_t = \{g_{1,t}, \cdots g_{M,t}\}$ respectively M sell electricity party of electricity sale price, sale of electricity and power transmission stability rating, $D_{i,t} = \{d_{1,i}, \cdots d_{3,i}\}$ said M sell electricity to the MGi power transmission distance. All of them constitute the state space $s_t = \{o_{1,t}, \cdots o_{N,t}\}$.

Action: The action space of each MG includes the electric quantity traded with each electricity seller and the charge and discharge amount of energy storage equipment, that is, the action of MG is $a_{i,t}$.

$$a_{i,t} = (x_{i,t}, d_{i,t}) \tag{14}$$

$x_{i,t} = \{x_{i,1,t}, \cdots x_{i,M,t}\}$ represents the transaction electric quantity of MGi and M sellers in trading time. All of them constitute action space $a_t = \{a_{1,t}, \cdots a_{N,t}\}$.

Reward: The purpose of each MG is to maximize its own utility, so the reward function can be designed as follows:

$$r_{i,t} = 1 - \frac{u_i(t)}{\max(u_i(t))} \tag{15}$$

$u_i(t) = u_i^1(t) + u_i^2(t) - u_i^3(t) - u_i^4(t)$ represents the utility function of buyer, which can also be referred to as the total cost for short. $\max(u_i(t))$ represents the maximum cost of buyer, so the reward vector is $r_t = \{r_{1,t}, r_{2,t}, \cdots, r_{N,t}\}$.

3.2 Multi-agent DDPG Algorithm

In the multi-agent scenario, from the perspective of each agent, the environment is dynamic and unstable, but this does not meet the convergence conditions of traditional reinforcement learning, so the MADDPG algorithm is proposed [9, 10]. The architecture of MADDPG algorithm is shown in Fig. 2.

Firstly, MADDPG algorithm adopts centralized training and distributed execution mode, allowing global information to be used for learning and local information to be used for decision-making during application [11].

The stochastic strategy gradient [12] (SPG) algorithm obtains the optimal strategy by directly optimizing the cumulative expected reward:

$$\nabla_\theta J(\theta) = E_{s \sim \rho^\pi, a \sim \pi_\theta}[\nabla_\theta log \pi_\theta(a|o) Q^\pi(o, a)] \tag{16}$$

where, $\pi_\theta(a|o)$ is the conditional probability distribution of the observed state o, and $Q^\pi(o, a)$ represents the state-action function of agent centralization.

In the stochastic strategy gradient algorithm, the complete state-action space needs to be traversed [13]. Deterministic strategy gradient (DPG) algorithm can be used to solve high dimensional action problems. The gradient formula becomes Eq. (17):

$$\nabla_\theta J(\theta) = E_{s \sim \rho}[\nabla_\theta \mu_\theta(a|o) \nabla_a Q^\mu(o, a)|_{a=\mu_\theta(o)}] \tag{17}$$

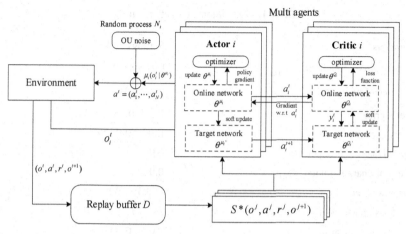

Fig. 2. Architecture diagram of MADDPG algorithm

The DDPG algorithm was obtained by using deep neural network to approximate the deterministic strategy μ_θ and $Q^\mu(o, a)$ in the above DPG algorithm [14]. Then extend DDPG algorithm from single agent to multi-agent, that is, MADDPG algorithm. Thus, the expected income gradient of each agent [15] is:

$$\nabla_{\theta_i} J(\mu_i) = E_{x,a \sim D}[\nabla_{\theta_i} \mu_i(a_i|o_i) \nabla_{a_i} Q_i^\mu(x, a_1, \cdots a_n)|_{a_i = \mu_i(o_i)}] \tag{18}$$

where, o_i represents the observation of agent i and $x = [o_1, \cdots, o_n]$ represents the observation vector. $a_1, \cdots a_n$ represents the actions of all agents. $Q_i^\mu(x, a_1, \cdots a_n)$ is the action value function established for agent i. D is an experience playback buffer. The centralized Critic network updates by minimizing the loss function:

$$L(\theta_i) = E_{x,a,r,x'}\left[\left(Q_i^\mu(x, a_1, \cdots a_n) - y\right)^2\right], y = r_i + \gamma \overline{Q}_i^{\mu'}\left(x', a_1', \cdots, a_n'\right)|_{a_j' = \mu_j'(o_j)} \tag{19}$$

$\overline{Q}_i^{\mu'}$ represents the target network and $\mu' = [\mu_1', \mu_2', \cdots \mu_n']$ represents the target policy. According to the above analysis, the model dynamics formula [16, 17] in MADDPG algorithm is stable:

$$P(s'|s, a_1, \cdots a_n, \pi_1, \cdots \pi_n) = P(s'|s, a_1, \cdots a_n) = P(s'|s, a_1, \cdots a_n, \pi_1', \cdots \pi_n') \tag{20}$$

4   Simulation Results

In this section, Python 3.6 and TensorFlow 1.8.0 are used to simulate the proposed model based on MADDPG algorithm, and the simulation results are analyzed.

Energy transactions and dispatching between ten microgrids with different load and demand are simulated. Table 1 shows the parameters in the experiment.

Table 1. Simulation parameters setting.

Parameters	Settings
Purchase price of main grid ρ_{grid}^{-}	0.15$/kWh
Sale price of main grid ρ_{grid}^{+}	0.25$/kWh
Seller's price	[0.15, 0.25] $/kWh
Battery capacity	[300, 500] kWh
Battery charging efficiency η_{ch}	0.9
Battery discharge efficiency η_{dis}	0.9
Battery wear cost c_ω	0.005$/kWh
Transmission line loss constant k_{ij}	5×10^{-6}
Power transmission stability	[A, B, C, D]
Penalty coefficient C_p	0.3

Assuming that the selling power of the microgrid of the six power sellers is [1000, 800, 1200, 1600, 500, 2000], the selling price is [0.18, 0.23, 0.16, 0.21, 0.17, 0.20], and the power rating is [A, B, B, C, D, D]. The power demand of the buyer is [1000, 1100, 700, 600], the power storage in the battery of the buyer is [500, 400, 200, 300], and the power demand rating is [B, C, D, D].

In order to compare and verify the performance of the proposed algorithm, two comparison schemes are also tested:

(1) Adopt DDPG: all power buyers are regarded as a centrally controlled agent.
(2) Adopt the strategy of random transaction: users randomly decide the purchase quantity and transaction object.

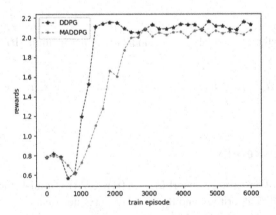

Fig. 3. Comparison of convergence results

Figure 3 compares the convergence effect of the proposed method and the DDPG. As the learning curve in the figure shows, the cumulative expected reward increases with the increase of training steps and both algorithms tend to converge. However, the final convergence reward value of MADDPG algorithm is slightly higher than DDPG. The reason is that the centralized agent can collect the state and action information of the whole system and make better decisions based on the global information, while the decentralized agent can only make actions according to its own state information. In addition, the convergence speed of DDPG algorithm is faster than that of MADDPG algorithm. The reason is that in MADDPG algorithm, each decentralized agent first needs to spend a certain time collecting information, and then trains the critical network based on the global state and action information, which slows down the convergence speed of the algorithm to a certain extent.

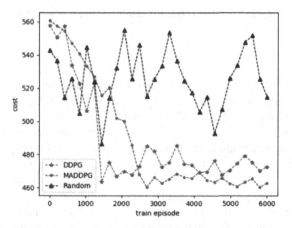

Fig. 4. The total cost of buying electricity for different scenarios

Figure 4 shows the comparison of the total cost of power buyers in the three methods. As shown in the figure, the total cost trend based on MADDPG and DDPG algorithms is the same. With the increase of training steps, the total cost of the buyer gradually decreases and then tends to be stable. The strategy cost of random trading fluctuates greatly, and is generally higher than the other two methods. Obviously, the method based on MADDPG proposed in this paper has the slowest convergence speed, but the total cost is the least.

Figure 5 shows the curve of total electricity purchase cost of four electricity buyers based on MADDPG algorithm. In general, each electricity purchase cost decreases with the increase of training steps and eventually converges.

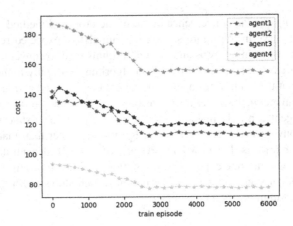

Fig. 5. MADDPG algorithm for the 4 buyers of total cost

5   Conclusions

In this paper, a power trading system model based on block chain is designed, and a P2P energy trading algorithm between microgrids based on MADDP is proposed. Simulation results show that compared with DDPG and random transaction algorithms, the proposed algorithm can maximize the overall utility function and reduce user costs. At the same time, the decision-making mode of multiple agents in the algorithm proposed in this paper is more consistent with the actual energy transaction scene, and easier to be applied to the actual production and life. However, the convergence speed of the algorithm proposed in this paper is relatively slow and costs more computing resources, which needs further improvement. In addition, trading systems using blockchain technology can ensure the security of energy trading data. In the future work, we can try to improve the algorithm to improve the convergence speed, and at the same time, we can consider applying the algorithm in this paper to more and more complex power trading modes to show the comprehensive advantages of the algorithm in this paper.

Acknowledgment. This work was supported by the Science and Technology Foundation of the State Grid Zhejiang Electronic Power Corporation: Research on Management and Control of Largescale Electricity Trading System Based on Blockchain Technology (5211JX1900CW).

References

1. Erol-Kantarci, M., Kantarci, B., Mouftah, H.T.: Reliable overlay topology design for the smart microgrid network. IEEE Netw. **25**, 38–43 (2011)
2. Zhang, L., Gao, Y., Liu, S., et al.: Multi-time slots real-time pricing for smart grid with time-coupled constraints. Syst. Eng.—Theory Pract. **39**, 2599–2609 (2019)
3. Tao, L., Gao, Y., Zhu, H., et al.: Optimal scheduling for smart grids with the integration of renewable resources and storage devices. Chin. J. Manag. Sci. **27**, 150–157 (2019)
4. Nakayama, K., Moslemi, R., Sharma, R.: Transactive energy management with blockchain smart contracts for P2P multi-settlement markets. IEEE (2019)

5. Yu, S., Yang, S., Li, Y., et al.: Distributed energy transaction mechanism design based on smart contract. IEEE (2018)
6. Morstyn, T., Teytelboym, A., McCulloch, M.D.: Bilateral contract networks for peer-to-peer energy trading. IEEE Trans. Smart Grid **10**, 2026–2035 (2018)
7. Xiao, L., Xiao, X., Dai, C., et al.: Reinforcement learning-based energy trading for microgrids. arXiv preprint arXiv:1801.06285 (2018)
8. Song, H., Liu, C.C., Lawarrée, J., et al.: Optimal electricity supply bidding by Markov decision process. IEEE Trans. Power Syst. **15**, 618–624 (2000)
9. Lowe, R., Wu, Y., Tamar, A., et al.: Multi-agent actor-critic for mixed cooperative-competitive environments. In: International Conference on Neural Information Processing Systems (2017)
10. Gu, B., Yang, X., Lin, Z., Hu, W., Alazab, M., Kharel, R.: Multiagent actor-critic network-based incentive mechanism for mobile crowdsensing in industrial systems. IEEE Trans. Ind. Inform. **17**, 6182–6191 (2021)
11. Awate, Y.P.: Policy-gradient based actor-critic algorithms. In: 2009 WRI Global Congress on Intelligent Systems (2009)
12. Lovatto, Â.G., Bueno, T.P., de Barros, L.N.: Analyzing the effect of stochastic transitions in policy gradients in deep reinforcement learning. In: 2019 8th Brazilian Conference on Intelligent Systems (BRACIS) (2019)
13. Mukherjee, A., Swindlehurst, A.L.: Jamming games in the MIMO wiretap channel with an active eavesdropper. IEEE Trans. Signal Process. **61**, 82–91 (2013)
14. ELamin, M., Elhassan, F., Manzoul, M.A.: Comparison of deep reinforcement learning algorithms in enhancing energy trading in microgrids. In: 2020 International Conference on Computer, Control, Electrical, and Electronics Engineering (ICCCEEE) (2021)
15. Sun, X., Qiu, J.: Two-stage volt/VAR control in active distribution networks with multi-agent deep reinforcement learning method. IEEE Trans. Smart Grid **12**, 2903–2912 (2021)
16. Schölkopf, B., Platt, J., Hofmann, T.: Natural actor-critic for road traffic optimization. In: Advances in Neural Information Processing Systems 19: Proceedings of the 2006 Conference (2006)
17. Cao, D., Zhao, J., Hu, W., Ding, F., Huang, Q., Chen, Z.: Attention enabled multi-agent DRL for decentralized Volt-VAR control of active distribution system using PV inverters and SVCs. IEEE Trans. Sustain. Energy **12**, 1582–1592 (2021)

Research on the Elements of Future Holographic Scene Design Based on Card Sorting-Fuzzy Comprehensive Evaluation Method

Wenjun Hou[1,2], Yujing Wang[1,2(✉)], and Lixin Zhang[1,2]

[1] School of Digital Media and Design Arts, Beijing University of Posts and Telecommunications, Beijing, China
739383223@qq.com
[2] Beijing Key Laboratory of Network Systems and Network Culture, Beijing University of Posts and Telecommunications, Beijing, China

Abstract. With the future application and deployment of holographic, it becomes essential to study the design elements of holographic scene. This article aims to explore holographic scene design elements and measure their impact on user experience. The integrated method of card sorting and fuzzy comprehensive evaluation can provide direction decision for future scene design. Based on obtaining the design elements, firstly, we used the card sorting method to analyze the attribute classification of each design element; secondly, we used the fuzzy comprehensive evaluation method to evaluate the importance of the design elements. Finally, we obtained the comprehensive weight of future holographic scene design elements through calculation. The results show that "Naturally reasonable function" has the highest impact on the future experience of holographic scenes, followed by "Interactive perception range", "Multi-sensory fusion", and "Intelligent prediction".

Keywords: Future holographic scene · Scene design elements · Card sorting · Fuzzy comprehensive evaluation method

1 Introduction

Nowadays, digital technology is constantly developing, and the holographic display has changed the way people perceive the world, visually changing from virtual two-dimensional to spatial three-dimensional. People gradually do not need the help of any exceptional eyepieces [1], and the way of interaction is shifting progressively from touch gestures to multi-modal and multi-sensory interaction. As a new virtual reality technology [2], holographic application shines in the field of holography [3]. At the same time, improving display quality and enhancing interactive performance has become the future development direction of holography. At this stage, most of the holographic scene design uses virtual aerial imaging as the starting point, and it has not realized the naked eye three-dimensional in the true sense. This paper also sets a threshold for people to try and use holographic applications and affects people's experience of holographic interaction.

The essence of design is to face the future and lead innovation. Because designers are not clear about the design elements of holographic scenes, they have no grasp when designing holographic scenes, which leads to problems such as lack of innovation, no bright spots, and bad experiences. Therefore, the mining and research of future holographic scene design elements have become the key to improving the user experience design of future holographic scenes.

Aiming at the problems of unclear design elements in future holographic scene design, lack of application of design research methods, and unsatisfactory results of scene design, this paper starts from the current research methods of actual scene design. It explores the application of design methods in future research on holographic scene design elements. We have summed up a comprehensive weighting system for the design elements of future holographic scenes. It can help people understand the key points of future holographic scene design and use the comprehensive weight of design elements to assist in decision-making on design priority. This article aims to explore the design elements of future scenes with innovative combination and application of current design research methods, help designers understand the design points, indicate design direction and hope to enhance the user experience of future holographic scenes.

2 Related Work

2.1 Holographic Scene Design

The current application of holography shines on the display, and the entire holographic field is in a preliminary exploration period. Researches are mainly about the user experience on the holographic display. Three-dimensional holographic display technology is also developing in a real-time, dynamic, larger size, and higher resolution. Dalvi et al. [1] realized a three-dimensional holographic projection with a sensor. The user can control the movement of the three-dimensional hologram and achieve a more exciting 3D holographic experience. Since current technology drives holography innovation, recent research is mostly the exploration of display technology. The holographic user experience primarily evaluates the usability of holographic products, and there is still insufficient research on how to design future holographic scenes. Jeongeun Song et al. [4] combined future research tools with design methods and proposed to shape future scenarios. But when shaping the future scenario, it did not indicate whether the factors considered were comprehensive.

2.2 Extraction and Rating of Holographic Scene Design Elements

At present, the extraction of design elements primarily uses POE (post-use evaluation) [5], interview method, observation method, and literature summary method. However, this classification of the extracted elements does not have the idea of comprehensive field experts. Most of them are unilateral subjective screening by researchers, and there are certain limitations. The traditional card sorting method is a design research method that does not consider time cost, takes people as the center, and weighs the average level of clustering results. Lin et al. [6] used the card sorting method to improve the information architecture of the campus portal website to make the website more user experience.

When prioritizing design elements or grading their importance, researchers mostly use the Kano model, Analytic Hierarchy Process, Fuzzy Comprehensive Evaluation Method, etc. Li et al. [7] used the Kano-QFD integrated method to analyze the attributes and rank the importance of the design elements of logistics services in colleges and universities. Wang et al. [8] graded the user experience points in the scene by Kano, using questionnaire surveys, factor analysis, and expert scoring to construct a virtual reality reading user interaction experience evaluation index system. Wang et al. [9] used the analytic hierarchy process to evaluate the effects of different augmented reality occlusion schemes and found the most suitable occlusion method. Su et al. [10] combined POE, Analytic Hierarchy Process, and Kano model to study the morphological design elements of printing equipment based on comprehensive user evaluation. Xu et al. [11] established a distribution map of satisfaction and importance of product social value elements using a fuzzy comprehensive evaluation method. Kim et al. [12] obtained design elements consistent with people's cognition of basic directions through experiments. Tondello et al. [13] used questionnaires to discuss user preferences and build design elements for the game.

Both the Kano model and the Analytic Hierarchy Process entirely rely on the evaluator's real and palpable feelings about the system to be evaluated. They are primarily used in areas where there are already formed products and large-scale civilian use. In the future, holographic scenes have not yet been applied on a large scale. Many users are not clear about their perceptions, which has led to the inestimability of the variability in user ratings. In addition, the Analytic Hierarchy Process requires a higher degree of expertise in the domain of experts. Among them, the Fuzzy Comprehensive Evaluation Method [10] is when people's evaluation of design objects is fuzzy. The application of fuzzy mathematics to evaluate things or objects restricted by multiple factors can get a better evaluation effect.

So this article fills in the vacancy of holographic scene design and makes up for the inadequacy of the predecessors in extracting design elements. This paper adopts more dimensions to obtain elements and integrates the existing open expert card sorting method suitable for future holographic scene design element classification and comprehensive fuzzy evaluation method of evaluation weight to carry out quantitative research on future holographic scene design elements.

3   Holographic Scene Design Element Extraction and Rating Method

This section introduces the research method of future holographic scene design elements based on card sorting and fuzzy comprehensive evaluation in detail and explains the overall process and calculation steps. The overall method process is shown in Fig. 1.

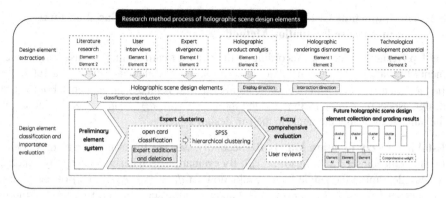

Fig. 1. Research method process of holographic scene design elements

3.1 Holographic Scene Design

Extract Design Elements. The innovation of information display and control is a basic theme of interactive experience. Since the scene we are designing is future-oriented, using grounded theory and other methods is impossible to construct a user experience evaluation system. At this stage, we extract elements through six dimensions: literature research, user interviews, expert divergence, holographic product analysis, holographic renderings dismantling, and technological development potential, considering the two dimensions of quantitative and qualitative. The extracted elements are classified and summarized to construct a preliminary element system for the future holographic scene.

Categorize Design Elements. We adopt the clustering method of open card sorting by experts, allowing them to add and delete elements. In this way, we can get the initial holographic scene design element set $U_0 = \{u_1, u_2, ..., u_m\}$, where m is the number of design elements. Before starting the experiment, use the "**rand** ()" formula in **Excel** to break up the initial elements sequence. As shown in Fig. 2, the construction process of the entire element system is as follows:

Calculate Symmetric Incidence Matrix. If the design elements were in the same category, the distance between them is 0. If the design elements were in a different category, the distance between them is 1. After that, we can obtain the M × M symmetric incidence matrix.

SPSS Hierarchical Clustering Import the processed symmetric incidence matrix into SPSS for hierarchical clustering. Analyze the generated pedigree diagram and aggregation coefficient.

Qualitative Analysis. We conduct qualitative analysis on the elements added and deleted by experts and finally get the set U of future holographic scene design elements.

3.2 The Important Grade Evaluation of Design Elements Based on Fuzzy Comprehensive Evaluation Method

Set Up Design Elements. According to the result of card sorting, we use various elements that affect the design of holographic scenes as elements to form a set $U = \{u_1, u_2, ..., u_i, ..., u_m\}$, where m is the number of first-level design elements. For the i-th design aspect, u_i can be further divided into $u_{ij} = \{u_{i1}, u_{i2}, ..., u_{ij}, ..., u_{ig}\}$, where g is the number of design elements in the i-th design aspect.

Establish Fuzzy Relation Matrix R. Secondly, we take the evaluation factors as elements to form a set $V = \{v_1, v_2, ..., v_n\}$. By evaluating each design element by experts, we can determine the single factor evaluation set $d_i = \{r_{i1}, r_{i2}, ..., r_{im}\}$ of the design element set U_i (i = 1, 2, ..., m) in a certain evaluation set $V = \{v_1, v_2, ..., v_n\}$. Among them, $r_{ij} \in [0, 1]$ (i = 1, 2, ..., m; j = 1, 2, ..., n) is the membership degree of the evaluation factor U_i to the evaluation grade V_j, and the fuzzy relationship matrix R is established:

$$R = \begin{bmatrix} r_{11} & r_{12} & r_{13} & \cdots & r_{1n} \\ r_{21} & r_{22} & r_{23} & \cdots & r_{2n} \\ \cdots & \cdots & \cdots & \cdots & \cdots \\ r_{m1} & r_{m2} & r_{m3} & \cdots & r_{mn} \end{bmatrix} \tag{1}$$

Calculate the Evaluation Vector B. We use the fuzzy relationship matrix R and the design element weight $W = \{W_1, W_2, ..., W_m\}$ to perform the relationship synthesis operation using the weighted average fuzzy synthesis operator and obtain the contribution of each design element to the comprehensive scene design system, which is the evaluation vector B. And the calculation formula is:

$$B = W \cdot R = \sum_{k=1}^{m} W_k r_{kj} = (W_1, W_2, ..., W_m) \bullet \begin{bmatrix} r_{11} & r_{12} & r_{13} & \cdots & r_{1n} \\ r_{21} & r_{22} & r_{23} & \cdots & r_{2n} \\ \cdots & \cdots & \cdots & \cdots & \cdots \\ r_{m1} & r_{m2} & r_{m3} & \cdots & r_{mn} \end{bmatrix} \tag{2}$$

Calculate Fuzzy Comprehensive Evaluation Score. We can calculate the fuzzy comprehensive evaluation score Q of the design elements according to our actual measurement scale H and evaluation vector B. The actual measurement scale H is the assignment of n evaluation levels, $H = \{H_1, H_2, ..., H_m\}$. The formula for calculating Q is:

$$Q = H \cdot B = (h_1, h_2, ... h_n) \bullet (b_1, b_2, ... b_m) \tag{3}$$

4 Research Experiment and Results of Holographic Scene Design Elements

4.1 A Set of Future Holographic Scene Design Elements

At this stage, we extract elements through six dimensions: literature research, user interviews, expert divergence, holographic product analysis, holographic renderings dismantling, and technological development potential. We have collected a total of 200 +

element data. We finally get 27 user experience elements of future holographic scenes through the classification and induction method in the two significant directions of display and interaction. A total of 15 experts (nine women and six men) who have a specific understanding of the field of holography were invited to conduct this open card sorting experiment. Through the SPSS hierarchical clustering analysis, we obtained the pedigree graph using the average connection and the line graph of aggregation coefficient shown in Fig. 2.

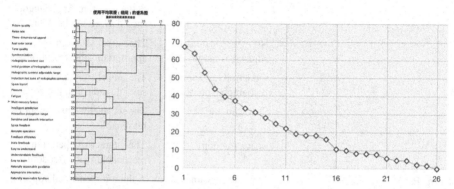

Fig. 2. SPSS hierarchical clustering pedigree graph and aggregation coefficient line graph

The aggregation coefficient line graph shows that the distortion degree changes significantly when the K value exceeds 5. So we can temporarily set the number of categories to 5. But in the pedigree diagram, when K = 5, the "**Spatial freedom**" is a single set of elements. Therefore, we set the number of clusters to 6 and then classify the "**Spatial freedom**" into the "**Spatial layou**t" group because they are in one group in most cases. Since "**Accurate operation**" evaluates user understanding and behavior, it is deleted based on expert experience. We finally get the final holographic scene design element set containing 26 elements, as shown in Table 1 below. The system has five primary types: the basic content of holographic space display, the quality of holographic space equipment, the efficiency of holographic interaction, the immersion of holographic interaction, and the natural holographic interaction.

Table 1. Future holographic scene design elements

Element type	No.	Element name	Element meaning
Type A The basic content of holographic space display	1	Holographic content size	The initial size of the 3D model is moderate, and you can see its complete picture
	2	The initial position of holographic content	Models and information should have a suitable default initial position. Any category should avoid too far away
	3	Holographic content adjustable range	The model should have an appropriate adjustment range
	4	Induction hot zone of holographic content	The model should have a suitable induction hot zone
	5	Space layout	The scene elements layout is reasonable
	6	Space freedom	The interactive operation has reasonable space freedom
Type B The quality of holographic space equipment	1	Three-dimensional appeal	A three-dimensional appeal is great
	2	Real color sense	Real color feeling, rather than sci-fi blue
	3	Picture quality	Holographic content with high resolution and clarity
	4	Tone quality	The source is consistent with the audio direction. The model and its related sounds should be bound
	5	Synchronization	Audio and video are synchronized
	6	Noise rate	Speckle noise should be as slight as possible
Type C The efficiency of holographic interaction	1	Interaction perception range	Expand the perception of interaction. The system can recognize user behavior from multiple directions. Users do not stand to maintain a specific angle or specific position

(continued)

Table 1. (*continued*)

Element type	No.	Element name	Element meaning
	2	Sensitive and smooth interaction	Interact smoothly, avoid loading too long
	3	State feedback	After completing the interaction, give the user successful feedback
	4	Feedback efficiency	Timely feedback
Type D The immersion of holographic interaction	1	Multi-sensory fusion	Integration of multi-sensory (taste, smell, touch, etc.) and multi-channel
	2	Intelligent prediction	Accurately guess and guide the user's following action
	3	Pleasure	The degree of pleasure during the experience
	4	Fatigue	Minimize the degree of fatigue during the experience
Type E The natural holographic interaction	1	Appropriate interaction	Set up appropriate interaction methods
	2	Easy to learn	Users can quickly understand the overall function
	3	Easy to understand	Interactive metaphors are appropriate and easy to understand
	4	Naturally reasonable function	Good fault tolerance. The logic of the scene function design is reasonable
	5	Naturally reasonable guidance	Guide content and form can help users quickly use the system
	6	Understandable feedback	Strong feedback intelligibility

4.2 Rating Evaluation of Future Holographic Scene Design Elements

We recruited eight users (four males, four females; six experts, two novice users) to experiment. According to whether the design elements "does not affect," "neutralize", or "affect" the user experience to complete the specific rating of each element. The specific words are: "how do you think this design element will affect the experience of future holographic scene design?". After rating the users, we statistically processed the data of 8 users. Finally, we obtained the fuzzy evaluation results of the users for the design elements of the holographic scene, as shown in Table 2.

The variance analysis of users' choice of influence degree shows that $F = 17.913$ and significance $p = 0.000 < 0.05$. This shows that users' judgment of levels is significantly different. Secondly, we choose whether there are significant differences in the influence of different scene design elements on user experience. Pearson's chi-square value obtained by Chi-square test is 296.457, $p = 0.000 < 0.05$. The results show that there are significant differences in the influence degree of the five types of scene design elements on user evaluation.

Table 2. Fuzzy evaluation results of future holographic scene design elements

Element type	No.	Element name	Does not affect	Neutralize	Affect
Type A The basic content of holographic space display	1	Holographic content size	25.00%	37.50%	37.50%
	2	The initial position of holographic content	25.00%	37.50%	37.50%
	3	Holographic content adjustable range	37.50%	37.50%	25.00%
	4	Induction hot zone of holographic content	37.50%	37.50%	25.00%
	5	Space layout	50.00%	25.00%	25.00%
	6	Space freedom	25.00%	37.50%	37.50%
Type B The quality of holographic space equipment	1	Three-dimensional appeal	25.00%	37.50%	37.50%
	2	Real color sense	25.00%	50.00%	25.00%
	3	Picture quality	50.00%	37.50%	12.50%
	4	Tone quality	37.50%	37.50%	25.00%
	5	Synchronization	50.00%	25.00%	25.00%
	6	Noise rate	12.50%	50.00%	37.50%
Type C The efficiency of holographic interaction	1	Interaction perception range	12.50%	37.50%	50.00%
	2	Sensitive and smooth interaction	37.50%	25.00%	37.50%
	3	State feedback	50.00%	37.50%	12.50%
	4	Feedback efficiency	50.00%	37.50%	12.50%
Type D The immersion of holographic interaction	1	Multi-sensory fusion	12.50%	37.50%	50.00%
	2	Intelligent prediction	0.00%	62.50%	37.50%
	3	Pleasure	37.50%	37.50%	25.00%
	4	Fatigue	50.00%	37.50%	12.50%

(*continued*)

Table 2. (*continued*)

Element type	No.	Element name	Does not affect	Neutralize	Affect
Type E The natural holographic interaction	1	Appropriate interaction	12.50%	50.00%	37.50%
	2	Easy to learn	37.50%	37.50%	25.00%
	3	Easy to understand	25.00%	50.00%	25.00%
	4	Naturally reasonable function	0.00%	37.50%	62.50%
	5	Naturally reasonable guidance	12.50%	50.00%	37.50%
	6	Understandable feedback	50.00%	25.00%	25.00%

4.3 Comprehensive Weight of Holographic Scene Design Elements

Since what we are studying in the future holographic scene, the specific manifestation and scale of the design elements are still uncertain, this article will temporarily set the weights of the design elements to be consistent. That is $W = (\frac{1}{26}, \frac{1}{26}, \ldots, \frac{1}{26})$. We assign 1, 3, and 5 to the three evaluation levels of "does not affect", "neutral", and "affect", respectively. Finally, the comprehensive weights of the design elements of the future holographic scene are calculated as shown in Table 3.

Table 3. Comprehensive weight of future holographic scene design elements

Element type	No.	Element name	Element weight
Type A The basic content of holographic space display 0.682692	1	Holographic content size	0.125
	2	The initial position of holographic content	0.125
	3	Holographic content adjustable range	0.105769231
	4	Induction hot zone of holographic content	0.105769231
	5	Space layout	0.096153846
	6	Space freedom	0.125
Type B The quality of holographic space Equipment 0.663462	1	Three-dimensional appeal	0.125
	2	Real color sense	0.115384615

(*continued*)

Table 3. (*continued*)

Element type	No.	Element name	Element weight
	3	Picture quality	0.086538462
	4	Tone quality	0.105769231
	5	Synchronization	0.096153846
	6	Noise rate	0.134615385
Type C The efficiency of holographic interaction 0.432692	1	Interaction perception range	0.144230769
	2	Sensitive and smooth interaction	0.115384615
	3	State feedback	0.086538462
	4	Feedback efficiency	0.086538462
Type D The immersion of holographic interaction 0.480769	1	Multi-sensory fusion	0.144230769
	2	Intelligent prediction	0.144230769
	3	Pleasure	0.105769231
	4	Fatigue	0.086538462
Type E The natural holographic interaction 0.75	1	Appropriate interaction	0.134615385
	2	Easy to learn	0.105769231
	3	Easy to understand	0.115384615
	4	Naturally reasonable function	0.163461538
	5	Naturally reasonable guidance	0.134615385
	6	Understandable feedback	0.096153846

From this, we can easily find:

The comparative analysis of each scene design element's comprehensive weight can help us take into account the constraints of time and space, human resources, and other factors in the future holographic scene design. When the design cannot be comprehensive within a certain time limit, the comprehensive weight of the design elements provides a basis for considering the design priority. Design elements with a relatively high comprehensive weight can influence user experience, and users will have a stronger perception of them. Therefore, when designing holographic scenes, we must focus on the negative effects it brings.

We have verified that the data are significantly different in the previous section. In terms of different element types, "**The natural holographic interaction**" is significantly higher than other elements. For different elements, the top elements are "**Naturally reasonable function**", "**Interaction perception range**", "**Multi-sensory fusion**", "**Intelligent prediction**", "**Appropriate interaction**", "**Naturally reasonable guidance**", "**Noise rate**". There are also quite a few elements at the same level. It requires us to make situational judgments. "**Intelligent prediction**" is more tailored to individual needs. It is necessary in situations like holographic fitting. However, in holographic collaborative communication design, which is biased towards user initiative, "**Intelligent prediction**" may not take priority over the other two elements of the same level.

At the same time, we must also pay attention to the factors that are not easy to affect the user experience, such as "**Picture quality**", "**State feedback**", "**Feedback efficiency**", "**Fatigue**". Although they are lower in this assessment, it is not certain whether the ranking will change as technology evolves.

In each element type, we can also analyze the elements according to the comprehensive weight. Among the basic content of holographic space, "**Holographic content size**", "**The initial position of holographic content**", and "**Space freedom**" have the same status as the first. In the quality of holographic space equipment, "**Three-dimensional appeal**" is considered by users as a factor that can more affect user experience. In the efficiency of holographic interaction, the "**Interaction perception range**" in which the scene can recognize user behavior from multiple directions and generate interaction is considered to have more impact on user experience. And in the immersion of holographic interaction, "**Multi-sensory fusion**" and "**Intelligent prediction**" are at the forefront. "**Naturally reasonable function**" is more concerned by users than "**Appropriate interaction**" in the natural holographic interaction.

5   Conclusion

Based on the integrated method of card sorting and fuzzy comprehensive evaluation, this paper extracts five types of future holographic scene design elements, a total of 26 design elements. It calculates the degree of importance of these elements, and also provides constructive guidance and improvement ideas for the design of holographic scenes in the future. We found that interactive control affects the user experience more than display content. Focusing on the functional design of requirements is the direction of future holographic scene design. During the application process of the research method, we found that many design research methods are not applicable because of the future characteristics of holographic scenes. However, with the advancement of science and technology, its scene characteristics are gradually changing, and the application of design methods should also be determined according to specific circumstances. At the same time, this article still has the following deficiencies. First of all, some of the design elements have the same comprehensive weight. If you are faced with a difference in design, the importance of these elements still needs to be further considered. Secondly, there are different classifications of future holographic scenes. For specific subdivision scenarios, whether the classification and importance structure of these design elements are different, we should continue to study in this direction in the future.

References

1. Dalvi, A.A., Siddavatam, I., Dandekar, N.G., et al.: 3D holographic projections using prism and hand gesture recognition. In: International Conference on Advanced Research in Computer Science Engineering & Technology. ACM (2015)

2. Nan, L.: The application of the holographic laser projection in the entertaining performance. In: International Conference on Advanced Materials for Science & Engineering. IEEE (2016)
3. Shein, E.: Holographic projection systems provide eternal life. Commun. ACM **57**(7), 19–21 (2014)
4. Song, J.: Design smart living scenario through future sensitive attached-it tools (2020)
5. Joiner, D.: Making POE work in an organization. In: Preiser, W.F.E., Hardy, A.E., Schramm, U. (eds.) Building Performance Evaluation, pp. 173–181. Springer, Cham (2018). https://doi.org/10.1007/978-3-319-56862-1_13
6. Lin, T., Li, X., Shaomei, W.: Improvement information architecture of campus website based card sorting method. Exp. Technol. Manag. **32**(10), 136–138 (2015)
7. Lin, S.: Research on design factors of university logistics service based on Kano-QFD integration method. West Forum Econ. Manag. **29**(04), 63–74 (2018)
8. Wang, X., Zheng, G., Wang, D., et al.: Construction and empirical research on evaluation indexes of user interactive experience in virtual reality reading. Libr. Inf. Work (16) (2020)
9. Wang, C., Hou, W.: Evaluation of augmented reality occlusion scheme based on analytic hierarchy process (2019)
10. Su, C., Fu, Y., Peng, W., Ma, Y.: Design elements of printing equipment form based on user's comprehensive evaluation. Packag. Eng. **41**(12), 111–116 (2020)
11. Xu, X., Dong, S., Zhang, X.: Product iteration design elements based on social value direction. Packag. Eng. **41**(420(06)), 194–199 (2020)
12. Kim, M.J., Morimoto, K., Kuwahara, N.: Study on design elements of cardinal direction based on cognitive analysis. In: Chung, W., Shin, C. (eds.) Advances in Affective and Pleasurable Design. Advances in Intelligent Systems and Computing, vol. 483, pp. 49–55. Springer, Cham (2017). https://doi.org/10.1007/978-3-319-41661-8_5
13. Tondello, G.F., Mora, A., Nacke, L.E.: Elements of gameful design emerging from user preferences. In: Proceedings of the Annual Symposium on Computer-Human Interaction in Play (CHI PLAY 2017), pp. 129–142. Association for Computing Machinery, New York (2017)

Fault Diagnosis Method of Automatic Sorter Equipment Based on Association Rules

Qiaohong Zu and Jiafan Gong[✉]

School of Transportation and Logistics Engineering, Wuhan University of Technology,
Wuhan 430061, China
920248875@qq.com

Abstract. Accurately diagnosing the cause of the failure type of the automatic sorter equipment is the basis for accelerating the efficiency of logistics sorting operations. Based on the research on the diagnosis problem of the parcel sorter equipment, based on the analysis of the fault text data, a method of parcel sorter equipment fault diagnosis based on association rules is proposed. First, build a two-layer fault diagnosis model based on the fault text information and expert experience; use the TF-IDF method to extract the semantic features of the fault text, and propose an improved Apriori algorithm on the basis of the traditional Apriori algorithm to mine the fault text information. The law of association between. The research results show that the evaluation indexes of the improved Apriori algorithm are higher than those of the Apriori algorithm, which proves the feasibility of the method.

Keywords: Automatic sorter equipment · Fault diagnosis · Association rules · TF-IDF algorithm · Apriori algorithm

1 Preface

This paper deeply researches the fault text data of automatic sorter equipment [1], and combines expert experience to convert the text fault diagnosis data into fault types and causes. First, the TF-IDF algorithm [2] is used to extract the features of the fault text, and the fault diagnosis model based on association rules [3] is established. Then, the improved Apriori algorithm is used to conduct data mining on the fault diagnosis results, and more practically meaningful hidden association rules are obtained. Finally, the equipment failure data of an automatic sorter in a logistics center from 2015 to 2020 is used for experiments to verify the validity and correctness of the fault diagnosis model based on association rules.

2 Failure Data Analysis of Automatic Sorter Equipment

2.1 Automatic Sorter Equipment

This article mainly researches and analyzes the cross-belt automatic sorter. Figure 1 shows its structural distribution, which mainly includes: 1-loading machine, 2-laser scanner, 3-belt pallet trolley, 4-grid and so on.

Q. Zu et al. (Eds.): HCC 2021, LNCS 13795, pp. 285–294, 2022.
https://doi.org/10.1007/978-3-031-23741-6_26

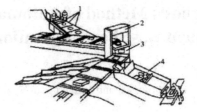

Fig. 1. Cross-belt automatic sorter

2.2 Description of Failure of Automatic Sorter Equipment

This article divides the automatic sorter equipment failure into two levels, as shown in Fig. 2. The first-level failure is a general description of the sorting equipment failure phenomenon, and the second-level failure is to locate the cause of the failure to a specific factor. In order to describe the relationship between equipment failures more clearly, some failure maintenance records are shown in Table 1.

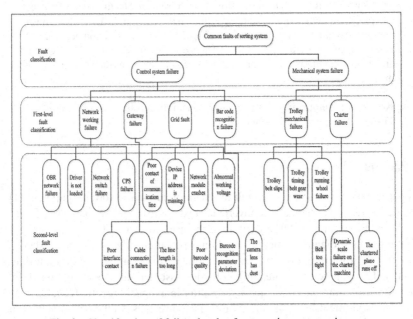

Fig. 2. Classification of failure levels of automatic sorter equipment

Because the fault phenomenon column in Table 1 only makes a simple description, there are many irrelevant redundant information in the actual text fault record, which will cause the meaningful regular information to be unable to be excavated. Therefore, this paper divides the automatic sorter equipment fault diagnosis into two steps: fault feature extraction and fault diagnosis. Firstly, feature extraction and vectorization are carried out on the fault text data of the automatic sorter, and the improved Apriori algorithm

Table 1. Some sample data of automatic sorter failure

Number	Failure phenomenon	First-level failure	Second-level failure
1	The barcode is not correctly recognized	Network working failure	OBR network failure
2	Data is unstable during transmission, and data packet loss	Gateway failure	Poor contact
3	Unable to count the number of messages	Grid fault	Abnormal working voltage
4	The dynamic scale of the charter machine is inaccurate	Charter failure	Dynamic scale failure
5	Abnormal car noise	Trolley mechanical failure	Trolley timing belt tooth wear

is applied to mine the association rules between the fault text information to obtain the association rules.

The overall flow chart is shown in Fig. 3.

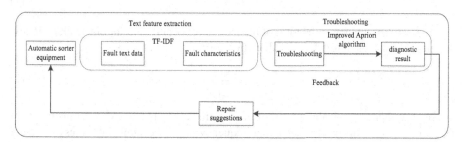

Fig. 3. Overall flow chart

3 Fault Feature Extraction of Text Data

3.1 Word Segmentation and Text Preprocessing

First, use the language cloud of Harbin Institute of Technology to perform Chinese word segmentation on the textual fault data of the equipment, and extract key words. After word segmentation, the text is transformed into a vector space model [4], which aims to convert the text content into a vector of feature words-feature weights and save it. The feature items $t_1, t_2, \ldots, t_n$ are regarded as an n-dimensional coordinate system, and the weights $w_1, w_2, \ldots, w_n$ are the corresponding. Therefore, $V(d_i) = (t_1, w_{m1}; t_2, w_{m2}; \ldots; t_n, w_{mn})$, as shown in Table 2.

Table 2. Vector space model of text

Feature vector	t_1	t_2	...	t_n
d_1	w_{11}	w_{12}	...	w_{1n}
d_2	w_{21}	w_{22}	...	w_{2n}
⋮	⋮	⋮		⋮
d_m	w_{m1}	w_{m2}	...	w_{mn}

3.2 TF-IDF Algorithm

TF-IDF model is a widely used weighting technology, which is often used for information retrieval and data mining. TF (term frequency) is the abbreviation of word frequency, which can be understood as the frequency of words in the text. The abbreviation of inverse text frequency is IDF, that is, the measurement of the universal key of a word. The core idea of the model is: assuming that a word appears more frequently in a text (TF is higher), but less frequently in the remaining text (IDF is higher), the word has a good ability to distinguish categories. The calculation formula of TF-IDF method is as follows:

$$w_{t,d} = tf_{t,d} \times idf_{t,d} \tag{1}$$

$tf_{t,d}$ word frequency is the ratio of the number of occurrences of eigenvalue t in text d to all eigenvalues in text D. the calculation formula is as follows:

$$tf_{t,d} = \frac{n_{t,d}}{\sum_k n_{t,d}} \tag{2}$$

Among them, $w_{t,d}$ is the weight of the feature value t in the text d; $tf_{t,d}$ is the word frequency; $idf_{t,d}$ is the inverse document frequency. $n_{t,d}$ is the number of times the feature value t appears in the text d; $\sum_k n_{t,d}$ is the number of all feature values in the text d.

The inverse document frequency formula $idf_{t,d}$ is as follows:

$$idf_{t,d} = \log \frac{N}{N_{t,d} + 1} \tag{3}$$

N is the total number of texts in the text database; $N_{t,d}$ is the number of texts with feature value t. If a word is not in the sample, it will cause the denominator to be 0. Therefore, the denominator plus 1 is to avoid this situation. After text preprocessing, an algorithm can be used to calculate the weight $w_{t,d}$.

4   Fault Diagnosis Based on Association Rules

Association rules can reflect the interdependence and correlation between things. If data mining can reflect a certain association between two or more things, it will help to further analyze the association mechanism between things, and even predict the probability of other things from one event. The application in this paper is: by mining the fault characteristics of automatic sorter equipment to obtain association rules, we can diagnose the fault from the obtained association rules.

There are two key indicators to evaluate an association rule: support and confidence [5]. Support indicates how likely a rule is to occur, and confidence indicates how trustworthy a rule is.

Let item set $I = \{i_1, i_2, \ldots, i_n\}$, and there is a data set D, each record T in it is a subset of I, then the association rules are all expressions of the form $A \Longrightarrow B$, A and B are both subsets of I, and the intersection of A and B is empty.

Support for this association rule:

$$\text{support}(A \Rightarrow B) = \frac{\text{count}(A \cup B)}{|D|} \tag{4}$$

Confidence of this association rule:

$$\text{Confidence}(A \Rightarrow B) = \frac{\text{count}(A \cup B)}{\text{count}(A)} \tag{5}$$

4.1   Apriori Algorithm

Apriori algorithm is one of the most commonly used data mining algorithms in association rule mining. Its core idea is to find frequent itemsets through candidate set generation and downward closure detection, that is, using the iterative method of layer by layer search and "k-1 itemset" to search "K itemset". The data mining process can be divided into the following two steps.

(1) Connection step

Let l_1 and l_2 be the two item sets in L_{k-1}, the j item in l_i is denoted as $l_i[j]$, and the connection operation of L_{k-1} is denoted as $L_{k-1} \oplus L_{k-1}$, for l_1 and l_2, only when the previous $(k-2)$ items in l_1 and l_2 are the same, can the connection operation be performed, and the result of the connection is the item set $l_1[1]l_2[2]\ldots l_1[k-1]l_2[k-2]$.

(2) Pruning step

If there are many items in the item set, the number of items in the candidate item set C_k generated by connection may be large, and the overhead of directly scanning the C_k row database will become very huge. Using Apriori property, we can eliminate the unlikely frequent itemset compression C_k before scanning, so as to reduce the overhead of scanning the database and improve the efficiency of the algorithm.

4.2 Improved Apriori Algorithm

With the continuous development of big data, the disadvantages of Apriori algorithm are also very obvious: the number of candidate frequent K itemsets is huge; When verifying the candidate frequent K itemset, the whole database needs to be scanned, which is very time-consuming. Therefore, according to the basic characteristics of Apriori algorithm, this paper improves its algorithm. The improved Apriori algorithm reduces the time spent by the traditional Apriori algorithm in scanning the transaction database.

Generally speaking, its improvement is mainly carried out in two aspects:

(1) A more superior strategy should be adopted for the steps of self connection and pruning.
(2) The purpose of simplifying the database itself is to reduce the complexity of Apriori algorithm.

Since the Apriori algorithm scans the database every time it is executed, in fact, this process can be optimized. During the calculation of C_k support, all kinds of things contained in C_k can be marked, and the marked things will not be considered when scanning again. After optimization, various databases in the support of the actual candidate set must be smaller than the real database. With the increase of K value, the difference will also increase, so the scanning time will be reduced, the calculation speed will be increased and the efficiency will be improved. The improved Apriori algorithm is as follows:

(1) Select the smallest support among them, scan the original database, you can calculate each 1-item set degree, and get 1-item set L_1.
(2) Connect pruning (this step remains unchanged).
(3) Mark the unmarked elements in C_k and delete the marked elements, thereby obtaining a new database D_k, and then rescan D_k, to calculate the support of each element in C_{k-1}.
(4) Search for C_k, and delete the smallest item set that cannot be satisfied, thereby forming a new item set L_k.

Repeat steps 2 to 4, until no new frequent itemsets can be generated, terminate this operation.

5 Test Verification and Result Analysis

In this paper, the equipment fault data of an automatic sorter in a logistics center from 2015 to 2020 are used for the test, of which 70% are used as the training set and verification set, and 30% are used as the test set. The proportion of training set and verification set is randomly divided by k-fold cross verification method. F-measure [6] is specially introduced as the evaluation and comparison index of the algorithm. Given the accuracy and recall, F-measure can be calculated. Accuracy refers to the percentage of the total number of correctly identified individuals in the total number of identified individuals. The accuracy rate can directly represent the proportion of accurate prediction samples in the prediction category.

$$\text{Precision} = \frac{1}{|C|} \sum_{i \in c} \frac{(TP_i + TN_i) \times TP_i}{TP_i + FP_i} \qquad (6)$$

Recall rate refers to the percentage of the total number of correctly identified individuals in the total number of individuals in the test set.

$$\text{Recall} = \frac{1}{|C|} \sum_{i \in c} \frac{(TP_i + TN_i) \times TP_i}{TP_i + FN_i} \qquad (7)$$

Among them, C is the total number of samples; c is the total number of classification categories; TP_i is the positive sample that is correctly classified into the i-th category; TN_i is the negative sample that is correctly classified into the i-th category; FP_i is the positive sample that was mistakenly assigned to the i-th category, and FN_i is the negative sample that was mistakenly assigned to the i-th category.

When considering the classification effect of each fault category separately, precision and recall sometimes conflict; F-measure is the weighted harmonic average of precision and recall, which can effectively solve this contradiction. Its expression is:

$$\text{F-measure} = \frac{2 \times \text{Precision} \times \text{Recall}}{\text{Precision} + \text{Recall}} \qquad (8)$$

5.1 Algorithm Comparison

In order to verify the effectiveness of the above-mentioned improved algorithm, a total of 956 pieces of data of automatic sorter equipment failure in a logistics center were used for verification and analysis. Among them, 70% is used as the training set and the validation set, and 30% is used as the test set. The K-fold cross-validation method [7] is used to randomly divide the proportion of the training set and the validation set.

According to expert experience, set min_sup to 0.2. It can be seen from Fig. 4(a) that the more fault data, the more obvious the advantage of the improved algorithm. Set different min_sup and compare the running time of the two algorithms. From Fig. 4(b), it can be seen that under different min_sup conditions, the improved algorithm has a shorter running time than the traditional algorithm.

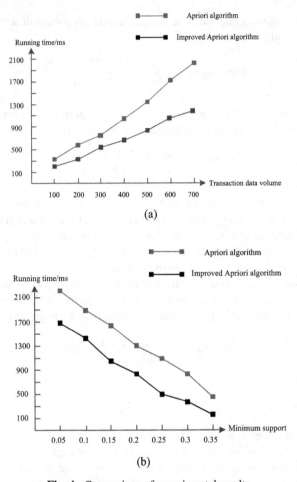

Fig. 4. Comparison of experimental results

After K = 5 times of training, 30% real samples are used to evaluate the Apriori algorithm and the improved Apriori algorithm. The evaluation results are shown in Table 3.

Table 3. Comparison results of K-fold cross-validation + algorithm evaluation

Method	Level	Precision	Recall	F-measure
Apriori	First-level fault	0.7653	0.7661	0.7588
	Second-level fault	0.7102	0.7257	0.7138
Improved Apriori	First-level fault	0.8842	0.8982	0.8715
	Second-level fault	0.7989	0.8017	0.7953

According to the comparison in Table 3, under the same parameters of the two algorithms, the evaluation indexes of the improved Apriori algorithm are higher than those of the Apriori algorithm. In the evaluation index of primary fault classification, the improved Apriori algorithm is improved by 12.12% on average compared with Apriori algorithm; In the evaluation index of secondary fault classification, the improved Apriori algorithm is improved by 8.21% on average compared with Apriori algorithm. The reason why the secondary fault classification evaluation index is lower than the primary fault classification evaluation index is that if the primary fault classification is wrong, the result of secondary fault classification will also be affected.

5.2 Fault Diagnosis Application and Analysis

Set the minimum support to 0.2 and the confidence to 0.6 to obtain 523 association rules. Among them, 219 meet the requirements. Due to space reasons, only five association rules with representative significance are listed as shown in Table 4.

Table 4. Association rules

Number	Rule	Confidence/%
1	Barcode identification system failure = barcode identification parameter setting error	78.49
2	Network working failure = The driver is not installed correctly and the network protocol is not added	75.91
3	Lattice failure = The corresponding indicator on the control circuit board of the Lattice device does not light up	83.52
4	The charter machine failure = the frame displacement causes the wall panel to collide with the dynamic scale	81.17
5	Gateway failure = the transmission distance of ordinary UTP twisted pair cable is greater than 100 m	71.09

After sorting out the association rules obtained from the above mining and deleting the association rules that are not meaningful in themselves, combined with expert experience, the maintenance scheme can be selected according to the diagnosis results. For example, according to rule 5, if the transmission distance of ordinary class V twisted pair is greater than 100 m, it can be deduced that it is a gateway fault, and then it is deduced that the communication line is too long by the gateway fault. If the reasoning is reasonable and the reason is correct, a scheme can be given according to the fault diagnosis results: reduce the length of the communication line. If the reasoning is unreasonable, another association rule is used for reasoning until the final result is deduced.

6 Concluding Remarks

According to the fault text data of automatic sorter equipment in a logistics center in the past five years, a fault diagnosis method based on association rules is proposed in this paper. TF-IDF algorithm is used to extract and vectorize the fault text, and classify it according to the fault diagnosis model; Through the improved Apriori algorithm, association rules with maintenance guiding significance are found. Experiments show that the improved Apriori algorithm is a method that can effectively improve the classification performance of automatic sorter equipment fault diagnosis model. The effectiveness of the proposed algorithm is verified by comparison with Apriori algorithm.

References

1. Wang, H.: Application of data mining technology in fault diagnosis of automatic mail sorter. Beijing University of Technology (2017)
2. Zhang, L.: Research on case reasoning method based on TF-IDF. Int. J. Syst. Assur. Eng. Manag. **12**, 1–8 (2021)
3. Zhang, X.: Research and improvement of association rule algorithm in data mining. Beijing University of Posts and Telecommunications (2015)
4. Tan, J.: Research on text similarity algorithm based on vector space model. Southwest Petroleum University (2015)
5. Wang, X., An, J.: Association classification algorithm based on Intelligent Optimization of support and confidence. Comput. Appl. Softw. **30**(11), 184–186+198 (2013)
6. Soleymani, R., Granger, E., Fumera, G.: F-measure curves: a tool to visualize classifier performance under imbalance. Pattern Recogn. **100**, 107146 (2020)
7. Wang, J.E., Qiao, J.Z.: Parameter selection of SVR based on improved K-fold cross validation. Appl. Mech. Mater. **2865**, 182–186 (2014)

Innovation Framework for Green Ports

Qiaohong Zu and Jingwen Yan[✉]

Wuhan University of Technology, Wuhan 430061, China
Ysslahplife@163.com

Abstract. In recent years, the development of green ports has attracted great attention from the academic circles, port management departments and port and shipping enterprises. In the past in the construction of port development, we have too much emphasis on port throughput and other economic indicators, although to a certain extent, contributed to the rapid development of trade, but due to global climate change and energy consumption problems intensified, the concept of green development widespread attention from the society from all walks of life, has been given to the mission of green port is imminent. At present, there are not enough literatures about green ports, and the few literatures remaining are mostly focused on a single dimension, which cannot deeply analyze the information about green ports. This paper attempts to explore green ports through innovative research and analysis, hoping to be helpful to the research on green ports.

Keywords: Ports · Green innovation methods · Green

1 Introduction

1.1 Green Ports

As an important infrastructure to promote national economic growth, the port is also an important transportation hub to ensure domestic and foreign trade. The trend of economic globalization in the 21st century has accelerated the efficient development of international trade, which is a great opportunity for port construction and development [1]. In this context, the scale of ports can continue to expand, port facilities can continue to update, port functions can continue to improve, port grade can continue to improve, while the ability of port to contribute to regional economy can continue to enhance, become a key part of regional economic development.

However, in the era of rapid port development, the negative impact of port on Marine and land environment is increasingly serious, so the need to build green port arises at the historic moment, which has become a favorable construction direction to solve the current port development problems. Green port requires port to achieve a good state of coordination, balance and sustainable development between economic benefits and environmental protection, and then realize the sustainable development of port. A green port maximizes economic benefits on the basis of maintaining a good production and living environment and pays more attention to environmental protection. Port environment includes not only ecological environment, but also atmospheric environment and

Q. Zu et al. (Eds.): HCC 2021, LNCS 13795, pp. 295–304, 2022.
https://doi.org/10.1007/978-3-031-23741-6_27

water environment. The destruction of the material basis on which the port relies will not only threaten people's survival and life, but also adversely affect port development in the long run.

Therefore, the economic development of the port must be based on the ecological balance and environmental protection of the port, and the coordinated and balanced development of the two can promote the sustainable development of the port. Chuansheng Peng [2] of the Ministry of Transport deeply discussed the nature and meaning of green ports. He pointed out that green ports are ports that meet the requirements in terms of energy utilization, low-carbon promotion, ecological protection, and resource conservation. In April 2013, the Ministry of Transport published the Green Port Grade Evaluation Standard, defining the concept of green port: "In production and operation, adhering to the development concept of resource conservation and environmental friendly, actively fulfilling social responsibilities, and comprehensively applying technologies and management measures conducive to resource and energy conservation, environmental and ecological protection and coping with climate change can meet the corresponding green grade standards". To establish evaluation index system of sustainable development of the port to be able to in the process of the construction of green port, provides the basis of the construction, timely, reasonably and accurately evaluate green port construction condition, provide the basis for port management strategy, is advantageous to the port of their own development and management of government department called for construction of environment-friendly society from all walks of life and green transportation, Among them, the promotion of green port is significant.

1.2 Concepts Related to Green Innovation of Port Enterprises

According to the results of Schiederig et al. (2012) using Google Scholar, database to search relevant literatures from 1990 to 2010, the concept of green innovation became popular in academic circles from 2005 [3].

Previously, the two concepts of environmental innovation and sustainable innovation were more adopted by scholars at home and abroad, and the concept of ecological innovation emerged together with green innovation. Although there are slight differences, the statistical results of Schiederig et al. (2012) show that there are only slight differences in the definition and description of these four concepts, which all refer to enterprises in order to:

- promote the economical use and optimal allocation of material resources, Or
- processes, technologies, practices, systems, and products adopted to reduce negative environmental impacts.

Therefore, it has been substituted in many literatures (Beise and Rennings 2005; OECD 2008; Kemp 2011; Schiederig et al. 2012; Xiangrong Wang 2012). In 2014, Karakaya et al. (2014) used Google Scholar database again to search literatures with high citation in related fields and got the same result.

The key words of literature review in this paper include green innovation, environmental innovation, sustainable innovation, and ecological innovation, but are not limited to green innovation. The term "green innovation" has a large extension. It can be said that all innovative activities that can save resources and be environmentally friendly can be called green innovation (Li Xu 2015) [4, 7]. Therefore, domestic, and foreign scholars of different disciplines have given the definition of green innovation based on different research perspectives. Kemp and Pearson (2007) [4] defined green innovation as a new product, technology or system that can minimize the damage to the external environment and reduce resource consumption during the enterprise's existence. The definition of "new" is relative to the enterprise itself. The European INNOVA group defined the evaluation standard of green innovation as using the least resources and emitting the least pollutants under a certain output target (Reid and Miedzinski 2008). Driessen and Hillebrand (2002), Foxon and Kemp (2004) and Bernauer et al. (2007) [5] relaxed the restrictions on enterprises' conscious pursuit of environmental benefits, arguing that enterprises need not develop products to reduce environmental burden (Figs. 1 and 2).

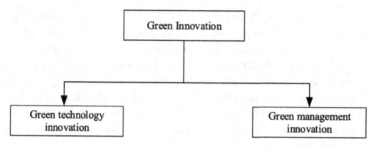

Fig. 1. Green innovation classification

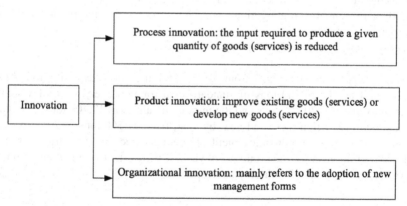

Fig. 2. Organization for Economic Cooperation and Development (OECD) classification of general innovation

2 Green Innovation Methods

2.1 Oil to Electricity

Gantry crane is short for gantry crane, which can handle container loading and unloading, hull splicing, valve opening and closing of hydropower station and many other operations. It is the most common and important mechanical equipment in ports (Lanqiang Zhang 2013). The traditional gantry crane generally uses diesel oil to generate electricity, which produces a lot of noise pollution and air pollution while the power generation efficiency is low, and seriously damages the port area environment. After "oil to electricity", the gantry crane is powered by the grid instead of the traditional diesel power generation, which can significantly reduce the adverse impact on the environment at the same time, but also save fuel costs, and achieve dual environmental and economic benefits.

In 2011, Longman crane "oil to electricity" project was again awarded provincial demonstration project. At this time, port has completed the transformation of 177 gantry cranes, the utilization rate of more than 80%, the annual carbon dioxide emissions decreased by more than 20,000 tons. In 2012, Port gantry crane "oil to electricity" project was completed, a total of 191 gantry cranes were renovated, the utilization rate of electric gantry crane was up to 90%, and the total investment reached 400 million yuan. It was the first port enterprise in China to fully use "oil to electricity" gantry crane and the first to recover the investment cost. The project has brought considerable ecological, social, and economic benefits to port [7]:

- zero emissions, no fuel power generation noise, no air pollution.
- Leading the country, highlighting corporate social responsibility, and improving corporate reputation.
- Energy saving rate up to 50%, saving fuel cost 65%.

Specifically, as shown in Fig. 3, from 2013 to 2017, the "oil to electricity" of Longmen cranes saved nearly 20,000 tons of standard coal for port every year, of which the maximum value was 20,600 tons and the minimum value was 17,400 tons. The annual CO_2 emission reduction increased year by year, from 41,500 tons in 2013 to 49,200 tons in 2017. In terms of economic benefits, Longman crane "oil to electricity" can save about 50 million yuan for the group every year, of which the maximum and minimum are 63 million yuan and 37 million yuan respectively.

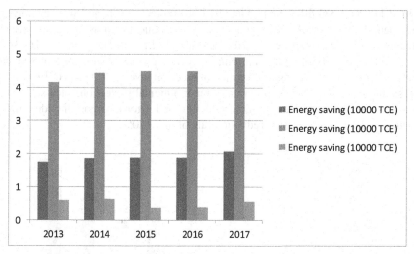

Note: TCE is equivalent to tons of standard coal

Fig. 3. Energy saving and emission reduction benefits of gantry crane "oil to electricity" from 2013 to 2017

2.2 Oil to Gas

Container truck is short for container truck, because of its small volume, flexible scheduling, become an important tool for container transportation inside and outside the port area, according to the different operating areas can be divided into internal container card and external container card. The external collection card is not owned or controlled by the container terminal and is only responsible for transporting containers to and from the container terminal. The main transportation area is the road outside the port area. The inner collection card is the container truck operating in the port area, which is owned and controlled by the container terminal. It is mainly responsible for the container transportation between the quay bridge and the yard bridge in the process of ship loading and unloading, and between the yard bridge and the yard bridge in the process of container turning (Wang Tao et al. 2015) [8].

The "oil to gas" project of port is the internal collection card owned by the port area, so it is also called "oil to gas" project of internal collection card. In 2009, port launched the "oil to gas" project of internal container card, to facilitate the timely and fast filling of LIQUEFIED natural gas (LNG) in the port area. Meanwhile, the LNG filling station infrastructure construction project was also launched. As shown in Fig. 4 and Fig. 5, by 2010, 23 LNG containers had been put into use in port, and the first LNG refueling demonstration station in Zhejiang province was successfully completed and put into operation.

In 2011, one LNG filling station and 91 LNG collector were added to the port area. Since then, the number of LNG filling stations and collector cards in the port area has increased year by year. By the end of 2018, a total of 11 LNG filling stations and 653 LNG collector cards have been built, with remarkable energy saving and emission reduction effects. In terms of cost saving, each collector card can save 53,400 yuan of fuel cost per year, saving rate up to 20.9%; In terms of environmental protection, each set of cards can achieve annual pollution emission reduction of 1.1 tons, carbon dioxide emission reduction of 19.4 tons, emission reduction rate of up to 20%.

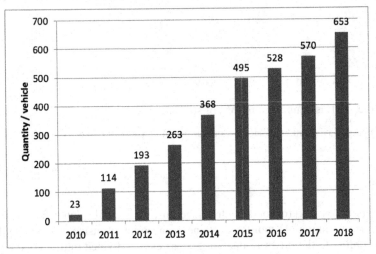

Fig. 4. Number of LNG trucks realizing "oil to gas" from 2010 to 2018

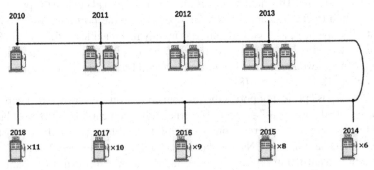

Fig. 5. Number of LNG filling stations owned by port from 2010 to 2018

2.3 Ships Rely on Electricity

Ship shore power refers to the replacement of traditional fuel oil power generation by connecting port ships with power supply devices. For a long time, the pollutants produced by oil-fired power generation from ships near the port are one of the main air pollution sources. As shown in Fig. 6, the PM2.5 emitted by a medium-sized container ship in a day is equivalent to that emitted by 500,000 ordinary cars in a day. Data show that the total number of ships calling at port can reach 35,000 times per year. By equivalent conversion, the PM2.5 emitted by ships at port in one year is equivalent to the daily emissions of 1.75 billion ordinary cars. Ship shore power has realized zero diesel oil, zero noise and zero exhaust gas for ships berthing at the port, which is a green technology innovation project promoted by port in recent years.

The frequency and voltage level of shore power equipment are also different according to different sailing areas. The mainstream classification method divides them into two categories: one is high voltage shore power equipment (frequency: 60 Hz), which is suitable for large ocean-going ships.

The second is low-voltage shore power (frequency: 50 Hz), which is suitable for offshore and inland ships (Jinbo Wang 2016). The low-voltage shore power project of port started earlier, and the utilization rate of wharf shore power facilities is relatively high (about 10%).

Figure 7 shows the annual number of ships connected to shore power project of port from 2012 to 2017. The figure for 2018–20 are missing, given that they have not been published officially for nearly three years. Compared with low voltage shore power, high voltage shore power started relatively late and developed relatively slowly. As shown in Fig. 8, in 2016, the first two high-voltage ship shore power points of port were completed and put into operation, marking that the ship-shore power project of port has been upgraded from "low-voltage" to "high-voltage". In the following three years, port added an average of 2 sets of shore power for high voltage ships every year and built an additional 5 sets in 2020.

Since the 12th Five-Year Plan, the state has vigorously supported the research and development, application, and promotion of shore power technology for ships. It has issued the "Guiding Opinions on Promoting the substitution of Electric Energy" and "Port Power Layout Plan", etc. At the local level, policies are also inclined to shore power by ships. For example, Transportation Energy Conservation and Emission Reduction Fund Management Measures clearly states that it will increase financial support for shore power projects by continuously increasing the number of financial subsidies from both shore power supply (port side) and shore power use (shipowner side). Strive for the smooth development and promotion of the project "escort". However, compared with the Longman crane "oil to electricity" and the collection card "oil to gas" projects, the development course of port ship shore power project is more difficult and bumpier. At present, many shore power equipment is idle, and the utilization rate of low-voltage facilities is only about 10%, while that of high-voltage facilities is even lower. The extremely low equipment utilization rate is in sharp contrast to the high equipment construction cost (about 8–10 million yuan per high-voltage equipment). Existing studies show that the potential influencing factors include:

- the high cost of ship power facilities renovation.
- Shore power price does not have competitive advantage.
- It takes a long time to connect shore power to ship and the effective power connection time is short.
- The lack of unified technical standards for high voltage shore power makes the ship connection process complicated.
- Immature high voltage shore power grid connection technology has potential safety risks (Wang Jambo 2016).

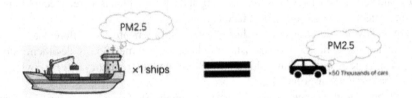

(a) PM2.5 emissions from a medium-sized container ship arriving at the port for one day

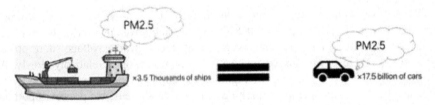

(b) Total PM2.5 emission from ships berthing at port in one year

Fig. 6. PM2.5 emission from ships berthing at port

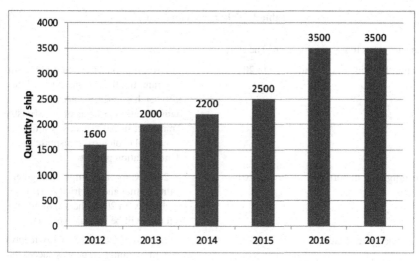

Fig. 7. 2012–2017 Number of ships connected to shore power project of port in a year

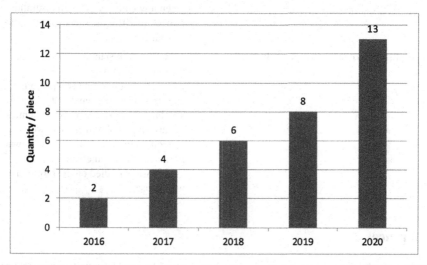

Fig. 8. Number of shore power for high-voltage ships completed in port from 2016 to 2020

2.4 Summary of Green Innovation

In addition to the "oil to electricity" of gantry crane, "oil to gas" of collector card and shore electricity of ships, port group has also carried out a series of green technology innovation projects such as "multiple towing of tractor", green lighting of port area, energy feedback of crane and distributed photovoltaic power generation. The basic information is shown in Table 1:

Table 1. Other green innovation

Name of green innovation project	The start time	The basic information
Tractor "Hanging at one end"	In 2010	In 2010, it piloted the "multiple deaths" program. In 2012, it was awarded the fifth batch of energy conservation demonstration projects of the Ministry of Transport. In 2013, it was awarded provincial ecological transportation demonstration project
Green lighting in port area	In 2010	In 2010, vigorously implement green lighting, fuel and electricity saving effect is obvious. In 2015, the use of green lighting will be further expanded
Crane energy feedback	In 2012	At the end of 2012, the energy feedback system of gantry crane was successfully developed with the support of Power Grid. In 2014, it was awarded the first green low-carbon cycle demonstration project. In 2015, the scope of renovation was further expanded
Distributed photovoltaic power generation	In 2017	In 2017, port began to implement the distributed photovoltaic power generation project, and two projects are currently being implemented: Taicang Wanfang Company plans to implement the distributed photovoltaic power generation project; In the Yue Qingwan Port area, a distributed photovoltaic system was installed on the roof of a warehouse

References

1. Wang, T.: Research on green port development in China. Dalian Maritime University (2014)
2. Peng, C.: Evaluation of green ports. Port Sci. Technol. **2014**(09), 1–6 (2014)
3. Peng, C.S.: Preparation of green port grade evaluation standard. Stand. Eng. Constr. **2014**(07), 29–33 (2014)
4. Abbas, J., Sağsan, M.: Impact of knowledge management practices on green innovation and corporate sustainable development: a structural analysis. J. Clean. Prod. **229**, 611–620 (2019)
5. Abdullah, M., Zailani, S., Iranmanesh, M., et al.: Barriers to green innovation initiatives among manufacturers: the Malaysian case. Rev. Manag. Sci. **10**(4), 683–709 (2016)
6. Acciaro, M., Vanelslander, T., Sys, C., et al.: Environmental sustainability in seaports: a framework for successful innovation. Marit. Policy Manag. **41**(5), 480–500 (2014)
7. Ahluwalia, R., Burnkrant, R.E., Unnava, H.R.: Consumer response to negative publicity: the moderating role of commitment. J. Mark. Res. **37**(2), 203–214 (2000)
8. Aoki, M.: The Cooperative Game Theory of the Firm. Oxford

Author Index